Previous studies of nineteenth-century Egypt have often been premature in identifying the existence of an independent nation state. In a way which will permanently affect our view of Egyptian history, this book argues that in the mid-nineteenth-century period Egypt was still an Ottoman province, with a provincial Ottoman elite which was only gradually becoming Egyptian.

Part one discusses the creation of a dynastic order in Egypt, especially under Abbas Paşa (1848–1854), and the formation of an Ottoman-Egyptian ruling class. It surveys the nature of government service and the dynamics of political power. Part two deals with the non-elite groups, the vast majority of Egypt's population. It investigates the pressures applied to the rural and urban orders and the degree of resistance which was given in return. A final chapter offers a convincing picture of the social and cultural life of the period in a way which has never before been attempted in a Middle East context.

The author's valuable knowledge of Ottoman and Arabic as well as European documents and his use of a wide variety of sources, including police and court records, chronicles and travel literature, have enabled him to make an important contribution to a neglected period of Egyptian history and indeed to our understanding of other provinces and dependencies in the region.

Cambridge Middle East Library: 22

The *Cambridge Middle East Library* aims to bring together outstanding scholarly work on the political, social and economic history, politics, sociology and economics of the Middle East and North Africa in the nineteenth and twentieth centuries. While primarily focusing on monographs by younger scholars based on original research, the series will also incorporate broader surveys and in-depth treatments by more established scholars.

STATE AND SOCIETY IN MID-NINETEENTH-CENTURY EGYPT

Cambridge Middle East Library

24 JILL CRYSTAL
Rulers and merchants in the Gulf: oil and politics in Kuwait and Qatar

23 DONALD MALCOLM REID
Cairo University and the making of modern Egypt

22 EHUD R. TOLEDANO
State and society in mid-nineteenth-century Egypt

21 FRED HALLIDAY
Revolution and foreign policy: the case of South Yemen 1967–1987

20 GERSHON SHAFIR
Land, labor and the origins of the Israeli-Palestinian conflict 1882–1914

19 MAHFOUD BENNOUNE
The making of contemporary Algeria, 1830–1987
Colonial upheavals and post-independence development

18 DANIEL J. SCHROETER
Merchants of Essaouira
Urban society and imperialism in southwestern Morocco, 1844–1886

17 TIMOTHY MITCHELL
Colonising Egypt

16 NADIA HIJAB
Womanpower
The Arab debate on women at work

15 BENNY MORRIS
The birth of the Palestinian refugee problem, 1947–1949

14 MIRIAM COOKE
War's other voices
Women writers on the Lebanese civil war

13 MARY C. WILSON
King Abdullah, Britain and the making of Jordan

12 SEVKET PAMUK
The Ottoman empire and European capitalism 1820–1913
Trade, investment and production

11 JOHN C. WILKINSON
The Imamate tradition of Oman

10 SAMIR A. MUTAWI
Jordan in the 1967 war

Series list continues on p. 320

STATE AND SOCIETY IN MID-NINETEENTH-CENTURY EGYPT

EHUD R. TOLEDANO

The right of the University of Cambridge to print and sell all manner of books was granted by Henry VIII in 1534. The University has printed and published continuously since 1584.

CAMBRIDGE UNIVERSITY PRESS

CAMBRIDGE

NEW YORK PORT CHESTER MELBOURNE SYDNEY

Published by the Press Syndicate of the University of Cambridge
The Pitt Building, Trumpington Street, Cambridge CB2 1RP
40 West 20th Street, New York, NY 10011, USA
10 Stamford Road, Oakleigh, Melbourne 3166, Australia

First published 1990

Printed in Great Britain at the University Press, Cambridge

British Library cataloguing in publication data

Toledano, Ehud R.
State and society in mid-nineteenth-century Egypt. –
(Cambridge Middle East library)
1. Egypt. Social classes, history
I. Title
305.5′0962

Library of Congress cataloguing in publication data

Toledano, Ehud R.
State and society in mid-nineteenth-century Egypt / Ehud R. Toledano
p. cm. – (Cambridge Middle East library: 22)
Bibliography.
Includes index.
ISBN 0 521 37194 5
1. Egypt – Social conditions. 2. Egypt – Rural conditions.
3. Social classes – Egypt – History – 19th century. 4. Egypt – Politics and government – 640–1882. 5. Egypt – History – 19th century.
I. Title. II. Series.
HN786.A8T65 1989
306′.0962′09034 – dc20 89–9755 CIP

ISBN 0 521 37194 5

WD

For Mira

Contents

Plates

Plates 1–9 are provided courtesy of the Middle East Project, the Open University, Israel; plate 10 is provided courtesy of the Victoria and Albert Museum, London.

Preface

This book was written during an extended sabbatical leave at St. Antony's College, Oxford. The Warden, the Fellows, and the College staff made my stay most fruitful and enjoyable. Above all, I owe a great deal to Albert Hourani and Roger Owen, who devoted much time and attention to my work. Their encouragement and kind hospitality are warmly remembered. They also read the full manuscript, and many of their valuable comments have greatly contributed to the final version of the book. Malcolm E. Yapp, of the School of Oriental and African Studies, carefully read a large chunk of the typescript and made many important suggestions.

Research for this book was conducted in Cairo during 1979–80 under the auspices of the American Research Center in Egypt. Most of the work was carried out at the Egyptian National Archives (*Dār al-Wathā'iq al-Qawmiyya*) and National Library (*Dār al-Kutub*). It was later expanded by work at the Public Record Office and the British Library in London, the Quai d'Orsay and Bibliothèque Nationale in Paris, and the Griffith Institute at the Ashmolean Museum, Oxford. Staff members of all these institutions were most helpful and gracious, for which I remain in their debt. Mrs. A. W. Field meticulously edited the typescript and suggested many useful changes. Richard Clarke, the History desk editor at Cambridge University Press, was as efficient and forthcoming as any author can hope for. And mother, at eighty-two, ran with great care through the final set of proofs.

This book is dedicated to my wife, Mira Ariel. While herself writing a book, she found enough love, warmth, and energy to sustain me through the toils of mid-nineteenth-century Egypt.

Note on transliteration, dates, and references

Transliteration from Ottoman Turkish follows modern Turkish spelling. Readers who are not acquainted with the pronunciation of some Turkish letters are advised that *c* is pronounced as *j* in *jam*, *ç* as *ch* in *church*, *g* as g in *goat*, *ğ* lengthens the vowel preceding it, *ı* sounds almost like the *u* in *radium*, *o* like the French *eau*, *ö* and *ü* like the German *könig* and *führer* respectively, and *ş* is pronounced as *sh* in *shall*. With minor modifications that are self evident, Arabic words are transcribed according to the conventions of the *International Journal of Middle East Studies*. Place names and terms with which the English reader is familiar by now appear in their English version. For definition of unfamiliar terms, the reader is referred to their first occurrence, which can be located through the index.

As a rule, the use of Turkish and Arabic in the text has been kept to a minimum and, following the first occurrence of a term, its English equivalent is used thereafter whenever possible. On first occurrence and when no adequate English equivalents have been found, Ottoman administrative and socio-cultural terms are cited in Turkish, concepts and usages current among the Arabic-speaking population are cited in Arabic. When warranted by common use, the Turkish and the Arabic are both cited. To minimize confusion, the plural of Turkish and Arabic terms is formed by adding *s* to the singular, not by giving the Turkish or Arabic plural form. Names of Turkish-speaking Ottoman subjects are given in Turkish, names of Arabic-speaking subjects in Arabic.

Hijrī dates are always cited with their Gregorian equivalent. The Ottoman abbreviations for the Muslim months have been adopted only in the notes. Accordingly, M = Muharrem (Arabic Muḥarram), S = Safer (Ṣafar), Ra = Rebiülevvel (Rabīʿ al-Awwal), R = Rebiülahir (Rabīʿ al-Ākhir = Rabīʿ ath-Thānī), Ca = Cemaziyülevvel (Jumādā al-Ūlā), C = Cemaziyülahir (Jumādā al-Ākhira), B = Receb (Rajab), Ş = Şaban (Shaʿbān), N = Ramazan (Ramaḍān), L = Şevval (Shawwāl), Za = Zilkade (Dhū al-Qaʿda), Z = Silhicce (Dhū al-Ḥijja).

Note references to books, articles, and theses consist of the author's name followed by the year of publication; full references are given in the comprehensive bibliography at the end of the book.

Introduction: the forgotten years

On 7 June 1841, late in the evening, a Russian steamer docked at the port of Alexandria. On board was Kâmil Efendi, emissary of the Ottoman government, bearing an historical edict (*ferman*) from Sultan Abdülmecit to the Governor of Egypt, Mehmet Ali Paşa. Its tone was firm but conciliatory:

The act of submission which thou hast just made, the assurances of fidelity and devotion which thou hast given, and the upright and sincere intentions which thou hast manifested, as well with regard to myself as in the interest of my Sublime Porte, have come to my sovereign knowledge, and have been very agreeable to me. In consequence, and as the zeal and sagacity by which thou art characterized as likewise the experience and knowledge which thou hast acquired in the affairs of Egypt . . . I grant unto thee the Government of Egypt within its ancient boundaries . . . together with the additional privilege of hereditary succession, and with the following conditions.

Three days later, before noon, the *ferman* was read in public throughout Egypt. A salute was fired from the Citadel in Cairo, and from the coastal forts of Alexandria and the Egyptian ships at harbor.[1]

As the guns of many past victories bid farewell to an era, Egypt was once again restricted to the natural bounds of the Nile Valley. To fully appreciate that striking swing of the pendulum, we should go back one year. By mid 1840, the stage was set for one of the more dramatic events in nineteenth-century Ottoman history. The Governor of Egypt, Mehmet Ali, a self-made *paşa* who had governed Egypt since 1805, seemed to have overstepped his limits. Having occupied Syria since 1832 and won a decisive battle against the sultan's troops at Nezip in June 1839, his forces were now deployed in eastern Anatolia. The Powers of Europe, with the exception of France, were preparing to defend the integrity of the Ottoman Empire, which in their eyes, was being threatened by the Paşa of Egypt. A joint European–Ottoman action was in preparation, and the viceroy, as he was known in Europe, vowed to fight it to the end. Early in January 1840, the British consul-general in Egypt had yet another difficult audience with him:

Mehemet Ali here burst forth violently, that "much words were useless: I dont [*sic*] deny the powers of England nor can I tie her hands; but if they pretend to confine me within the limits (meaning I presume of Egypt) I swear that I will do anything before I submit to be thus sacrificed . . . I am an old man, upwards of seventy one, but I will never consent to the cession of them [the territories he occupied outside Egypt] during my life time." The Pasha confirmed this determination with a solemn oath.[2]

Within the following months, however, Britain, Austria, Prussia, and Russia would coordinate their action and, finally, on 15 July 1840, would sign a convention which, in effect, enjoined Mehmet Ali Paşa to withdraw from all territories held by his forces, in return for the hereditary governorship of Egypt and the Sudan, to be ruled as an autonomous Ottoman province within a few restrictions. "The conditions imposed are dishonourable to me and I will never submit to them," the viceroy told Count Medem, the Russian consul-general in Egypt. "After eight years of labour in Syria," he added, "I will not yield to such humiliation." On an earlier occasion, he spoke of himself as the "oppressed" party, demanding justice and placing his confidence in "Divine Providence". But the Old Paşa knew when the time was ripe to accept reality. He finally succumbed to a joint European task-force which landed in Syria and recovered the occupied territory in the last months of that year.[3]

After some negotiations between the Ottoman government, Mehmet Ali, the signatories to the convention, and France, who had not forcibly resisted the action of the other European Powers, the Edict of Hereditary Governorship was promulgated by the sultan on 1 June 1841. *Inter alia*, it limited the size of the Egyptian army, stipulated that all Ottoman legislation and treaties would apply to Egypt, and prohibited the conclusion of international agreements by the viceroy without prior Ottoman consent. The rapid fall of the Egyptian mini-empire was followed by a gradual, not immediate, political and economic decline. His hopes dashed, his wings clipped, for the remainder of his reign the Paşa would not be the man he had been. Less than three months later, the once-defiant and insolent man meekly responded to a new British consul-general, who inquired about his relations with the sultan: "Oh! everything is now settled, everything is finished, and we shall only have to talk upon commercial matters."[4] The drama ended in a whimper, attention shifted from foreign to domestic affairs, and Egypt entered a new era.

Prelude to the middle years

Mehmet Ali's expansionism was not unique in the rich annals of Egypt. Rather, it was yet another attempt – and a fairly successful one – in a long series of similar moves by past and future Egyptian rulers to achieve regional hegemony. Indeed, the swinging of the pendulum beween the status of a province in an external empire and that of an imperial center dominating the region is a familiar motif in Egyptian historiography. The very occupation of Egypt by Sultan Selim I in 1517 altered the position of Cairo as the capital of the Mamluk sultanate, reducing her to the center of an Ottoman province ruled from Istanbul. Between 1250 and 1517, the country was governed by an elite of emancipated military slaves – the mamluks and their households – which was being constantly replenished by new recruits imported from central and western parts of Asia. The Mamluks, who dominated the region from Cairo, variously controlled the Nile Valley, Syria and Palestine, the Hijaz, and areas along the Red Sea.[5]

The history of Egypt as an Ottoman province is largely the story of the scramble between the central Ottoman government and the Egyptian elite for political power and access to the considerable economic wealth of the province. Through most of the period leading to the nineteenth century, the Porte – or the Sublime Porte, as the central government was referred to in Western sources – was mainly concerned to appropriate that wealth and reallocate it within the Empire. Egypt was administratively and economically incorporated into the Ottoman sphere and, at least during the sixteenth century, was effectively governed from Istanbul. The seventeenth and eighteenth centuries witnessed a changing relationship between the center and Cairo. For nearly two hundred years, the various local forces in Egypt assumed a dominant role *vis-à-vis* the

1 Mehmet Ali Paşa (ruled 1805–48)

Porte. At the same time, the Istanbul government engaged in a subtle power play involving its official representatives in the province, mamluk warlords, and officers of the imperial regiments – most notably the Janissaries – that had become localized over the years.

The political history of Egypt during those two centuries has been dominated by the internal strife among the major factions mentioned above. Until relatively recently the picture was confused, consisting of an endless inventory of battles among little-known mamluk *beys*, obscure commanders of Janissary units, and unfamiliar Ottoman *paşas*. Battles, massacres, exiles followed each other in a series that seemed unpromising to many historians. The important works of P. M. Holt and André Raymond have changed that historiographic chaos and given much meaning to a period that had been generally deemed stagnant and dull. Holt was mainly concerned with the political story, while Raymond explored the economic and social aspects of life. As often happens, the cultural and intellectual sides remain to be studied, although some beginnings have already been made.[6]

During much of the seventeenth century, the mamluk *beys* appear to have held effective political power in Egypt. In the last third of the century and the first third of the eighteenth century, power shifted to the regiments, especially to the senior Janissary officers. The rest of the century saw what Raymond termed "la domination des beys"; that is, the mamluk households, the Ottoman regiments, and the Ottoman administrative apparatus had merged into a single system controlled by men holding the rank of *bey*. It has been recently suggested that the process might be described as consisting of two general phenomena. In terms of structure, the Ottoman administration assimilated all other structures into its ranks. At the same time, the mamluk pattern of recruitment and socialization predominated within the Ottoman structure. It became a major mechanism of social reproduction for the ruling elite. In other words, the mamluk household was being replicated also in essentially non-mamluk structures, such as the regiments and the provincial administration.[7]

Raymond estimates that the elite, which he calls "la caste dominante/dirigeante," numbered about 10,000 men and women, while the population of Egypt in the eighteenth century was about 3.5 million. The overwhelming majority consisted of peasants, better known as the *fallāḥīn*, with an urban "proletariat" of artisans, craftsmen, and shopkeepers. The merchants, especially those engaged in long-distance, lucrative trade (Arabic, *tujjār*), and the upper stratum of the religious–judicial–educational hierarchy (Arabic, *ʿulamā*) formed the local notability. A complex and shifting relationship existed between the military-administrative elite and that notability; its purpose was to ensure the appropriation of the surplus and its unequal distribution among the partners.

Thus, during the ascendancy of the Janissary corps, its membership formed close ties, of the exploitation/protection type, with the urban population. The leading officers colluded with the wealthy merchants and, to a lesser extent, the top *ᶜulamā*, while rank-and-file Janissaries cooperated with artisans and shopkeepers in a mutually beneficial symbiosis. When the mamluk *beys* held effective political power, their allies and conduits to the producing population were mostly the *ᶜulamā*, but also, as the political system merged, members of the regiments and their urban artisanal and commercial associates. Generally speaking, the mamluk *beys* derived most of their revenue from rural tax-farms, whereas the Janissaries relied on urban sources of income. The surplus was appropriated through various mechanisms, the most common of which were the urban *muqāṭaᶜa*s and the rural *iltizām*s. Essentially, these were contracts which delegated to their holders the right to collect taxes for the government in return for the difference between what they managed to exact and the amount owed to the treasury.

The upper echelon of the merchant community owed its wealth to trade in coffee and spices. The better-off *ᶜulamā* thrived on the management of public and private endowments (Arabic, *waqf*s), and their less-fortunate brethren engaged in small-scale commercial activities or lived on low income from religious–judicial–educational services which they rendered. Intermarriage along horizontal lines was common; it strengthened the ties within the elite and forged alliances among the lower ranks of the urban and rural population. Raymond observes, however, that because they relied much more on rural revenue and support, the mamluk *beys* were less integrated into the urban fabric than the Janissaries and the other regiments, who better understood the utilitarian limit of exploitation. Hence, the mamluks' ascendancy over the Janissary coalition during the last three decades of the eighteenth century resulted in unmitigated oppression of the urban population. The French occupation (1798–1801) dealt a major blow to the power of the *beys*, which Mehmet Ali Paşa terminated a decade later.

In socio-political terms, Egypt was not much different from other Ottoman provinces during the seventeenth and eighteenth centuries. Throughout the empire, the balance between center and periphery was shifting, and a concomitant integration of imperial forces into provincial society was taking place. Istanbul adjusted her policy accordingly, playing her hand with due flexibility in order to retain as much revenue as was possible in the new circumstances.[8] However, relations between the central government and the provinces were to assume a closer, more direct nature in the nineteenth century. Under the governorship of Mehmet Ali, Egypt was a striking exception to that rule. The viceroy increased his autonomy and carved out a mini-empire inside the Ottoman state. Operating within the political culture and playing by its rules of conduct, he took over the state, strengthened it, and reshaped in many ways the nature of its relation to society.

During the first decade of his reign, Mehmet Ali Paşa gradually eliminated his rivals, actual and potential, concentrating all political and economic power in his own hands. Moreover, at the same time he recaptured for the sultan the important Ottoman possessions in Arabia – lost to the Wahhābīs – thereby acquiring recognition as the major regional power. From that enviable but dangerous position, Mehmet Ali launched the most ambitious, bold, costly, and painful program of reforms implemented in the Ottoman lands until then. His reforms were inspired by the Western model and guided by European experts. They centered around the army, but also induced economic, social, and cultural changes mainly on the upper echelons of Egyptian society that won for the Paşa the debatable title – "Founder of Modern Egypt."[9]

However, Mehmet Ali was no benign reformer, nor was his "revolution from above" a white one. Rather, he was an ambitious political and military leader who dragged Egypt into a series of bloody regional wars. By the end of the 1830s, his rule had spread from the Sudan in the south to Eastern Anatolia in the north, with an offshoot in the Isle of Crete. The Egyptian army and navy were stronger than any other Middle Eastern military configuration, and the Paşa seemed virtually unstoppable. His network of independent contacts took his emissaries to the Yemen and to Muscat and the Persian Gulf. His pressing demand for a considerable measure of independence from the Porte was a challenge to his Ottoman sovereign that could no longer be contained. Thus, in the final reckoning, we must take account of the enormous human and material cost of his unrelenting desire to extend his power and dominions.

If the historical Edict of 1841 marked the limit of Mehmet Ali's political accomplishments, it also created the first dynastic rule in a major, Muslim, Asian territory of the Ottoman crown, though Egypt still remained under Ottoman sovereignty. Whereas sovereignty and power are related, the former is a legal concept, the latter is practical and has to be measured by capability. Ultimately, Mehmet Ali's power could win for him no more than political autonomy, the governorship of Egypt for life, and a promise of hereditary rule. The long-term degree of political autonomy and the consolidation of hereditary rule remained to be thrashed out between his heirs and the Ottoman government. Although against the letter and the spirit of the edict, symbols of statehood were gradually being adopted by Egyptian rulers. Full sovereignty, however, would still elude them for many decades to come.

Themes of mid-nineteenth-century Egyptian history

Mehmet Ali cast a giant shadow over the fortunes of his successors. His image loomed larger than life, dwarfing his grandson Abbas (ruled 1848–1854), his son Sait (1854–1863), and, to a certain extent, even his grandson Ismail (1863–1879); only Ibrahim (1848), survived by his father, seemed to have escaped a similar fate. The model that the Paşa had set for reform and glory was rejected by Abbas, who tried to proceed along a different path. To him fell the difficult task of entrenching a dynastic order in Egypt and making hereditary government a permanent reality. To him, too, was left the struggle with the central government over the degree of autonomy which Egypt would continue to enjoy. And, finally, it was he who had to steer the wheel of reform in a realistic direction, adjusting it to the needs and capabilities of the people.

If the first years of the middle decades were marked by the declining powers of Mehmet Ali Paşa, the rest of the period belonged to the reigns of Abbas and Sait. Before we attempt to characterize the social and political realities of the time, a word about the careers of the two men in order. The following are only brief sketches of two little-known figures, whose lives were lost somewhere between the heroism of Mehmet Ali and the extravagance of Ismail. Indeed, the substance of the present work as a whole is the flesh of these skeleton biographies. It also attempts to show that, contrary to received wisdom, the reign of Abbas was of pivotal importance in the middle years of the nineteenth century, much more so than the longer and favorably viewed reign of Sait.

Born in Alexandria on 1 July 1812, Abbas was the son of Tusun Paşa. Tusun, Mehmet Ali's second son, who successfully led the Egyptian expedition to the Hijaz between 1811 and 1814, died in his twenties. The Old Paşa prepared his grandson for a career in government, and, from an early age, appointed him to various military and administrative posts, both in the provinces and in the capital. Abbas was trained at the military *lycée* of al-Khanqāh and served as general in the Egyptian army under the command of his uncle, Ibrahim Paşa, during the first Syrian war in 1831. When Mehmet Ali went to the Sudan in 1839, he appointed Abbas as governor-general of Egypt *ad interim*. On 12 November 1849 Abbas assumed supreme power in Egypt until his mysterious death at Binha on 16 July 1854. Most textbooks of Egyptian history tell us that under his rule the first railway in Egypt was constructed between Alexandria and Cairo from 1852 to 1854, that roads were paved and improved, notably the one from Cairo to Suez, that he built the military-administrative complex of ᶜAbbāsiyya, now a suburb of Cairo, and established the famous mosque of as-Sayyida Zaynab in Cairo.

Even his many Western critics admit that Abbas relaxed, though did not abolish, economic control through state monopolies and, in 1851–2, successfully resisted Ottoman attempts to curtail his power within Egypt. In 1853, the viceroy dispatched a contingency of 20,000 men, with naval support, to assist the sultan in the Crimean War. He is widely considered to have been a closer and more loyal subject of his Ottoman sovereign than both his grandfather and his uncle. At the expense of France and her interests in Egypt, Abbas's foreign policy was overtly pro-British. His reign was generally peaceful, the roads were safe, the economy prosperous, and the impositions on the lower classes seem to

2 Ibrahim Paşa (held effective power for less than eight months in 1848)

3 Abbas Paşa (ruled 1848–54)

4 Sait Paşa (ruled 1854–63)

5 Ismail Paşa (ruled 1863–79)

have been somewhat lighter. In the area of reforms, his approach, based on utility and cost, was clearly conservative.

At an early stage in his reign, Abbas alienated most members of the ruling family, who strongly opposed him at home and in Istanbul. With the active support of European observers, they portrayed him in Ottoman elite circles and in Europe as reactionary, fanatic, cruel, indolent, and incompetent. There was little relation between the performance of Abbas as ruler of Egypt and the "demon-image" he thus acquired, a topic that will be discussed in chapters 5 and 6 below. By sharp contrast, Sait Paşa enjoyed the support of his family and the European Powers. Consequently, he acquired the reputation of an enlightened, progressive ruler and the public image of a friendly and jovial man. Atmosphere aside, however, Sait's reign brought little positive change to Egypt. As an administrator, he was not as capable and thrifty as Abbas was, for which the country paid dearly.

Sait, one of Mehmet Ali's younger sons, was born on 17 March 1822. He was brought up by French tutors and trained for a career in the navy. Under his father, his brother Ibrahim, and his nephew Abbas, Sait served as commander-in-chief of the Egyptian navy. During the reign of Abbas, Sait was the unofficial leader of the opposition to the viceroy. He was recognized as the legitimate and desirable heir to the throne by all members of the ruling family who wished to have Abbas deposed. Although Sait was accused of plotting to overthrow Abbas, the latter still allowed him to retain his position as chief of a neglected and neutralized navy. When Abbas died in July 1854, Sait succeeded him to rule Egypt until his own death in 1863. With his reign ended also the pace and mood of the middle decades, giving way to the energetic, eventful, exciting, and painful years of Ismail.

Nineteenth-century accounts and modern historiography are generally favorable to Sait Paşa. He is remembered mostly for allowing the launch of the Suez Canal project, after Abbas had resisted it for years. The Land Law which he promulgated in 1858 is widely considered as an important step towards the formation of *de jure* private land ownership in Egypt. Sait is also credited with the final phasing out of the monopolies, and with improving conscription policies, the irrigation network, and the transport and communications system. All these were begun under Abbas, but the maligned viceroy received no kind words for his contribution. In the reign of Sait, Egypt's gates were thrown open to European immigration, foreign loans were contracted on a large scale, and the influence of the foreign consuls in economic matters and domestic affairs greatly increased. All these crippled the Paşa's ability to act as he saw fit.

During the middle years of the nineteenth century, Egypt was still part of the Ottoman Empire, but the sultan's actual power over his Nile Valley dominions was limited. Although the governor-general of this semi-autonomous province (*vilayet*) was appointed by the Ottoman sovereign, he had to be the eldest surviving male member of Mehmet Ali Paşa's family. An annual tribute continued to be remitted from Cairo to Istanbul, Egyptian military units could be – and on one occasion were – summoned to fight Ottoman wars, and Egypt was restricted in its relations with foreign states. Nevertheless, in domestic matters the viceroy enjoyed a great deal of independence from the central government. The Paşa ruled Egypt with the help of a small governing elite of a few thousand bureaucrats and army officers. They spoke and governed in Turkish, and their culture, which was distinctly Ottoman, was gradually acquiring an Egyptian tinge.

The ruling family and that Ottoman-Egyptian elite disposed of all the country's material and human resources. In what basically still was an agrarian economy, a land-holding urban elite appropriated the surplus produced by a vast peasant population, the *fallāḥīn*. Through an improved network of roads and newly introduced railways, agricultural produce was being delivered to government warehouses and market towns in perfect security. With Egypt's rapid incorporation into the world economy, cash crops took over, and exportation of agricultural products was constantly rising. Although social and economic gaps were not narrowing, the 1840s and 1850s were, by and large, a good time to be alive in Egypt for members of all strata. What Western observers described as decline in the passion for comprehensive reforms, and the destruction of past achievements, was for most Egyptians a much-needed relief from a costly and demanding policy, which society seemed no longer able to sustain.

The countryside flourished and cities were full of commercial hustle and bustle. In 1850, a visitor, who was also a physician and a botanist, marveled at the beauty of rural Egypt. "Our path," he wrote,

> lay between richly cultivated fields of Guinea corn, cotton, &c. among date palms growing in clumps, or standing singly, interspersed with beautiful tufted tamarisks, and gum trees, (*acacia nilotica*,) generally called Sant. Here the doum palm is a most conspicuous feature of the landscape, and noble specimens intermixed with the date, and the two other trees just mentioned, constitute beautiful groves and glades . . . In lower Egypt the date palm forms vast groves both native and artificial, and every village almost stands in, or by, a planted palm wood . . . I had no previous idea of the lovely features of the superior parts of the valley of the Nile, in innumerable places, as between Siout and Thebes, which are so much bolder than anything I expected to see.[10]

Leaving that lush and serene environment, visitors often found themselves amidst the hubbub of Cairo, or Alexandria. There, the great variety of colors and sounds rarely failed to leave a strong impression on Europeans. A keen observer of Egypt in the early 1850s conveyed some of the impact of Cairo, as he described his walk to the Citadel, enjoying a treat of unparalleled bustle and confusion, amid throngs of horses, camels, donkeys, dogs, carriages, bullock carts; funeral and marriage processions; beys, sheikhs, effendis, fellahs, soldiers, policemen, beggars, santons; Turks, Egyptians, Arabs, Ethiopians, English, Americans, French, Germans, Italians; women, boys, and girls; Greek, Barbarians, Scythian, bond, and free.[11]

With a population of about 250,000 in the early 1840s and nearly 300,000 in the early 1860s, Cairo was one of the great urban centers of the Middle East. Its real upsurge, however, occurred later, under Khedive Ismail. In the middle decades of the century, the total population of Egypt increased from over 4.3 million to around 5.6 million. Governed by an elite of few thousand men, Egypt was defended and policed during most of the period by a force that oscillated between 80,000 and 120,000 men. Literate adults were estimated by one source to have constituted 3 percent of the total population – another source asserted that about one-third of the male population of Cairo was literate – but literacy was on the rise. About 5 percent of children aged six to twelve were receiving some formal education, Islamic, Western-influenced, or European. The government issued an official gazette, but no other newspapers were published regularly. Steam navigation and the telegraph, introduced in the 1850s, improved contact with the outside world, and visitors continued to flock to Egypt from various countries.[12]

But despite continued international interest, both economic and political, in her affairs, "the story of Egypt" in the middle years was no longer about Egypt *and* the world; it became much more – though not exclusively – about Egypt herself. Following the imposed settlement of the "Egyptian Question" in 1840–1, Egypt gradually receded from center stage, leaving it to other "questions," the Lebanon, the Straits, the Crimea. For some twenty years she would supply no major drama for the world to watch, sport no hero on the battlefields of the Middle East, excite no deep emotions at the "Gate of Felicity" in Istanbul or in the courts of Europe. Her strategic importance remained the same, but for a while was not a double-edged sword in the hands of ambitious rulers. Rather, as an issue of international politics, it was contained and, during the middle decades, the "Egyptian Question" was laid to rest.[13]

True, from time to time Egyptian issues surfaced to occupy the attention of the Powers, but those were only brief, pale reminders of a glorious and costly past. From 1850 to 1852, Abbas Paşa challenged the Porte's demand that penal legislation be applied in Egypt without modifications. This would have curtailed some of his prerogatives, most notably the right to execute condemned murderers without recourse to Istanbul. Into the whirlpool was thrown the issue of the Alexandria–Suez railway concession, which Britain had sought for a long time and ultimately obtained. This had the making of an international crisis, but exhausted itself before reaching alarming proportions. At the end of the day,

Abbas came out on top, and the Ottoman government resigned themselves to the fact that the clock could not be turned back to its pre-1841 position. In 1856, Sait Paşa granted De Lesseps the concession to dig the Suez Canal, but the project was only completed thirteen years later. Its grave international implications were not felt before the reign of Ismail.[14]

On the domestic scene, the bold, Western-inspired reforms slowly ground to a halt. Although the destruction of Mehmet Ali's military and economic enterprise is usually attributed to Abbas, the evidence clearly indicates that Abbas had little to destroy by the time he came to power. If the Old Paşa and his son Ibrahim – who held effective power for less than eight months, before dying – continued to profess Westernism, they benevolently allowed the edifice of industry to fall into disrepair, so that by the time of their demise few factories remained in operation.[15] Much reduced in size, the armed forces no longer provided a captive market for products produced by the Paşa's industries. There was not enough money to replace worn-out machinery, not enough energy and zeal to carry on a frustrating undertaking. Abbas, who was never imbued with much enthusiasm for his grandfather's industrial experiment, phased out what was left, sparing only very few profitable plants. In spite of his avowed adoration for European culture, Sait was no great reformer. Though his style was markedly different from Abbas's, inertia carried the day, and the phenomenon which Charles Issawi called "deindustrialization" continued.

Economic historians seem to agree that agricultural monopolies were gradually being abandoned in Egypt in the course of the middle decades of the nineteenth century. This, however, did not mean the loss of economic control by the rulers and their dependent elite. Other means were found to ensure that, such as the concentration of large tracts of land in the hands of the viceregal family and its allies and the demand of taxes in kind. In the mid-1850s, following Abbas's death, expenditures overtook revenues, and by the end of 1861 the floating debt was as high as £11,000,000. It was only in the early 1860s, and much more after that time, that European capital began to play a major role in the Egyptian economy, transforming and affecting power relations beyond recognition. Abbas contracted a relatively small British loan in 1852, but Sait, before his death in 1863, borrowed over £3,000,000. During his reign, Egypt became the reluctant host of large, enterprising, powerful, and practically immune "minorities." At the turn of our "forgotten period," many ingredients of Egypt's late-1870s malaise were already present.[16]

Most historians are also in agreement about the constant expansion of the state in nineteenth-century Egypt. The instruments of power created and implemented by Mehmet Ali Paşa proved effective and served the viceroy well in imposing his will and policies on the population. From its consolidation during the early 1810s, the might of the centralized state sufficed to crush the attempts to resist authority. Rural revolts and brigandage between 1820 and

1846 were put down and failed to seriously threaten the stability of the regime. The viceroy did not suffer the emergence of potentially rival centers of power, which accounts for the absence of political urban notability in Egypt, as Albert Hourani pointed out.[17] His control was efficient enough to enable him to mobilize Egypt's human and material resources to fight and win several major campaigns. In spite of great human suffering and enormous material cost, the *paşa* was secure on his throne throughout his reign.

Abbas inherited that strong and interventionist state, which, within a short time, he made his own. He, however, perfected the instruments of control to promote different policies from those his grandfather strove to achieve. Sait's government was not different in concept and practice, but towards the end of his reign, burdened, harassed, and fatigued, he became somewhat lax, though the basic patterns remained. The persisting power of the state notwithstanding, the reigns of Abbas and Sait were in fact a much-needed respite for the population. The middle years of the nineteenth century were peaceful, and the effect of peace was felt throughout society. The rural population benefited from fewer and smaller levies, interrupted only once during the Crimean War. As already mentioned, between 1853 and 1856 Egypt raised and maintained an expeditionary force of about 20,000 men to assist the sultan in that war.

A modest, thrift, less-ambitious attitude to reform, as well as neglect of some irrigation projects, also meant a reduction in public works. For the *fallāḥīn*, this spelt less forced labor (*corvée*). In addition, both Abbas and Sait abolished some rural and urban taxes, though it is not clear if workers could keep a relatively greater share of their income than before.[18] On the whole, it seemed as if the old Ottoman concept of the relation between state and subjects – what Halil Inalcı̂k called the Ottoman "economic mind" – was being restored. The 1850s saw highways being paved and expanded, the Alexandria–Cairo–Suez railway inaugurated, international trade developed, and the cultivated area extended. The army ensured calm and security, and, at least in the reign of Abbas, official injustice to the powerless majority was checked. As a true Ottoman, Abbas was well aware of the concept of "prosperity and security" (*rahat ve asayiş*) and, in his fashion, tried to apply it as best he could.

If the poor did not become poorer in the "forgotten years," the rich certainly got richer. Again, social and economic historians agree that large, private ownership of land was clearly rising. If the nature and history of private ownership of land in Egypt had given rise to some controversy, the emergence of large landed estates controlled by powerful individuals is not in dispute. Such men were members of the ruling family, high officeholders in the government, and favored court figures. Viceroys bestowed these estates on them as part of their efforts to form a loyal and totally dependent elite. Hence, they did not constitute an independent, competing group which could limit the ruler's absolute power. Not until the latter part of Ismail's reign, in the second half of the 1870s, did large landowners in Egypt act to check the viceroy. They could do that mainly because of the unprecedented influence of Europeans and European capital in Egyptian politics at the time. It was during the 1840s and 1850s that the foundations of such large landownership were laid.[19]

Mehmet Ali Paşa, who began the process and pushed it forward, bequeathed to his successors a basic confluence of social forces which held throughout the middle years. Having replaced the eighteenth-century alliance of mamluk *beys* – at times backed by merchant capital – and *ᶜulamā*, a central bureaucracy and a conscript army continued to be the mainstay of the state. The urban notability, which was depoliticized by Mehmet Ali, remained neutralized and did not play a role in the political life of Egypt. The rural notability, however, proved a useful ally of the viceroys and gradually worked its way to prominence in the administration. For a brief moment early in the reign of Abbas Paşa, a temporary realignment of forces appeared imminent. In circumstances that will be discussed in part I, the Viceroy alienated many members of the governing elite who had served his grandfather and looked for new sources of support.

He made a few gestures to the *ᶜulamā* and struck a special relationship with the bedouin chiefs. But once he managed to consolidate a loyal elite of his own, he reverted to the earlier pattern. Nevertheless, throughout his reign, Abbas was not the favorite of the Ottoman-Egyptian elite. He had to contend with strong opposition within the ruling family and was unable to rely on his uncles and cousins in the daily administration of the country. But he continued to employ Armenians and Europeans in some key positions, coopted a number of Mehmet Ali's men, and brought in his own aides. At the same time, his policies were said to have been popular with the *fallāḥīn* and the urban lower strata, and his Islamic-tinged conservatism curried the favor of the *ᶜulamā* and their ready flocks. The accession of Sait Paşa, Abbas's younger uncle and leader of the opposition, re-ingratiated the elite and the fast-growing European communities.

In appearance, at least, Mehmet Ali's style of reform regained main-stream respectability under Sait. Abbas's conservative type of reform lost out because it was so much identified with one man, Abbas Paşa, because his character was so maligned, and because of the rapid rise of European influence in Egypt during the reigns of Sait and Ismail. Consequently, a more sensible, measured, less disruptive approach to reform was not again contemplated by Egyptians for many decades thereafter. The latter part of Sait's reign already manifested many of the negative effects of the loss of such alternative. Foreign debt, an alarming degree of consular interference, and constant European pressure were very much part of reality in the late 1850s and early 1860s. This trend only intensified during the reign of Ismail Paşa, but was at least compensated by rapid development in all spheres of life. However, for the better part of the middle decades, Egyptian society was spared the mixed blessing of aggressive reform.

Egyptian society during the middle decades

Whatever the *political* alignment of social groups in mid-nineteenth-century Egypt, each group was going through different *social* processes. Egyptian society at the time was not segregated, but segmented, and interaction between its various groups was common. In socio-cultural terms we can speak of a number of sub-cultures. While each sub-culture had a distinct core, their peripheries overlapped in a noticeable measure. In the middle decades, the two most apparent sub-cultures were what I call the Ottoman-Egyptian elite and practically everybody else, or the non-elite groups. This definition replaces ethnic-based categories such as "Turks," "Turco-Circassians," and "Egyptians." It combines a lingual distinction, that between Turkish and Arabic, with a cultural one, that between Ottoman and Arab-Egyptian. This definition is not based purely on language, as not all Turkish speakers belonged to the elite. Nor is it an ethnic definition, for, despite ethnic awareness, in an Ottoman context group identity was clearly *supraethnic*, as well as constrained by political and economic circumstances.

Nor does this concept hinge on economic differentiation alone, since there were quite a few middle-income earners in the elite and a distinct group of rich merchants and rural notables among non-elite groups. This notion is somewhat closer to that of governing-elite, or power-elite; it marries power to culture. Succinctly put, core members of the Ottoman-Egyptian elite spoke Turkish; shared the values and heritage of Ottoman culture; were mostly, though not exclusively, Muslim; came from various parts of the empire, though some were born in Egypt, and from various ethnic backgrounds; were committed to serve in Egypt under an Ottoman-Egyptian dynasty; held office either in the military or in the bureaucracy; tended to be well-off and gradually came to hold agricultural land. Farther from the core, lower-level bureaucrats and army officers had lower income and less access to power. But, significantly, even they were "Ottoman gentlemen" and their wives were "Ottoman ladies," with all that these notions implied in dress, etiquette or manners and customs, and in verbal forms of entertainment.

In spite of internal differentiation, the Ottoman–Egyptian elite was fairly homogenous, which is in striking contrast to the nature of the non-elite groups. This is hardly surprising, if we remember the small size of the elite *vis-à-vis* the rest of the population. In the middle years, probably no more than one in six hundred Egyptians, that is permanent residents of Egypt, belonged to the elite. Hence the common denominator of the non-elite core was much lower, though still quite meaningful. All core members spoke Arabic and shared the values and traditions of Arabic-Egyptian culture. Unlike Ottoman-Egyptian elite culture, which was imperial, universal but Istanbul-centered, and literate, Arab–Egyptian culture was rooted in the Egyptian locale, replete with themes and images of both village and city life in the Nile Valley. Most core members were born in Egypt, and were either Muslim or Copt.

Beyond that socio-cultural core, diversity prevailed. Members of this sub-culture ranged from rich and mid-market urban merchants to shopkeepers and artisans, from the established rural notable families to the *fallāḥīn*, from rich to poor *ʿulamā*, from junior officers to their conscripted soldiers. They included speakers of Turkish, Greek, Maltese, Pashtu, and other languages, who found their way to Egypt or were brought there in various circumstances, mingled with the lower urban strata, and gradually adopted Arabic. This rich human mosaic was set apart from the Ottoman-Egyptian sub-culture. It might be cogently argued that this non-Ottoman-Egyptian milieu had its own elite group, a kind of "sub-elite." That group was distinguished by the wealth and prestige of its members, as well as by its power relation to the rest of the non-elite sub-culture. Rich merchants, high-ranking *ʿulamā*, the leadership of the *ṣūfī* orders, and the rural notability were the most prominent members of that top group outside the governing Ottoman-Egyptian elite.

We must bear in mind, however, that such a "sub-elite" had no political power and only a limited say in the running of government. Whatever influence its members had on political and economic matters had to be exercised *through* the Ottoman-Egyptian elite. Moreover, even the most influential individuals in the non-Ottoman-Egyptian group did not feel culturally at home with core members of the elite. Given the high correlation between cultural and other kinds of domination in mid-nineteenth-century Egypt, this was a significant factor. As the cores were distinct, the boundary between peripheries was drawn through a dynamic process of exclusion and inclusion. Still, where the cultural peripheries overlapped, bilingualism existed, and social mobility occurred through education and service to the state. This was also greatly facilitated by a belief system which most members of Egyptian society shared. That system was saturated with the occult and mixed with Islamic tradition and lore. As elsewhere, a simplistic dichotomy between "high" and "low," or "learned" and "popular" culture – once popular among scholars – is untenable.

The socio-cultural process of boundary drawing and redrawing was constantly acted out in mid-nineteenth-century Egypt. A long-term, everyday happening, it was a Braudelian *structure* which permeated Egyptian society on all levels.[20] If we explore the processes that occurred in the socio-cultural "twilight zone" between the two cores and examine how they affected the cores themselves, we may gain insight into the social and political history of Egypt in the whole of the nineteenth century. For one thing, during the middle years, the elite core was undergoing dynamic re-formation. For another, movement began to appear across the boundary, as members of non-elite groups were acquiring technical skills and higher government appointments in the provinces as well as in Cairo. Also, lower-strata urban society remained fairly conservative in its attitude to change. It continued to favor what I call the "known faces" and to reject anonymity, which impeded, though not prevented, migration from village to town, movement from town to town, and movement within the two large cities.

If *change* is what one looks for, then the Ottoman-Egyptian elite during the reign of Abbas Paşa is the group to observe. First, it was torn apart in a bitter struggle between the viceroy and a disloyal opposition. Regrouped and transformed, its second generation took part in a comprehensive drive to entrench a dynastic order in Egypt. Patronage networks were being reshuffled as a result of separation from the Istanbul-based Ottoman elite and the split within Mehmet Ali's family. Part I of this book describes the royal ceremonialism, power symbolism, and identity building that accompanied the emergence of dynastic order. Whereas Abbas, who initiated and directed the process, gave it a distinctly Ottoman character, Sait and Ismail preferred to emulate the courts of Europe. The entrenchment of the dynasty of Mehmet Ali was not only the most dynamic, but also the most successful political process in the middle decades. It established a trend of growing independence from the Porte and paved the way for an Egyptian monarchy that lasted until July 1952.

However, if one is attracted by early formation of long-term processes, then the educated and the rural notability are the two most interesting groups. As for the educated, the middle years were the period in which the exposure to European ideas and technology began to yield the first synthesis with the Ottoman-Egyptian and learned Islamic cultures. Those years witnessed the coming of age of men like Rifāᶜa Rāfiᶜ aṭ-Ṭahtāwī, ᶜAlī Mubārāk, and Maḥmūd al-Falakī, whose inspiration would guide generations of Egyptians on their bumpy road to nationhood. Although they and many others were to flourish in the reign of Ismail, their work was well in progress already in our period. Their contribution was not just intellectual, but mainly practical, as they actively developed and ran the first schools in which European material, translated and reworked by them, was taught to generations of Egyptians.

The rural notability, which by the turn of the century was one of the major sources of political leadership in Egypt, was modestly beginning its sociopolitical climb in the middle decades. Its members were gradually attaining mid-level positions in the provincial administration and receiving higher officers' ranks in the armed forces. Some held high office even in the central government. While Abbas preferred to rely on the services of the Ottoman-Egyptian elite, he did not indiscriminately block the way of Egyptians who did not belong to that group. Quite a few of the men who later reached prominence started their careers in his service. Sait Paşa had a deliberate policy of granting the rural notables and their sons a larger share in provincial government and the army. In 1858, he appointed the first provincial governor from that group, and in 1860, he promoted Aḥmad ᶜUrābī, future leader of the famous 1881 revolt, to the rank of colonel. Using their local power base and the apparatus of the state, members of better-off rural families were amassing the resources and attaining the skills which would propel them to the forefront of Egyptian politics.

If change and the early formation of long-term patterns have been the subject of many historical inquiries, continuity has been under-studied. The urban and rural lower strata offer an opportunity to study a section of Egyptian society whose life did not change much at mid-century. As pointed out above, peace and scaled-down development reduced the demands put on these groups by the state. But the basic patterns and realities of their life did not alter much. The state continued to appropriate their time through taxation, low pay, conscription, and the *corvée*. If the rise of Mehmet Ali replaced previous "unregulated exploitation" by "regulated exploitation," to use ᶜAlī Barakāt's phrase,[21] his successors retained the practice, albeit in a mitigated form. Part II of this book examines how the state "squeezed" the *fallāḥīn* and the urban lower strata, how some resisted and others succumbed, and how all adjusted to reality.

Members of these large groups in Egyptian society appear to have held what might be called "conservative views" – they did not seek modernity but rather tried to resist it. The degree to which they had been exposed to Mehmet Ali's reforms and their negative experience of the effects of Westernization can, perhaps, explain their attitude. A study of the two decades immediately after that great period of reform reveals that for the vast non-elite groups, it was not what some eager observers likened to nothing short of a total revolution. In part, this is because the reforms were so compartmentalized and goal-oriented that they affected only the Ottoman-Egyptian elite and those involved in the army and the new industries. In other words, the spill-over of reform to everyday life and to the social behavior of the population was far more limited than we have been led to believe.

The benefits of modernity were to be accrued as a result or direct or indirect contact with European technology, products, and daily comforts. These could be found at the new schools, in military service, on public works, in government factories, or through trade with European merchants. But only a minority among members of the lower strata had access to any of these. Much of the reformatory drive centered around the army, which was a relatively self-contained organization, especially during the long colonial wars it fought away from home. Hence, although at its peak size the army directly engaged close to 10 percent of the population, the modernizing impact of military reform was confined and short-lived. The industrial experiment, too, was fairly limited, not only in scope – involving about 40,000 workers – but also geographically; it did not encompass the whole country. In addition, for most of the period, trading with Europeans was restricted by the system of monopolies, and few merchants managed to penetrate the Delta or Upper Egypt and have any contact with the population.

Thus, for members of the lower strata of society, Mehmet Ali's modernization had mostly negative consequences which worsened their condition. Those men and women bore the brunt of the Paşa's reforms and paid the heaviest price for his wars and ambitions. In fact, the demise of his empire and the ebbing of the drive towards Westernization were a much-needed respite for these vast groups, the overwhelming majority of Egyptians. Conscription and forced labor on public works disrupted village and family life. Agricultural reform and large irrigation projects benefited not the *fallāḥīn* but the large-estate holders, foremost among whom were the viceroy himself, his family, and his loyal elite members. Perennial irrigation and the massive introduction of cash crops, particularly cotton, changed the rural ecology and displaced many *fallāḥīn*. As a result of perennial irrigation, diseases such as bilharzia – Dr. Bilharz himself worked in Egypt during the 1850s – only increased.[22]

Perhaps the only areas of development which benefited the lower strata to some extent were public health and education. However, progress in these areas was, by nature, cumulative and slow to yield results. The creation and deployment of a competent medical corps under the Frenchman Clot Bey, the opening of a medical school (1827), the introduction of quarantine measures (1831) and vaccinations (1836), and the establishment of provincial health services and hospitals in the 1840s were all important beginnings. However, they were specifically intended to care for the viceroy's bureaucrats, soldiers, factory workers, and students. Except for the control of the plague and smallpox –

6 The Nile Barrages, one of the main projects of the middle years

which were replaced by cholera – all other measures failed to reach the vast majority of Egyptians, who, in any case, tried to avoid them because they came from the government and were alien to local culture.[23] Several decades had yet to pass before the lower strata began to accept European medicine and benefit from its accomplishments.

Thus, in the final analysis, it seems that the broadest-ranging, most-enduring impact of the Old Paşa's reforms was in the area of education. That impact was primarily felt by those who benefited directly from Western education, either in Europe itself when sent to study there, or in Egyptian schools with tailored and somewhat diluted European curricula. In addition to sons of Ottoman-Egyptians, student missions to Europe and the new schools in Egypt also included sons of rural notables and other native Egyptians, members of the lower strata, who showed talent, or were fortunate enough to be selected by men of high standing and given European education. However, members of non-elite groups did not make a significant leap forward until well into the reign of Ismail. One may certainly doubt whether these seeds, sown by Mehmet Ali, would have lasted much beyond the middle decades without the resumption of aggressive reform by Ismail.

The Ottoman character of mid-century Egypt

Before we round up these introductory notes about the composition of Egyptian society and its history, a brief comment about the Ottoman character of nineteenth-century Egypt is in order. Most of what has been written on Egyptian history of the period tends to stress Egypt's growing independence from the Ottoman Empire and her development towards the modern nation-state. The nineteenth century thus assumes the role of "precursor," and its history becomes subservient to and explanatory of twentieth-century history. This is partly because the sources used by most writers are either external (i.e. European) or internal, but in Arabic and written by men who did not belong to the Ottoman-Egyptian elite. European consular reports emphasize the weakening of Ottoman political control over Egypt from the reign of Mehmet Ali until the British occupation. The impact of Egyptian sources in Arabic is twofold: first, they are external to the governing elite and the dominant culture of which they seem to have little knowledge; second, by Arabicizing Ottoman Turkish terms, they distort the Ottoman nature of government in Egypt at the time.

Some writers have used the Turkish material in the Egyptian National Archives, but rather through the Arabic translation available there and not directly in the original. This has created a barrier to an understanding of the profoundly Ottoman nature of both the administration and the Ottoman-Egyptian elite. Thus, high members of the elite – who spoke Turkish, considered themselves and were considered by others as Ottomans, and would be completely at home in an Istanbul salon – are introduced in Arabic as *adh-dhawāt al-kirām*, not in Turkish as *zevat-i kiram*, as they were called. *Efendi* becomes *afandī*, *kethüdâ* becomes *katkhoda*, the suffix *-baş* (+ ı), which denotes "head of," usually in ranks, becomes *bāshī*, which soon deteriorates to *bāshā* and is then mistaken for the title of *paşa*, as happens in colloquial Egyptian (e.g., *binbaşı* → *bikbāshā*). The *vali*, or governor-general, appears as *al-wālī*, or the *Bāshā*; his common title *veliyünimet*, or benefactor, quite familiar to students of Ottoman history, appears as *wālī an-niʿma* (sometimes *veliyüniâm* becomes *wālī an-niʿam*); his and his family's estates are now *shaflik*, or *jiflik* (with an Arabic plural *shafālik*), instead of *çiftlik*. Mehmet Ali, of course, will for ever be known as Muḥammad ʿAlī.[24]

The case I wish to make here is not for elegance nor for purist accuracy, but against the imminent loss of the Ottoman historical context. Not only are the terms distorted, but gone is their clear relation to the past and contemporary Ottoman background, which can explain and present them for what they were. Lost are also the nature of a dynasty, of an elite culture, of a rich and complex bureaucratic tradition. Our ability to trace the fascinating interaction between the Ottoman and the local, the central and the provincial, is thus much impaired. A mere glossary reference to the Turkish origin of terms, or a cursory acknowledgment in the text that the elite was "Turkish," are clearly not enough; they do not change the general impression left with the reader. If we "Arabicize" the government and elite of Mehmet Ali Paşa, we are bound to misapprehend the gradual process of Egyptianization, which made the Ottoman elite in Egypt at the beginning of the nineteenth century into the Ottoman-Egyptian elite of the middle years, and finally, at the turn of the century and beyond, into an Egyptian elite.

This story, which is crucial for the understanding of nineteenth-century Egyptian history as a whole, is graphically told by the records of the Egyptian National Archives. The registers of the Cairo government well into the reign of Sait Paşa are mostly in Turkish, with the Arabic records forming a small minority. The reign of Abbas Paşa is perhaps the most "Turkish," while that of Ismail is beginning to manifest a preference for Arabic. Obviously, this is not merely a technical point, but a significant social indicator. For it clarifies the process by which Egypt became the heir to an Ottoman bureaucratic heritage, with all its advantages, limitations, and implications for the Republican era. This is yet another instance of what Albert Hourani called the "Ottoman background of the Middle East."[25] As we move from the realm of elite and government, Arabic becomes all-important. Thus, parts I and II of this book duly reflect this transition from Turkish to Arabic in both terminology and sociocultural interpretation.

A word on scope and method

The present book deals with political, social, and cultural themes that lie at the crossroads of state and society in mid-nineteenth-century Egypt. It does *not* pretend to offer an *histoire totale* of the period, if such a goal is at all attainable. Rather, my intention is to consider the main features of an interesting and formative, but much neglected, period of Egyptian history. These features bring together the political, the social, and the cultural, not necessarily in causal relationships, but as complementary facets. Economic matters are considered on a "need to know" basis, not for the sake of writing an economic history of the period. The works of Roger Owen, Charles Issawi, and others make this luxury possible. I have not dealt with intellectual developments either within Islamic or Westernized circles, as these seem to have had but a limited effect upon the groups and issues which concerned me most in this book.

A few important groups in Egyptian society are under-represented in this study. This does not stem from the mere limits of space or sources, although quite naturally these had to be taken into account. Rather, I believe that the state of the historiography justifies the omission. In recent years, a number of good studies have appeared that make it unnecessary to belabor certain aspects of nineteenth-century Egyptian history. Women, the bureaucracy, the *ᶜulamā*, the *ṣūfī* world, and the emerging native Egyptian intelligentsia and intellectuals have been variously treated by Judith Tucker, Robert Hunter, F. De Jong, Chris Eccel, Gilbert Delanoue, and Anouar Abdel-Malek. I have relied on their works when relevant to the middle years, reviewed some points of contention when such arose, but found it on the whole unnecessary to recapitulate their theses just in order to "cover" an entire society. Instead, I focused only on those social groups whose history during the middle decades appeared especially interesting and seemed to reflect the mood of the period.

Given the considerable amount of excellent source material available for the period, the extent to which it has been neglected by historians is indeed striking. The most important source for the present book is the material contained in the Egyptian National Archives in Cairo. Registers of the central government, police files, administrative court records, and occasional papers form the bulk of documents consulted and adduced here. Much of what I have to say is derived from that material, which has been evaluated and interpreted with the assistance of other archival sources, notably British, French, and American consular reports, as well as Ottoman records and Amīn Sāmī's valuable collection of documents from the Egyptian Archives. Greek, Italian, and Russian consular reports have also been published. Some of the high officials of the middle decades left invaluable private papers and memoirs, as did others who were just beginning a career then and later rose to prominence. Nubar Paşa, Hekekyan

Bey, ᶜAlī Paşa Mubārak, Clot Bey, Linant de Bellefonds, Yusuf Kâmil Paşa, and Cevdet Paşa come to mind as the main examples.

The middle years were also blessed with a number of high-quality travel accounts, some by well-known and talented writers, such as Gustave Flaubert, Maxime Du Camp, and Anthony Trollope. Other travellers have also proved to be meticulous observers, most notably Nassau Senior, Bayle St. John, John Gadsby, and the guide-book compiler John G. Wilkinson. *The Times* had a permanent correspondent in Alexandria who sent communiqués from Egypt almost every fortnight through most of the period. Not a few of the first photographs ever to be taken are of ancient Egyptian monuments, but also of mid-century Egypt in whose midst they were located. Du Camp, Francis Frith, and Felix Teynard's pictures date from the 1850s. Some excellent collections of drawings are also available for the period. David Roberts and Edward Lear are better known, but Edwad James Hawker's collection also injects life into a society long gone.

All these have been used to retrieve as much as is still possible of mid-century life. My aim has been to paint a picture, to convey an atmosphere, to open a crack through which one can see a world gone by. The required evidence does not have to be concocted, it abounds in the sources. There is no need to contrive a reality that cries out to be recovered. Rather, the difficulty lies in the wealth of information, in the great detail, and in the necessity to make sense of data that greatly impedes, if not outright defies, quantification. Having plunged into the anthropologically "thick"[26] records of the Egyptian Archives, one can appreciate Bayle St. John's reaction, in the early 1850s, as he was trying to describe Cairo: "It is most difficult to convey a general idea of a city, the very charater of which is infinite variety." It is equally easy to understand Flaubert's response to the sounds and scenes of Cairo in January 1850:

> each detail reaches out to grip you; it pinches you; and the more you concentrate on it the less you grasp the whole. Then gradually all this becomes harmonious and the pieces fall into place of themselves, in accordance with the laws of perspective. But the first days, by God, it is such a bewildering chaos of colours.[27]

To overcome the problems presented by the material, I chose, for parts of the narrative, what is sometimes called an anecdotal style of writing. This method is not original; it has been used by many historians with similar problems, mostly for conveying "everyday life." An eminent historian who made extensive use of anecdotes, which he also called "snapshots," believed that "sometimes a few anecdotes are enough to set up a signal which points to a way of life."[28] As a rule, anecdotes have been used in this work only when supported by other cases and deemed representative. All anecdotes are specific instances and, in many cases, are taken from the police and court records. It is important to note, however, that such records do not reflect a marginal world of offenders, but the entire society. The men and women in these records came from all walks of life. They were witnesses, relatives, neighbors, employers, or the victims of crime, while those who committed an offense, or were accused of transgressions, formed only a small minority. Through their investigators, even illiterate men and women, who could not leave a written record, tell us of the world they inhabited.

The historiography of the middle decades

The conventional periodization of nineteenth-century Egyptian history is dominated by rulers and political events. It is still very much about grand policy, foreign and imperial relations, battles, conquests, and large-scale economic ventures. In most history books, all these are arranged by reigns, the underlying assumption being that the Viceroy's personality molded the period of his rule. According to main-stream historiography, the French occupation of 1798 is thought to have ended a "dark age" and inaugurated the modern era. The reign of Mehmet Ali Paşa is described as an heroic period of conquest and reform. The renewal of grand-scale Westernization by Khedive Ismail is presented as yet another great reign, which, however, ended in a bad way. The rest of the century belongs to colonial history, an age that heralded Egyptian nationalism. The rise of the nation-state in its various aspects still dominates the study of twentieth-century Egyptian history.

Sandwiched between the reigns of Mehmet Ali and Ismail is the most neglected period in the study of the modern history of Egypt. The reigns of Abbas and Sait have acquired dubious reputation as a dull interregnum, attracting few interested scholars. All the authoritative textbooks reflect and perpetuate the notion that nothing "important" happened in those years, nothing that is worth remembering. In fact, the period I call the "forgotten years" began well before the reign of Abbas. After the collapse of his Syrian empire and the end of his challenge to the central Ottoman government, Mehmet Ali became less interesting to writers and historians. The reaction to his declining political importance was not immediate, as the decline itself was not. Hence, most worthwhile accounts of his reign peter out around 1843–4, providing very little information and interpretation for the remainder of the decade. The time unit proposed in this work is, thus, both historically and historiographically coherent.

To put things in perspective, the traditional periodization needs to be somewhat revised. Rather than following the well-trodden path arranged by reigns of viceroys, we ought to consider as one historical unit the period from about 1841 through the reigns of Ibrahim, Abbas, and Sait, until about 1863. That period shall hereafter be referred to variously as "the middle years," "mid-century," "the middle decades," and in historiographical terms, "the forgotten years." The gist of the argument is that the period thus marked had an historical coherence, pace, and air quite different from those of either the preceding or succeeding periods. This work will attempt to show that not only in terms of political history, internal and external, but also in terms of economic, social, and cultural history, that period should be studied as one unit. Whereas the first two parts of Mehmet Ali's reign and much of Ismail's reign were dominated by large-scale, energetic, Western-inspired reforms and expansionism, the middle years were quiet, relaxed, withdrawn.

If Mehmet Ali's expansionism ended in defeat, ushering in the mood of the middle years, Ismail's galloping Westernism led to bankruptcy, deposition (1879), revolt (1881), and British occupation (1882). Though certainly not devoid of interest or action, the middle years, by comparison, lacked in heroism, enthusiasm, and excitement, but managed to avoid past and future disasters. In part, this is why so little is known about the period, indeed why it has been "forgotten" by historians and students of Egyptian history. But in part, the middle decades suffered from the repelling reputation of the reign of Abbas Paşa. The hold of his demon-image over the historiography made his reign unattractive to scholars and students alike. And that, in turn, impeded the study of the middle years as a whole. Though popular with European writers for obvious reasons, Sait Paşa did not cut an impressive figure by any standard. Above all, Sait aroused benign indifference that could not kindle interest in his reign nor generate studies of the preceding period.

The following pages will tell, in chronological order, the story of the historiography of Abbas and his reign. For the reader's convenience, a great deal of information has been removed to expansive notes. It is hoped that the evidence and interpretation offered in the rest of the book will prove the inadequacy of the writings about the period. This, in turn, may open the middle decades to fresh research. Our sample includes not only scholarly works by historians of modern Egypt, but also material composed by what might be termed writers about Egyptian history. Considered in this section are works from the 1880s until the present, in Egypt and abroad, in Arabic, Turkish, French, English, German, and Italian. The writers come from different backgrounds: European, Ottoman, and Egyptian. Only few of the sources devote much space to the reign of Abbas – or to the middle decades – but all mention him and evaluate his character, often in quite unequivocal terms.

The first volume of *La Grande Encyclopédie* was published in Paris in 1887. It contained a detailed article about Abbas Paşa, written by the publicist Maxime Petit.[29] The author was mostly interested in the foreign policy of Egypt under Abbas, and in the power play between Istanbul, Cairo, and the major European caitals. However, a few words were also devoted to the character of the Paşa. As a youth, we are told, Abbas preferred drills and games to studying. But when he first assumed a position of power as provincial governor in Lower Egypt, the ugly side of his nature became apparent. He ordered two innocent women to be drowned in the river for a trivial matter, and had one of his mistresses flogged 500 times. He then exiled her to Esna, the city to which prostitutes had been banished. "In one word," the author summed up this character sketch, "the spoiled child became a capricious, cruel, and unjust tyrant, and since he attained any power, his haughty nature did not permit him to suffer the smallest contradiction [of his word]." With the authority of *La Grande Encyclopédie*, this image became part of the historical record, and was then transmitted on.

At the turn of the century, Louis Brehier incorporated that text into the book he wrote about Egyptian history from 1798 to 1900. In a short chapter about the reigns of Abbas and Sait, we read that Abbas was bent on destroying his grandfather's modernizing endeavors, and that if his government had lasted longer Egypt would have returned to the "beaux jours" of the mamluks. Brehier believed that Abbas was as fanatic as he was cruel. As a finale, Brehier recounts the story, attributed to the *fallāḥīn*, that the excessive heat that prevailed when Abbas died was due to the opening of the gates of Hell to receive his soul. About the same time, a rather more mixed account of the reign of Abbas appeared in D. A. Cameron's work *Egypt in the Nineteenth Century*. The book was published in London in 1898, and is fairly representative of the less passionate treatment of Abbas across the Channel. However, in what became a common attitude to the middle decades, Cameron lumps together the reigns of Abbas, Sait, and Ismail, and asserts that there is little to admire in that period, in which Egyptian history becomes "emphatically dull."[30]

The first time an item devoted to Abbas appeared in the *Encyclopaedia Britannica* was in the eleventh edition of 1910. It occupied only a third of a column and contained the following sentences:

> He has been generally described as a mere voluptuary, but Nubar Pasha spoke of him as a true Turkish gentleman of the old school. He was without question a reactionary, morose and taciturn, and spent nearly all his time shut up in his palace. He undid, as far as lay in his power, the works of his grandfather, good and bad.

This unsigned entry clearly benefited from Cameron's book, though his more balanced approach was somehow lost on the way.[31] In any event, what may be overlooked in a general encyclopedia is more difficult to excuse in a specialized one.

The first edition of the *Encyclopaedia of Islam* was pubished in Leiden and London in 1913. In this major enterprise of Western orientalism, J. Oestrup wrote the article about Abbas. As the following passage reveals, the article is quite startling in its strong language:

> the beginning of that brutality of character which he later showed so strongly could already be seen in his childhood. Having been at a very early age entrusted with important

> office, he behaved as a full-blooded despot of the best oriental type . . . As to the internal government of Egypt, ᶜAbbas acted as a narrow-minded and stupid fanatic. He gave up the costly experiments of his two predecessors to introduce European civilization into his country, only it was not from any economical motive, but purely out of hate of the Franks and his hostility to culture.

No sources are adduced in the bibliography to support these harsh words, published in what became one of the main reference works for almost half a century.[32]

During the middle and late 1920s, George Young, C. G. Elgood, Ettore Rossi, Joseph Cattaui, and Henry Dodwell all wrote about Egyptian history. In varying degrees, they all contributed to the dislike of Abbas Paşa and the middle years of the nineteenth century.[33] To Young, whose book *Egypt* first appeared in 1927, Abbas's reign was "a calamity." The Paşa was "a born reactionary," whose revolt against Mehmet Ali's modernism was, nonetheless, a genuine Egyptian reaction to foreign exploitation. Much the same view is taken by C. G. Elgood. The contrast between Mehmet Ali and Abbas, as between progress and reaction, light and darkness, is reflected in many works, but is perhaps especially significant for the main argument of Dodwell's famous book *The Founder of Modern Egypt*, published in 1931. Dodwell was one of the scholars who benefited from King Faud I's encouragement of the study of nineteenth- and twentieth-century Egyptian history. In a way, his book inaugurated the "New History" of Egypt, which was being written during the 1930s.

The king was interested in promoting a scholarly – and preferably favorable – studies of the royal family from the time of its illustrious founder, Mehmet Ali Paşa, until his own reign. He opened the state archives to approved Egyptian, French, Italian, and British scholars. The king also financed the publication of voluminous works, both independent historical studies and edited texts of state and consular records. As far as Abbas is concerned, these works did not yield any substantive alteration of the basic views we have encountered thus far. The received wisdom about Abbas and the record of his reign was woven into the respectable pages of modern historiography in both western and Eastern languages. The few changes that may be discerned are in the more serious historical studies conducted during the formative 1930s. Such changes concerned only the assessment of Abbas's reign, but not the harsh treatment of his character.

In his much quoted *ᶜAṣr Ismāᶜīl*, which he published in 1932, ar-Rāfiᶜī devotes a twelve-page chapter to the reign of Abbas. To remove any possible doubts, the title of the chapter already includes the term "reaction" (*rajᶜiyya*). According to ar-Rāfiᶜī, Abbas had none of the good qualities required to govern Egypt, and during his reign "the movement of progress and renaissance which had been launched in Mehmet Ali's time came to a halt." He credits Abbas with the construction of the railway, the improvement of the Cairo–Suez road, and, significantly, his refusal to dig the Suez Canal, or grant foreigners concessions to exploit Egypt's natural resources. On these issues, the author adds, Abbas's record was better than those of Sait and Ismail, and history should remember him well for it. Ar-Rāfi^{c}ī also shows some historiographical sensitivity when he states that the excessive criticism levelled at Abbas by French writers is due to the decline of French influence in Egypt during his period.[34]

Sabry's lengthy *L'Empire égyptien sous Ismail* was published in Paris in 1933. His concept of nineteenth-century Egyptian history is vividly demonstrated in this scholarly work. Sabry produced two huge volumes dealing with the Egyptian Empire, one under Mehmet Ali, the other under Ismail. By his own admission, the middle decades were a "discredit," like the period between Louis XIV and Louis XVI in French history. Accordingly, they merited only a few dozen pages, based mostly on French and British consular reports. Abbas, says Sabry,had many faults with no redeeming quality. He was lazy, frivolous, superstitious, mistrustful, dissimulating, cold, taciturn, cruel, despotic, reactionary, an enemy of innovations, extravagant, fond of luxury and pleasure, capricious, and unstable. However, Abbas checked the spread of European influence in Egypt. Sait Paşa later reopened the country to Europeans, but was faced with the harsh consequences of his policies. Willy-nilly, Sabry concedes that Abbas managed Egypt's foreign affairs with skill and success, but strongly condemns him for having destroyed the life work of Mehmet Ali and for ruling Egypt in silence and terror.[35]

Even the limited and reluctant credit that Sabry bestowed on Abbas drew sharp criticism from Angelo Sammarco, whose book on the reigns of Abbas, Sait, and Ismail was published in 1935. This work became one of the four authoritative texts for reference to the much neglected middle decades. In the text, we are told that from the moment of his accession, Abbas's mind was set on destroying all the good and useful work of Mehmet Ali. Abbas wished to erase the "action civilisatrice" of his grandfather, but it had already gone too far for him to be able to drag the country back to barbarism. Abbas not only destroyed, but derived real pleasure from personally supervising the work of destruction, as in the case of the Barrage. Not much that is new or different seems to be presented by Sammarco. However, with the weight of scholarly prestige, the demon-image of Abbas receives in this work its most ringing endorsement, though certainly not the only one.[36]

About a year later, in 1936, the fourth volume of the *Histoire de la Nation Egyptienne* appeared in Paris.[37] Authoritative and officially endorsed, the *Histoire* portrays, in the words of Charles-Roux, an Abbas whose reputation in history is that of a "prince borné et d'instincts mauvais." Reading the text, one might get the impression that during his reign the country was on the verge of disintegration: security was neglected, finances fell into disarray, and while important projects were being abandoned for lack of funds Abbas was spending on luxury like mad. However, the viceroy's handling of foreign affairs was quite skilful, admits the author. This goes some way towards a more balanced view, but surely not enough. The condemnation of Abbas in the opening part is so strongly worded that the impact is carried throughout the entire discussion. The final, positive passage is too hedged and feeble to improve the general impression. Especially so, as it ends in a quotation from a report of the French consul-general in Egypt, who asserts that there was not one person who was not happy to be relieved of the "système de compression" which weighed upon Egypt during the reign of Abbas.

Also in 1936, Amīn Sāmī published another volume of his celebrated work *Taqwīm an-Nīl*, with seventy pages dedicated to the period of Abbas Paşa. This valuable collection of edited documents from the Egyptian archives occasionally contains some observations by the editor and compiler on various issues treated in the documents. At the end of the chapter devoted to Abbas, Amīn Sāmī provides a one-paragraph evaluation of his reign.[38] Half of that paragraph eulogizes Mehmet Ali's reforms, while the other half consists of a short list divided between Abbas's accomplishments and his faults. Abbas is credited with the construction of the railway and with leaving behind a treasury free of debt. However, he is blamed for destroying many educational institutions, of which only few remained in the country after his time. He is also accused of neglecting the navy, and of intending to deny members of his family their share in Mehmet Ali's inheritance. In that affair, we learn, the Sultan had to intervene in order to protect the lawful rights of the princes. So, Amīn Sāmī censures Abbas for both omission and commission: he blames him, by implication, for failing to measure up to his grandfather in reformatory zeal; and quite directly, he accuses him of being a tyrant, who actively destroyed much of Mehmet Ali's progressive work.

Thus, already by the mid 1930s, with the disparaging notes by recognized authorities such as Sabry, Sammarco, Charles-Roux, and Amīn Sāmī, Abbas was decidedly relegated to a sad place of notoriety in the annals of Egypt, from which it would be almost impossible to extricate him in generations to come. With him and his reign, the reputation of the middle decades as a whole was set. It, too, was quite unattractive. Even those who, for whatever motive, praised Sait could not change the general picture, or make his reign more interesting to students of Egyptian history. These mid-1930s scholarly notions were canonized in M. Colombe's article about Abbas, published in 1960 in the new edition of the *Encyclopaedia of Islam*.[39] Still, over the years, a few writers dissented from the predominant anti-Abbas view. They were, however, a small minority unable to change the tide. A brief reminder of their dissenting view is in order here.

In 1886, A. Vingtrinier published in French a biography of Süleyman Paşa, formerly Joseph Sève, a French colonel in Napoleon's army who reorganized Mehmet Ali's armies and became one of the most celebrated Egyptian generals.

In this detailed and laudatory biography, we find the first dissenting view about the reign of Abbas Paşa. Vingtrinier does not consider Abbas to have been any worse ruler than others. True, Europeans were estranged from his government, but debts were paid and the treasury operated without deficit. Abbas was "léger, insouciant, personnel" – almost the opposite of what his character was supposed to have been according to received notions – and in the eyes of many orthodox Muslims, he governed better than Mehmet Ali. Thus, concludes Vingtrinier, his reign was not, as claimed by many, a period of death, but rather a repose, "recueillement de la terre pendant l'hiver."[40]

In 1895, Ismail Serheng Paşa launched his important work on the history of Egypt. The second volume, out of three, was published two years later; it contained five pages on the reign of Abbas Paşa.[41] The author's father was a ship's captain in the Egyptian expeditionary force sent by Abbas in 1853 to assist the Ottoman armies in the Crimean War. Serheng himself was an army officer, and his information on military affairs is particularly valuable. But he also had historiographical awareness, for he was the first of our sources to point out that Abbas was severely criticized by writers because he drove out of service many French experts, cut their pensions, and revoked their work permits. This is the first time, as far as I am aware, that the evaluation of Abbas's reign and personality, in this case by French authors, is treated critically. Serheng's book also contains one of the earliest and fullest accounts of the assassination of Abbas, in which the page who betrayed his master is condemned as a traitor (*khā'in*).

From the last decade of the nineteenth century onward, with the growing interest among educated Egyptians in local history, a number of useful reference works made their appearance. This is, of course, in addition to historical works, which had been published sporadically during the century. Mubārak's monumental bio-geographical dictionary, the *Khiṭaṭ*, is the most important of this genre. We should note also the appearance, beginning in 1876, of the first encyclopedia in Arabic – Bustānī's *Dā'irat al-Maᶜārif*. In 1897, Elias Zakhūra published his *Mir'āt al-ᶜAṣr*, sub-titled "History and Pictures of Great Men in Egypt," and a number of biographical dictionaries, of varying quality, appeared in the following years. Several history books, notably those written by Jurjī Zaydān, were published from the second decade of the twentieth century onwards.

As far as the treatment of Abbas's personality is concerned, these works have one thing in common: they all describe the defamed Paşa in commendatory terms. Abbas receives high marks for almost every phase of his career, beginning with his school days, through his years as military commander in Syria, to his performance as governor-general of Egypt. Indeed, the compilers seem to have been virtually unaware of what Europeans had been writing about Abbas for nearly half a century. Here, unanimity is not the result of independent reseearch leading to the same conclusions, for some of these men merely copied Abbas's biography from each other with minimal variations. The common source for most of them was probably Zakhūra and Bustānī.[42] The treatment of Abbas, and for that matter of Sait and the rest of the viceroys, is quite stereotyped, avoiding negative information and providing very limited evaluation. That genre had no noticeable impact on the historiography of the middle decades.

Thus, until the publication of ar-Rāfiᶜī's comments on Abbas (1932) and of Amīn Sāmī's assessment of the viceroy's reign (1936), the biography of Abbas in Arabic was quite positive. That was to change, not only because of what such authors had to say about Abbas, but even more because Egyptian writers and historians were now consulting accounts in European languages. Actually, some of the histories in European languages were written by Egyptians who taught Egyptian history in Egypt. The views of Sabry, Rifaat, or Ghorbal, were often as "progressist" and Western-oriented as those of their European teachers and colleagues. So the fundamental world view that produced the demon-image in European writings was internalized by Egyptian writers. In their works, they reproduced Abbas's image often with reinforced zeal.

In 1938, a short while after these works first appeared, J. Heyworth-Dunne published his much-quoted, pioneering work, *An Introduction to the History of Education in Modern Egypt*. If we consider that some of the main charges against Abbas were based on his alleged destruction of the educational system in Egypt, we could expect Heyworth-Dunne's book to provide a major indictment of the Paşa. In fact, however, this book offers the strongest defense of Abbas's rule that I have come across, not only of what he did in the field of education, but also of his overall record. After a brief survey of the prevailiang view of Abbas, Heyworth-Dunne asserts that "self-interest and personal feelings have been allowed to inspire many of the pens that have described Abbas."[43] Whereas one can hardly find a book dealing with education in the Middle East that does not cite Heyworth-Dunne's book, often extensively, his view about Abbas Paşa has left almost no impact on the literature.

The Awakening of Modern Egypt, published in 1947 by Muhammad Rifaat, devoted a chapter to the reigns of Abbas and Sait, significantly entitled "Stillness after the Storm." To the author, a British-trained professor of history and a director-general of the Ministry of Education in pre-revolutionary Egypt, stillness was not a positive term, for it actually meant that almost nothing of note happened in those middle years between the two great movements of reform. In 1961, Helen Rivlin wrote a sympathetic account about the way Abbas handled his foreign relations in trying times. However, her paper does, on the whole, very little to revise the way in which the Paşa and his reign had been presented in the literature. In 1966, ᶜOmar ᶜAbd al-ᶜAzīz ᶜOmar surveyed the introduction of railways during the middle decades. He, too, based his main theses on European archival sources without questioning their strong anti-Abbas bias. Thus, with Rivlin and ᶜOmar having no interest in an historiographical re-evaluation, a rare opportunity to challenge the accepted view of the middle decades was lost.[44]

Not that such a challenge would have been inconceivable. When ᶜOmar submitted his dissertation (1966), his supervisor at the School of Oriental and African Studies, Professor P. M. Holt, published his widely circulating textbook, *Egypt and the Fertile Crescent, 1516–1922*. Almost thirty years after Heyworth-Dunne called in question the prevailing view of Abbas, Holt raised his own doubts about the validity of received notions. His discerning sensitivity on this point is unique in scholarly writings. Holt pointed out the too-heavy reliance on accounts written by contemporary partisan observers about Abbas, Sait, and Ismail. He attributed the unsympathetic views of Abbas to the fact that the Paşa's traditionalist rule and mistrust of European reforms ran counter to the modernizing current in Egyptian history between 1805 and 1882. Holt further believed that Abbas's attitude

> was an intelligible point of view, but it was not likely to commend itself either to the Europeans who found themselves deprived by ᶜAbbās of lucrative employment, or to writers who regarded the westernization of traditional society as synonymous with progress.

Holt's view remained, however, a minority view and was not incorporated into future textbooks on the modern history of Egypt.[45]

For Egyptian writers and intellectuals, Abbas remains the man who dealt a blow to the development of Egyptian national consciousness by exiling to the Sudan Rifāᶜa Rāfiᶜ aṭ-Ṭahṭāwī, the hero of the national and intellectual renaissance of Egypt. In 1969, for example, Anouar Abdel-Malek published his *Idéologie et Renaissance National, l'Egypte Moderne*, which he dedicated "pour le peuple égyptien et, en son nom, pour Rifāᶜa Rāfiᶜ al-Ṭahṭāwī (1801–1873)." The author faults Abbas for obstructing Egypt's progress in all areas.[46] After Abbas died, aṭ-Ṭahṭāwī was recalled by Sait Paşa, while ᶜAlī Mubārak, who prospered under Abbas, was sent away from the capital. For this "change of the guard," Sait was assured a much better press in Egyptian intellectual circles, though not his reign or the middle years. The fact that aṭ-Ṭahṭāwī flourished in the reign of Ismail made it even easier to look back on the middle decades as a "dark age" in terms of intellectual life and national education.

How, then, did the blackened record of Abbas's reign, his demon-image, and the dismal view of the middle decades survive the scrutiny of modern scholarly research on Egyptian history? The answer is fairly simple. First, there was no need to revise the character evaluation of Abbas, as long as the record of his reign remained so tarnished. Second, his reign and record as ruler were seriously examined only in the formative works of the 1930s. The influential works of

Sabry, Sammarco, and Charles-Roux were based on hostile consular material, mostly French, but also some British. These scholars also shared a world view with their sources, which prevented them from questioning the basic assumptions and biases of the material. There was little doubt in their minds that Mehmet Ali was the model of the ideal Egyptian ruler, and that his reforms were the best thing that ever happened to Egypt. It is true that Sabry criticized the European presence in Egypt for obstructing Egyptian independence. Yet, he, too, shared the view that European civilization had all the cures for Egypt's woes. Those writers were not all French, but they wrote in French, had French education, and – most importantly – thought French.

Heyworth-Dunne was clearly the odd man out among the scholars of the 1930s. To be able to look at Abbas in a different way, one had to doubt the basic interpretation of the meeting between East and West; that is, to question the very paradigm of modernization. If one believed, as did Bayle St. John and a few other observers, that European activities caused a great deal of damage to the social and economic equilibrium in Egypt, only then could one approach the role of Mehmet Ali, Abbas, and Sait afresh. In the eyes of such observers, the Old Paşa tried to introduce unrealistic reforms in a brutal way that tore apart the social fabric of Egyptian society. He brought more disruption and suffering than progress and happiness. To them, Abbas only tried to restore the balance, heal the wounds, and re-adjust the pace of life in Egypt. This was clearly a minority view among Egyptian writers during the century that followed Abbas's reign. Among the scholars of the formative 1930s, Heyworth-Dunne's was a lonely voice.

At the same time, the traditional biographies of Abbas in Arabic maintained a separate existence well into the twentieth century. These show no awareness of the standing of their subject in Western literature, and their approach is not critical. Only in the 1930s do the writers in Arabic and European languages cross paths and, in fact, merge into a single current. As seen above, the resulting account is quite negative. In those years, only few politicians and intellectuals, in both Egypt and Europe, dissented from the traditional view of modernization. That was conceived essentially as a process through which the East was gradually becoming like the West, denying its self-identity in order to assume a "progressive" posture. A serious re-evaluation of modernization theory had to wait until the 1960s. As no original research has been done on the reign of Abbas since the 1930s, the historiography of the period had not been revised. Rivlin and ʿOmar, who did work on that period, were interested in specific topics, not in a general re-evaluation, and surely not in an historiographical revision. Again, as in the case of Heyworth-Dunne, P. M. Holt's view of the middle years was the exception.[47]

Writing in 1910 about the nature of historical knowledge, the editor of the eleventh edition of the *Encyclopaedia Britannica*, Hugh Chisholm, wished to assure the readers that, in spite of certain doubts, the product of historical research was sound and trustworthy. He further emphasized that "what *has been*, if accurately recorded, remains permanently true as such."[48] Looking at the historiography of the reign of Abbas and the middle decades, we may slightly revise his assertion to read that whad has been, even if *inaccurately* recorded, *might* remain permanently true as such. The trouble, of course, is that the negative nature of that historiography cast a shadow on the whole period, making it unattractive to prospective students of nineteenth-century Egyptian history. Upheld by default, the false notions about the middle decades have remained unchallenged.

PART I

The Ottoman-Egyptian elite in the middle of the nineteenth century

Introduction

We begin with a history of the Ottoman-Egypt elite, neither because of any preference for a hierarchical order of things, nor because the history of any social group is inherently more important or interesting than that of another group. Rather, the choice of the elite is predicated on the view that the most dynamic and significant developments during the middle years of the nineteenth century in Egypt happened at the top of the socio-political ladder. It was within the Ottoman-Egyptian elite that the nature of government was determined for the following seven or eight decades. The shift of generations from the reign of Mehmet Ali to that of Abbas, the struggle inside the ruling family, the survival of hereditary governorship and the emergence of dynastic order were not only politically important, but also economically, socially, and culturally significant. It is through these processes that we may learn how an Ottoman khedivate became an Egyptian monarchy and understand some of the major features of Egyptian political culture before 1952.

1 Dissent and opposition

Abbas's dissent from Mehmet Ali's style of reform

Although historians have paid little attention to the reign of Abbas, it is in fact hard to overestimate the impact of his administration on the makeup and character of the Ottoman-Egyptian elite. Not until the accession of Ismail in 1863 was a ruler faced with such a challenge to his ability to govern effectively. It is commonly assumed that in patrimonial household politics ideological issues tended to be of little significance. Personal loyalties were the dominant element, it is further argued, and articulation of political controversy was limited. While this may have been true in the Ottoman Empire until late in the eighteenth century,[1] the situation changed with the introduction of Western-inspired reform. In this respect, too, Egyptian history is much a part of Ottoman history. What appeared as mere rivalries between mamluk households for domination and access to economic resources took on an added dimension with the advent of reforms in the second decade of the nineteenth century.

Even within the tight patrimonial household government of Mehmet Ali Paşa, the introduction of modernization along Western lines proved a divisive political issue; in fact, it became a rallying point for opposition. However, during most of his reign, opposition was not directly aimed at the viceroy, but rather found expression in factions which developed within his household among potential heirs to the throne. Thus, the first major cleavage occurred between Ibrahim Paşa, son of Mehmet Ali and heir presumptive, and Abbas Paşa, grandson and next in the herditary line after Ibrahim. In the last few years of Mehmet Ali's reign, the Old Paşa and Ibrahim had bitter disagreements and greatly mistrusted each other. This, however, did not bring Abbas into alliance with either of them. The reasons were partly personal, but an undeniable ideological element was also present – a marked difference in attitude to European-inspired reform.

Perhaps too much has been made of Abbas's alleged rejection of his grandfather's aggressive Westernization. What is certain, however, is that Abbas offered an alternative attitude to reform. His approach was different from that commonly identified with the views of either Mehmet Ali or the Tanzimat reformers in Istanbul. The most obvious and mobilizing aspect of opposition "counter-culture" was its rejection of the prominent role, and consequent high visibility, of Europeans in Egypt. Another aspect was a different view regarding the pace and scope of reform the country could sustain. Succinctly put, Abbas and like-minded people in the Ottoman-Egyptian elite believed that too many Europeans were carrying out too many and too expensive reforms in Egypt too fast. It must be understood that even Abbas and his men did not advocate a return to a golden age in some remote, idyllic past. They had immediate grievances and sought to redress them within the context of a modernizing society, not outside it.

As often happens, Abbas's known dissent from mainstream reformism *à la* Mehmet Ali and Ibrahim attracted the disaffected and malcontents. But these were not merely seeking alternative patronage, they also had a common political view. It is difficult to know who these people actually were. Ottoman-Egyptian sources are unlikely to record such information, for this was not an open, declared opposition with known adherents or formal organization. No such opposition could conceivably exist during the reign of Mehmet Ali. Rather, it was a sentiment embodied in the person of Abbas and shared by the people of his patrimonial household. During the late 1840s, that ideological tinge distinguished Abbas's household from any of the households of the ruling family. European sources noticed that difference and described the phenomenon as the formation of a "Fanatical Party."

Mehmet Ali Paşa was certainly aware of his grandson's views. In fact, on several occasions they aroused his suspicion. The British consul-general reported in March 1840 that there was popular opposition in Cairo to the Viceroy's levies in the area and "other arbitrary acts."[2] Abbas was then Governor of Cairo, and Mehmet Ali felt that he did not do enough to check that public reaction. The Paşa, reported the consul-general, "even expressed some suspicions of his [Abbas's] tempering in intrigues." It is unlikely, however, that in those years Abbas, or anybody else, could seriously contemplate taking even indirect action against the government of Mehmet Ali. This is not to say that he could not make his criticism known in political circles and serve as a "benign focus of opposition," as he did. For his conservative approach to reform, Abbas was branded a "reactionary," and the consequences of his future accession were dreaded by supporters of the reforms both within the elite and among the Europeans.

In a sympathetic contemporary account of that "opposition," Bayle St. John compared Abbas and his group favorably to the other actors in the political scene of mid-century Egypt. In an odd way, he himself appears to be sharing, at least in principle, the sentiments commonly associated with that unique phenomenon in the Egyptian body politic of the time. "It must be confessed," wrote St. John, that Abbas Pasha alone had the good sense to take up a position of his own. Whether he was as crafty and politic as some pretend before his elevation to power, it is difficult to decide; but the plan at that time generally ascribed to him, of forming what was called a Turkish or bigoted party, – a party of discontented great folks, and fanatical Ulemas, – a party which should appeal to the religious prejudices of the good Caireens, and oppose itself to the inroad of European adventurers and improvements, – this plan, if distinctly formed, was certainly a very sagacious one. Let us be frank: Europeans have done more harm than good in Egypt.[3]

The author then went on to describe the negative effects that European involvement in Egypt had. He also believed that Abbas had planned to deal a fatal blow to European interests in the country, but that such an option did not exist politically. Ironically, it was the aging Paşa and his pro-European son Ibrahim who carried out much of what Abbas had preached. The 1840s witnessed a real scaling-down of Mehmet Ali's reforms, and many of the projects were either completely abandoned or retrenched. The same trend continued through the short reign of Ibrahim, in which, Nubar wrote, "the work of destruction continued uninterrupted." Taking advantage of a rare moment of calm, Abbas requested leave to go on a pilgrimage to Mecca, so as to distance himself from the center of tension and personal danger. His wish was granted and he departed. A short while later, Ibrahim died, and in mid-November 1848, Abbas was recalled to assume power. The Greek consul reported that the accession of Abbas was greeted with general public rejoicing.[4]

A major reshuffle in alliances was expected as a result of this change.[5] Normally, this would have occurred during an interim period, after which new alliances would be formed and stability restored. Nevertheless, what happened to the Ottoman-Egyptian polity in the reign of Abbas, especially in its earlier period, was both traumatic and far-reaching. Instead of going through a process of smooth realignment of forces, the elite was torn apart. A long-drawn-out bitter struggle for hegemony ensued, while the autonomy and hereditary governorship of the province were being challenged by the Ottoman government and nearly lost. In fact, it is not so difficult to understand why this happened, though the extent of its implications has not been fully appreciated. Without going into cumbersome detail, the following section will attempt to outline the main features of the struggle within the Ottoman-Egyptian elite.

Opposition to Abbas within the ruling family

The Islamic and Ottoman preference for passing hereditary political power to the senior male member of the ruling family meant that when Ibrahim Paşa died Abbas possessed the acknowledged right of succession. Although a grandson of the Old Paşa, he was thirty-five, and older than Sait, Mehmet Ali's eldest surviving son, who was then only twenty-five. Other potential contenders were also much younger. There were two younger sons of Mehmet Ali, Abdülhalim, aged seventeen, and Mehmet Ali, still a minor. But the more troublesome candidates were the three sons of Ibrahim Paşa: Ahmet Rifat, who was thirty-three, Ismail (later khedive) and Mustafa Fazîl, who were both eighteen. Though not in the line of succession, Nazlî and Zeynep, daughters of mehmet Ali, were also involved in the politics of the time. As women, they were limited in their public activity, but both they and a certain Gelin Hanîm, an elite figure, appear from time to time in the accounts of the period. Nazlî was by then a widow, while Zeynep was married to Yusuf Kâmil Paşa, one of the leading figures of Mehmet Ali's household. When the septuagenarian ruler became mentally incapacitated, Ibrahim was not only the legitimate successor; he was much more than that – he was the natural and indisputable one.

Abbas's position was markedly different. From a legal standpoint, the right of Abbas to succeed was not challenged. However, owing to his reputation as a leading opponent of Mehmet Ali's style of reform, and because of his known alliances, his accession was feared by many members of the elite. Though younger, Sait Paşa was certainly of age, and his philo-European sentiments were widely known. With the temporary exception of Mustafa Fazîl, it was the households of the late Ibrahim and of Sait which formed the backbone of the opposition. Still, all waited to see the direction in which Abbas would steer his government. At first, there was a hint of continuity, with the retention of key figures in their high positions. Kavalalî Mehmet Şerif Paşa remained as *Kethüdâ*, or Deputy Governor-General, Artîn Bey continued as Commerce and Foreign Minister, Ali Burhan Paşa stayed as head of the Finance Department, and Sait Paşa, the main contender, was renewed as Commander of the Navy. Foreign, mostly French, anxieties were temporarily alleviated with the extension of Süleyman Paşa as Chief-of-Staff, while some of the top French officials, such as the Director of Engineering Linant Bey, were also allowed to remain in office.[6]

Soon enough, however, these proved to be merely the cover for a drive to remove from positions of influence all those who had served in prominent positions in the administrations of Mehmet Ali and Ibrahim. Abbas feared that these men were not reconciled to having him as complete master of the land, and would soon try to turn him into a figurehead and run the government on their own. He believed that their services were not indispensable and sought support in Istanbul for their recall to other imperial duties. With the honeymoon between Abbas and the Porte in the offing, his wish was granted. Meanwhile, a property dispute flared up between the sons of Mehmet Ali and Abbas.[7] The viceroy refused to release to their possession a great deal of property, which they claimed as private and he as state domain. The vast amounts of money involved became the focal point of contention between Abbas and the rest of the family. In consequence, a number of the leading figures and their retinues moves to Istanbul to obtain justice.

By May 1849, the French consul was having contacts with Sait Paşa, Artîn Bey, and the French ambassador in Istanbul, General Aupick. Weighing the gravity of the situation and the growing threat to French interests in Egypt, he proposed to his government that steps might be taken in Istanbul and Cairo to have Abbas deposed. A few months later, a major conflict erupted between the Porte and Abbas over the application of Ottoman legislation in Egypt and the concession of the railway. During that conflict, the last remaining family ally of Abbas, Mustafa Fazîl, defected to the opposition. In 1851, Hekekyan could list in his diary notes twenty-seven names of high-ranking officials alienated by Abbas since the beginning of his reign. The list included five *paşas*, among them prominent names such as Mehmet Şerif, Sami, Yusuf Kâmil, and Hasan, and twenty-two *beys*, among them Artîn, Clot, Lambert, Gaetani, and Bedan. In those years, Abbas came to rely on the services of Manastîrlî Hasan Paşa, Diramalî Ahmet Paşa, Manikli Ahmet Paşa, Stefan Bey, and Nubar.[8]

With the settlement of the dispute between Abbas and the Porte, late in May 1852, hopes of deposing him were finally shattered – not, however, before a plot led by Sait was uncovered earlier that month. It was organized in the hope of destabilizing the country while the Porte's emissaries were still in Cairo trying to resolve the conflict. In one of the villages belonging to Sait Paşa's estate in the district of Sharnūb, near Alexandria, a group of household members and auxiliaries was assembled, armed, clad in military uniforms, and trained for combat.[9] Some of the men were recruited from other opposition households; that of Ahmet Rifat Bey, son of Ibrahim Paşa, was mentioned specifically. Friendly bedouin tribes and naval units – Sait was still chief of the navy – provided the rest of the troops. The actual size of the force is not clear, but estimates reached several hundreds. Rumors that spread among the villagers regarding that unusual activity were reported to the governor of the province.

The governor moved in immediately, but could track down only one contingent of men. Some twenty bedouins on horseback managed to escape, leaving at the hands of the governor sixty men in uniform, sixty-three rifles, six fully equipped field guns, and a considerable amount of ammunition. Some of the men had served as stablemen, running footmen, messengers, and gardeners in Sait Paşa's household. Others were recruited from various provinces in the Delta, from Giza near Cairo to Buḥayra near Alexandria. Five naval officers were in charge of military instruction. The case was reviewed by the military court and treated as a serious offence. Accordingly, it was recommended that the instructors be sentenced to ten years' hard labor in the mines of Feyzoğlu in the Sudan. The remaining men were to be dispersed among different regiments stationed in the Sudan. However, when the case came before the Council of Justice, the sentences recommended by the military court were seen as insufficient. Consequently, all men were sentenced to fifteen years in the mines of Jabal Fezzan, deep in the Sudan.

Ironically, in this case the Council of Justice was already applying the provisions of the penal section of the law enacted as a result of the settlement reached between Abbas and the Porte. Sait Paşa, however, was allowed to remain as navy chief, and continued to be the focus of opposition to Abbas throughout his reign. From time to time, rumors circulated regarding tensions within the Ottoman-Egyptian elite. In May 1853, the French consul-general reported that an attempt had been made on Abbas's life and that many arrests were being made in Cairo. To his credit, it must be said that the diplomat doubted the possibility of any serious challenge to Abbas from the opposition. He further observed that, if Abbas was ever hit, it would be by one of the members of his entourage, at a moment of anger caused by insult, which, he added, was common from Abbas. Abbas continued to restrict the movement of his rivals, at times refusing Sait an extended yachting trip to Europe, at others forbidding Mustafa Fazîl to leave Egypt for several months.

Referring to those years, Sait told Senior in 1856 that they, the opposition, were all "as sweet as a lamb" under Abbas.[10] However, even if we accept this self-effacing description of reality in the reign of Abbas, we should note that important precedents were being set at the time. The fact that leading households within the ruling family were alienated from government had far-reaching implications for nineteenth-century Egyptian history.

Sait Paşa: end of the alternative approach to reform

After the unexpected death of Abbas, his arch-rival Sait came to the throne. As the attempt by members of Abbas's household to foil the order of succession failed, a complete changeover was expected to take place. "Sait," wrote Edwin De Leon, "collected the scattered sticks of the faggot which Abbas had divided; but on his death they were scatteed again." In fact, although room was made at the top for members of the alienated branches of the ruling family, the change was not so dramatic. True, men like Sait's brother Abdülhalim Paşa, and his nephews Ahmet Rifat, Ismail, and Mustafa Fazîl, Ibrahim's sons, held from time to time important positions in government. However, they were not a dominant force in the administration, nor did they work as a team. There was little love lost among the princes, and, with time, rivalries impeded cooperation. After the first wave of recriminations, members of Abbas's cabinet found their way back to high offices. Middle-level officials like ʿAlī Mubārak, or Nubar and his brother Arakel, lost their positions. But men such as Manastîrlî Hasan Paşa, Manikli Ahmet Paşa, Stefan Bey, and others who had been considered close to Abbas, still managed to play a role in Sait's government.[12]

Most striking in its absence during the reign of Sait was a real challenge from a rival faction. No opposition similar to the one Abbas had to contend with existed. The natural candidate to lead such a faction was Abbas's son, Ilhami

Paşa.[12] Yet Ilhami was too young – about seventeen years old – isolated within the ruling family, and incapable of providing the needed leadership. The beginning was "promising," though. As Sait entered Cairo to assume the governorship of Egypt, Abbas's *kethüdâ*, Ibrahim Elfi Paşa, and some military commanders refused to surrender the Citadel to him. They hoped to stall the accession until the return of Ilhami from Europe, but, under consular pressure, they gave up almost immediately and dispersed. When Ilhami returned to Egypt, he entered into a prolonged dispute with Sait over the inheritance of his father, similar in many ways to the one between Mehmet Ali's heirs and Abbas. But this was where the similarities ended. Without a leader, and without support, there was to be no opposition to speak of. As Sait reintegrated many of Abbas's men into his administration, even the cause for opposition was gone.

Not until the reign of Ismail was a viceroy faced with the difficulties that Abbas was faced with. But Ismail had the benefit of hindsight, which Abbas did not. Thus, the reign of Abbas had a crucial importance in the history of Mehmet Ali's dynasty and in forging the political culture of nineteenth-century Egypt. For one thing, it placed the hereditary government of Egypt firmly in the hands of the House of Mehmet Ali. As pointed out earlier, Ibrahim's succession was not the real test. He was known to be very ill and not expected to live long. The Porte clearly saw the reign of Abbas as the test of the whole arrangement for the governorship of its Egyptian *Vilayet*. The fact that Abbas, unlike Ibrahim, was controversial and unpopular within the Ottoman-Egyptian elite and among Europeans gave the Ottoman government a chance to manipulate the opposition and weaken the dynastic principle as the best idea for Egypt.

As a direct result of the intra-family struggle, a new generation of administrators and military commanders replaced the one that served Mehmet Ali and Ibrahim.[13] Abbas, Sait, and Ismail relied on men who emerged out of the rift between Abbas and Sait during the early 1850s. The fact that the Porte played such an important role in the rivalry helped to "drain" the outgoing group, or first generation. While hoping to benefit from the power struggle in Egypt, Istanbul actually served as a "safety valve," preventing Egypt from becoming a "pressure cooker," with no alternatives for members of the losing party. Although the patrimonial style of government did not change much during the 1840s and 1850s, a basic notion in the political culture did. It was during the reign of Abbas that, for the first time, large households, those in opposition to the viceroy, operated outside the core of government. Indeed, they managed to survive as organizations and patronage networks while receding into the periphery of the body politic.

This was certainly one of the effects of the Porte's special position in Egypt. Egypt's attachment to the Empire provided the checks and balances that prevented Abbas from applying to his relatives the same methods used by his grandfather against the chief Mamluk households. As ultimate arbiter of power,

Istanbul set the limits of viceregal rapacity *vis-à-vis* the other households in the ruling family. The fact that even the dispute over the inheritance of Mehmet Ali had to be settled by a legal opinion of the Şeyhülislam in the capital meant that, in economic as in political matters, Abbas could do only so much. Left with their large estates, factories, and palaces, his uncles and cousins continued to maintain large households. These required the services of accountants, managers, engineers, skilled and unskilled workers, and servants. They thrived on patron–client relations and led an almost autonomous existence.

When a similar dispute arose between Sait and Ilhami over the estate of Abbas, the outcome was distinctly different.[14] Sait deprived the young prince of his government position as Minister of War, but allowed him to retain a large share of his father's property. This would have enabled Ilhami to fade quietly into household activity outside the scope of government. However, Ilhami claimed a larger chunk of property, and later, in 1856, even sued Sait for the expenses of the Alexandria–Cairo railway. Through waste, fraud, and frivolity, an almost legendary estate dwindled rapidly. In a few years, the prince, if not exactly a pauper, fell into debt and began to borrow heavily from European bankers. With the involvement of Ilhami's bankers, the continuous dispute acquired a financial and political nuisance-value for the viceroy. Wishing to enlist in his favor old and trusted mechanisms, he tried to have the issue referred to Istanbul for adjudication. By then, however, his European policies had backfired and he was too vulnerable to consular pressure. In the meantime Ilhami died, but the final settlement of the matter proved a painful and costly business for Sait, nonetheless.

Another consequence of the intra-family strife during the reign of Abbas Paşa can be seen in the realm of ideology, or political thinking. Because the rivalry between Abbas and the rest of the ruling family did have an ideological aspect, its outcome decided, to a great extent, the course Egypt would take for the rest of the century, if not beyond. As stated before, the difference between the camps lay in the approach to Western-style reform. In opposition to the costly and extravagant reforms implemented by Mehmet Ali and Ibrahim, Abbas proposed to scale down the move, apply cost/benefit calculations, and reduce the direct involvement of European experts in executive positions in government. He had no ambitions of military expansion and was willing to strengthen his ties with the Porte. With hindsight, his alternative policy made sense. It was also quite successful. However, with his death and the defeat of his "party," the policies propagated by them lost out completely. They did not constitute an option in Egyptian politics until the 1930s.

The reason is simple. Abbas managed to antagonize the constituencies that might have supported his policy and could, in due course, espouse and perpetuate at least some of its major components. His failure to integrate leading members of the ruling family into government absolved such men of all responsibility for his policies. Thus, discontinuity became an almost inevitable consequence of any change of government. Abbas also failed to build bridges to the European powers through their consuls and the foreign community in Egypt. Even his attempt to sugarcoat the pill he administered to French interests was too clumsy to be effective. Hence, Europeans in general sympathized with the opposition, and the opposition became increasingly identified with European-style reform. Abbas was depicted by both groups as a reactionary of the first order and as an inveterate hater of Europeans and European civilization. Though he was far from being so, his policies came to be seen as a threat to Egypt's progress.

When Sait succeeded, he not only made changes in the administration, as any new ruler would have, introducing a completely different personal style and opening his court to Europeans. He did more than that: he made every effort to demonstrate that the reign of Abbas were a mere aberration. It was made to look as if it had been no more than a nightmare, a dark episode in Egyptian history, and that there would be a return to the "right course" charted by Mehmet Ali and Ibrahim. Though in many ways he continued the policies of Abbas, the image created was of a complete break, a clean cut with Abbas, both the man and his way.[15] In this he was enthusiastically assisted by his family and the Europeans. Very soon, however, style yielded substance, and Mehmet Ali's approach to modernization eclipsed the only viable alternative – that offered by Abbas. Only neither Sait nor Ismail were as strong and skilful as Mehmet Ali; rejecting Abbas and his ideas, too eagerly rushing to modernize, they soon found themselves in the hands of European bankers.

In this chapter, we followed the development of dissent into open opposition. Abbas's "party" became the government, and for four and a half years put many of its ideas into practice. Consequently, some ruling-family and old elite figures lost much of their influence, while French and other European interests were jeopardized. For almost three years, an overt effort to overturn the government of Abbas was mounted in Egypt and Istanbul. Although the challenge of the opposition occupied and aggravated the viceroy, it did not tie his hands. Far from it, his efforts to stifle the opposition did not prevent Abbas from launching a formidable campaign to entrench a dynastic order in Egypt. In a way, it was his response to the attempts of Sait and other prominent family members to discredit him and his policies. As we shall see in the following chapter, although his approach to reform was abandoned, some of the main elements of his dynastic style of government were eagerly adopted by his successors.

2 Creation of a dynastic order

There should be little doubt that in the socio-political history of mid-nineteenth-century Egypt, the process of institutionalization of a dynastic order – with the contemporaneous emergence of a new civil bureaucracy – was the most significant process that occurred within the Ottoman-Egyptian elite. Essentially, it was all about entrenching a center of power and legitimating it. True, Mehmet Ali was granted hereditary rule over Egypt, but the *ferman* of inheritance was only the first step to legitimacy. His heirs had to win legitimacy for an Ottoman-Egyptian dynasty, a task made all the more formidable by the unquestioned, charismatic legitimacy of the House of Osman. It was accomplished nevertheless, and again, in many ways, the pattern was set during the reign of Abbas. The first thing he did as governor-general of Egypt was to accept the sultan's invitation to come to Istanbul to receive in person the edict of investiture. That very act, which was confirmed in numerous ceremonies and rituals in the Ottoman capital, was an act of submission to one's undisputed sovereign. It strengthened the bond that had been weakened by Mehmet Ali and Ibrahim, and gave the Porte more than a ceremonial position *vis-à-vis* the government of Egypt. But that act of submission was equally a part of the drive to legitimate the dynasty in Egypt itself.

Writing about the symbolics of power, Clifford Geertz observed that at the political center of any complex society

> there is both a governing elite and a set of symbolic forms expressing the fact that it is in fact governing. No matter how democratically the members of the elite are chosen (usually not very) or how deeply divided among themselves they may be (usually much more than outsiders imagine), they justify their existence and order their actions in terms of a collection of stories, ceremonies, insignia, formalities, and appurtenances that they have either inherited or, in more revolutionary situations, invented. It is these – crowns and coronations, limousines and conferences – that mark the center as center and give what goes on there its aura of being not merely important but in some odd fashion connected with the way the world is built.[1]

It is precisely that "symbolic character of domination," in Geertz's terms, which was being developed during the reign of Abbas and accentuated under his successors, Ismail in particular. Rituals and ceremonies of different kinds and on various levels served as a form of communication that became part of mid-nineteenth-century Egyptian realities. The stereotyped, public, and politic nature of those rituals was unmistakable. Especially under Abbas, and to countermand the absence of Mehmet Ali's heroic government, ceremony not only legitimated authority, but also mystified it.[2]

Abbas's ceremonial court

Charles Murray, Britain's consul-general in Egypt, referred to the new style of the viceroy's court as "Abbas's follies." In fact, this was a serious matter. Although festivities were celebrated in the courts of Mehmet Ali and Ibrahim, their general style of government was rather austere. There is little evidence to indicate any conscious effort to involve the public at large in a ritualized ordering of society. Both the Old Paşa and his son were above all military men and state builders. They were "self-made men" who fought their way to glory. Hence they were less given to lavish spending and criticized "spoiled" and "soft" men like Abbas and Sait. They were drawn to European technology more than to European luxuries and comforts. A change of attitude to ceremonies and ostentation was noticeable almost immediately upon Abbas's accession at the beginning of 1849, as ceremonies became more frequent and spectacular. These were not limited to the person of the ruler, but extended to all members of Abbas's immediate family.[3]

Thus, for example, a major procession – pageantry and all – took place upon the return of Abbas's mother from Istanbul.[4] The sound of cannons accompanied the entry of the Paşa's mother (*Valide Paşa*) into Cairo, announcing her passage through the city all the way to the Citadel. The procession consisted of the following: at the head rode high military and civilian officials in their uniforms, then came two squadrons of cavalry, then more than forty closed carriages, presumably containing harem personnel, and then, at the end, in an elegant carriage with six horses, rode the viceroy's mother. The carriage was flanked on all sides by eunuchs and cavalrymen. For three days the city remained adorned with street decorations and illuminations, a bonfire was lit in Azbakiyya Square, and every hour a cannon fired.

Two months later, in September, a much more elaborate ceremony took place – the circumcision rites of Abbas's eldest son Ilhami. Young princes of the Ottoman family were circumcised between the ages of eight and sixteen, and the occasion was usually celebrated in public by all social strata. The tradition was emulated in Egypt, though festivities for Ilhami surpassed even what could be expected for a sovereign's son. The celebration lasted for fourteen days and nights, with lavish balls for the court and elite, and charity feasts of sheep and buffalos for the poor. The final procession paraded through the streets of Cairo, displaying the treasures of the viceregal family. Early in January 1850, Flaubert recorded in his travel notes impressions of yet another ceremonial procession. It marked the return of Abbas's mother-in-law from the pilgrimage to Mecca.

We went to see the ceremony of her arrival at the palace, which is at the edge of the [Suez] desert . . . Desert maneuvers by the irregular infantry . . . Bekir Bey invites us in with the staff; the band plays polkas . . . the poor Turkish *pasha*s, grotesque in their tight European uniforms. The Princess's camels wear knee-pads decorated with pieces of mirror framed in rows of pearls; around their necks are triple bell-collars, and on their heads tufts of colored feathers. The windows of her litter are shaped like a ship's portholes and lined inside with mirrors. On the lances carried by the irregulars, the tips of the shafts are trimmed with bristles of feathers.[5]

The frequency and ostentation of such ceremonies, and their being associated with figures not widely known to the public, were a new phenomenon in mid-nineteenth-century Egypt. The Greek consul remarked that the public did not react enthusiastically to the elaborate and lavish reception accorded to Abbas's mother. But Murray, the British consul-general, described the large masses that filled the streets during Ilhami's circumcision procession, adding that "no serious accidents have occurred, nor has there been any appearance of disaffection, or disturbance." Gradually, people learnt to accept the new style of government. Officials were ordered to don their full uniforms on holidays and state occasions, and public life in Egypt became markedly more ceremonial. Because of the challenge to his rule from within, and the need to use the trappings of dynastic rule, Abbas relied on ceremony and ritual. He was thus acting out his legitimate status. After 1852, Abbas gradually withdrew from the public eye. Although he himself attended only the most significant ceremonies after that, Abbas did not abandon the use of ritual as a political tool.

A major component in the legitimacy of the Mehmet Ali dynasty, at least in the eyes of Abbas and the Ottoman-Egyptian elite, derived from the charisma of the Ottoman sultans. Therefore, it was necessary to demonstrate the continuous flow of symbolic support even in times of strained relations between Istanbul and Cairo. Abbas was perfectly happy to pose as a "sub-monarch" to the sultan, though he was unwilling to relinquish Egypt's autonomy and become a figurehead, or just another governor-general in the empire. At the beginning of June 1850, three large portraits of Sultan Abdülmecit arrived in Egypt and were presented to Abbas.[6] Accompanied by a senior emissary of the Porte, they were received in Cairo with much pomp and paraded through the city in a great procession. The portraits were exhibited in the Citadel for three days amidst ceremonies and celebrations, and were finally hung in the three most important public offices. The event served the Porte as a public affirmation of sovereignty, while Abbas could pose as the delegate of the sultan, who exercised power in Egypt in his name.

Even when Abbas and the Porte were at loggerheads, the ceremonial semblance of legitimacy was not removed. In fact, one can argue that the conflict over the introduction of Ottoman legislation itself acquired a symbolic dimension. To both insiders and outsiders, it was presented as a rift over the right to execute murderers after due process of law, that is, the question of *lex talionis*, or *kīsas*. Nubar observed that the issue was perceived in terms of what the exercise of that authority *implied*.[7] It became a question of prestige, a symbol of sovereign power threatened to be withdrawn. The viceroy would become an impotent ruler, it was argued by his agents as by foreign diplomats supporting his cause, if he were to be deprived of the right to take the life of legally convicted murderers. Needless to say, it was precisely that kind of symbolic effect that the Porte was meaning to achieve. Yet, amidst all that, in April 1851, an envoy arrived from Istanbul with a special imperial sermon for the inauguration of the new mosque in the Citadel.

The mosque, which still dominates Cairo's skyline today, is known as the Muḥammad ᶜAlī Mosque. It was intended by Mehmet Ali Paşa as a "cathedral mosque" and family mausoleum. Much of the work had already been done when Abbas came to power, but it was he who completed the final stage. In a symbolic act reflecting the change of attitude from grandfather to grandson, Abbas named it the Mecidiye, in honor of the reigning sultan, Abdülmecit. In the circumstances that prevailed, the Ottoman envoy who carried the festive sermon also conducted political negotiations with Abbas. However, the official reason for his visit was stated in terms of the ceremony at the Citadel. After the resolution of the conflict, relations between Abbas and the sultan warmed up considerably. In March 1854, a messenger arrived from Istanbul to announce the betrothal of Münire Sultan, daughter of Abdülmecit, to Ilhami Paşa, son of Abbas. Large public celebrations were proclaimed and the viceroy was reported to be highly pleased with the news.[8] As we shall see below, it formed a part of his grand plan to alter the order of succession, for which the Porte's consent had to be obtained.

Construction of new palaces

An essential part of dynastic symbolism during the reign of Abbas was the construction of palaces. Mehmet Ali had a small number of them scattered in various spots in the country. When in Cairo, he usually moved between the palaces of Shubrā and the Citadel. At the Citadel, he normally worked, receiving officials and guests, transacting the business of government. The furniture was mostly European, and not very ostentatious at that. "There was throughout a universal mixture of meanness and extravagance, magnificence and dirtiness," wrote a visitor in 1847. "Marble floors, and shabby stuccoed walls; rich couches and curtains and some pieces of furniture that might have been picked up in Broker's Alley, London." The same visitor, however, was taken with the beauty of the Shubra palace, especially known for its gardens. "Turn which way I would, the scene was enrapturing," he wrote, though here, too, he found the interior unworthy of particular notice.[9]

With Abbas, palaces were a passion. He built and rebuilt at least seven, some in remote and isolated places. The best-known ones, which he frequented most, were the very large one in ᶜAbbāsiyya, north-east of Cairo, an area that was then in the desert, and Binha, in the Delta, where he also died. Foreigners often mentioned with wonder the palace of Dār al-Bayḍā', in the middle of the Suez desert, which they observed on the road from Cairo to Suez, not far from station no. 8. Before he became viceroy, Abbas built the palace of Kharanfish, inside the city of Cairo. Al-ᶜAtaba al-Khaḍrā', another palace, was built on an historically significant site. The mansion which Abbas bought in the luxurious area of Azbakiyya had belonged to two famous mamluk *beys*, Riḍwān Kethüdâ al-Jilfī and Muḥammad Bey Abū adh-Dhahab. Abbas tore it down and built a palace instead, which he later gave to his mother. Some government business was conducted from time to time in the palace of Ḥilmiyya, and there were also less-used palaces in Birkat as-Sabᶜ and Alexandria.[10]

Much effort was involved in these construction projects. Because some of them were in uninhabited areas, water and building materials had to be hauled by camels and carts, often causing the workers great hardship. These were either soldiers, convicts, or *fallāḥīn* serving on *corvée*. At the same time, roads were paved to facilitate access to these palaces, trees were planted, and bridges constructed. The large palace in ᶜAbbāsiyya was designed as the nucleus of a government center, with barracks, a hospital, and military schools around it. High-ranking members of the Ottoman-Egyptian elite were given free land and ordered to build their homes in ᶜAbbāsiyya. Under much pressure from the viceroy, many did. Gradually, the area witnessed a growth in commercial activity, but Abbas's unexpected death was detrimental to the developing town. Sait had different ideas and a markedly different style of government, so he branched out westward to the banks of the Nile and built Qasr an-Nīl. As for ᶜAbbāsiyya, it was used by British troops from 1882 on, and was finally incorporated into the city at the beginning of the twentieth century.[11]

Ironically, in spite of Abbas's secrecy, we possess no less than four insiders' accounts of the interior of his most guarded palace of ᶜAbbāsiyya. Kâmil Paşa, later grand vezir, was an apprentice in the palace inner service and tutor to Abbas's son Ilhami. We shall later return to his notes about the internal organization of the palace (pp. 56–7 below). Nubar, who was often at the viceroy's side, and ᶜAlī Mubārak, who also had been to the palace on official matters, both made passing remarks on the style of ᶜAbbāsiyya. Mubārak commented only that great attention was devoted to the structure and luxury of the palace. Nubar wrote that it was furnished and decorated with "exquisite taste, by real artists." It was somber as a structure and somber in its decor, he added. And Sait Paşa, who visited some of his arch-rival's palaces and bought the one at Binha, told

Senior that Abbas, "fond as he was of building, lived always in the most uncomfortable houses."[12]

Abbas's construction zeal cannot be explained away as mere frenzy. The giant scale that it assumed, both in size and in numbers, was a sharp departure from the austere style of his two predecessors. I suggest that it, too, symbolized to Abbas dynastic grandeur. As a highly private person, the Paşa had little social use for the large palaces he built and lavishly furnished. Visitors were not welcome in their splendid rooms, and no high-society balls were given there by the ruler. Rather, the size and magnificence of palaces represented sovereign power, royal prestige. ᶜAbbāsiyya was thus meant to project splendid isolation, at once removed from the city, and elevated on a hill. In a symbolic way, it reflected Abbas and his style of government, which, like his palace at ᶜAbbāsiyya, were aloof, gloomy, and commanding. Sait's personality and government were different; they required a different habitat too. Dynastic grandeur remained and flourished throughout his reign, but he tore down the walls, opened the palace gates, and filled the ballrooms with song and laughter. So ᶜAbbāsiyya was abandoned and new palaces were built.

But there remained a common architectural style throughout the period. Actually, a change had already begun to occur in the 1830s, during the reign of Mehmet Ali, as more houses were being constructed according to an Ottoman-Mediterranean style, called in Arabic *Rūmī*.[13] By the 1840s, wooden lattice windows (*mashrabiyya*s) were gradually giving way to European windows with rectangular framed panes. The Mamluk style was being replaced by a mixture of Greek, Italian, and Spanish styles, often seen along the Ottoman-dominated littoral of the Eastern Mediterranean. Abbas's buildings were mostly in that style, which was also adopted by Sait and Ismail. However, while Sait turned to Europe, wholeheartedly embracing her culture, Abbas looked to Istanbul. As his palaces point out, nonetheless, he imbibed European influence through the Ottoman pipe. If Sait and Ismail were more like European princes, Abbas saw himself as "a vezir, the son of a vezir, the grandson of a vezir." He tried to apply that view in every sphere of life, and, as the Ottoman center was slowly modernizing, so was he.

Emulation of the imperial court

It was also to Istanbul that the viceroy turned for a model of a royal court. Not only the ceremonies, but the basic structure of the patrimonial household of the Paşa was modelled on the imperial one. Much in the way that grandees of the Ottoman elite tried to emulate the sultan's household, so did the viceroys of Egypt and the prominent members of the Ottoman-Egyptian elite. Mehmet Ali and Ibrahim also fashioned their households on the sultanic model, but Abbas, Sait, and Ismail aspired to attain a closer approximation of the original. It is not merely in size and wealth that resemblance has to be measured, but in content and quality as well. Both Findley and Hunter have shown that the patrimonial household as a model was organized on a kin base, extended through marriage and slavery. Beyond that core, a vast network of patron–client relations existed through the institution of *intisap*. Such households were personally dependent on their respective heads, who disposed at will of all political and economic power in their spheres of influence.[14]

With his efforts to institutionalize dynastic order, Abbas upgraded the status of his court. Although role relations remained the same, the outlook seemed different. Thus, his mother was cast in the role of the sultan's mother (*Valide Sultan*), the top figure in the harem and the most prominent woman at court. The harem itself became socially and politically more important, and the influence of the chief eunuchs rose. "The most powerful and high-ranking men," wrote Aḥmad Shafīq in his late-nineteenth-century pamphlet on Islamic slavery, "used to fawn and grovel before Elmas Ağa, head eunuch of Abbas Paşa's mother, Halil Ağa, head eunuch of Sait Paşa['s mother], and later before the famous Halil Ağa, head eunuch of the former Khedive [Ismail]'s mother." Spread in various palaces, harems became large social and administrative structures.

Even the palace service under Abbas resembled, in more ways than one, the classical structure of the imperial palace. The internal organization in the newly constructed ᶜAbbāsiyya palace was "very strange," at least to the young and impressionable Kâmil Paşa, who would later become Ottoman grand vezir.[15] The palace consisted of three huge wings, each having a different purpose. The first wing constituted the harem, and no one outside that wing was allowed to enter it. The second wing housed the Paşa's young mamluks, being trained for their future career as the most loyal personal guard of the viceroy. It resembled the palace school, in which the sultan's servile elite was trained in the classical period. That section of the palace was also inaccessible to outsiders. The third wing was the *selamlık* of Abbas, or the public – hence male – quarters. The viceroy's apartment was on the top floor. It was to that section that officials came to report and receive orders. On rare occasions, foreign visitors were received there too. On the middle floor lived mamluks who had graduated from the palace school, some young pages, and a few sons of high-ranking members of the Ottoman-Egyptian elite.

Most of these young men, too, were kept in isolation from the outside world. They were assigned to the personal service of the Paşa much in keeping with the pattern of palace service in Ottoman tradition. Our informant. Kâmil Paşa himself, was assigned comfortable quarters in that section, along with a personal black slave to serve him. Unlike other inmates, he was allowed to leave the palace for his language training during the day, though he was expected not to have contact with anybody but his teachers. The ground floor in the third wing housed the chancery and those officials having direct contact with the viceroy.

Given that nature of palace organization, it is hard to escape the feeling that Abbas was trying to recreate the Ottoman palace tradition at his own court. Strict division into harem, inner service (*enderun*), and outer service (*birun*), was characteristic of the Ottoman palace service as late as the nineteenth century.[16] The terminology was carefully different to avoid any overt pretense, but the usage was quite suggestive.

Trainees in the palace school were young white slaves imported specifically for the mamluk corps of Abbas. They, and harem inmates in training for their duties, were called *çǐrak*, the traditional term for apprentice in the palace system. When they graduated, the men were placed into the "inner service," on the second floor, and called pages (*iç ağalarǐ*, singular *iç ağasǐ*). In the classical imperial capital, the best graduates of the palace school, levied through the *devşirme* system, were also placed into the *enderun*, but more often called ịç oğlanǐ. In the harem, similarities were even greater. Mothers of rulers were entitled to be addressed as Valide, and, as in the imperial harem, when an heir to the throne was born during the lifetime of his grandmother, the latter would become Büyük ("Senior") Valide, and his mother Küçük ("Junior") Valide. The daughters of Mehmet Ali were referred to as Hanǐm, unlike daughters of sultans, who were called Sultan. But the wives of the viceroys were called Kadǐn Efendi, just as wives of sultans were.[17]

It appears that the basic elements in Abbas's view of khedivate-turned-sultanate were embodied in the three segmented wings of the palace, the compartmentalized floors in the third wing, and the segregation of the whole complex from the outside world. In his version of the Privy Chamber – the imperial *Has Oda* – another Ottoman reality was in evidence: the mixing of slaves, who had been trained in the palace school, and free-born sons of prominent elite members. Clearly, the role of mamluks in Abbas's idea of the newly emerging dynastic order was quite different from the practice in the reign of Mehmet Ali. It is certainly true, as Hunter points out, that the eradication of the mamluks as a political force in Egypt did not mean that the tradition of the mamluk household disappeared completely. It is estimated that in 1825, Mehmet Ali and some of the top officials in his government owned about 1,610 mamluks. According to that estimate, Mehmet Ali possessed 500, Ibrahim 300, and Abbas 150 mamluks.[18] However, the reign of Abbas was the mamluks' "swan song."

The mamluk contingent as a royal symbol

During the middle years of the nineteenth century, the style of grandee households changed both functionally and architecturally. The vast, mamluk-like houses were replaced by the smaller, north-Mediterranean mansions of the *Rūmī*, or Istanbul type. There was no room for large contingents of mamluks in those households, except for one – Abbas's. Owning and training mamluks after the imperial pattern of olden times was one of the dynastic attributes of Abbas's government. To his grandfather and uncle, the mamluk contingent was merely a reliable bodyguard, but for Abbas it became a symbol of power, royal status, and imperial replication. After his accession, Abbas assigned some of Mehmet Ali and Ibrahim's mamluks to the military school he created, the Mefruze, while others were dispersed in various army units. Hekekyan relates that, in 1851, when Abdülhalim Bey, son of Mehmet Ali, asked for four or five of his father's mamluks who were then serving as officers at the Mefruze, Abbas refused. Moreover, he pulled out of the Mefruze the whole contingent of Mehmet Ali's mamluks – more than 120 – and sent them as privates to regiments of the line.[19]

The nature of the mamluk institution was not alien to Ottoman-Egyptians. However, members of the elite knew the phenomenon in its contemporary Ottoman context rather than in its eighteenth-century Egyptian one. Even in mid-nineteenth-century Istanbul, it was not impossible for household-trained white slaves to rise to the highest posts in the Empire. That was still one of the ways one could be integrated into large households, though that avenue was certainly declining in importance. Slaves were being purchased and carefully raised for military and bureaucratic careers, which were opened to them through patronage links. That was quite different from eighteenth-century mamluk households in Egypt, though quite similar to common practice during the reign of Mehmet Ali. In 1856, Hekekyan told Senior that "in fact, Stephan Bey and Edhem Pasha are the only ministers that occur to me who have not been slaves." Though Hekekyan was probably exaggerating, the phenomenon was still fairly widespread at the time.[20]

The practice created bonds of loyalty between master and slave and solidarity among ex-slaves who had been trained at the same household. Nubar writes about his own guilt feelings towards Abbas for having resigned his position following the demotion of his brother Arakel. Nubar felt that he had shown ingratitude to the viceroy, who "*sans être son esclave* . . . m'avait admis auprès de lui, avait fait de moi un homme de sa maison!" The emphasis is in Nubar's own text, expressing astonishment and admiration. Another aspect of those complex relations is brought out in Ismail Serheng's version of how Abbas was murdered. It combines treachery towards the master and loyalty within the peer-group. According to Serheng, Abbas's mamluk pages (*iç ağalarī*) had mocked their supervisor, a eunuch, for which the viceroy deprived them of rank and elite status, and sent them away to work in the stables.[21]

This humiliation had tragic consequences for Abbas. After the pages had been sent away, a prominent official in the Paşa's service, Hazinedar Mustafa Paşa, tried several times to intercede in their favor. It was because they were his "class mates" (*khushdāsh*s, in Arabicized Persian), that Mustafa Paşa was impelled to beseech Abbas to pardon the banished pages. His efforts did not bear fruit. But ultimately, when Mustafa enlisted the support of the *kethüdâ*, Abbas gave in and reinstated the culprits. The pages then asked to see the viceroy in order to pay homage. When their request was granted, they rode to his palace at Binha, worked out a plot, and killed him in his sleep. Such a blatant violation of master–mamluk trust was, however, quite rare. Indeed, intimacy and affection between a patron and his mamluks, rather than this kind of treachery, appear to have been the norm.

Intimacy and utmost loyalty figure also in another, quite revealing story about the relations between Ibrahim Paşa and one of his mamluks. It was related to Nubar by the mamluk himself, who had commanded the irregular forces in the Syrian War under Ibrahim's command. Years later, Ibrahim was summoned to see his infuriated father. At the time, Ibrahim feared that the father-turned-foe might order to take his life. With such trepidation at heart, he and his mamluk mounted a carriage and rode to the Shubrā palace. As they arrived in front of the stairs, Ibrahim said "draw," and the mamluk asked "whom?," and Ibrahim answered: "him who would give the order." Nubar explains that the two men were so close and shared the same thoughts and feelings, that they had no need for elaborate sentences. What Ibrahim actually meant was "draw your sword," to which the mamluk responded by asking "whom shall I strike?" The answer he received was "the one who would give the order to strike," i.e. Mehmet Ali. Nubar adds that it is hard to convey in French the laconic Turkish speech.[22] In Turkish, the whole exchange consisted of just three words.

However, it is difficult to imagine that Abbas, or for that matter Mehmet Ali or Ibrahim, had such intimate relations with all their mamluks. Still, recruitment and socialization into grandee households through the mamluk pattern carried with it strong ties of loyalty and often much warmth. Among the hundreds of mamluks owned by Abbas, he probably had close relations with a few dozen, but the others must have felt that they were linked to the viceregal household by a very special bond. The intensity of their training, as well as their seclusion, had to produce a distinct sense of group identity. Kâmil Paşa relates that the mamluks in training at the second wing of the ᶜAbbāsiyya palace used to avoid contact with all men and women. During the morning they studied indoors, but in the afternoon, they put on "Egyptian" clothes and mounted horses that were prepared for them. They then rode into the desert and trained until the evening. Hekekyan reports that instruction in a similar style took place also at the palace of Binha. According to his source, about fifty mamluks used to ride at night under their tutor and black supervisors, clad in strange attire.[23]

Training troops was considered strictly the privilege of the state. This was one of the arguments used against the anti-Abbas activities carried on the estate of Sait Paşa and exposed in mid 1852. In that case, the court ruled that military instruction was "a matter [reserved] solely for the government." Such a policy made the building up of mamluk contingents virtually impossible, though individuals in small numbers could still join grandee households as mamluks.

There was, of course, one exception, that of the viceregal household, which was synonymous with the state. Maintennce and training of a mamluk corps were expensive.[24] It was a long-term project, which required much care and attention. For Abbas, who harbored strong sentiments for Ottoman tradition, it was an essential symbol of dynastic power. A tradition revived, it was one that combined cherished Ottoman and Egyptian ways. Just like the ceremonies and the palaces, it represented to society the right to rule, cast in and legitimated by old institutions. It set the viceregal household above – and apart from – those of other figures in Mehmet Ali's family.

Primogeniture – an attribute of dynastic order

As argued above, the middle years of the nineteenth century were crucial in legitimating the privileged position of the ruling family in Egypt.To the vast majority of the population, might was right. That is, whoever held power, within very broadly defined lines, was obeyed and considered legitimate. However, that was not so within the Ottoman-Egyptian elite. In many ways, Mehmet Ali's position was unique. Originally not the choice of the Porte, he actually wrested the governorship of Egypt in battle with other contenders. In 1805, the Porte recognized the fact that he was virtually in control of the province. It was not unusual for the Ottoman central government to live with reality and, for practical reasons, endorse it. For more than forty years, Mehmet Ali Paşa was the sole, autocratic ruler of Egypt. In those years he carved out a patrimony and freely disposed of its economic resources. The Porte, whose representative in Egypt he was, had little effective say in the running of the province. But that, too, had happened before in the empire.

In the late 1830s, Mehmet Ali directly challenged the central government, and his troops defeated its armies in the heart of Anatolia. It was not new for rebellious *paşa*s to try – and sometimes succeed – to affect the political scene in Istanbul by marching with their soldiers towards the capital. Yet the outcome of the conflict between that rebellious provincial governor and his sovereign introduced a major element of discord into the Ottoman imperial system. Under European pressure, the Porte agreed to establish hereditary rule in Egypt, thereby forgoing its basic right to appoint the governors of the province and change them at will. It was also European pressure that, only a decade before, resulted in hereditary rule for a local prince in Serbia, an arrangement tended by much trouble and infighting. Indeed, the consent of the Ottomans to a similar idea in Egypt – a much graver case – was secured only under the more dire circumstances. The Porte's historical pragmatism suggests that Istanbul probably hoped to withdraw the concession at some point in the future, should an opportunity present itself.

Indeed, the reign of Abbas gave the Porte precisely that kind of opportunity.

As already mentioned, the succession of Ibrahim was not, in a real sense, a test of the hereditary principle. Both Ibrahim's prominence and his illness made it unwise for the Ottoman government to mount a serious challenge. Rather, it offered the European guarantors of the settlement an example of goodwill on the part of Istanbul. But the case of Abbas was completely different, as indicated by some of the features of the conflict between the Porte and the viceroy described in chapters 5 and 6 below. Here we are concerned rather with some of the implications of the Porte's failure to alter the hereditary principle of government in Egypt. The most significant of these was the creation of a dynastic core within the Ottoman-Egyptian elite, with the concomitant structural and cultural effects. It meant that ultimate power became ascriptive, that it was limited to an agnatic core-line, and that supreme power passed in that line according to a principle of seniority.

From the first half of the seventeenth century, seniority (Turkish *Ebkeriyet*) became the preferred principle of succession in the Ottoman House.[25] Until then, authority passed from father to son, though not necessarily to eldest son. In 1617, Mustafa I became the first uncle of an heir presumptive to be alive at the time of succession. Before that, fratricide ensured that brothers of sovereigns would be eliminated to avoid challenge to the reigning monarch and a possible fragmentation of the ruling family. Mustafa I thus succeeded his brother before Osman II, his thirteen-year-old nephew, came to the throne. The precedent became the rule of succession until the demise of the Ottoman dynasty in 1924. Accordingly, power passed to the eldest surviving male member of the ruling family. During that period, several abortive attempts were made to resume a father-to-son succession, and even to introduce primogeniture, in which the core-line ran from father to eldest son.

The obvious advantage in a system of seniority is that minors rarely reach the throne, and that men attain power at a relatively mature age, having acquired sufficient political and administrative experience. Though the system does not necessarily ensure such a situation, it creates conditions favorable to it. In a case of a minor on the throne, regents, harem figures, and grandees of various sorts could vie for power and strain the political system. Another advantage is that, by keeping alive the hopes of the major branches of a ruling family to attain power some day, seniority encourages cooperation and a measure of unity among them. On the other hand, there are also clear disadvantages in a system of seniority. For one thing, it tends to fragment the ruling elite into patrimonial households that continue to have a potential for attaining ultimate power. Hence alliances and patronage links are more tenuous, and a major realignment of forces has to take place upon each succession.

In addition, as pointed out by Roger Owen, seniority had an important economic drawback. Unsure of the political prospects of their offspring, rulers attempted at least to secure their financial future. They did this by assisting their children to accumulate enormous fortunes by diverting to them large amounts of public funds. In nineteenth-century Egypt, argues Owen, all viceroys after Mehmet Ali did precisely that at the expense of state resources.[26] This situation does not usually happen under primogeniture, which consolidates a hierarchical order within the elite by according clear preference to the core-line over all other households. Thus, it substantially reduces the need to divert public resources to safeguard the future of offspring, though some measures are normally expected to ensure the prosperity of those children who do not inherit the throne. In sum, if hereditary monarchy tends to stabilize the political system, primogeniture is supposed to take the succession question off the political agenda. It thus became an almost natural next step for the House of Mehmet Ali, too.

The Edict of Hereditary Governorship devised in 1841 stipulated that power would pass according to seniority. But from the outset, primogeniture loomed as an alternative, thereby playing an important role in political thinking and planning in Cairo. Ibrahim was not only the most senior member of the family, but also Mehmet Ali's eldest son. Yet, he himself already began to explore the possibility of substituting seniority for primogeniture in favor of his son Ahmet Rifat Paşa. Much more time and concerted efforts were required, however, to obtain such a major change of terms in the Edict. Ibrahim was too ill and alienated from Istanbul politics to be able to achieve that, so it was Abbas who succeeded Ibrahim, not Ahmet Rifat. After Abbas had settled his conflict with the Porte in 1852, he began to prepare the ground for a change in the principle of succession in favor of his son Ilhami, and to the detriment of Sait and Ibrahim's sons. He, too, died before the plan got off the ground. Sait had similar thoughts after he ascended the throne, but as Nubar put it, like with many ideas that Sait had, "it [too] remained in an embryonic state."[27]

Finally, it was Ismail who, in 1868, after much effort and spending, obtained the Porte's consent to establish primogeniture as the rule of succession.[28] He thereby disinherited his brother Mustafa Fazıl and his uncle Abdülhalim in favor of his son Tevfik. However, primogeniture was not strictly adhered to in the following years. After Ismail had been deposed in 1879, Tevfik succeeded him. When Tevfik died in 1892, his eldest son Abbas Hilmi II became khedive. Yet, when Abbas Hilmi II was removed by the British in 1914, he was succeeded by his uncle Hüseyin Kâmil, who died three years later. It was then that his younger brother Fuat I, later king, came to the throne. After two successions, primogeniture was abandoned, and a strict core-line from Ismail down was not followed. Thus, despite the change in the principle of succession, three of Ismail's sons became rulers of Egypt. But historically these deviations from the principle are far less important than the significance of its establishment.

For, it seems that the establishment of primogeniture as the principle of succession in the House of Mehmet Ali was seen by Egyptian rulers – and by the Porte, who opposed them – as a necessary step towards the institutionalization of dynastic order in Egypt. It is not surprising that once he won his victory over the opposition and the Porte, Abbas began to prepare for a campaign to change the order of succession. It was he, more than any other member in the ruling family, who suffered from opposition within the elite core. That opposition was made possible by two seemingly contradictory factors. One was the desire of the Porte to wreck the hereditary arrangement in the government of Egypt. The other was the hope of some prominent members of the family, notably Sait and Ibrahim's sons, to discredit Abbas and induce the Porte to replace him by one of them. Thus, a partial community of interests existed between the parties, though ultimately, they would have clashed. That temporary convergence of interests made possible the sustained existence of opposition to Abbas's rule.

Therefore, it is necessary to understand that the institutionalization of dynastic rule in mid-nineteenth-century Egypt was much colored by the bitter experience of opposition and challenge to authority. Not only Abbas learnt from that experience. Those who opposed him also drew similar conclusions. Abbas,

7 Ilhami Paşa, Abbas's son

Sait, and Ismail believed, as their actions point out, that primogeniture would lend greater legitimacy to their rule, and would make the possibility of royal opposition smaller. A contender was much more likely to pose a threat to authority under a system of seniority than under primogeniture, in which a challenge would be conceived as aimed against the dynasty as a whole. To be sure, all three wanted to secure the future of their direct offspring and were also motivated by a deep dislike towards those whom they wished to exclude. But the main motivation was more practical than personal, stemming from their common experience during the reign of Abbas. In that experience, the accumulation and denial of wealth – mostly of landed property – proved a major political asset.

Land as a tool in intra-dynastic struggle

Perhaps the most important implication of the internal strife within the ruling family was in the redistribution of land. The use of land as a political tool was not a new phenomenon in nineteenth-century Egyptian history.[29] In a largely agricultural economy, where land was the main source of wealth, this is hardly surprising. The natural connection between power and land was vividly demonstrated by Mehmet Ali's struggle against the mamluks during the first decade of his reign. In the process, he not only stripped those *ancien régime* grandees of their landed tax-farms (*iltizāms*), but also seized land that religious officeholders administered as tax-free Islamic endowments. By so doing, Mehmet Ali deprived all potential challengers of their independent power-base, thereby making all elite members totally dependent on the viceroy for income and position. Subsequently, he began to redistribute land to himself, his family, and close political allies. By the end of his reign, Mehmet Ali was the largest land owner in Egypt, while his relatives and officials held estates of landed tax-farms of various sizes.

ʿAlī Barakāt has shown that by 1846, the Paşa had concentrated in his own hands close to 250,000 feddans (one feddan is about one acre), while granting to various members of his family close to 85,000 feddans.[30] These lands formed a category known as *çift*, or *çiftlik*. That category was tax-exempt. It became synonymous with viceregal estates. In July 1846, Abbas received from his grandfather a high quality estate in the area of al-Maḥalla al-Kubrā. It covered more than 13,000 feddans and brought the holdings of Abbas alone to 16.5 percent of the total *çift* land. Mehmet Ali's example was followed by his successors, who also realized the importance of land as a political tool. When Ibrahim succeeded his father, he almost immediately appropriated about 34,000 feddans of his lands, which he later divided equally among his three sons. However, his reign was short, and the most significant changes in the land holdings of the viceregal family occurred under the rule of his nephew.

Early in his reign, Abbas began to deprive top members of the Ottoman-

Egyptian elite of their main capital asset. Revision of the new tax-farming system (called in Turkish *ühde*, in Arabic *ᶜuhda*) meant that large tracts of land, previously administered by members of the elite, reverted to the treasury, via the provincial governorates. Partly through that procedure, partly through other measures, land was taken away from one group of people and given to another. "La reprise des fiefs territoriaux avait terrorisé les fonctionnaires," wrote Nubar.[31] Fully realizing his sovereign powers, Abbas granted estates to his supporters and top officials. He, his sons, and other members of his household gradually accumulated vast estates in various parts of the country. But medium-size estates were also granted to lower-level officials. Thus, it was Abbas, more than Sait, who gave the incoming generation of officeholders their base of landed property. Land had great symbolic value for the ruling family and the elite, and, with the great increase in the value of cotton during the reign of Abbas, it began to be regarded also as an economic asset.

Already within the first few months of his reign, Abbas appropriated more than 29,000 feddans of Mehmet Ali's *çift* lands and distributed it among his closest relatives. His mother and his son Ilhami received more than 10,000 feddans each, the mother of his son Mehmet Sĭddĭk somewhat less than 6,000 feddans, and his wet-nurse more than 2,000 feddans. A few months later, he gave Ilhami's mother 5,000 feddans. By the end of his reign, Abbas had reallocated close to 100,000 feddans of Mehmet Ali's *çiftliks*, including land grants to some high officials who were not family members. Sait appropriated only a little over 10,000 feddans during a reign that was twice as long as Abbas's. Both rulers also created new *çiftliks* by appropriating cultivated land known as *mamur* in Turkish, *maᶜmūr* in Arabic. Abbas designated as *çift* land more than 22,000 feddans, including more than 18,000 feddans in one estate which he took to himself. Sait created somewhat more, or larger, *çiftliks*, over 27,000 feddans in all, but again, we have to consider the length of his reign.

Another type of land grants consisted of surveyed but uncultivated land, known as *abadiyat* (Arabic *abᶜadiyyāt*). These were also exempted from taxation and granted to officials on the condition that they be brought into cultivation. They were usually given to government officials, and in the early 1860s were distributed in lieu of pensions owed to retired personnel. Such lands were not considered a great asset, as they required investment in agricultural infrastructure and close supervision. In 1854, Sait imposed the tithe on these lands – and on *çiftliks* – which made them even less attractive to recipients. In all kinds of land, by the end of his reign, Abbas and his immediate family held over 67,000 feddans, as compared to just below 14,000 when he became viceroy. Of this amount, Abbas himself held over 32,000 feddans, the rest belonging to his two sons, his mother and his first wife. In his reign, Sait amassed close to 77,000 feddans, while Ismail surpassed them all, reaching over one million feddans, or more than 22 percent of the arable land in Egypt.

However, in spite of Abbas's large-scale manipulation of land holdings, he did not disinherit members of the opposition within the ruling family. For example, in April 1849, Sait himself received a valuable plot in Azbakiyya in order to build a palace. On 12 June 1849, he granted 50,000 feddans to the prominent women in the family not belonging to his branch. Among the recipients we may note Sait's mother (6,000 feddans), mothers of sons and daughters of Mehmet Ali (5,000 each), mothers of Ibrahim's three sons (5,000 each), and other wives of former viceroys (1,000 each). At the same time, Abbas also provided a mechanism which enabled members of the opposition to protect their estates against confiscation. In August 1849, he abrogated Mehmet Ali's prohibition on turning certain types of land into *vakıf* (Arabic *waqf*). Consequently, the creation of large *vakıf*s became a safeguard against re-appropriation of land by the state. This device, however, was used sparingly by members of the ruling family in opposition to Abbas, since the Porte provided them with adequate protection against "unreasonable" recrimination by the viceroy.[32]

Through the creation of large estates, Abbas – like Mehmet Ali, Sait, and Ismail – manipulated the agricultural economy and maximized his own profits. The appropriation, accumulation, and redistribution of land was used by Abbas to establish his authority and weaken the opposition. Mehmet Ali used his vast land holdings to create the wealth he needed for his military campaigns.[33] Abbas continued to expand the viceregal estates, still refusing to relinquish effective control of prices in the agricultural markets. Like his grandfather and uncle before him, he too used land grants as rewards to loyal officeholders. And, not least important, his lands produced the surplus to support the expensive symbolic aspect of his reign – the lavish palaces, the ceremonies, the maintenance of his large household, mamluks and all. Perhaps more for Abbas, but also for other viceroys, large estates were a major power symbol. In the countryside, they represented mass domination: the *fallāḥīn* obediently toiling under an all-powerful landlord. In the city, palaces, carriages, processions, large retinues served a similar purpose.

Thus, in mid-nineteenth-century Egypt, land was the main capital asset of a dynasty working to carve for itself a patrimony. But in his efforts to provide his household with means with which to act out their new role, Abbas was generous not only with land. He also handed out cash. On 10 September 1849, for example, he ordered the Treasury Department to pay his mother 100,000 *kuruş*; to his first wife and a favored relative, Gelin Hanım, 40,000 each; to his second wife 30,000; to his wet-nurse 25,000; and to various female relatives 30,000. Altogether the grants amounted to 265,000 *kuruş*. Less than three months later, the same Gelin Hanım received 25,000 *kuruş* to cover the expense of her trip to Istanbul. At the same time, he doubled the monthly salary of his mother's household manager, and granted a large amount to two harem eunuchs of his great aunt, who went to retire in the Hijaz, as was customary among the imperial eunuchs, too.[34]

However, with time, Abbas became more frugal in his cash advances to family members. On 20 October 1851, his mother applied in writing for a raise in the salaries of five of her harem female attendants. Those five slaves, she explained, had just completed their training and attained new status. The total cost was estimated at 75,000 *kuruş*. However, concerned that such a raise might encourage similar requests by other sections in the household, Abbas turned his mother down. He wrote to the director of her household: "When this order reaches you, you shall convey to my mother special greetings and kiss her noble hand. After carefully communicating my message, you will tell her not to spend even one additional penny."[35] Conscious as he was of cost and benefit, Abbas clearly recognized the importance of spending large amounts of money on the maintenance of the viceregal harem. The figures cited above clearly indicate that this was indeed an expensive matter.

As with land grants, so with cash; Abbas also granted various sums of money to members of opposition households. However, those amounts only helped to maintain members of the family above the standards of other elite households, not in any way to rival the style of the court itself. In September 1849, he gave eleven women, widows of former viceroys, the total sum of 190,000 *kuruş*. In March 1851, it was reported that he raised the salaries of the young princes from 150,000 *kuruş* a year to 350,000. At the same time, of course, Abbas refused to acknowledge the right of Mehmet Ali's heirs to the full estate of the Old Paşa. The amounts involved in that case were considerably higher. The final settlement of the dispute by the Şeyhülislam in Istanbul forced Abbas to pay each heir half a million pounds sterling.[36] In the struggle against the opposition, liquid assets, as much as land, had their importance. Both set the court above other family and elite households. They supported a royal lifestyle, with all its appurtenances, its pomp, its lavishness. That style served to bolster Abbas's dynastic claims. It remained a feature of the viceregal court during the reigns of his successors, ever groping for more ostentation to keep up with their self-image and to carry on the symbols of absolute power.

3 The mainstay of dynastic order – the elite

The composition of the Ottoman-Egyptian elite

An office holding elite – size and components

Four viceroys ruled Egypt in the 1840s and 1850s: Mehmet Ali, Ibrahim, Abbas, and Sait. There can be hardly a doubt as to the centrality and dominance of these men in the life of Egyptian society during that period. Each one had his own character and style of government. Each one left his mark on the history of Egypt in the nineteenth century. Economic retrenchment and scaled-down reform became a policy already in the last years of Mehmet Ali's reign. After Ibrahim's short time on the throne came the stormy and important reign of Abbas, which witnessed the entrenchment of dynastic rule in Egypt and a different, perhaps more sober approach to Westernization. The reign of Sait purported to be an antithesis to that of Abbas, but was more so in style than in substance. A return to aggressive reform and expansionism occurred only in the reign of Ismail, more precisely from the second half of the 1860s onward. His government collapsed in the late 1870s, bankrupt and disgraced, leading to foreign occupation which, in various forms, would last seventy years.

In those days in the middle of the nineteenth century, a whole society lived under the viceroys. Men and women of various cultural, ethnic, and religious origins worked to make a living, to build a home, to raise a family. Some made a name and a fortune, others died anonymous and destitute. As we attempt to comprehend the realities of their lives, we must resort to abstractions. Much as we rely on metaphor to make sense of life around us in the present, so must we impose similar, though historically adjusted, metaphors on past society. It is at such junctions that concepts like "center," "class," "elite," "power," "culture," and others readily spring to mind. The literature of the social sciences is full of various definitions for each term according to ideological preference or theoretical persuasion. Historians have tended to use the terms somewhat eclectically, not always paying due respect to their theoretical implications. Consequently, not a few among us have incurred the wrath of social scientists, whom they in turn accused of preaching an ahistorical gospel.

As the pitfalls of concept and terminology seem hopelessly unavoidable, I shall simply try to reduce them as much as possible. Thus, we ought to recognize at the outset, that all efforts to conceive mid-nineteenth-century Egyptian society in rigid categories are doomed to fail; they are bound to miss the shades, the grey areas, and hence the very flavor of society. Instead, I propose to describe both the core elements of each social group and its periphery, or the twilight zone where limits are blurred, where boundaries overlap. In addition, I shall try to remain as close as possible to terms and concepts used by the actual members of the social groups concerned. Part I deals with what I broadly define as the Ottoman-Egyptian elite, whereas part II treats the vast majority of the population, all those not enjoying elite status. Such a definition of social groups emanates from a concept that is both cultural and socio-political. In the period under consideration, effective power in Egypt was held by the viceroy alone. But it was delegated to and exercised by a power-elite. In a variant of patrimonialism, that elite was organized along the lines of grandee households, modelled after the Ottoman imperial household and replicated on a reduced scale by the viceroy of Egypt, by members of the ruling family, and by a number of other leading personages.

In various forms, some not immediately recognizable, the notion of a privileged elite and of patrimonial households existed in the culture itself. Such households were called *daire*s (Arabic *dā'ira*s), and their pecking-order was also a familiar idea. This is amply reflected in government documents. For example, in an order issued by the Council of Justice in May 1853, tax-farm holders were warned to comply with instructions and supply manpower for public works when required. Failure to do so, it was stated, would result in the concession being forfeited, regardless of how elevated the holder was: Ilhami Paşa, who was the son of the viceroy; members of the ruling family (*familya*); members of the elite (*zevat-i kiram*); and so on. It is significant that in this case, the household of the viceroy himself was not mentioned. In other cases, it appeared at the beginning of the list. Those referred to as *zevat* were all officials holding the top two ranks in the bureaucracy and the top three in the military. They were addressed by the honorific titles of *paşa* or *bey*, also familiar to all members of society. Middle- and lower-level bureaucrats were called *efendi*s. In both the civil and military hierarchies, the income and status borderline which distinguished between middle-level and low-level officials was drawn below the fifth rank.[1]

During the middle years of the nineteenth century, it was the ruling family and the *zevat* who formed the core of the Ottoman-Egyptian elite. Owing to the principle of hereditary governorship, members of Mehmet Ali's family were assured both status and wealth. However, they did not necessarily hold office, nor did they automatically have a say in the running of government. As for the *zevat*, high office was a prerequisite of status, without which one could not belong to the elite. It was through office that rank was attained, after which one could be temporarily, or even permanently, out of office without losing elite status. That office elite consisted of two major branches of service – civil and military. It was rather small in numbers. In his study of the bureaucratic elite, Robert Hunter estimated the aggregate total of men appointed to high office by Abbas, Sait, and Ismail as exceeding 300. On the basis of data provided by Amīn Sāmī, Hunter calculated that between the years 1848 and 1879, 983 *paşa*s and *bey*s were in the manpower pool from which high-level appointments were being made.[2]

It is difficult to provide similar figures for the military. The size of the army and its regiments changed considerably during the 1840s and 1850s, and the available data are conflicting and equivocal. Thus, only a very tentative approximation of the number of officers in the top five ranks can be attempted here. Sarūjī provides a detailed list of all field commanders in the Egyptian army at the accession of Ismail Paşa in 1863. According to him, there were at the time sixty-eight officers with third, fourth, and fifth rank. The size of the army was then about 26,000 men. At the height of the Crimean War, the army peaked to about 130,000, with an officers' corps averaging more than 4,000. In the earlier years of Abbas's reign, before the war, the army fluctuated around 100,000 men. It began to decline in numbers during the reign of Sait, after the war, and maintained a strength of about 70,000 to 80,000 men, finally plummeting to about 24,000 from 1860 on. The number of officers declined less rapidly, reaching just over 2,000 in 1857 and about 1,000 in 1860.[3]

We may, then, put the number of officers with third, fourth, and fifth rank during the peak years of the early and mid 1850s at about four times their number in 1863, or approximately 270. The number of officers belonging to the top two ranks retained a similar ratio. During the 1850s, the general staff contained from sixty to seventy men. It declined in the early 1860s to less than fifteen. It is not clear how many of these were actually brigadiers and generals. In any event, we may estimate with caution that, at mid-century, there were no more than about 300 officers in all five top ranks of the armed forces. This would come to approximately 8 percent of the average number of officers during the same period. Of course, only a minority among these were *paşa*s and *bey*s, but they all had sufficient income to live comfortably in elite style. We cannot simply add these estimates to the figures provided by Hunter for the bureaucracy, because careers overlapped and the pool contained both civil and military men.

These estimates ought to be raised by adding the families of *zevat*, including also adopted children as well as educated and trained slaves. Thus, as Hunter correctly suggests, the elite probably included several thousand members. In a total population of about four million people – Cairo alone accounting for close to 250,000 – this was, indeed, a very small and highly privileged group. On the periphery of this core, bordering on the periphery of the large non-elite groups, there existed a socio-cultural environment which mixed a diluted elite culture with distinctly non-elite cultural characteristics. But a social divide still distinguished the cores of these two subcultures, drawing soft, interrupted lines between their respective peripheries. It is virtually impossible to estimate the population which inhabited that doubly peripheral social zone. The groups that might be included in it were the lower echelons of the officers corps and the bureaucracy, religious officeholders (*ᶜulamā*) of middle and lower rank, and not least, rural and urban notables.

In his seminal paper "Ottoman Reform and the Politics of Notables," written in 1966, Albert Hourani argued for the crucial importance of the role of urban notables in the political history of the Muslim provinces of the Ottoman Empire.[4] His analysis of more than a century of Egyptian history raised the question of the complete absence of urban political activity in the middle decades of the nineteenth century. That "political vacuum," Hourani observed, resulted from the successful monopolization of power by Mehmet Ali and his heirs, which virtually eliminated any social group that might have posed a threat to their absolute power. The viceroy's appropriation of tax-farms and religious endowments, the introduction of legal and educational reforms alongside more effective policing of streets and markets, and the changing patterns of commerce, mostly towards Europe, all contributed to the erosion of notable power. The old mamluk establishment, the great religious families, and the leadership of guilds and mystic orders lost their standing.

The gap was filled by Mehmet Ali's centralized household government, based on a strong army and a personally loyal bureaucratic elite, whose members had benefited from European technology and education. "It is these two factors," wrote Hourani, "the preponderant power of the government and the absence of instruments of political action, which explains why politics (except for 'court politics') virtually disappeared in Egypt, during the period from the 1820s to the 1870s."[5] Extensive study of Egyptian archival and other sources from the 1840s and 1850s fully bears out Hourani's view. The records examined at the Egyptian archives often refer to individuals belonging to the group identified by Hourani as urban notables. Heads of guilds, Azhar *shaykh*s, leaders of mystic orders, and wealthy merchants are familiar figures to readers of such records. However, they never appear as a corporate body or a socio-political group. They seem to have functioned strictly within the sphere of government control, never as organized opposition.

As a social group, urban notables had lost their political role and maneuverability as a result of the emergence of a strong and centralized state under Mehmet Ali Paşa. There is no indication that they had any significant role in Egyptian politics in the 1840s and 1850s independent of the central authority. In times of tension, however, the government used notables for public mobilization. Such a case occurred during the first half of 1840, when Mehmet Ali came under European pressure to give up his Syrian territories and submit to the sultan. Fearing European attack, orders went out to raise militia forces in Cairo. Two *ᶜulamā* and a merchant were among those appointed to levy and command these regiments. Faced with popular discontent and protest, the men mentioned were charged with a difficult task, in which they were to employ their influence in the service of the viceroy.[6] Even those trying circumstances did not give rise to an independent urban notability.

However, for a brief period during the reign of Abbas, a kind of new "social pact" emerged as a result of the struggle within the ruling family. Wishing to break away from the established elite of Mehmet Ali and Ibrahim, which he deeply resented and mistrusted, Abbas sought political allies outside the groups that traditionally supported his predecessors. It was then that he turned to the Azhar and mystic *ᶜulamā*, many of whom also shared his criticism of European influence in Egypt, and to the bedouin chiefs. He restored the right to create religious endowments, suspended by Mehmet Ali, thus reviving one of the *ᶜulamā*'s main sources of power. Abbas himself created such endowments, restored mosques and mystic lodges, and showed greater deference to the religious establishment. In March 1849, as a renewed gesture, for this was not a precedent, Abbas appointed the three highest ranking *ᶜulamā* in the land to a newly formed Privy Council.[7]

With the bedouins Abbas had a special relationship that went back to his childhood experience and his preference for the solitude and dry air of the desert. In a way continuing his grandfather's policy, Abbas granted large tracts of land to bedouin chiefs. Out of mutual respect, he reached a tacit understanding with them, which kept Egyptian roads and the countryside in complete tranquility throughout his reign. However, having entrenched his own loyal elite, Abbas seemed inclined to resume his predecessors' policies. Thus, at mid-century, the only vestige of the traditional role of notability could be found in rural areas. There, the village headman (the *ᶜumda*, or *shaykh al-balad*) played a role reminiscent of notability. Although in government employ, *ᶜumda* families often had a broad local base. They used their dual position in an intricate game of interest-balancing, often to their own advantage. A number of leading figures, most notably Muḥammad Sulṭān, rose to prominence from such a background.[8]

It is indeed the "political vacuum" in Egyptian urban politics which helps to explain the structural deviation of the Ottoman-Egyptian elite from the traditional Ottoman model. That model consisted of three, rather than two, branches: the military service (*seyfiye*), the scribal service – later the civil bureaucracy (*kalemiye*), and the religious service (*ilmiye*).[9] These were not segmented services, but rather intersecting career tracks with movement between them, the extent of which varied from period to period. The striking absence of religious officeholders from the ranks of the Ottoman-Egyptian elite was the direct outcome of Mehmet Ali's policies. We must remember that, contrary to the Istanbul religious establishment, the Egyptian *ᶜulamā* did not belong *culturally* to the Ottoman-Egyptian elite. The overwhelming majority of them did not speak Turkish, nor regarded themselves as heirs to high Ottoman elite traditions. Moreover, they had a strong local base and could vie for power in the newly emerging state.

Therefore, Mehmet Ali chose to liquidate their political assets rather than co-opt them into his elite as junior partners. Their absence left the Ottoman-Egyptian elite with just the military and scribal branches. Crossing over between career tracks was not uncommon, though it was mostly military men who moved to civil positions, rather than vice versa, with a considerable number of them receiving commissions in the provincial administration. This is one of the reasons why we must not artificially separate the two services in any socio-cultural consideration of the Ottoman-Egyptian elite. The other major reason is the considerable lowering of the functional and political divide between these two bodies during the middle years of the nineteenth century. Save for two years of the Crimean War, in which an Egyptian expeditionary force participated, those were quiet and peaceful years in Egypt. Even the Crimean episode had a limited, and mostly external, impact on social realities within the elite.

In the years following the settlement of the "Egyptian Question" in 1841, the size of the army was substantially reduced. It was still a large force, much in excess of the 18,000 men allowed by the Edict of Hereditary Governorship. From the mid 1840s to the early 1860s, the number of soldiers fluctuated between about 80,000, during most of the period, and approximately 130,000, at the time of the Crimean War. These numbers include all branches of the armed forces – infantry, cavalry, artillery, navy, and irregulars. A less dramatic, though still substantial, reduction also occurred in the size of the officers corps. There were no wars to fight and simply not enough money to keep the huge forces of the 1830s. With much of the economy geared to supply the needs of the army, that reduction in size meant some significant readjustments in many sectors of the economy. In the course of a few years, large numbers of discharged soldiers and factory workers of a collapsing industry were dumped on the labor market. However, more relevant to our discussion here are the changes that took place within the army in that period of retrenchment.

In his comparative study of European and Middle Eastern armies, Malcolm Yapp points out the multidimensional demands put on the Ottoman army in the nineteenth century.[10] That army had to police vast territories, fight European battles, and conduct colonial-type wars within the Empire. It was this, not the inadequacy of weapons or the superiority of arms industrial base, that accounted for Ottoman military inferiority *vis-à-vis* contemporary European armies. Major technological and tactical developments, Yapp observes, occurred only in the 1860s, while the post-Napoleonic European armies of 1815–60 were smaller, with a less open officer corps and distinctly domestic tasks of keeping public order and upholding the state. This description fits very well the situation of the Egyptian army in the 1840s and 1860s. Abbas and Sait did not wish to challenge the Porte on the battlefield, but at the same time were not trusted to be called upon to assist the central government in its colonial wars – unlike Mehmet Ali who, before rising against the sultan, restored Ottoman rule in the Hijaz and Greece. Yet when international war flared up, both Abbas and Sait sent troops to aid the Empire against the Russians.

Thus, in the middle years of the nineteenth century, the reduced but still sizable Egyptian army was inward- rather than outward-looking. However, it too, like the Ottoman army, was multi-functional. While retaining a fighting capacity against European-type armies and a colonial-type capacity for the subjection of the Sudan, its main task was to serve as the mainstay of dynastic power and assist the police in maintaining law and order in Egypt. In addition, the army supplied manpower to government projects of public works, such as the Alexandria–Cairo railway, the Cairo–Suez road, the Barrages, and the construction of viceregal palaces and public buildings. Since the government did not have a regular unskilled labor force which it could readily use on such projects, the oversized and mostly idle army shouldered the burden. This relieved some of the yoke under which the *fallāḥīn* labored during the reign of Mehmet Ali. Concomitantly, conscription of fresh troops from that population was reduced to a minimum, with a noted exception during the Crimean War.

The fact that there were no wars to fight and that, instead, the army was so much involved in civilian tasks also reduced the differences between actual military and civilian careers. Differences of training and skills remained, but in practical terms, many officers found themselves involved in public-work projects, more on the managing than on the professional side. Even in barracks routine, aside from occasional drills and maneuvers, their jobs resembled those of bureaucrats more than those of combat officers. If an artillery officer was appointed director of an excavation project in Heliopolis in 1851, by 1856 Nassau Senior recorded the complaint of a certain *bey* to the effect that Abbas had turned the troops into carpenters and masons.[11] Thus, until Ismail augmented the army and gave it a military *raison d'être*, in the mid-1860s, the concerns of civilian and military *zevat* seemed almost the same.

To these increasingly similar tasks, we can add the resemblance in living conditions. Military *zevat* and their families lived in the cities, not in segregated barracks or garrison towns. They received salaries almost equivalent to those of civilian *zevat*, except when away on expedition, and were part of the same economy. There were almost no differences between households of military and civilian *zevat*. They formed the same patron–client relations and partook of the same political networks. When Abbas developed ᶜAbbāsiyya – about one mile north-east of Cairo – he ordered both military and civilian dignitaries to build their houses there. They moved in the same social circles and undoubtedly belonged to the same Ottoman-Egyptian elite culture.[12] Yet it is likely that, in the eyes of many elite members, military rank and commission still had greater prestige – a carry-over from the "heroic age" of Mehmet Ali and Ibrahim. The following case may shed light on what went on in the mind of one bureaucrat and elite member.

On 16 October 1852, after sundown, a certain Ahmet Efendi entered the police station at as-Sukkariyya in Cairo and asked to see the captain in charge of the station.[13] Although just a scribe in the household of Mehmet Ali Bey, youngest son of the Old Paşa, he presented himself as a *bey* sent for inspection by Selim Paşa, head of the police of Cairo. Assuming the tone and air of authority, Ahmet told the surprised captain and sergeant that, under his supervision, they were to enforce a new regulation. The regulation required that every two individuals walking outside after dark had to carry one lantern. All those not complying with the said ratio of persons per lantern were to be detained at the guard station. After a short while, five men passed by carrying only one lantern, as required before. Ahmet ordered them to stop, told them of the new regulation, dismissed their protests, allowed two of them to go and fetch additional lanterns, and detained the remaining three at the station.

After abusing the three and beating one of them with a stick, Ahmet gave them a lantern and sent them off. A short while later, he left the station and went home. Before retiring, he also hit two patrolmen, whom he accused of not making their rounds properly. As the evening wore on, both the policemen and the men harassed by Ahmet became increasingly suspicious until they finally discovered they were dealing with an imposter. In the morning, Ahmet was summoned to police headquarters and interrogated there. He admitted all and asked for clemency, claiming that he had been under the influence of arrack (Turkish *rakı̂*, Arabic *ʿaraq*, a rasin-based liquor). His paternal uncle, retired major Ömer Efendi, testified that Ahmet was not prone to drinking, and that indeed he had consumed half a bottle of arrack before assuming a false identity. At the end of the process, the Council of Justice convicted Ahmet and the viceroy confirmed the penalty. But socially, the story may be more significant than that.

All we have here is a low-level bureaucrat who, under the liberating influence of alcohol, posed as a middle-level military officer. For a brief but eventful moment, Ahmet Efendi acted out a fantasy, which might or might not have had a social meaning. If it did, which is a reasonable speculation, then it indicates that crossing over from bureaucratic to military service was both thinkable and desirable. That it was possible to fool police officers and civilians by assuming the right posture and using the right tone is evident from this case. That at least one bureaucrat envied the power and status of military men is also a fact. How common such sentiments were within the elite at mid-century is quite difficult to determine. In any event, a military career carried more prestige in the "heroic age"; that lingered on, though at a lessening degree, in the period covered by the present work. One of the reasons for this was the fact that all the viceroys of the time – Mehmet Ali, Ibrahim, Abbas, and Sait – were trained in the army and held high commissions.

However, not only the rulers but also many of their top ministers have had a strong military background. Such career patterns demonstrate the dual nature of the Ottoman-Egyptian elite in the middle years of the nineteenth century. The growing complexity of the administration, the increasing need for professional skills, and the fact that all viceroys had extensive administrative experience contributed to the rising prestige of the bureaucracy. Those who were at home in both services were the "cream of the crop," since their careers embodied the duality of the elite. It is clear that the experiences of this core were shared by members of both branches, and that the military was not less susceptible to political developments. Thus, military *zevat* were also exposed to intra-family politics, such as the serious challenge posed by Sait and others to the rule of Abbas during the early years of his reign.[14] Not surprisingly, that struggle for ultimate power in the state also had important ramifications for the military.

Perhaps the most important implication of the rift within the ruling family concerned the size of the army. Why were not more soldiers discharged, when there was no immediate need for them? Indeed, it was only in the early 1860s that Sait finally reduced his army to about 25,000 men. One of the reasons is that perception of needs naturally lingered after real needs, and real needs often depended on self-perception. Thus, Abbas felt that his position *vis-à-vis* the domestic opposition and the Porte was not secure until some time in 1852–1853. By then, he already needed to send troops to assist the sultan against the Russians. He therefore wished to keep as many men within the army as he possibly could. Abbas even explained his position to Sait, then commander of the navy, as he ordered him to transfer soldiers to the merchant marine. Abbas believed that in that way marines could retain their skills and might be used without delay when need arose. In doing so, Abbas also weakened the navy, which he considered as being loyal to Sait and, therefore, opposed to him.[15]

In addition, Abbas also believed that a large army was required to police Egypt effectively. In that, too, he was probably guided by his fear of subversive activities. He must have felt, and rightly so, that it would be easier to keep well-trained men mobilized and working on various projects than to discharge them and, in a state of emergency, recruit them – or untrained substitutes – again. to Hekekyan, who said that the vast Roman Empire had an army of only 4,000 or 5,000 men, Abbas replied that there were no firearms in Roman times. The ministers present at that meeting concurred in his view.[16] For Sait, the army was both power and amusement. He liked to dress his soldiers in fancy European uniforms, drill them, and parade them in public for prestige and symbolic power. But as the bullion in the state coffers dwindled, he realized that cost had to be weighed against benefit and discharged two-thirds of his officers and soldiers. Incidentally, when Sait became viceroy, he did not restore the navy to its previous strength, not even to make a point.

The Ottoman-Egyptian elite – a socio-cultural concept

Before we examine the main social and cultural features of the Ottoman-Egyptian elite, we ought to consider what were the groups of which it was made up. On this issue, two types of explanations have been advanced in recent years. Findley's study of bureaucratic reform in the Sublime Porte during the *Tanzimat* and Hunter's work on the bureaucratic elite in mid-nineteenth-century Egypt both treat a central element in the Ottoman and Ottoman-Egyptian elites.[17] In spite of great similarities, these two excellent works adopt a somewhat different approach to the internal division of the elite groups which they examine. This is not merely due to the nature of their subject matter – the central versus the Egyptian government – but also reflects a more general difference in historical explanation. In this section, I shall point out the difference and offer another approach to the question. It should be noted at the outset that elements of both theses will figure in the interpretation advanced here.

Findley breaks down the bureaucrats of the Porte according to a "religio-ideological" criterion. Hence he sees among them three groups: traditionalistic Muslim officials, non-Muslims, and modernist Muslim officials. This division is based on the attitude of each group to reform and suggests a certain relation between religious affiliation and attitude to reform. Muslims belonged to two distinct groups in terms of approach to reform, while non-Muslims supported reform. In this way, Findley avoids the stereotyped view that muslims opposed reform because they were fanatic and backward, while non-Muslims carried the reforms on their shoulders because they were advanced and forward-looking. The main distinguishing mark, status symbol, and mobility channel in Findley's view was mastery of French, which split the Muslim bureaucrats, joining the substantial French-speaking group among them to the non-Muslims. This analysis stresses the differentiating impact of Western culture and its stratifying effect in career patterns within the bureaucracy to the detriment of economic considerations. It is more "superstructural" and less "infrastructural."

Hunter, on the other hand, divides the Ottoman-Egyptian elite along ethnic lines. The dominant group was that of Turks. Then came two groups of Egyptians – technicians, who served mostly in the central administration, and notables, who served mostly in the provincial government. The fourth group was made up of the Armenians, and the fifth of European officials. Attitude to reform and cultural criteria are introduced as a subordinate category, since knowledge of French or English – as opposed to the lack of such knowledge – divided Turks and Egyptians and, to a large extent, conditioned their view of reform. Armenians and Europeans, of course, had Western education and strongly supported modernization. Hunter stresses the ethnic rivalries among the various groups to the point of asking, "why did not the differences between elite subgroups lead to rivalries so fierce as to threaten the stability of the state?" His answer is that the political/administrative order was not purely competitive, there being enough for everybody. And, that all elite members, regardless of group, shared strong material interests – mostly land-bound ones – which held them together in a common bond. Hunter's division is, then, more "infrastructural" and less "superstructural."

It is pointless to deny that economic factors, and certainly the acquisition of land, played an important role in class formation in Egypt during the middle years of the nineteenth century. In addition, Ottoman-Egyptians were certainly not "ethnicity blind." However, we need to move away from an economic and ethnicity-based definition of the elite towards a more socio-cultural one. It is for this purpose that the term "Ottoman-Egyptian elite" is introduced.[18] Accordingly, it is maintained throughout part I that the common bond of that elite consisted in high Ottoman culture, loyalty to the House of Mehmet Ali, and special attachment to service in Egypt. Such a concept enables us to reduce the importance of ethnicity and, to a lesser extent, of economic factors, without denying their relevance to elite formation. There are several reasons why this concept explains in a better way the nature and socio-political behavior of the Ottoman-Egyptian elite.

An ethnicity-dominated explanation is objectionable on two grounds. First, there were many more ethnicities which are subsumed in Hunter's "Turks" and in the more familiar, by now defunct, "Turco-Circassians."[19] Turks were only one – albeit important – ethnic group represented in the Turkish-speaking population of Egypt. As will be shown in part II, there were Turkish speakers also in non-elite groups. Besides Turks, there were ethnic Albanians, Greeks, Circassians, Georgians, Kurds, Bosnians, Laz, and others on both sides of the social divide. One look at Hunter's own tables of "Turkish" officials in high government positions (nos. 4 and 10) reveals a great variety of origins. But the frequent occurrence in the records of names such as Arnaut, Çerkes, Gürcüoğlu, Lazoğlu, Kürt, or Manastırlı, Moralı, Diramalı, Kavalalı, and many others, should prove the point beyond dispute.[20] Secondly, there were strong intra-group rivalries in all ethnic groups, at times so intense that it is quite difficult to talk of ethnic solidarity within the Ottoman-Egyptian elite.

A few brief examples may serve to illustrate the point. Being smaller and more cohesive minorities, Armenians and Europeans were most likely to show ethnic solidarity. Many Armenians were also related to each other by kin, and therefore expected even further to prefer the ethnic group as a basic unit of identification. However, it is not too difficult to find examples to the contrary. When his brother was demoted by Abbas, Nubar resigned from his post as personal aide and interpreter to the viceroy. He risked a great deal in doing so, but owing to Abbas's generosity towards him, Nubar was spared, and both brothers received new commissions in Vienna and Berlin.[21] Yet, to other Armenians, Nubar was less loyal, if we take Hekekyan's word. In 1850, Artîn Bey, Abbas's Armenian Director of the Commerce and Foreign Affairs Department, fled to Istanbul after the viceroy had accused him of embezzlement. Artîn's brother Hüsrev Bey and his brother-in-law Hekekyan Bey, remained in Egypt and, at least partially, in Abbas's service.

Hekekyan's situation was more awkward since he did not have foreign protection, whereas Hüsrev had French protection. His correspondence with Artîn and other members of the family in Istanbul was being opened and scrutinized by state agents. Hekekyan's prime suspect was Nubar. Incidentally, when letters were written in Armenian for secrecy, they could be read only by an Armenian. Hekekyan also believed that Nubar was responsible for the downfall of another Armenian – Vichen Ağa. Vichen came from one of the wealthy and influential Armenian families of Istanbul. He arrived in Egypt after a financial dispute with his uncle. Artîn introduced him to Mehmet Ali, and he was gradually promoted to responsible positions in the administration. Vichen was retained by Abbas, but when Artîn fell from grace, he, too, was discarded. Hekekyan blamed Nubar for using his close relations with Abbas in order to get rid of Vichen,[22] perhaps a future potential rival. But Armenians were no worse than Europeans, or others for that matter.

Consider, for example, the two most eminent Frenchmen in the service of Mehmet Ali, Ibrahim, and Abbas – Süleyman Paşa, formerly Colonel Sève, and Clot Bey. The former was the distinguished Chief-of-Staff of the Egyptian army, while the latter created and developed the Egyptian health service. In October 1832, Clot returned to Marseille for a home visit. Upon his arrival, he was greatly dismayed to learn that rumors were circulating in town to the effect that he had been converted to Islam. In order to refute such allegations, which he and his family found most offensive, Clot wrote a sharp letter to the press, denying the "accusations" and denouncing apostasy and renegades "en termes violants," according to his own admission. To his regret, he had not realized that his published statement would reach Süleyman, who had embraced Islam, and gravely offend him. Returning to Egypt, Clot found Süleyman's attitude towards him greatly changed. He never forgave me, wrote Clot in his memoirs, and twenty years later he even proved it. That remark was a reference to Clot's belief that it was Süleyman who induced Abbas to dismiss and practically banish him from Egypt.[23]

Within the European group, rivalries across national lines were even more frequent than within the same national group. Since both Europeans and Armenians competed for the same positions in government – those requiring knowledge of foreign languages and technical education – it is hardly surprising to find rivalries within these groups, as well as between them. It seems that the drive to excel and achieve higher rank and economic reward was stronger than the realization, if Hunter is correct, that at the top there was enough for everybody. Generally speaking, there was natural competition for high office among French, English, and German officials, which was often keen and, at times, nasty. Throughout the middle years of the century, a number of cases became better known than others. In April 1850, for example, the French consul-general reported that there was deep hatred between Artīn Bey and the Austrian physician Pruner Bey, who had replaced Clot Bey. Hekekyan described the rivalry between Nubar and Bonfort, a French expert, during the reign of Abbas, and alluded to the ill-feeling which Benaud, a French doctor dismissed from the Board of Health, harbored against Artīn, though in fact, it should have been directed at Hekekyan himself. And Nubar described with great disgust the Frenchmen that surrounded Sait, naming some names in the process.[24]

There can be little doubt that the dominant and largest group within the Ottoman-Egyptian elite, which Hunter calls "Turks" and others called "Turco-Circassians," did not function as an ethnic group. The internal struggle within the ruling family pitted one faction against another within the dominant group with no regard to ethnicity, Turkish or other. To a lesser degree than in that major cleavage, rival factions, patronage networks, and coalitions were part and parcel of the social fabric and cultural code of the Ottoman-Egyptian elite. Even within the growing but still small "Egyptian" group of technicians, rivalries sprang up as a natural consequence of political competition for position and wealth. The case of Rifāᶜa Rāfiᶜ aṭ-Ṭahṭāwī and ᶜAlī Mubārak is only one, perhaps the best known, case. Much as intra-group rivalries were common, so were alliances across ethnic barriers. There were "Turks," Armenians, Europeans, and Egyptians on both sides of the Abbas/Sait struggle, which is, again, hardly surprising. All this is inexplicable if we insist on the *primacy* of ethnic identities within the Ottoman-Egyptian elite.

Yet, a socio-cultural approach can provide a more satisfactory explanation. If we accept the notion that the Ottoman-Egyptian elite was drawn together by a common, well-articulated socio-cultural and political heritage, then "Turks" and "Turco-Circassians" are absorbed into the wider group of Ottoman-Egytptians. Already at this stage, we should stress three points. First, that all ethnic groups in the elite, excluding the Europeans and non-Turkish-speaking Egyptians, were bound together by the core components of that heritage.[25] Second, that loyalty to the ruling dynasty transcended all group loyalties and ensured that intra-group rivalries would not be suppressed, while inter-group alliances would be constantly formed. And third, that commitment to a life-long service in Egypt in effect separated the Ottoman-Egyptian from the Ottoman pool of officeholders, thereby localizing the elite, though still retaining its kin and social ties with the "parent," mostly Istanbul-based, Ottoman elite.

As mentioned before, a socio-culturally based definition of the Ottoman-Egyptian elite neither contradicts nor precludes economic factors. at the pinnacle of that elite stood the viceroy, who possessed the absolute means of appropriating and redistributing the surplus and all assets in the economy. Since the reign of Mehmet Ali, viceroys used this enormous power in the process of forming and entrenching a loyal elite. Thus, the rewards of office were never purely status, honor, and prestige, but wealth too. The partnership between the viceroys and their dependent elites, until the last phase of Ismail's reign, was one in which loyalty and services were exchanged for status, land, and cash. However, it must be emphasized that elite status and wealth were not synonymous. There were middle-level officials who were culturally Ottoman-Egyptian, but whose economic means were modest. Conversely, there were wealthy individuals and families, mostly local merchants and village notables, who did not belong – by their own, as by elite view – to the Ottoman-Egyptian elite.

The boundary between elite and non-elite groups was not necessarily a confrontation line. It signified a sphere of belonging in which one felt comfortable, abided by the same social code, and shared a similar value-system. On the peripheries of both cultural cores, groups and individuals negotiated their own *modus vivendi*. In that environment, liquid and non-liquid assets were an important currency, but in and of themselves could not buy elite status. At the same time, elite status and high office were an open invitation to accumulate such assets. In the last third of the nineteenth century, wealth and elite status became increasingly tied to each other. This was the outcome not only of the emergence of an enriched land-holding Ottoman-Egyptian elite. It was also the result of the social expansion of that elite, which in a gradual process became more Egyptianized. These two phenomena must be seen in conjunction, if we are to understand the full range of the processes which the Ottoman-Egyptian elite was undergoing from the 1870s to the First World War.

To round up our discussion of the makeup of the Ottoman-Egyptian elite, let us return briefly to Findley's "religio-ideological" division of the Ottoman bureaucratic elite in the nineteenth century. Findley's categories combine an essentially religious distinction between Muslim and non-Muslim officials with a subdivision of the Muslim group into traditionalists and modernists. With regard to the Ottoman-Egyptian elite, the ideological classification seems less pertinent than the religious, though both should be given some consideration. Owing to the strong impact of Mehmet Ali's attitude to reform, and the fact that he handpicked many of his officials, the overwhelming sentiment in his government was modernist, to use Findley's categories. Opposition to Mehmet Ali's *style* of reform, not to reform *itself*, centered around Abbas, and a conservative approach to reform predominated during his reign.

However, after the reign of Abbas, attitude to reform lost much of its vigor as a divisive political and ideological issue within the Ottoman-Egyptian elite. Men like Mehmet Şerif Paşa were known for their conservative views,[26] but under Sait and Ismail a modernist *élan* predominated, at least in style. Other conservative elements, such as the *ᶜulamā*, were not part of the Ottoman-Egyptian elite and possessed limited political influence. In the middle years of the nineteenth century, save for a brief interlude during the reign of Abbas, they remained politically incapacitated and quite reluctant to engage in opposition to a powerful state run by strong autocratic rulers.[27] This was markedly different from the situation in Istanbul, where the religious establishment was culturally and politically integrated into the Ottoman elite. Conservative and modernist alliances could thus be formed *within* the elite, joining together civil, religious, and military officeholders around ideologically defined political issues.

If attitude to reform was a less important divider in the Ottoman-Egyptian elite than in the Ottoman bureaucratic one, religious categories were as relevant in both cases. In the same way that Ottoman-Egyptians were aware of ethnic divisions, they also distinguished between Muslims and non-Muslims. Though this much is not disputed in the literature, a vivid example from an Ottoman-Egyptian context may further illustrate the point. At the beginning of March 1851, Hekekyan was waiting in an antechamber at the ᶜAbbāsiyya palace for a meeting with Abbas.[28] Also waiting were Nubar, Hurşit, the French physician Benaud, and two elderly men, "*beys* in appearance." After some time, Abbas's Armenian Director of Foreign Affairs, Stefan Bey, entered the room. Hurşit and the Christians, relates Hekekyan, got up in respect, but the two *beys* remained seated. Aware that they were being deliberately discourteous, Hekekyan decided to teach them a lesson.

Turning to the two, he began to tell them in Turkish an anecdote which he had just invented. Once, he intimated, a party of Arab *shaykh*s paid a visit to some distinguished French officers in their camp. The officers noticed that the private soldiers did not stir an inch to show respect to the *shaykh*s and asked them to explain "such a want of civility." The soldiers replied that the visitors were Muslims who made a point of not stirring before a Christian. One of the officers then exhorted them to behave otherwise, saying "if these people are asses and do not know how to behave themselves, you should not make yourselves asses [too]." Hekekyan believed that the two got the point. In any event, it is quite obvious that the common bond of language and culture enabled Hekekyan to convey an unpleasant message without directly offending the men. He did that as a Christian demanding that Muslims respect the marks of seniority and higher status of another Christian, and fellow Armenian, Stefan Bey. In keeping with the code, it was Stefan who was called in first to see Abbas, the rest remaining outside.

All those involved in that case were aware of religious categories. But these categories, too, were subordinate to socio-cultural ones. In the evolving Ottoman-Egyptian culture at mid-century, ethnic and religious sub-divisions were submerged. While a dynastic order was gradually taking hold, both as a political reality and an image, a loyal elite was being formed. As part of the process, shared notions about Egypt, her place in the Empire and the region, and who ought to govern her were being inculcated in the minds of Ottoman-Egyptians. In other words, elite formation was not only a political and economic process, but a socio-cultural and psychological one too. As will be argued in the next part of this chapter, a second generation of officeholders did not merely "emerge," or was simply "formed," but was "educated" or "socialized," as elite members were being given a new, distinct Ottoman-Egyptian identity.

The emergence of elite identity

It has been commonly observed that Abbas Paşa substituted Mehmet Ali's European orientation for an Ottoman one. He is reported to have said that Egypt was no longer part of the Ottoman Empire, and that it had become a Christian country. His grandfather, he allegedly added, was an absolute master to his servants and children, but to the European consuls, he was a slave. According to another version, Abbas said that he would rather be a servant to his Ottoman sovereign than, like Mehmet Ali, a servant to the consuls.[29] In full agreement with these statements, Abbas was depicted as an enemy of Western civilization and a self-effacing subject of the sultan. However, realities during his reign were far more complex. There is ample evidence that Abbas continued to maintain relations with the major European powers and benefited from the advances of Western technology. At the same time, far from a cringing servant of the padişah, he bravely engaged in a long-drawn-out conflict with the Porte during the years 1850 to 1852.

Sabry was perhaps close to an understanding of Abbas's intentions when he wrote that the viceroy did not seek a *dépendence étroite* with the Porte, but a *solidarité étroite*.[30] Even so, this was regarded as a major departure from the path taken by Mehmet Ali and Ibrahim. Their policy relied on intense political, economic, social, and cultural contacts with Europe and Europeans; to Istanbul they were merely rebels. In European eyes, they stood and fought for an independent Egypt, while Abbas was an Ottoman vassal. The record shows, however, that by the middle years of the nineteenth century, all three were committed to the same idea: a fiercely autonomous Egypt, though still within an Ottoman Empire. It was Mehmet Ali Paşa who carved a patrimony for his family out of the sultan's domains. His children and grandchildren protected and strengthened it. Here we are not concerned with the political process through which all this came to be. Instead, we wish to explore the social and cultural process that accompanied the political one.

A crucial step towards autonomy was the creation of an Ottoman-Egyptian elite committed to a long-term service in the province and having a distinctly Ottoman-Egyptian identity. To accomplish that, Mehmet Ali had to lure away high and middle-level officeholders from the imperial pool of administrative manpower and, then, retain them in Egypt. This he did by offers of higher and more regular pay, as well as through land grants. We have already noted how land that had been appropriated by the viceroy was redistributed to members of his patrimonial household. Estates that had accumulated tax arrears were granted to officials as *ühde*s, so that their holders became tied to Egypt and its treasury by mutually beneficial ties.[31] By the end of Ibrahim's reign, there was a distinct and committed Ottoman-Egyptian elite, whose members saw their future and the future of their children as linked to the country. Deeply mistrustful of these people, Abbas considered them as loyal to his enemies – the sons of Mehmet Ali and Ibrahim – and did not wish to rely on their services.

Hence, he set out to disperse the top echelon of the elite without betraying the ultimate goal of his grandfather and uncle – a fully autonomous Egypt under dynastic rule. In other words, what Abbas had to do was to reintegrate that group into the Ottoman pool by inducing the Porte to appoint them to positions elsewhere in the Empire. He then had to promote a new generation of officeholders, who would be both loyal to him and attached to Egypt. He accomplished the first stage of his plan within the first year or so of his reign. A number of key figures lost their positions in government, and not a few others were made to feel unwelcome in Egypt. Many *ühde*s were revoked due to unpaid taxes, on which previous viceroys had turned a blind eye. As part of this drive, the Porte consented to appoint some of the top men in that group to other imperial positions, thereby signaling that reintegration was possible. Sami Paşa was appointed governor of Salonika, Hasan Haydar Paşa became governor of Biga, and Yusuf Kâmil Paşa, husband of Mehmet Ali's daughter Zeynep, began his gradual rise to the grand vezirate in Istanbul.[32] In due course, some of those who remained in Egypt were allowed a share in Abbas's new government.

Thus, while Mehmet Ali and Ibrahim's men were broken up as a group and a generation of officeholders, not a few of them, mostly on the middle levels, were absorbed as individuals into the second generation, which emerged under Abbas and matured under Sait. That new group of officials was to dominate the government of Egypt throughout the middle years of the nineteenth century and well into the reign of Ismail. An important achievement of the transition period of the late 1840s and early 1850s was that, despite the generational shift which occurred, the Ottoman-Egyptian identity of the elite remained virtually intact. In fact, it was even being strengthened. For his part, Abbas continued to inculcate in his officials a sense of loyalty to "Paşa and Country," as an essential element of his endeavors to base his dynastic order on firm ground. That identity was Ottoman-Egyptian in the full sense of the combination. It did not deny the Ottoman component, certainly not on the cultural level. Rather, it contained an additional dimension, namely a commitment to bind one's future to Egypt and the House of Mehmet Ali.

Consolidating an Ottoman-Egyptian identity

Because they made a lifetime commitment to serve in Egypt, elite members gradually came to regard Istanbul as a cultural center to which one looked for example and inspiration, where one went on vacation to seek the latest social and cultural fashions. It became more of "the old country" and less a political center where the "action" was. The process was gradual, but it was nonetheless real. So much so, that it is noticeable even during the reign of Abbas, that supposedly most Ottoman period in the nineteenth century. Abbas was certainly proud of his predecessors' record in making Egypt autonomous and prosperous. When the conflict with the Porte was at its peak, he reportedly told the Ottoman government that they should compare the state of Egypt and Iraq before meddling any further with the internal affairs of his province. Governed by a Mehmet Ali, he argued, Iraq would have been as prosperous as Egypt, not in ruins as she was. Mind the affairs of Iraq and let Egypt be, Abbas told the Porte.[33]

However, the most revealing evidence concerning the viceroy's sentiments can be found in his correspondence with Selim Paşa, commander of the Egyptian expeditionary force to the Crimean War. The letters exchanged between the two spanned the period from June 1853 to July 1854, roughly the last year of Abbas's life.[34] Its actual background puts matters in relief. For, Egypt's participation in the Ottoman war effort was an act of identification with and submission to the sultan. And yet, what clearly comes out of the letters is Abbas's insistence on a separate Ottoman-Egyptian identity. In most of his dispatches, the viceroy kept demanding full and accurate reports of the condition of the Egyptian troops, while censuring the commander for not providing sufficient information. Procedure decreed that a scribe (*kâtip*) and a day-book keeper (*jurnalcî*) accompany the commander in battle. These officials had to provide the viceroy with detailed reports of the condition and daily routine of the Egyptian forces. That was the practice in the time of Mehmet Ali, when Ibrahim kept his father up-to-date through such reports.

There were at least two kinds of *jurnal*s. The first dealt with camp routine (*dâavi*, literally "complaints"), and contained specific data on "conditions, strength, food, dress, administration, discipline, and well-being." The second type reported on movement of forces, battles, victories, and defeats (*vukuât*, literally "events").[35] Abbas was more keen on receiving the first kind of *jurnal*s than the second, for it was mainly through these that he could really follow the well-being of his troops. By giving or denying assent to initial rulings of his commander-in-chief, the viceroy retained ultimate, albeit delayed, control of the situation. Those *jurnal*s were a sort of barrier against an Ottoman take-over of the Egyptian expeditionary force. Abbas was constantly, and zealously, on guard against such encroachment upon established precedents. When the veteran Selim Paşa once again failed to send detailed *jurnal*s as ordered, Abbas reprimanded him, though this time in a personal, pleading manner. The viceroy addressed him in the familiar second person, using the affective form (*canım paşa, sen* . . .) along with some sarcasm recalling Selim's experience under the command of Ibrahim Paşa in various campaigns:

> I wonder, have you not seen the *jurnal*s written by . . . [the scribe's name] and sent to my grandfather by my uncle from the Morea? And, if you did not see them, have you not heard of them? . . . One look at your *jurnal*s will show that I cannot possibly learn what is happening or how you deal with daily matters . . . Have you got something against me? If not, is it, then, that the scribes in your command refuse to write?[36]

With regard to manpower, Abbas insisted that casualties be replaced by fresh troops from Egypt, to maintain the integrity of the force. He also demanded that all promotions be confirmed by him in person, which meant that Selim Paşa had to apply for permission before making any promotion. In one case, Selim reported that he had promoted two officers from the rank of colonel to that of brigadier. Abbas castigated him for so doing and reminded him that there were enough brigadiers in Egypt. Should he require brigadiers, Abbas continued, he ought to apply to him and the officers would be sent promptly. In yet another case, Abbas remarked cynically that he had read in a recent *jurnal* about the death of a certain captain, but that he did not recollect that a request for replacement followed. "This truly surprised and astonished me," remarked Abbas. "You have a *jurnalcı* with you," he continued, "not merely to report from what place to what place you moved or provide an official account of events. Rather, it is in order to report in great detail everything. From now on you must do precisely that, and request permission for every appointment you wish to make."[37]

Control over the expeditionary force was partly exercised through the payment of salaries to the troops. Payments were made every four months by a special officer who was sent from Egypt to disburse the money to officers and soldiers. In September 1853, Selim Paşa wrote to Abbas requesting that his army be paid on a monthly basis, just like the Ottoman imperial forces. Abbas refused for practical reasons, the salient one being that the Egyptian treasury was based on a system of four-monthly budgets. He added that it had been decided in previous cases, such as the expeditions to Arabia, Crete, and the Morea, that for the Egyptian what counted was what the Egyptian practice was. Abbas phrased this in Ottoman Turkish in an interesting, and possibly more generalized way: "What comes first for an Egyptian is Egypt" (*Mısrına evvel Mısırdır*). Though the immediate context may suggest a limited interpretation of this statement, the wider one allows for a broader understanding of it.[38]

Herein lies the notion that Ottoman-Egyptians – significantly referred to in this case as "Egyptians" – were loyal Ottoman subjects, but for them, a commitment to Egypt and Egyptian ways (*usul-ı Mısriye*) came first. In conformity with their Ottoman loyalty, they fought alongside the imperial army in the Crimean War. Indeed, when news of his troops' success on the battlefield reached Abbas, he warmly commended Selim Paşa and stressed that it was "a service for Islam, the Muslim community, and the Ottoman Empire" (*din ü-millet ü-devlet hizmeti*). At the same time, a loyalty to viceroy and Egypt coexisted with a loyalty to sultan and Empire. Accordingly, when Abbas congratulated his forces on a successful naval operation, he reminded Selim Paşa that he, the viceroy, always demanded of his men the utmost exertion for the protection of Egypt's honor and prestige (*Mısrın şani ve namusı*). Obviously, such sentiments could exist in harmony only in times of mutual understanding and cooperation between the sultan and the viceroy of Egypt.[39]

When conflict erupted, however, the loyalty of Ottoman-Egyptians had to rest with Egypt and its ruler, for that was basically what dynastic rule in Egypt was all about. To the first three viceroys, a commitment to an Egyptian autonomy was an overriding consideration. Mehmet Ali and Ibrahim made Egypt an autonomous Ottoman province. For his part, Abbas ensured the longevity of dynastic rule in Egypt. All three, their different natures and worldviews notwithstanding, imparted to the governing elites they created and worked with a sense of an Ottoman identity peculiar to Egypt. In their view, that identity was permanent, something you took with you wherever you went. The concept of an Egyptian self-rule was thus extended to Ottoman-Egyptian personnel even when outside Egypt and in the service of the sultan. These remained Egyptian soldiers (*asakir-i Mısriye*), never again to become imperial ones (*asakir-i şahane*). The same commitment was shared also by later viceroys – Sait during the remainder of the Crimean War,[40] Ismail in his unprecedented expansion of the Ottoman-Egyptian elite and in making it more "Egyptian" than ever before.

The consolidation of an Egyptian component in the identity of Ottoman-Egyptians must not be taken as any form of nascent nationalism or proto-nationalism. If a connection could ever be established between the phenomenon described above and the rising of the modern Egyptian nation-state, it would probably be a complex and tenuous one. That identity – by the time of Abbas indeed a reality – emerged within the context of an elite culture and had very little to do with any sympathies towards the vast non-elite groups in Egypt. It was only when growing numbers of culturally non-Ottoman Egyptians joined the Ottoman-Egyptian elite, that a shift in focus occurred. Only then, towards the last decade of the nineteenth century, genuine Egyptian nationalism began to arise. It was carried on the shoulders of an urban middle class, the *efendiyya*, which imbibed, through education and reading, the teachings of politicians and intellectuals affected by European nationalism.[41]

Historical self-awareness

Almost as a necessary corollary of the growing sense of Ottoman-Egyptian group identity in the middle years of the nineteenth century, it is possible to detect an interest in Egyptian history, both modern and ancient. In the formation of a dynastic order, precedent was a crucial element. The pattern of independence from the Porte was set by Mehmet Ali and Ibrahim, but Abbas had to prevent any impingement on the measure of autonomy that had been reluctantly granted to his predecessors. His elite had to be enlightened as to the limits of Ottoman encroachment on Egyptian "rights," and was expected to assist the viceroy in his relentless efforts to defend the status quo. Since many of the officials had no personal historical experience, they had to be told. But it was not only recent history that gained respect in the time of Abbas. The ancient past of Egypt, the relics of its glory scattered unheeded across the country, was beginning to attract some, though still limited, attention. All this was part of the process of forging the bond between the elite and Egypt.

A strong sense of historical continuity is evident in Abbas's correspondence with Selim Paşa. When the official codes of conduct and regulations of the Ottoman imperial army were sent to Selim for application in the Egyptian expeditionary force, he forwarded them to Abbas, mocking Ottoman pretense. The viceroy replied with an historical account of the situation in the Morea war of 1824, when Mehmet Ali dispatched Ibrahim with Egyptian forces to assist the sultan against the Greeks. This was before the edict granting hereditary government to Egypt, remarked Abbas, yet even then Ibrahim would not take any orders regarding his troops from anybody but Mehmet Ali. "Now that Egypt has been entrusted to me," he wrote, "I am in charge of everything that takes place in the army. I receive the *jurnal*s, and I [alone] confirm the policy [to be followed]." If you are told that all forces are now imperial forces (*cümlesi asakir-i şahanedir*), added Abbas, you shall reply: this is how things are nonetheless.[42]

Another indication of growing historical awareness is in the often neglected area of archeology and antiquities. The relevant context here is the rise of Egyptology as a field of both scholarly and popular interest. The discovery and excavation of the Memphite Serapeum at Saqqāra in 1850–3 is considered as the first major achievement in Egyptian archeology. The French Egyptologist Auguste Mariette is most widely identified with that project. This and other important discoveries during the reigns of Abbas and Sait gave the field of Egyptology the public exposure which made it so attractive to Europeans for the rest of the century and beyond. Contemporary developments in the technology of photography in France were closely connected with the scholarly interest in Egyptian monuments. They brought Ancient Egyptian sites to the awareness of Europeans in a way that landscape painters could not. Maxime Du Camp's photographs, taken in 1849–50, when he travelled in Egypt with Flaubert, were published in 1852. They are, perhaps, the most striking example of that development.[43]

A by-product of mid-century discoveries was an increase in the ransacking of Egyptian archeological treasures. To be sure, the phenomenon was not new to the Egyptian countryside. For centuries, the inhabitants of the Nile Valley had used derelict temples as dwellings, after some modifications, or taken materials from such temples for building their new houses. Moreover, interested European travelers helped themselves to archeological items from temples and tombs well before the new discoveries. However, only from the last years of Mehmet Ali's reign, did this phenomenon become a profitable business. It was then that Egyptologists began to protest at the lack of archeological supervision in Egypt which would have prevented local inhabitants and greedy tourists from jeopardising the future study of Ancient Egypt. To appease protestors, Mehmet Ali issued orders to stop the destruction of ancient monuments, but according to one of his top European officials – who was himself a major collector – such orders were never seriously carried out until the reign of Sait.[44]

With the growing interest in Europe, many invaluable historical items were taken out of Egypt to adorn private collections and museum holdings in all the major Western capitals. Many of the Europeans residing in Egypt, including some of the highest ranking government officials, built up large collections over the years of their service in the country. The French Director of the Health Services Clot Bey, Director of Engineering Linant Bey, Director of the Giza Cavalry School Varin Bey, the Belgian consul-general, Zizinia, and the British doctor Abbott owned some of the largest and best-known collections. There were also recognized dealers in antiquities, such as the Cairene Fernandez, who made a handsome living by catering to this rapidly developing market.[45] The lack of interest in preventing the outflow of historical objects reflected an apparent indifference among Ottoman-Egyptians towards the ancient past of Egypt. This was to change in the reign of Abbas, whose concept of dynastic patrimony in Egypt encompassed the whole range of Egyptian history, including antiquity.

On 10 May 1849, only a few months after he assumed power, Abbas issued revealing instructions regarding antiquities.[46] According to his orders, two engineers were appointed to conduct a survey of archeological sites in Upper Egypt. They were to compile a detailed register of all sites, inform the provincial governorates of sites located in their jurisdictions, and report the results of their efforts to the Council of Justice. Provincial governors were charged with the protection of sites in their respective governorates, and sites in the vicinity of Cairo, such as the pyramids, were entrusted to the care of the Director of the Department of Education. The purpose of these instructions, as stated by Abbas, was to preserve Egypt's heritage and prevent archaeological sites from being robbed. It was explained that offenders were either travelers coming from faraway countries, or local inhabitants who used precious remains as construction materials.

Abbas's orders were intended to correct a situation in which the instructions of his predecessors on antiquities were not enforced. The viceroy believed that the reason for that was the inefficiency of centralized supervision. There was a supervisor of antiquities, but he did not have the means to cover all sites in Egypt. Therefore, responsibility was given to local authorities, which were thereafter to possess detailed information on known sites under their protection. The motive for Abbas's action was not only the desire to protect "Egyptian heritage." It was stated in addition, that "the archeological remains and other antiquities found in the territory of Egypt bring the country both beauty and pride; they [also] serve to discover and study the conditions of the past." In this spirit, restrictions were also placed on the exportation of antiquities from Egypt. These were enforced, but it seems that pressures from European consuls induced Abbas to allow, from time to time, some exceptions.[47] It is also quite likely that smuggling occurred as prices abroad rose, posing irresistible temptations to merchants and customs officers alike.

The notion of Egypt as a "mini-empire"

Another aspect of the emerging Ottoman-Egyptian group identity at mid-century was what might be termed the "mini-imperial" self-view. That is, the view that Egypt was not only part of the great Ottoman Empire, but that it was in itself the core of a smaller empire within the Empire. That notion was approximated to what is nowadays termed a "regional power." Until the defeat of 1840–1, the immediate sphere of domination of such a "mini-empire" consisted of Egypt and the Sudan, with a desirable expansion towards the Syrian provinces. A *cordon* of influence, or at least of special relations, engulfed the province of the Hijaz and the *beylik* of Tunis. The latter had an autonomous status under a strong *bey*, and was considered in a similar position *vis-à-vis* the Porte as Egypt. Geographically and historically, a special relationship had existed between Egypt and the Hijaz since the time of Mehmet Ali, who in 1811 crushed the Wahhābī movement and restored the province to Ottoman rule.[48] Following the events of the early 1840s, the "mini-empire" did not include provinces more closely administered from Istanbul, such as Damascus, Sidon, or Tripolitania (Trablusgarp, today's Libya).

The reign of Abbas witnessed further manifestations of Egypt's special relations with Tunis and the Hijaz. The French were concerned that the viceroy's contacts with Ahmet Bey, governor-general of Tunis, were the prelude to an alliance between the two, or at least an attempt to formulate common policy towards the Porte. During the conflict over the application of Ottoman legislation in Egypt, the Bey, too, refused to extend the relevant codes to his realm. With the settlement of the dispute, Abbas advised him to adopt a similar policy, which he did. The French, who had suffered a major setback in Egypt because of Abbas's policies, were worried that similar fate might befall their interests in Tunis. At the end of July 1849, the French Foreign Minister expressed his strong disapproval of Abbas's meddling in Tunis, defining it as an act of hostility against France.[49]

Abbas's special relations with the Hijaz were of both a personal and a political nature. These sentiments went back to his father, Tusun Paşa, who commanded the Egyptian troops in the Hijaz between 1811 and 1815. It was in June 1812, during his father's long absence from Egypt, that Abbas was born. There are conflicting versions as to where he was actually born. According to the prevailing one, he was born in Egypt, and his father did not see him for nearly three and a half years, not until he returned from the Hijaz. On the other hand, Hekekyan tells a different story. According to him, Abbas was born in the Hijaz, had a Meccan wet-nurse, and spent the first four years of his life there.[50] In any event, Abbas was intimately linked to that province, and his special relations with the bedouins of Egypt might well have stemmed from that attachment too. It was to the Hijaz that Abbas went at the end of Ibrahim's reign, in order to keep at a safe distance from his hostile and ailing uncle.

It was from there that he was recalled to assume power in Egypt after the death of Ibrahim at the end of 1848. One of the first things Abbas did upon his return from Istanbul, where he was invested as Governor of Egypt, demonstrates his feelings towards the Hijaz and its most prominent family – the Şerifs of Mecca. In February 1849, Abbas ordered his deputy and the officer in charge of the Egyptian dock works in Jidda to present the Egyptian frigate *Atiyetürrahman* as a gift to the son of the Şerif of Mecca. The frigate had been built under Mehmet Ali and was one of the best Egypt possessed. It used to patrol the Red Sea, forming part of the fleet that served as a symbol of Egyptian power in the region. One of the arrangements concerning the Red Sea was Egypt's control of the two important ports of Massawa and Sawakin. These belonged to the province of the Hijaz, but the collection of customs was farmed out to Mehmet Ali. In June 1849, upon the expiration of the grant's term, the ports reverted back to the Hijaz.[51] Contrary to his general attitude, Abbas did not try to prevent the secession. They were returned to Egyptian control only in 1865, during the reign of Ismail. To him, they were important as part of a policy of regional expansion towards Ethiopia.

Perhaps because of the special relations between Abbas and the Şerifian family, and certainly owing to Mehmet Ali's record of rebellion aigainst the sultan, the Porte did not use Egyptian forces when trouble arose in the Hijaz. In August 1851, the central government sent several detachments of Ottoman soldiers to pacify the Hijaz, which Abbas allowed to pass through Egyptian territory. The same occurred during the disturbances of 1856–8, in the reign of

Sait, although he did not have a similar attachment to the Hijaz.[52] Unlike its willingness to use Egyptian forces against an external enemy, as in the Crimean War, the Porte refrained from using them to settle internal affairs. In a way, this represented a *de facto* recognition of Egypt's position as a regional power. It could not be trusted to serve wider imperial interests overriding her own, regional ones.

The middle years of the nineteenth century also saw the reassertion of the Egyptian position in the Sudan.[53] During the last years of Mehmet Ali's reign, Cairo's control over the affairs of that province was weakened. The decline in the quality of government gave rise to local, peripheral forces. Not many of the reforms introduced in Egypt reached the Sudan, and service there came to be regarded by members of the Ottoman-Egyptian elite as a sort of exile. Sudanese mines continued to absorb convicts sentenced to long imprisonment with hard labor. It was believed, though hard to document, that not many of those who went to "convict colonies" in Jabal Fezzan or Feyzoğlu returned. Abbas and Sait were both concerned with the situation in the Sudan, and tried to change things there. In September 1849, Abbas regulated the rank and term of service of district governors in the Sudan. He ordered that such governors be appointed for no less than three years. They also had to have higher rank, at least that of *Mir-i Liva* (roughly equivalent to brigadier).

The reason for this upgrading was stated to be the desire of the viceroy to give the Sudan proper government according to its importance and the large amounts of money invested in it. In the course of his reign, Abbas also reorganized the administration of the Sudan, initiated a wave of construction in the capital Khartoum, opened some major roads, developed the trade through relaxation of monopolies, and established the first modern school under the directorship of Rifā^{c}a Rāfi^{c} aṭ-Ṭahṭāwī. During his reign, Egyptian forces in the Sudan repelled a number of attempted incursions from Ethiopia.[54] In fact, histories of the Sudan in Arabic, especially those based on archival material, usually praise Abbas as a great reformer, which is not quite what has been written about him in Egypt. Sait, too, took an active interest in the Sudan. He personally led an expedition to the province to deal with local rebels, appointed his brother Abdülhalim Paşa as governor-general there, and prohibited the slave trade from the Sudan into Egypt.

Our interest here lies in the significance of these policies as they relate to the self-view of the viceroys and their elite. The reassertion of Egyptian power in the Sudan, it is suggested, should be seen also within an Ottoman-Egyptian context. That is, as part of the emerging identity of the elite, as it was trying to negotiate a regional role for an autonomous, though still Ottoman, Egypt. This is what I termed the notion of "mini-empire." Together with a loyalty to the House of Mehmet Ali, a commitment to live and serve in Egypt, and a sense of belonging to Ottoman culture and an Ottoman Empire, this notion formed part of a distinct

Ottoman-Egyptian identity. Yet this identity was only one aspect of the daily life of officials in Egypt during the middle years of the nineteenth century. Chapter 4 explores the realities of officeholding, its benefits and limitations, and describes the ways in which officials adjusted to those realities.

4 The realities of office holding

In this chapter, we shall follow some of the more pertinent aspects of the life officeholders led. The dependent nature of the elite and the consequent view among officials that their careers were ever subject to the whims of the ruler are, perhaps, the most apparent feature of elite life. Although there is evidence that decision making and appointments became less "irrational" at mid-century, the sense of insecurity, both of office and property, still lingered in the minds of people. Nevertheless, the great benefits attached to office and "survival mechanisms," such as patronage, decidedly tipped the scales in favor of the viceroy's service. All these produced a distinct officeholders' culture, a certain mode of behavior, and a set of values which became identified with the Ottoman-Egyptian elite of the time.

The viceroys and the elite – a "moody" relationship

In the middle years of the nineteenth century – though certainly not only then – the lifestyle and structure of the Ottoman-Egyptian elite were deeply affected by the viceroys' personality. Although Mehmet Ali, Ibrahim, Abbas, Sait, and Ismail each governed in his own way, they all served as a focal point for their respective elites. Structurally, very little could be done without their personal assent. That assent was granted in writing by the issue of an *irade*, or a decree embodying sovereign will. The stylized text of *irade*s conveys the nature of the process. It reads as follows:

> I [the viceroy] have perused this . . . [type of document presented by a government body], dated . . . Since it accords with my will (*muvafık-ı iradem bulunmuş olduğundan*) that it be implemented as required, notice is hereby served to apply [the measure] promptly and as stipulated.[1]

There is good reason to believe that the written record encompassed a great deal of the business transacted by government. This was so especially with regard to internal matters during the reign of Abbas, but to a large extent also during the reign of Sait. Understandably, the record is deficient on foreign relations and maneuvers *vis-à-vis* the Porte; these were highly sensitive matters, and leaks were greatly feared. In domestic matters, registers containing recorded decisions of the viceroys often refer to verbal instructions and oral arrangements. It seems that Ottoman record-keeping traditions and greater bureaucratization resulted in a detailed written practice. This enabled the ruler and his high officials to follow the various stages of policy-making and communicate more efficiently through the various branches of a steadily growing government apparatus. We often come across some variation of the following phrase, here addressed by Abbas to the Director of the Education Department: "In a recent conversation with Your Excellency, I drew your attention [to the matter] and instructed you to . . . "[2]

In orders sent to various government agencies and to provincial governors, Abbas sometimes addressed his officials in the familiar form, using "I" (*ben*) and "you" (*sen*) rather than "we" (*biz*) and "thou" (*siz*). This might mislead the casual reader to assume intimacy between the viceroy and his bureaucrats. Although in some cases this was indeed so, the rule seems to have been rather the opposite. The use of that style created an immediacy and a sense of personal responsibility, which the distanced and more elevated address tended to soften. It underlined a personalized style of government, blatantly conveying the message of authority. In a rather colloquial manner, we might render it as: "Let us leave niceties aside and get down to business. *You* are responsible for carrying out this order, and *I* shall see to it that *you* do."

Personal style was so intrinsic to the concept of state and government that it was at times used even in matters concerning Egypt's relations with the Porte. In this, too, it was Mehmet Ali who set the pattern. At times, the style reached the absurd, as in the tense moments of the crisis over Syria in 1840. When the Old Paşa wanted to communicate to the Porte his proposals for a settlement, he chose to entrust the papers to his daughter-in-law, who was supposed to deliver them to the harem of the grand vezir in Istanbul. She went there twice, but on some excuse was not received, so the proposals were not delivered. "I am laughed at by the Court of Constantinople," complained Mehmet Ali to the British consul-general. This mode of operation became less frequent with the passage of time, but the personal word of the viceroy continued to be law; it committed the government of Egypt as a whole.[3]

There can be little doubt that a gradual process of bureaucratization was taking place in the government of Egypt during the middle decades of the nineteenth century. At the same time, one can hardly overemphasize the personal predominance of the viceroys within the administration. From Mehmet Ali through the first part of Ismail's reign, departments and conciliar bodies were set up, reorganized, abolished, and re-created. Both the civil and military administrations grew in size, ranks and salaries were changed, army and police formations were recast, hierarchies and chains of command were elaborated. That much is not disputed. However, not before the second phase of Ismail's reign, towards the early 1870s, do we observe a qualitative change in the role of the viceroy *vis-à-vis* the administration and the military. Before that – and certainly not during the 1840s and 1850s – we cannot speak of any meaningful qualification of either the power-base or the manner in which power was being wielded in government. Nothing resembling the uneasy balance between sultan and Porte during the *Tanzimat* emerged in Egypt. Authority emenated solely from the Paşa, his presence and his will reverberated throughout the administration.[4]

Because of this dominance, much of the discourse within the Ottoman-Egyptian elite revolved around the person and actions of the viceroy. The political fate of bureaucrats and army officers depended so much on his will that decision-making was almost inevitably taken to be capricious. Though often based on clear policy guidelines, with well-articulated long- and short-term goals, the style of personal government seemed to participants and contemporary observers to be whimsical. It was this widely held belief that centered attention on the ruler's mood and external behavior rather than on substantive analysis. Consequently, what people sought to obtain was information about the personal life of the viceroys, or what we would perhaps call "political gossip." Demand for that "commodity" became more acute when circumstances, or the personality of the ruler, made it particularly scarce, as happened at various times in the middle of the century.

Such a situation occurred when Mehmet Ali's mental capacity deteriorated in the latter part of the 1840s, during the short reign of Ibrahim, and in the reign of Abbas. It was less felt in the reigns of Mehmet Ali, Sait, and Ismail, whose open court provided sufficient information and accessibility. Unwittingly, Hekekyan provides an interesting and typical example of how that actually worked.[5] In 1850–2, Abbas and the Porte clashed over two issues – the application of Ottoman legislation in Egypt and the Alexandria–Cairo railway concession. Hekekyan's analysis of the situation depended entirely on mood-guessing. As Abbas was reported to be in a gloomy mood, Hekekyan concluded that his position *vis-à-vis* the Porte was being weakened. However, only days later, Hekekyan's brother-in-law, Hüsrev Bey, reported that Abbas was seen in good spirits. This led Hekekyan to reverse his previous, well-argued assessment of the political situation. He then advanced the theory that there was actually a grand conspiracy between Abbas and the Porte to deceive Britain.

It matters little that neither of these conflicting interpretations was particularly insightful or accurate. What is significant is that this was a perfectly logical deduction within the cultural terms of the Ottoman-Egyptian elite at the time. A whole arsenal of stories was readily available to support that kind of reasoning. Some were probably true, or at least had a grain of truth in them, others were no doubt a figment of the imagination. In many, however, a recurring motif was the mood element in decision-making. Men in government learned to accept this element as part of reality and adjusted to it. In the lore of the time, whims could decide the personal fate of high officials. In noted cases it cost them not only position and rank, but their lives too. The agent was usually poison mixed with coffee and offered to the ill-fated. Kapudan Ahmet Paşa, Nubar relates, quietly drank the cup and died. It was administered to him by the governor of Alexandria on Mehmet Ali's orders. Yusuf Kâmil Paşa did not, fearing a similar order by Abbas. And Nubar himself, when summoned to an important audience with Abbas, was warned by his brother not to drink water or coffee.[6]

While accompanying the ailing Ibrahim Paşa on his return from Istanbul in 1848, Nubar was again involved in a comparably hazardous situation. He was on deck, conversing with Hasan Paşa and Bedan Bey, all close associates of Ibrahim. It was then, not far from Alexandria, that Şirin Bey, captain of the vessel, approached the three and calmly said that the viceroy regarded them as traitors. You, he told Hasan Paşa, you betrayed him with Abbas; you, he said turning to Bedan Bey, betrayed him with Artin Bey; and you, he said to Nubar, betrayed him with his father Mehmet Ali. To prevent you from carrying out your conspiracy, continued the captain, he would have you beheaded and thrown into the sea before reaching the port. Pale and trembling, they looked at each other. Hasan Paşa then asked the captain if he would indeed do it, should Ibrahim give him such orders. "No," replied Şirin in a quiet voice, "for when I do that, by the same order my lieutenant would kill me and push my body down after yours." Their fears, however, were not over until they finally landed safely on shore.[7]

The insecurities of office

Another aspect of life ostensibly subject to viceregal caprice was that of appointments in the army and bureaucracy. The common perception was that men were appointed and dismissed almost regardless of how qualified they were to do the job. One could rise and fall fast, it was believed, but that depended more on the viceroy's personal liking than on actual performance. At least that was the prevailing notion. In fact, however, the kind of promotion pattern Şerif Mardin called "Aladdin's lamp mobility" and Carter Findley "wheel-of-fortune mobility,"[8] namely the meteoric rise based on a fortunate encounter with the sultan or one of his grandees, became unlikely in Egypt by the middle of the nineteenth century. Training, education, and patronage through long-term association with an elite household (*intisap*) were far more important in shaping the careers of officers and bureaucrats. It is true, however, that frequent changes in high office tended to obfuscate this reality.

As Hunter has shown, viceroys used frequent changes in order to manipulate office granting and increase their control over the government. He calculated that department directors served on average twenty months under Abbas, sixteen under Sait, and thirteen under Ismail; town and city governors averaged fourteen months under Abbas, eighteen under Sait, and eleven under Ismail; and governors of provinces lasted an average of twelve months under Abbas, eighteen under Sait, and only eight months under Ismail.[9] The major shifts which resulted from the struggle within the ruling family during the reign of Abbas were still alive in the minds of many elite members. Such memories, too, did not help to enhance confidence among officeholders. But it was not only in office itself that officials had a deep sense of insecurity. Many felt that their property and earnings might arbitrarily be taken away. Hence, they tried to conceal from others what they had, though not by sacrificing living conditions, which also served as status symbols. In addition, officeholders tended to hoard money, while carefully diversifying investment and savings to minimize what they perceived to be the hazards of their position.

Hekekyan, for example, called this insecurity "the calamity of Egypt." In a conversation with Senior, which took place in 1856, he described the feeling in vivid terms:

> Nothing that I or any other Egyptian possesses is really mine. I have a house: the Pasha can take it from me. I have a village [as *ühde*] – its taxes now amount to 50,000 piasters a year: he may raise them to 80,000 or to 100,000; he may require it to furnish him with camels, oxen, or corn; he may take all its inhabitants – men, women and children – and send them to dig a canal in the desert; when he has rendered it incapable of paying its taxes he may seize it for arrears, and grant it to one of his friends. No property, no rank, no institution is stable, except the few that enjoy European protection.[10]

Nubar conveys a similar feeling when he describes his decision to quit Abbas's service after the demotion of his brother Arakel. The first thing he did was to assess his financial situation. Pooling their resources together, the two families had 3,000 francs in cash and some more in assorted currencies. Nubar also had a house, especially built for him by Abbas as a wedding present. But it was, as he put it, "*non-valeur*," for no one would dare to purchase or rent the house of a man who had fallen from grace. Nubar's wife came to the rescue, chipping in her dowry. It consisted of diamonds worth 60,000 to 70,000 francs. At that, they all sighed with relief: "we were rich, and with God's help, independent."[11] Though Armenian, Hekekyan and Nubar do not reflect merely the insecurity of a non-Muslim minority. In fact, there can be little doubt that they echoed widespread sentiments among members of the Ottoman-Egyptian elite.

The regimented life of officials

Almost in contradiction to job insecurity, the rest of the officials' lives was becoming more regimented at mid-century. Concomitantly, although differences continued to exist between civil and military spheres, the borderline was becoming increasingly blurred. External elements such as uniforms, titles, ranks, salary tables – despite variations in all of them – and converging career patterns, tended to level the barriers between the two services.

As mentioned above, in times of peace, as during the 1840s and 1850s, even the tasks performed by the two services became increasingly similar. When soldiers and marines were being employed in public works of all sorts, in cleaning and construction, their commanders were more managers and project directors than combat officers. Abbas's tendency to regiment the bureaucracy narrowed the gap even further. A more typical division of labor re-emerged only during the reign of Ismail, whose imperial designs gave the army a role in battle and conquest. In his turn, Abbas attempted to regulate public appearance of officials, giving the bureaucracy a more distinct corporate look. Government officials were ordered to grow beards, according to the Istanbul fashion. Specialists were invited from the imperial capital to advise *fez* (*ṭarbūsh*) manufacturers in the art of making hats for officials *à la turca*. Civil and military officeholders were instructed to wear their uniforms on Islamic holidays and on public occasions.[12]

The trend, however, was not confined to appearance. Behavior was also regulated. For example, smoking was prohibited in government offices.[13] When a code was drafted for a newly established council, it stipulated that members were not allowed to smoke or drink coffee in the conference hall. A special cabinet room was designated for smoking and drinking coffee, where members could take a break during meetings. Scribes, however, were allowed to drink coffee in their offices. An attempt was also made to control leaks from sensitive council deliberations, as these were considered harmful to state interests. The spreading of rumors about political matters was deemed reprehensible, and potential leakers were warned that they would be severely punished. In an increasingly regulated environment, refusal of an appointment or resignation from office were almost inconceivable. They brought upon an individual the wrath of rulers and could mean social decline and financial ruin.

Hekekyan took great pains to convince his superior, and through him Abbas Paşa, that his chronic ophthalmia, not his unwillingness, prevented him from supervising a mining expedition to Upper Egypt. Nubar felt that in resigning his post after the demotion of his brother Arakel, he committed a grave offense, for which he was prepared to incur the lasting indignation of Abbas. He was astounded when the viceroy offered the two of them new and attractive positions abroad. Mubārak complained about the insecurity of government employ and even tried his luck in commercial enterprise. But offered a chance to return to the service, he accepted, although it had been some time before he was given a suitable appointment.[14] It was that insecurity of position and wealth that created a distinct culture of officeholders in mid-nineteenth-century Egypt. Although a living response to specific, taxing circumstances – in many ways a "survival code" – that culture was, at the same time, part and parcel of Ottoman elite traditions.

Obedience, conformity, and exclusion

In the cultural code of officeholders, obedience and conformity were widely believed to win approval and, therefore, reward and promotion. They were symbolically codified and highly ritualized. The way one sat before and addressed a superior, the form in which submission to orders was indicated, and how one took leave, were all dictated by convention, with little room for variation. Entrance of a senior official into the room called upon all present to rise in respect; the hand of a dignitary offered to a subordinate to kiss meant that the interview was over; and bowing down with a gesture of the hand expressed readiness to obey orders. The offer of coffee, or water-pipe, as much as the want of such offer, were symbolic of status, favor or disfavor. These rituals were acted out and replicated in government offices, in bureaus, military headquarters, and council chambers. The question of their sincerity hardly ever arose; they were meant to represent to the elite the reigning order of things.

In that representation, modes of differentiation and exclusion played an important role. One of the most conspicuous ways of putting one in his place occurred regularly in the ante-chambers of high officials. It was there that people waited to be admitted to the presence of a grandee whose favor or attention they needed for the conduct of government business. There were always those who were kept waiting for hours, visibly humiliated in front of all those sitting in the ante-room. And there were those who walked in immediately upon arriving, also visibly favored by the man in charge. The winnowing process was subtle and smooth, the attendant of the *paşa* or *bey* announcing to his master each arrival and receiving a hint as to how long the newcomer should be made to wait. The length of interview also signified favor or disfavor, especially when measured against the time spent in the ante-chamber beforehand. Not infrequently, dignitaries would deliberately summon a person for a meeting in order to inflict upon him precisely that kind of public humiliation, which was usually promptly reported around.

During the intra-family strife in the reign of Abbas, Ibrahim's sons Ahmet Rifat and Ismail bitterly complained to the viceroy that he would summon them and make them wait hours before being admitted. Two consuls-general complained that their interviews were constantly delayed by Abbas. And Hekekyan, his standing in government on the wane, waited long for an audience with Abbas, but finally had to leave the palace without being received, when the attendant announced that the viceroy had retired to his apartments for the night. In different circumstances, but with a similarly negative interpretation, Nubar bemoaned four "deadly hours" of ante-chamber before an interview with

Stratford Canning in Istanbul, which lasted less than an hour.[15] These experiences were shared by all members of the elite, were easily interpreted by them, and were disseminated for public consumption as indicators of status and prestige. Thus, internal differentiation was both public and painful; exclusion was even more so.

The word about an official's falling from grace with the viceroy, and similarly on lower levels with his superiors, spread around quickly. It immediately affected the way in which that official was to be treated by peers and subordinates. Acting towards him otherwise would be taken as going against the will of the ruler, who had, in a manner of speaking, "cut him loose." Hekekyan described his own experience in vivid terms.[16] Not only was he made to wait long hours for an audience, to no avail, but when he roamed the palace in the meantime, he was treated almost like a pariah. As he wandered into the office of Talat Bey, one of the viceroy's secretaries, Hekekyan was ignored by all who were working there, although they knew him very well. A drawing that was being passed around with much admiration was not shown to him. A hint was given to a young man who was telling Istanbul news not to continue his political story in Hekekyan's presence. This kind of treatment was not unique to Egypt in the middle of the nineteenth century, however.

Cevdet Paşa, in the early 1850s only an assistant at the Porte, relates an equally unpleasant experience. When he was working under Fuat Efendi, later Paşa, a rivalry developed between Fuat and Mustafa Reşit Paşa, who had lost his position as grand vezir to Âli Paşa. Because of the association of Cevdet with Fuat and Âli, he was ostracized by members of Mustafa Reşit's household. They began to observe him "with a crooked look" (*keç nazarla*). Worse still, protégés of Mustafa Reşit Paşa simply refused to have any dealings with him, although he had had excellent working relations with them before. They imposed on him, Cevdet wrote later, a boycott and made him "quarantined-like" (*karantineli gibi*). Sensitive issues were never raised in his presence, and if he would enter a room where men of the ousted grand vezir were talking on politics, the conversation would be abruptly interrupted. This last scene is particularly reminiscent of Hekekyan's experience in Talat Bey's office.[17]

Another example of this kind is, ironically perhaps, the case of Ilhami Paşa, son of Abbas. When Sait came to power, he revoked a large number of villages from Ilhami's tax-farm, or his *ühde*. The interesting point is the description, given by one of Senior's interlocutors, of what befell an *ühde* in such circumstances.[18] The announcement of the reversion of an *ühde* to the treasury, he said, was regarded by provincial governors, *kadis*, and villagers as evidence that its previous holder was out of favor and his property might be plundered with impunity. "Old claims are raked up against him, new ones are forged; his crops are destroyed, his cattle are stolen; he becomes, in the language of the Arabs, 'a thing to be eaten'". Although there may well be some exaggeration in this depiction, an official who had lost the protection of his patron, the viceroy, was not in an enviable predicament. As mentioned above, Nubar expected to be unable to sell or rent his house after resigning his post. It was as if the same code that had granted officials so many privileges before, now turned against them to strip them and their families of both status and wealth. However, officeholders were not completely helpless.

Intisap – a form of partial protection

Some protection against the insecurity of office was provided by the institution of *intisap* (Arabic *intisāb*), which may loosely be translated as attachment, affiliation, or association.[19] A time-honored Ottoman tradition, *intisap* described the link between a grandee household and a person, extending to his or her family, and implied a form of patron–client relations. It was formed across class divisions and aligned to such households individuals of both elite and non-elite status. For high-ranking members of the elite, *intisap* was a power-base, providing professional assistance, bureaucratic or military, and a network of information and influence throughout the administration and the army. For those who were "attached," *intisap* was a form of guarantee against utter office insecurity for elite members, and a means to avoid loss of livelihood for all others. When position was lost, which often happened as a result of clashing patronage networks, one relied on one's patron to provide an alternative post.

Although attachments to households were switched when circumstances made it necessary or expedient, some were lifelong commitments. Indeed, major realignments of patronage networks on the highest level took place only upon the accession of a new viceroy, until a balanced system was renegotiated. Otherwise, the frequency of appointments and reappointments in government required equally frequent readjustments of alliances, which also affected attachments to households. But these seemed to have been limited mostly to the elite, while affiliations by members of non-elite groups to elite households were fairly stable and long-term. A certain amount of *intisap* relations stemmed from kin, "suckling (*süt*, literally 'milk') relations," adoption, or slavery – either domestic or of the mamluk type. Some such relations led to marriage with another household member. Reenforced attachments of this kind tended to be stronger, better enduring the fluctuations of office. In any event, attachment to a grandee household was a social marker that one carried around as one of his or her foremost attributes.

Thus, for example, one would be referred to as being attached to the household of Abbas (*mansūb al-ᶜAbbāsiyya*), as in the case mentioned below (pp. 176–7). Or, as with Rifāᶜa Rāfiᶜ aṭ-Ṭahṭāwī's family, would have a reputed "special attachment" (*intimā' khāṣṣ*) to Ibrahim Paşa's household. One was taken to be "a man of" as an essential form of identity in society, and was expected to enjoy the benefits derived from that identity, or pay a price for it. Upon the accession of Sait Paşa, Nubar and his brother Arakel were recalled from their respective missions in Vienna and Berlin and dismissed from government service. "Why?" Nubar asked himself. Explanations were useless in such cases, he later wrote in his memoirs, "nous étions les hommes d'Abbas."[20] Moreover, *intisap* was often carried from one generation to the next, heavily drawing on old commitments. Sometimes, *intisap* sentiments were almost irresistible, even when admission of their existence was clearly detrimental. This is evident in the following conversation between Nubar and Ibrahim Paşa on the boat which returned them from a European visit.

Ibrahim feared that his father, Mehmet Ali, might wish to obtain detailed information on his European tour. Since he believed that Nubar, who had accompanied him on that trip, would be summoned for questioning, he asked him how he would resist the Old Paşa's queries. Ibrahim seemed convinced that his young interpreter could withstand Mehmet Ali's wrathful insistence, but he was worried that his father might resort to another approach. What would you say, asked Ibrahim, if he tried to exploit your sentiments and implored you thus:

> "Are you not the nephew of Boghos [Mehmet Ali's confidant and Director of Foreign Affairs], the son of Meguerditch, the brother of Carlo, are you not [one] of my [men]? Are you not attached to me?" "Oh! in that case," I naively replied, "I shall obey [him]."[21]

At that, continues Nubar, Ibrahim changed the subject. This anecdote quaintly reveals Ibrahim's realization, eventually confirmed by Nubar's answer, that his young Armenian interpreter owed a kind of "hereditary allegiance" to Mehmet Ali, via the attachment and services of his uncle, father, and brother Arakel, for whom Ibrahim used the dimunitive "Carlo," to boot.

Although *intisap* was the great neutralizing mechanism of office hazards in mid-nineteenth-century Ottoman Egypt, it could only provide limited protection. Obedience and conformity were essential, but the rest was up to individual skills. A prerequisite for success was good information from reliable, highly placed sources. With the right contacts, such information could be utilized to gain bureaucratic and economic advantage. Put in negative terms by Hekekyan, one had to be a "clever villain" to be successful in Egypt in those years. He thought that Abbas's Foreign Minister, Stefan Bey, was too honest and lacking in duplicity to keep his job for long.[22] However, the record shows that Stefan held office for more than three years under the demanding leadership of Abbas. This was also the usual term in that position during the reigns of Abbas and Sait. So honest men could survive in that system, and duplicity alone was not enough. Other qualities were also required.

Hekekyan's observation might be rephrased to read: in order to succeed in government, one had to be clever, alert, and well-versed in the cultural code of officials. Penal legislation to curb corruption existed since the reign of Mehmet

Ali. The files of the Council of Justice show that the law was applied and that flagrant offenders were duly punished. Skill was no doubt needed to maneuver in the grey area between the letter of the law and actual practice. But, while such social skills were necessary, they were not sufficient. An aptitude for business was also useful, for it could maximize the benefits of office and build up capital. One had to diversify both contacts and investment in order to minimize damage on a rainy day. There were growing opportunities for commercial activity as monopolies were being relaxed and Egypt was further integrated into the world economy. Concomitantly, knowledge of European languages became a key to success, even in the reign of Abbas. His son received tutoring in English, and at least one of his ministers, Abdi Paşa, took up English while in office. A governor for Suez was appointed by Abbas on the merit of his knowledge of European languages, as the number of travellers passing there increased.

In short, the more skills one had, the less vulnerable one became in the system. To begin with, literacy became indispensable for many positions in government, including some low level technical jobs.[23] Moreover, in the 1840s and 1850s, technical skills became increasingly important in attaining and retaining high office. Those sent abroad by Mehmet Ali, Abbas, and Sait returned home and were given positions in the bureaucracy and the army. Students educated in the new schools in Egypt itself were also being absorbed into government service. Still, though increasing professionalization of the service in effect mitigated office insecurity, the feeling among elite members persisted nonetheless. The process was clearly gradual, and views were slow to change. In any event, social status and economic opportunity were so inextricably bound to office, that officeholders were prepared to endure a great deal in order to remain in the viceroy's service. In that sense, they certainly had an accurate perception of reality. In the middle of the century, many advantages accrued with office, which greatly offset the hardships attached to it.

The benefits of office

Despite the growing burdens of indebtedness after the reign of Abbas, the Egyptian economy at mid-century was stable and prosperous.[24] This was clearly reflected in the living standards of the elite and the easier yoke born by the rest of the population. Under Abbas, the dynastic order emerged with a distinct mark of grandeur and ostentation; Sait and Ismail adopted and elaborated that style. The benefits that derived from high and middle-level office, both directly and indirectly, enabled most members of the Ottoman-Egyptian elite to support a material lifestyle that followed viceregal example and was significantly higher than that of non-elite groups. Their income derived from relatively high and regular salaries, handsomely supplemented by access to surplus-generating sources. The combination of the two made the *nişan* – insignia of rank that served as the symbol of office – virtually irresistible. Not merely a status symbol, the *nişan* had great pecuniary value; it was the key to a better world.

By mid-century, salaries were being paid on the basis of rank rather than of position or performance. This was commensurate with a tendency towards greater regularity in an increasingly rationalized administration. According to policy, officeholders enjoyed a fixed and fairly regular pay, calculated monthly but disbursed every few months – on principle every four months. All others not in the government pool were hired and paid on a daily basis. These were normally menial laborers, skilled and unskilled, since the government did not maintain a regular menial workforce. Instead, workers were recruited when needed, often by decree to provincial governors, who in turn referred the demand to village *shaykhs*. Nubar claimed that in the reign of Mehmet Ali, pay arrears amounted to fifteen and even twenty months. During the reign of Abbas, he observed, salaries were regularly paid with no arrears. Retired officials and relatives of deceased officials were given pensions, according to different systems, from 1844 on.[25]

Under Abbas, Sait, and Ismail, pay scales for civil and military officeholders reflected extreme inequality. The top salary was approximately 300 times the bottom one. The first four ranks, five on some scales, formed a distinct privileged group, and salaries below that mark fell sharply. It was in that top echelon that the Ottoman-Egyptian elite was concentrated. Although that category was internally differentiated, gaps within it were considerably narrower. In addition to fixed salaries, officeholders received food and fodder allowances and uniforms. Food allowances were often a meaningful supplement to salaries. However, as Hunter has shown, high officials had ample opportunity to avail themselves of public funds, well in excess of what they were officially entitled to receive. They took advantage of a loose administrative structure and the absence of effective controls in order to embezzle funds and gain undue "fringe benefits."[26]

One of the main sources of such benefits was the central economic-administrative mechanism of concessionary grants. Through that method, various state-controlled assets were granted to individuals by contract, in return for a fixed, usually pre-determined sum. Any amount in excess of the fixed sum belonged to the contractor. This way of managing state resources was normally applied to assets or enterprises which were not income-yielding, such as uncultivated and abandoned land, mismanaged manufactories, and services which required organization of labor or financial investment. If we adopt this broad definition as a framework, we could accommodate within it such phenomena as tax-farming systems (*ühde*, and *iltizam* of land or customs houses), concessions to provide food supplies or clothing for the army, contracts to supply gold and silver to the mint or building materials for public works, and agreements to run *fez*, chintz, or spirits factories for the government.[27] This system offered great opportunities for all involved.

It was mostly to members of the Ottoman-Egyptian elite that landed tax-farms were granted. Among grantees of "operational" concessions and contracts, non-Muslims were disproportionately represented. Many of these were rich merchants who were not part of the elite. But even so, elite members were involved in the procedures leading to such grants, which meant that they could expect remuneration for promoting the interests of those bidding for concessions. Furthermore, contacts with the bureaucracy did not end when a concession was granted. Difficulties could arise as time progressed, arrears could accumulate, and terms might need to be renegotiated. At the end of the grant period, applications for extension and improvement of terms were expected. In all these, there was always need for some help or intercession. Not only bureaucrats were courted; police and army commanders often proved useful in carrying out the grant terms and facilitating access to resources and, not infrequently, also to cheap, that is, forced, labor. Throughout, pockets were filled to make things easier.

Still on the income side of the equation, we ought to add land granted to high- and middle-level officials by the viceroys. As we shall see later, there were several types of land grants. Suffice it here to say that although some of these grants were actually a financial burden on their holders, with the dramatic rise in the value of cotton and cereals during the middle years, land became an economic asset, not just a status symbol or a political base. Thus, with access to government funds and to surplus-producing sources, many officials lived quite comfortably. Not a few owned large houses, had many servants, ate and dressed well, and surrounded themselves with amenities modelled on Istanbul and Europe. Archival sources are peppered with evidence that not only the chosen few at the top enjoyed material affluence. A bureau chief owned a three-story house in Cairo; a *binbaşı̂* (fourth rank from top in the bureaucracy) and his wife had a number of female slaves and even a young mamluk; a treasury official had a harem large enough to employ a eunuch. These are but a few examples.[28]

Abbas encouraged his officials, military and civilian, to spend money in constructive ways rather than save it. As if he had premonitions of the fate of his own son, the viceroy told officeholders that if they saved money, their children would waste it in no time after they die. Instead, if they built houses, they would enjoy them during their own lifetime, and their children would enjoy them afterwards. Abbas used this argument as he granted officials plots in the newly developed suburb of ᶜAbbāsiyya and ordered them to build houses for their families there. At that time, he was still trying to reason with them. However, as officials were slow to comply with his wish, the viceroy resorted to another, safer method. On 4 July 1849, he gave his men forty days to commence building, sixty if absent from Cairo at the time of the order. The heads of the civil and military services were instructed to lower by one rank all those failing to obey the instruction.[29]

The benefits of office and the cushioning effect of *intisap* went a long way towards compensating officials for the insecurity and other hazards of office. Their standing in society, their livelihood, indeed their identity, were bound to office so much, that they did all they could to remain on the "civil list" even when they did not hold a position in government. However, during the reign of Abbas, intra-elite strife and the viceroy's unusual personality weighed more heavily on most members of the Ottoman-Egyptian elite. The alienation of almost all the ruling family from the government of Abbas Paşa rendered them and their protégés virtually powerless in political terms. That powerlessness impelled them to resort to indirect resistance, that familiar tactic of the weak. Unable to confront Abbas directly, they demonized him in order to discredit his reputation and induce the sultan and the European Powers to depose him. The process through which the demon-image of Abbas was created and propagated by Ottoman-Egyptians and Europeans is a most telling story. As it unravels in the following pages, so does the *mentalité* of the dominant social group in Egypt and the essence of its political culture.

5 The demon-image of Abbas Paşa: evidence and counter-evidence

Few historians dispute the fact that the reign of Abbas was generally peaceful, the roads were safe, the economy prosperous, and the burden on the lower classes much reduced. The government was stable and the position of the dynasty secure. Yet, students of Egyptian history are well aware that Abbas Paşa has been portrayed in the most negative terms. Reading what contemporaries and historians wrote about him, one cannot escape the impression that everybody loved to hate Abbas Paşa. Indeed, it is hard to find another person in nineteenth-century Egyptian history who enjoys a worse reputation. This apparent unanimity with regard to both character and performance is even more striking if we consider the controversy which permeates almost any discussion of Egyptian rulers in the nineteenth century and beyond. For the inquisitive reader of Middle Eastern annals, this discrepancy between record and image is an open invitation into the mysteries of *terra incognita*: the emergence and afterlife of a demon-image.

Before we begin to describe the genesis of the demon-image of Abbas Paşa, it may be opportune to sum up briefly the main features of that image. For the sake of convenience, we can classify the qualities attributed to Abbas into two categories – those related to his performance as viceroy of Egypt, and those related to his character. As governor-general of Egypt, Abbas was said to have been incompetent, idle, inconsistent, erratic, and hesitant. His political outlook was portrayed as backward, reactionary, fanatical, and opposed to European ideas of progress. As a person, Abbas was said to have been suspicious, mistrustful, apprehensive, superstitious, capricious, vain, haughty, reserved, and inclined to solitude. He was reputed to be merciless, murderous, and capable of extreme cruelty. He was also commonly believed to have been homosexual and to have engaged in bestiality. His love of birds, horses, and wild animals was interpreted in deviant terms.

All these qualities were united in one person, the most powerful individual in Egypt from the end of 1848 to his death in mid 1854. What made the image demonic was the combination of all these qualities. The demon-image was a coherent whole; it admitted of no redeeming feature. During his reign and for a while afterwards, Abbas aroused fear, hate, curiosity, and occasional ridicule.

His desert palaces, imposing and isolated, came to represent his personality. "Abbas est le héros du mal de notre siècle," wrote a French visitor to Egypt in the mid 1860s, "un ange de l'enfer, celui qui représente tous les vices du monde réunis en un seul être."[1] But to understand the formation and survival of that demon-image is really to understand the cultural code of the Ottoman-Egyptian elite and the social realities that made the life of its members in the middle decades. Moreover, it is also to understand the interaction between elite members and the European consular and commercial communities in Egypt.

To make a convincing case in matters of images, one obviously requires a great deal of supporting evidence. This is so because at least part of the argument rests on sheer quantity and its overwhelming impact. To avoid burdening the narrative, a great deal of additional information is provided not in the text, but in extended notes.

8 Abbas Paşa – note the contrast with plate 3

Contemporary Ottoman-Egyptian observers

When Ibrahim Paşa died in October 1848, Abbas was in the Hijaz. Disturbed by the political embroilment in Cairo, he preferred to await the death of his uncle at a safe distance. His return to "the city of the thousand minarets" was the cause of genuine popular celebration, as the short reign of Ibrahim, with its fear and uncertainty, was not much lamented.[2] The Ottoman-Egyptian elite was bracing itself for a major reshuffle of alliances. An interim period began, in which new political and economic networks were laid down and allegiance was redefined at the top echelon. The viceroy was expected to strike a new balance of power and bring in his own men, but also create a *modus vivendi* with the party that lost out. The events that ensued in Cairo and Istanbul were crucial in molding the image of Abbas Paşa within that elite. His failure to come out well from the initiation phase proved most costly for the rest of his reign. It set in motion a process that gave life to the demon-image. This and the simultaneous disaffection of the French were to cast a giant shadow over his reputation and tarnish his standing in Egyptian historiography.

In the early 1850s, after a respite of nearly a decade, Egyptian affairs once again preoccupied the Sublime Porte. The government of Grand Vezir Mustafa Reşit Paşa, one of the imposing leaders of the *Tanzimat*, was engaged in a move calculated to restrict the special status enjoyed by Egypt under the stipulations of the Edict of Hereditary Governorship. It will be recalled that the Edict was granted to Mehmet Ali Paşa in 1841, with European endorsement, as part of the settlement of his long-drawn-out conflict with the central government. Our concern here is to point out that between 1849 and 1852 the Egyptian issue again came to life in an Ottoman context, attracting attention among political and social circles in Istanbul. There was at least one interest group whose business it was to keep the topic on the agenda.

At the beginning of his reign, Abbas took political and economic measures which had a direct negative effect on the interests of some members of the ruling family. Consequently, a few of them, and a number of high-ranking officials aligned with the old regime, left Egypt and came to the Ottoman capital. They hoped to induce the sultan and his ministers to depose Abbas, or at least to curtail his powers and stature. These men and women were highly connected in the city both through their extended families and their vast social and economic contacts. Many of them had considerable means, entertained lavishly, spread money and gifts, and were entertained in return by friends and relations. They constantly flooded the court and the many salons of the elite with stories about Abbas and his maladministration of Egypt. A major component in their campaign was the character assassination of the Paşa. To be sure, Abbas had his own Istanbul connections, which he used to gather information about the activity of his opponents and to protect his interests at the Gate of Felicity. He, too, had vast means and used what he could with much political skill.

At this stage, we are not concerned with the political implications or the final score of that war of words, a war waged in parlors and harems by well-dressed and polished men and women over fine food and drinks. The outcome obviously depended on weighty strategic considerations, though one should not scoff at the power of calculated gossip imbibed with bubbly water-pipes. For our purposes here, we should note that horror stories about Abbas incessantly travelled the Mediterranean route from Cairo and Alexandria to Istanbul. There were constant ties between the Ottoman elites of Egypt and Istanbul, through visits of relatives and business associates, and through letters which took two to three weeks in each direction. And there was regular contact between political circles in the capital and the influential European diplomatic community, through which information flowed freely. The European ambassadors in Istanbul maintained close links with their respective capitals, but also received updating reports from their own consuls-general in Cairo. This was so especially in times of pressing problems involving Cairo and Istanbul, such as the early 1850s.

It was in those years that a crisis evolved around Abbas's refusal to apply the Ottoman penal code of 1850, unless it was modified to meet Egyptian needs.[3] After long-drawn-out negotiations and a seeming impasse, growing European pressures on both sides to reach a settlement yielded the mission of Fuat Efendi. Better known later at Fuat Paşa, this celebrated Foreign Minister and Grand Vezir of the *Tanzimat* period was then a close adviser to Grand Vezir Mustafa Reşit Paşa. At the end of March 1851, he was sent to Cairo to deal directly and continuously with Abbas until white smoke came out of the Citadel chimney. After three months of bickering, a compromise was reached and the conflict resolved much to Abbas's advantage, though the Porte's face was saved. Our pursuit of the story of an image leads us to a junior member of Fuat's delegation to Cairo, a man who would later become one of the most prominent Ottomans of the nineteenth century – Cevdet Paşa.

In his collection of memorials, *Tezakir-i Cevdet*, the author describes the events surrounding Fuat's mission to Egypt and his own experience there.[4] In those days, Cevdet was deeply involved in the life of middle-echelon Porte bureaucrats and well-versed, it may be safely assumed, in political and social gossip. His account of the rivalry that developed between Mustafa Reşit Paşa and Abbas Paşa bears witness to his aptitude in that area. Cevdet was, of course, familiar with what was said about Abbas. His evaluation of the man in the *Tezakir* text clearly implied common knowledge, there being no incongruity with an immediate or more distant context. In Cevdet's notes, Abbas is described as given to imagining things and obsessed with suspicion (*vehham ve müvesvis bir zat*).

This unusual frame of mind, observes Cevdet, led Abbas to seek the support of Britain, who was then also the great defender of Reşit Paşa himself. Abbas began to mistrust Reşit following the cooling in their relations, which resulted from Reşit's support of claims put to the sultan against Abbas by members of his family, who flocked to Istanbul.[5] To court the English away from Reşit, Cevdet intimates, the viceroy promised to build the Alexandria–Suez railway, which impelled Reşit Paşa to seek Abbas's dismissal. That Reşit's hostility towards Abbas pre-dated the dispute over the railway, that Abbas's fears were quite real, and that his reliance on British support against the Porte indeed helped him win the decisive battle, all these did not matter much. Because everyone who knew anything about politics and society in the Ottoman Empire – even outsiders to the Egyptian scene – knew that Abbas was imagining dangers that did not exist, and was exceedingly suspicious by nature.

Sait Paşa, Abbas's jovial successor and life-long enemy, while chatting with a few of his European employees and some important visitors, described Abbas as having been haunted by the occult. His predecessor, alleged Sait, surrounded himself with astrologers who kept threatening him with assassination, which could only be averted by strange and costly rituals. Abbas's reputed aversion to Alexandria was often attributed by Westerners to his dislike of Europeans, who were represented in growing numbers in that city. However, the correspondent of *The Times* offered a different explanation, not much more flattering to the viceroy: Abbas was told by a certain venerable *shaykh* that he would die in Alexandria, and consequently tried to avoid the city as much as possible. It should be noted, nonetheless, that ᶜAlī Mubārak praised Abbas's contribution to the development of Alexandria.[6]

Construction was one of the main activities undertaken by the government of Abbas Paşa. It is also true that the viceroy liked to build palaces and spent large sums of money on them. But even something which is not laudable *per se* received an added twist, so that it would suit the oddity of the image. When visiting Bani Suwayf after his accession, Sait Paşa complained to his European guests about the way in which Abbas had the local barracks built. He positioned the horses' stables to the north, remarked the viceroy, and the men's quarters to the south, so during ten months of the year the smells of the stables would blow towards the men. Sait then began to ridicule Abbas's architectural ideas as applied in his palaces. His much-hated uncle would build staircases so that a person climbing them could be seen by the guards but not see them, and that after seemingly mounting towards nowhere, would find himself suddenly facing the Paşa. Abbas also liked each room to have three or four doors, said Sait, so that he could escape in one of several ways if an attempt was made on his life.[7]

A prominent member of the Ottoman-Egyptian elite who bequeathed a great deal of material to the student of Egyptian history is Yusuf Hekekyan Bey. Like most members of his social stratum, Hekekyan fed on rumors which were passed from one person to another and served as the indispensable lubricant of social contact among men in Egypt. Among women, political gossiping was probably much less important in social discourse, though stories about the personal life of men in high office, and of influential women, circulated in all elite harems, and some of them even originated in those establishments. Thus, through Hekekyan's eyes, we gain a closer, more intimate glimpse of the image of Abbas and the stories that were told about him in that milieu. However, this Ottoman-Egyptian gentleman found himself in a delicate situation during the early 1850s, which must have colored his perception of events and personalities. His story and family connections were not atypical of elite realities.

In 1851, Yusuf Hekekyan was removed from the Presidency of the Board of Health, to which he had been appointed by Abbas in 1849, and relegated to non-importance in the administration of the viceroy. His wife, Banuma Nekava, was the sister of Artīn Bey, the once all-powerful Commerce and Foreign Minister under Abbas. In September 1850, Artīn fled Egypt to avoid prosecution for financial irregularities, which Abbas had discovered, or trumped up, as some would have it. He settled in Istanbul among the disgruntled Egyptian contingent, and was one of the main opponents of the viceroy at Court and Porte. Hüsrev Bey, the brother of Artīn and of Banuma Hekekyan, remained in Egypt after his brother's flight. But as Hüsrev enjoyed French protection, the only members of the family to be left in a vulnerable position were Hekekyan, his wife, and child.[8]

One of the most fascinating documents in the Hekekyan Papers is a detailed account of a political consultation held by Abbas at the palace of ᶜAbbāsiyya, a meeting in which Hekekyan Bey took an active part.[9] When summoned to the meeting in March 1851, Hekekyan was probably quite anxious, vacillating, as it were, between hope and despair. There he was again, facing the ruler of the land, perhaps getting a chance to re-ingratiate himself with Abbas. Although there were six other men present besides himself and the Paşa, Hekekyan managed at some point to sneak in a comment with that end in mind, but Abbas seemed to ignore it. Then came a few trying moments, when the viceroy signaled to our *bey* and they both withdrew to a side room for a tense *tête-à-tête*. Hekekyan emerged from that exchange with a strong sense that the Paşa mistrusted him and suspected his loyalty in relation to Artīn's activities in Istanbul.

Thus vexed, Hekekyan rushed to his house and poured out his heart to his diary. About Abbas, he wrote then that he

> had no dignity. He is not regular in his ideas. He is the very emblem of inconsistency. He may be cunning; but he is very impolitic, and momentarily rash and headstrong. He fears, hopes, condemns and pardons in an instant. He is very distrustful and I think he is deficient in moral and animal courage. He talks much and high in order to persuade others that he is not that which he well knows himself to be.

At the end of the private interview, Abbas gave Hekekyan his hand to kiss and dismissed him. When, full of trepidations, our *bey* was finally at a safe distance from the palace and the viceroy, he reviewed the bizarre details of the conversation, and contemplated "the mountebank coward strutting about in his 'meshlah'[10] afraid of his [own] shadow."

The sense of total insecurity regarding his present and future life, and the well-being of his wife and son, was extremely hard for Hekekyan to bear, as it would be for anyone in a similar predicament. However, Hekekyan's way of coping with his situation was quite interesting, though by no means unique. It is possible that in order to be able to control his fear, he unconsciously chose to belittle and ridicule the source of his anxiety: he made Abbas into a mountebank coward strutting about in an unbecoming garment. That was his own private way of avenging himself. Thus, the distinguished *bey*, humiliated and – in his mind at least – threatened with his life, turned the tables around. From a situation in which "I got on my street donkey and galloped down the road [from the ᶜAbbāsiyya palace to Cairo] as fast as possible fearing the Viceroy might overtake me in his carriage," Hekekyan resumed control, and *the feared viceroy in his carriage* became *the mountebank coward in his meşlah*.

However, this exercise supplied only temporary relief to his stress. Not long after that encounter, a former colleague told Hekekyan about other enormities committed by Abbas. According to that man, whom Hekekyan describes as an official favored by the viceroy, Abbas had one of his attendants eaten up by hounds for having "displeased him." He also beat to death several people in the desert, near his palace, for slight offenses.[11] In Hekekyan's mind – as in the minds of many who heard and believed these stories – such information only increased the strain he had already experienced by the cooling of his relations with the Paşa. Whereas for Hekekyan such horror stories were a real cause for alarm, they were quite familiar to members of his cultural milieu. Still, we may use the political gossip peddled by our "favored official" in order to introduce a fresh element of Abbas's demon-image: the weird practices associated with the training of his mamluks.

Now, most outsiders took "mamluks" to mean, more or less, a contingent of bodyguards personally loyal to the Paşa. While this is not entirely wrong, one certainly loses the real importance of Abbas's attempt to restore some elements of this historical institution. We have already dealt with the significance of the mamluk corps for the dynastic image of Abbas's court (see pp. 57–60 above). For our purposes here, we ought to note that the description of the practice provided by Hekekyan's source is a classic piece of evidence. It vividly reflects how insiders viewed the mamluk aspect of Abbas's demon-image. The mysterious and almost unnatural character of this phenomenon filled with horror the hearts of government officials throughout the reign of Abbas. The complete seclusion of the viceroy's mamluk corps gave rise to some of the most ghastly stories about him, the sexual aspect of which is reflected in the hospital scene described by Flaubert below (pp. 120–1). The mere mention of Abbas's mamluks conjured up in people's minds an image of fair and young devils, answerable to none but the Paşa, riding at night into the middle of the desert to commit all sorts of ungodly abominations.

Almost in the same way as foreigners try nowadays to gauge the popular mood by talking to their Cairene cabbies, so did Hekekyan sound out his donkey driver in an attempt to discover how Abbas was viewed by the lower strata.[12] Not unexpectedly, Abbas emerged as both the idle ruler and the heartless oppressor. Whether or not that was indeed the sentiment of the *fallāḥīn* and the urban poor is another matter. For our purposes here, it is important to note that the coherent, fully rounded nature of the demon-image of Abbas could admit of no exception: he had to be perceived as evil with no mitigating circumstances. Abbas could not be the oppressor of the powerful and the saviour of the poor, for it might mean he had a heart, at least for somebody, and that would make him human, at least partly. Since neither the *fallāḥīn* nor the urban poor, who were illiterate, left any written record, it is through the tainted, anti-Abbas prism of the educated that we read of their views. The harmony of evil and deviancy was thus made to look as if perceived by people from all walks of life, cutting across barriers of wealth, education, and social prestige.

Since we mentioned the cohabitation of evil and deviancy within the demon-image of Abbas, we might also add that Hekekyan, too, was in no way oblivious to the rumors concerning Abbas's alleged erotic preference. In the cultural code of the Ottoman-Egyptian elite, sexuality was not something a respectable person would commit to paper in any but an indirect manner. It is, therefore, rather through insinuation that the allegation was made. The first example is a note in Hekekyan's diary, entered on 2 March 1851,[13] reporting that, two days earlier, Abbas had said that "the Arabs in his Mafrouzeh [school he had established] were of a spurious race. They were too handsome, he said, to be the sons of the husbands of their mothers." There is no further comment or contextual reference in this case.

Now, it might be argued that this quotation was used by Hekekyan to point out Abbas's ethnic prejudice against the local Arabophone population. Not that this does the Paşa much credit, but Hekekyan himself was not a great admirer of Arabic-speaking Egyptians either. In fact, in this regard, he had similar views to those which prevailed among members of the Turcophone elite of Ottoman Egypt, to which he belonged. His British education could do little to disabuse him of such biases, for these were shared, in large measure, by many Europeans. Actually, Europeans did not have kind words for the Ottoman-Egyptian elite either. So it seems that what Hekekyan had in mind when he inscribed that entry in his diary was, in fact, that Abbas was physically attracted to those handsome boys in the Mefruze.

That this is not a wild speculation may be gathered from another note entered into the same diary two months later. On 7 May, Hekekyan reported that Abbas was very unpopular throughout the country and hated by all strata. So much so, that during the conscription drive in Upper Egypt, the *fallāḥīn* said: "He does not want men, but handsome youths for himself and household." This conveniently leads to the next anecdote in Hekekyan's text, as we firmly remain within the realm of sexuality. We read that when a Cairene lady was told that Abbas had been carrying on intrigues with a certain Mrs. Badrāwī, she exclaimed: "Is then Mrs. Badrawi a *bardash* [a male homosexual]?[14] Thus, through the handsome school boys of the Mefruze, the protest of the *fallāḥīn* against the draft, and the comments of the Cairene lady, Hekekyan guides us to the inevitable conclusion about the tastes of the viceroy.

Quite apart from that, these stories also vividly bring out the flavor of political and social gossip around Abbas within the Ottoman-Egyptian elite. Again, our purpose is not merely to investigate how members of the elite created the demon-image, but to recover the socio-cultural milieu in which the elite throve. Yusuf Hekekyan's papers are but a mirror that reflects the dynamics and subtle mechanisms of that milieu. It is from coded innuendo and discourse topics that the *mentalité* of the elite can be gleaned. In our context, "gossip" was a powerful political weapon, and Ottoman-Egyptians were not the only ones to realize its potential. Europeans in Egypt and outside, who had their own motives, also endeavored to destroy Abbas's reputation. In certain ways, Europeans made the image even worse, harping on sentiments dear to Western audiences. So, in order to complete the emergence of the demon-image during the reign of Abbas, we ought to examine some of the writings of contemporary European observers.

Contemporary European observers

When Abbas acceded to the throne, the consular corps was anxiously watching the new ruler, bracing itself for years of attrition and alienation. The new Paşa had the reputation of a European-hater, and was not regarded as a "true heir" to Mehmet Ali – the great Westernizer. Of the Europeans, the French had the most to lose, for they enjoyed a clear preponderance in all spheres of public life in Egypt. Therefore, in recognition of their preeminence among the foreign groups in Egypt and their position as the most injured party, we shall begin by describing the French attitude towards the Paşa. As in the previous section, here too the evidence will lead us beyond the demon-image of Abbas. Indeed, it should reflect the involvement of Europeans in Egyptian society, their broad connections with the Ottoman-Egyptian elite, and the meeting of two cultures during the middle years of the nineteenth century.

Even before the reign of Abbas, the French were constantly on their guard against non-French "progressive" trends, which might favor other European powers, and against "reactionary" elements, which opposed Westernization altogether. Abbas was targeted as a potential source of problems as early as 1833, when he was only twenty years old. A prominent French visitor, Baron de Boislecomte, wrote to the Minister of Foreign Affairs at the time that Abbas had no communication with Europeans and "est resté très croyant et très zélé dans sa foi."[15] This uneasiness about the young prince was set aside during the years of French ascendancy in Egypt. It was hoped then that, through some unexpected development, he might not come to the throne after all. Barring that, the French believed that, once in power, Abbas might prove more flexible and, perhaps, see the "light."[16]

However, when Abbas eventually became viceroy, the worst French fears seemed to have come true. The reshuffling of department heads and other senior officials immediately displaced some of the prominent Frenchmen in government service. Although a matter of routine with the change of administration, this was generally perceived as the first salvo announcing the beginning of an anti-Western age. Understandably, it heightened the anxiety of the French both in Egypt and at home. A number of previously supported projects – synonymous in European parlance with progress – were abandoned, and European consuls, accustomed to bask in the joys of Ottoman hospitality, were not as welcome at the court of the new viceroy. But the initial reaction of the French consul-general to the changing times was moderate and rational. On 12 April 1850, when he reported the situation to Paris, Le Moyne still wrote favorably of Abbas.[17] He defended the decision to discontinue some of the projects, complimented the Paşa for improving living conditions, explained that the blow to French officials and interests had been exaggerated, and counseled caution.

In less than six weeks, however, patience yielded to frustration. From then on, the critical note struck in the consul-general's correspondence of late May[18] would reflect the French view of Abbas for the duration of his rule and thereafter. The following example suffices to convey the gist of what French diplomats felt about the man and his ways of governing:

> Abbas Pacha est un grand enfant qui, malgré beaucoup d'esprit et d'intelligence, ne sait jamais ce qu'il veut et qui, par faiblesse de caractère, se laisse, la plus part de temps, conduire en aveugle par son entourage. Il oublie volontiers ceux qui sont loin.[19]

Other Frenchmen, not constrained by diplomatic language, found harsher terms to describe the viceroy. Clot Bey, the famous physician who planned and directed the health services under Mehmet Ali, was among those whom Abbas forced to retire. In his memoirs, he described the Paşa as "the unworthy grandson" of "the immortal" Mehmet Ali. Writing about the Azbakiyya Hospital which Ibrahim Paşa, "the illustrious" son of Mehmet Ali, had established in 1837, he complained of its deterioration "sous la main impuissante et barbare d'Abbas Pacha." In 1856, Mougil Bey, an engineer employed by Mehmet Ali on the Barrages and other projects, talked to Nassau Senior. About Abbas, Mougil had to say that he "was *mauvais idéal* of selfishness. He cared for nothing but the gratification of his sensuality, vanity, and spite."[20]

Dr. Bourguières, a French physician employed by the ruling family and prominent members of the elite, told the same interlocutor the following story about Abbas Paşa:

One day an Englishman, admitted to an audience, saw some blood on his hand. "I got it," said Abbas, "half an hour ago as I was sewing up the mouth of a woman whom I found smoking in the hareem."[21]

These observations and stories reiterate a vital element in the demonization of Abbas: extreme cruelty and moral depravity. This was joined to the familiar charge that Abbas was an incompetent administrator and an enemy of Western-inspired reforms. Full development of these traits in Abbas's image had already taken place during his lifetime; as we shall soon see, the "icing" was added to the "cake" by later generations.

The Englishman mentioned above in Bourguières' story is not entirely out of place. For even if he never existed, but was just invented by the French doctor to lend credence to his story, Abbas was not the darling of the British either. This is more difficult to understand, since the viceroy was generally regarded as having abandoned the French for the English in what became known within Istanbul political circles as the *İngiliz Politikası*, or "English Politics," of Abbas. We must remember, however, that Europeans shared basic cultural assumptions and measured Eastern society by the same yardstick. Differences emerged when political interests intervened. That is, Frenchmen, Austrians, or Britons were inclined to show greater tolerance of reprehensible acts when committed by an Egyptian viceroy whose policies favored their respective national interests. We can discern, of course, a more lenient tone in British accounts of Abbas's reign, but when it came to his character, their pens maligned him almost as much as did the *plumes* of the French.

It was his fearsome reputation that ultimately won Abbas the endorsement of the British consul-general, Charles Murray. Typically, it came as a left-handed compliment, at the time of the viceroy's accession. Murray was concerned for the safety of the overland passage to India through Egypt, a long-standing British interest in that part of the world. In his correspondence with Lord Palmerston, then Foreign Secretary, during the second half of 1848, Murray expressed his preference for strong government and mentioned his doubts about the competence of Mehmet Ali's heirs. In one of these dispatches, we find the following comment concerning Abbas:

Although he has the reputation of being selfish and tyrannical in the extreme, and although he is notoriously addicted to the filthy sensualities which degrade so many of his

Caste, he is, nevertheless, a man of considerable shrewdness and energy, and he might be able to control the jarring elements of disorder which are here so rife; the very fact of his being so much hated is a proof in this country that he is somewhat feared.[22]

Murray, who would later force a close working relationship with the Paşa, here reiterates Abbas's alleged homosexuality, a feature of the demon-image already mentioned above. This is obviously what the consul-general meant by the euphemism "filthy sensualities." In time, the viceroy would make Egypt as safe for transit as she ever was, pave the road from Cairo to Suez, grant Britain a concession to construct the railway from Alexandria to Cairo, which she so much desired, and favor her commercial interests in Egypt. Yet all this will fail to win him more than a reluctant approval from Her Majesty's highest representative in Egypt. With time, Murray became a source of envy for the entire consular community, but his reports did little to dispel the demon-image; because of his favored position, they even reinforced it. Frederick Bruce, who replaced Murray in 1853, did not have the same privileged status with the viceroy. Resentful of that, he naturally had no good words for the Paşa.[23]

Several times a month throughout the reign of Abbas, the London *Times* printed interesting information about the viceroy. In general, the paper's Alexandria correspondent reported favorably about the way Abbas managed Egypt. But readers of *The Times* in Britain and in the European community in Egypt could read also about the more amusing and odd side of the Paşa's life: his passionate love of animals and horse racing. In February 1850, they learnt that Abbas had challenged the English horse-racing community to a match between the fastest horses in England and Egypt. In May of the same year, the public learnt that Abbas's agent in Britain had shipped to Egypt twelve race horses, eight ponies, five dogs, about twenty pheasants, four swans, six rabbits, and some barndoor fowls. All were of the highest quality and beauty. Two months before, the Zoological Society had presented the viceroy with twelve greyhounds. The correspondent bemoaned the plight of the dogs who, after inspection, were sent to Alexandria, where they would remain unnoticed until they died: "like a spoilt child, he [Abbas] soon gets tired of what he has, and wants something new."[24]

These follies, however, were surely mild when compared with some horror stories linked to Abbas's building enterprises. When Senior visited Suez in December 1855, Abbas had been safely in his grave for nearly a year and a half, though his memory still inspired terror. Senior was told by the wife of Consul West, the British representative in town, that if Abbas's palace at Binha were pulled down, strange things would be discovered. For he used to punish men by "building" them into a wall. Although he had heard much about Abbas by then, Senior reacted skeptically and asked: "Is there any proof of that?" To which the consul's wife unabashedly replied: "It is currently reported; and I believe it because it is only a counterpart of a story which I know to be true." She then cited the story of how Abbas had ordered the mouth of a slave woman in his harem to be sewn up for having smoked in contravention of his orders.[25] While such stories rarely found their way into consular reports, the air was saturated with them nonetheless. They undoubtedly reflected and reinforced the popular view of the Paşa's personality.

As we leave the relatively restrained realm of diplomacy and respectable newspaper reporting, we should note that most of the essential features of Abbas's image have by now come to the surface. The love of animals and the Paşa's deviant building schemes have been the latest brush strokes on our canvas. These, as the rest of the portrait, will soon assume a life of their own, as the pens of travelers and visitors to Egypt take over. It should be said, however, that Egypt in the period of Abbas was blessed with an exceptionally interesting, observant, and talented bunch of European visitors. Their descriptions of society and culture are sometimes surprisingly insightful. However, about the personality of Abbas Paşa, what most of them had to say is of a markedly different quality. We shall now take up some of the more interesting travel accounts, and while so doing, various familiar themes will recur. As they do, it will be noticed how the lines intensify to darken the features of the portrait, how the notions transgress the grotesque and the gruesome.

In a letter from Cairo, dated 15 January 1850, Flaubert wrote to Dr. Jules Cloquet: "Abbas Pasha – I whisper this in your ear – is a moron, almost a mental case, incapable of understanding anything or doing anything." And in a letter to his mother a short while later, he speaks of a ceremony he attended at Abbas's palace. The French consul-general presented his credentials to the viceroy, and Flaubert was invited to watch the event. He had obviously expected the brilliance of "oriental splendor" and evidence of the enormous wealth Abbas was amassing behind the walls of his isolated palaces. However, we are told that the ceremony was "pathetic," the Paşa's mamluks were dressed "like servants supplied by a caterer," and the coffee was "execrable." One thing, however, caught Flaubert's eye: "the Viceroy's pipe was splendid – encrusted with enough diamonds to satisfy the lust of a hundred marquises." The lesson Flaubert drew from that experience was not that Abbas's ceremonial style was modest, unassuming, plain – as might be suggested – but rather that it was shabby, mediocre, and on the whole "exceedingly flat."[26]

In his Travel Notes, Flaubert wrote a few sentences describing his impressions from a visit to Qasr al-ᶜAynī Hospital. It is there, in passing, that we encounter again the shared underlying assumption about Abbas's sexual preferences:

> Pretty cases of syphilis; in the ward of Abbas's Mamelukes, several have it in the arse. At a sign from the doctor, they all stood up on their beds, undid their trouser-belts (it was like army drill), and opened their anuses with their fingers to show their chancres.[27]

At a second glance, one might argue that the insinuation is perhaps not as direct, for only the mamluks are implicated, not Abbas himself. But at first glance, when association between context and story is intuitively made, the innuendo is very much there. The immediate context being, of course, the prevailing view that Abbas was homosexual. In another place, Flaubert is less ambiguous when he writes about the restrictions which Abbas imposed on brothels: "Abbas Pacha, who is fond only of men, makes things difficult for women."[28]

Wild ideas about the Paşa were by no means restricted to the French community. English travelers also imbibed a fair share of "Abbasiana" and constantly perpetuated the demon-image with almost precisely the same ingredients. Thus, in his otherwise interesting and informative travelogue, John Gadsby is quite critical of the viceroy.[29] With other observers, the author believed that Abbas's death was caused by two of his slaves. In a description that accords with the stereotype of the demon-image, Gadsby relates how the slaves, "who had witnessed the execution of several of their brethren, and had themselves been threatened to become victims to the cruel caprice of their master, are said to have strangled him in the midst of his debauches." All that notwithstanding, Gadsby expressly believed that, on the whole, Abbas's rule was mild by comparison with his predecessors.

While Flaubert's attendance at a palace ceremony helped shatter his previous notions of the wealth and splendor of Abbas's court, the legend remained much alive among those who observed it from a distance. Paradoxically, while Gadsby is trying to defend Abbas's extravagant expenditure on his palaces and horses, he is in fact helping to perpetuate the negative image. "But it is the custom of the country," he writes, "and, if [Abbas were] spoken to on the subject, he would doubtless say as one of our nobles did, 'May not a man do what he will with his own?'" To which Gadsby immediately adds: "I heard it stated that a single room in one of his palaces cost 100,000 pounds for furniture and drapery alone, and he is reported to have upward of 3,000 horses." This surely sounds a mild exaggeration when compared, for example, with the following statement culled from a fairly useless contemporary travel account: "We came to anchor not far from the Pasha's steam-yacht, built for him at Glasgow, and to all appearance seems to be made of solid gold."[30]

Was Abbas himself aware of how he was being demonized during his lifetime? Did he actually realize the extent to which his reputation was being "dragged through the mud"?

The answer is certainly positive. It is highly doubtful whether he fully recognized the intricacies and the complex mechanisms which molded his image. But in his sharp political senses, he realized that he was being consistently misrepresented, and that a great deal of malice was behind all that. Very much at home in Ottoman-Egyptian elite culture, Abbas must have been keenly aware of how the discourse of the elite was being employed against him. Indeed, he believed that the motive for his defamation was political and that the aim of his defamers was to have him deposed. At the beginning he even tried to refute the allegations. Sensing that the French were the prime movers against him, Abbas wrote to the French government and instructed his Minister of Commerce and Foreign Relations, Artīn Bey, to write as well.

Early in June 1849, only a few months after the viceroy came to power, Abbas and Artīn wrote to Odilon Barrot, then Président du Conseil des Ministres.[31] From the letters, it is quite clear that Abbas was fully aware of the charges that he was driving Egypt back "to the age of barbarism" by destroying the work of his grandfather, Mehmet Ali Paşa. So he tried to explain that he had no such intention and that the institutions created by the Old Paşa had to be cleansed of abuses and made to suit the needs of the country. Egypt does not need developed industry with which it cannot cope, nor advanced schools when its sons lack proper primary education. Emphasis will be placed, asserted Abbas and Artīn, upon basic needs which will be catered for piecemeal from the foundation upwards. At that point, the viceroy still believed that he could reason with his critics and with time, perhaps, even persuade them to accept his views.

However, as the attacks intensified and the breach with the French seemed a *fait accompli*, Abbas no longer attempted to affect his image in France. He maintained the necessary diplomatic contacts and communicated with the French when political expediency so required, but that he did with great reluctance. In February 1852, the French consul-general in Egypt reported to the Foreign Minister that Abbas had told him that the French press and government were taking a negative view of him and working against his interests in Istanbul. The British press and government were doing the opposite, which is why he was more favorably disposed towards England, added the Paşa. The Foreign Minister responded by asking his consul-general to assure Abbas of French friendship and explain to him that the French government had no control over the press in France. He added that on the issue of the *Tanzimat*, the French supported Abbas's demands and believed that a compromise would soon be reached.[32]

At the time, Abbas had probably realized that there was not much he could do about the French press, though he was sorely wounded by how he was being portrayed by it. Towards the end of 1852, the viceroy tried once again to explain his foreign policy to a new French consul-general, as he vented his frustration with the way he was being treated:

> My enemies had at first made me [both] a tiger and an imbecile, then they accused me of having been bought by England. I am not, nor do I wish to be, either [pro-] English or [pro-] French, because I understand very well that it is in my interest to be supported by both of these powers. Therefore, I try very hard to treat the one and the other with a

balance, precisely in order not to disaffect them. You can write to Paris and you will immediately see if I am sincere. Here is France and here is England . . . but for the good of Egypt I have to stay in the middle.[33]

Thus, it is clear that Abbas was aware of how his character and views were being distorted by the French. He also identified the motive as political, and rightly believed that it stemmed from the blow he had dealt to French interests in Egypt and his close relations with England. However, as he was not at ease with Europeans and European culture, he failed to court the French and, consequently, could not alter the way he was being perceived in the West. With the Ottomans, Abbas was much more skillful, for he maneuvered very well indeed in his own culture. In political Istanbul, he used the strength of his strategic position, and did not hesitate to spread the necessary funds. When his standing with the Porte was secure, he seemed to care little for what people actually said. Ultimately, Abbas's foreign policy triumphed over his image even in Europe. Britain proved to be a reliable ally, and the French did little to upset his plans. At the time of his death, Egyptian troops were fighting alongside Ottoman, English, and French forces, as allies against Russia in the Crimean War.

In July 1854, Abbas Paşa was found dead in his palace at Binha, a town in the Delta, north-east of Cairo. It was widely believed that he was strangled by his attendants, though the official report attributed his death to an attack of apoplexy.[34] Thus, even the Paşa's death was violent, shrouded in mystery, unnatural, virtually tailored to fit the image. But unlike the man himself, his image had a vivid afterlife. No new elements were added to the portrait in the years following the reign of Abbas. Yet, time accentuated its features, the lines growing rougher, the colors stronger, the monster more monstrous. So our next step is to view the aging of the demon-image, not a graceful process, but an ugly one, in which the evil and the deviant drove out of cognition all counter-evidence, silencing any kind words. This was done gradually, not overnight, and the first few years tell a rather complex and interesting story.

Consolidation of the demon-image after Abbas's death

We shall now follow the process described above, allowing our sources to guide us, with the help of a few examples, through the twilight zone between reality and perception. A French engineer, J. Barthélemy Saint-Hilaire, visited Egypt in 1856, about a year and a half after Abbas's death, in connection with plans to dig the Suez Canal. He would later become Public Affairs Officer to the Canal administration. His information came mostly from the French commercial and diplomatic community in Egypt, which was still very hostile to the memory of Abbas. However, his account is more differentiating than might be expected, and he certainly tried to be "fair" to the dead viceroy:

Abbas Pasha, although mild in his conduct to the people (we must do him this justice), made himself execrated and despised by his excessive cruelty to the great, his abominable licentiousness, his mad expenditure, the unbounded terror he inspired in all who approached him, and his implacable hatred of civilization. It is probable that he paid the forfeit of crimes, which nothing could excuse, by a violent death. The exercise of his power had been so odious that, as the heat was excessive at the time he died, the Fellahs affirmed that the gates of hell had opened to receive his soul.[35]

Two points are worth mentioning with regard to this passage. The first is that almost all the major ingredients of the demon-image are present here to produce in the reader great revulsion towards Abbas. The context is, of course, praise for Sait Paşa, great friend of French civilization and supporter of its darling project in Egypt at the time – the Canal. Sait shines here, as in many similar accounts that juxtapose the two men; whatever faults he may have had are attributed to the general character of government in these parts of the world. Thus, we are made to sympathize with the ruler – here Sait, not Abbas – who has to conquer the vices of the system, and whose position is "far more arduous than enviable."[36] The second point is that the "justice" done to Abbas by mentioning his mild conduct with the people, is not carried even to the end of the paragraph: it is undone immediately by citing what the *fallāḥīn* supposedly said about him when he died. This comes at the end of the reference to Abbas in the text, a privileged position marking significance and usually retained by the reader. There is no need to assume malice on the part of this or other writers, but they do reflect the grip that the image had on them even when they meant to do Abbas justice.

Another French admirer of Sait Paşa was Paul Merruau, whose *L'Égypte Contemporaine* was published in Paris in 1858. Merruau later replaced Barthélemy Saint-Hilaire as Public Affairs Officer to the Suez Canal administration. Not surprisingly, his book is adorned with a ringing endorsement by De Lesseps. It purports to describe Egyptian history from Mehmet Ali to Sait, but in fact ignores the intervening reign of Abbas. The few references to Abbas are *ad hominem*, and demonstrate how the author internalized the demon-image in its most horrifying version. Merruau asserts that Abbas's reign was disastrous, and opines that if that fanatic and cruel prince had lived, he would have opened the gates of Egypt to Oriental barbarism. Abbas was a true specimen of the Oriental prince, mistrustful, somber, uninterested in the destiny of the country which God had confided to his care. His heart was not energetic enough to have done much harm, his spirit too retrograde to have done much good. And, in a nutshell,

il aimait à se retirer dans le secret de ses palais et à *s'isoler au milieu de ses gardes* pour vivre de cette vie des *despotes ombrageux et voluptueux* de l'Orient, où *le sang* se mêle à *l'orgie* [italics mine].[37]

Thus we have despotism, mysterious isolation in remote desert palaces, the mamluk guard, the blood and orgy: the image encapsulated. But, as the following views of Olympe Audouard clearly indicate, this was not the worst passage written about Abbas Paşa.

The French writer Olympe Audouard visited Egypt in the mid 1860s, during the reign of Ismail Paşa, more than ten years after the death of Abbas. Unlike so many of her countrymen, she was not enamored of Ismail, and strongly rejected the brilliant image he still enjoyed at the time in the eyes of Europe, especially in France. Audouard complained bitterly about his autocratic rule as manifested in the excessive use of the police force. She herself was subjected to surveillance and harassment for her known disapproval of his methods of governing.[38] Those Europeans who admired Ismail as an enlightened reformer saw him as the true and worthy heir of Mehmet Ali. They denigrated the rules of Abbas and Sait, though many treated Sait with great leniency. The fact that Audouard rejected the prevailing view of Ismail's reign did not lead her to upgrade the rating of Abbas, nor to question the validity of his demon-image. Quite the contrary, she embraced the image wholeheartedly, and, in fact, perpetuated it in a worse form.

In her depiction of the defamed Paşa, Audouard certainly reflected the views current in the European – mostly French – community in Egypt. By then, we may add, those views were already well integrated into European common knowledge about Egypt and its modern history. Nevertheless, the intensity with which the memory of Abbas was retained in that public's mind is quite amazing. Audouard reported that everybody she had talked to maligned Abbas in the worst fashion and considered him to be the incarnation of evil. She was told by her interlocutors that whatever she could write about him would pale in relation to what he was in reality. The *fallāḥīn* say, she was informed, that it was Hell which spewed him out upon the earth ("C'est l'enfer qui l'a vomi sur cette terre").[39] This, of course, coheres with the story – also attributed to the *fallāḥīn* – that Barthélemy Saint-Hilaire and others relate about the gates of Hell which opened to receive Abbas's soul. Quite naturally, the connection between Abbas and the dark forces of Hell was an essential part of his demon-image.

The passages cited above from Barthélemy Saint-Hilaire, Merruau, and Audouard are but a few examples of the writings about Abbas. They, and the folk tales that were adduced to back them up, bear witness to the fact that Abbas's demon-image – created and developed during his lifetime – vigorously survived in European writings about Egypt long after his death. These writers are generally hostile to Abbas, and toehr observations are fairly consistent throughout their works. It is interesting to note, however, that even writers who mention the reign of Abbas favorably, do not challenge the basic features of his image. A brief example may illustrate the point. Writing a short time after the British occupation of Egypt in 1882, Sir Donald Mackenzie Wallace, who was quite familiar with Egypt, describes in very positive terms the condition of the *fallāḥīn* under Abbas. He is essentially saying that the burden they felt was lighter and their life better than in the reigns of Mehmet Ali, Sait, and Ismail. However, when he writes about the character of the viceroy, we read the following sentence: "gloomy, savage Abbas, who was strangled in the recesses of his hareem by the habitual victims of his tyrannical cruelty."[40]

In another place, the author explains that Abbas had a bad reputation among Europeans because of his "reserve, haughty demeanor towards the few foreigners whom he admitted to his presence," but also because of "certain private vices regarding which Europeans are much more severe than Orientals." Still, when he admits that Abbas "was a much better master to the peasantry," Wallace, too, is impelled to qualify his evaluation by "perhaps without intending it." This is yet another manifestation of the umbrella that protected the demon-image from any substantive revision even by those observers who made positive statements about Abbas's rule and were clearly aware of his "unjust" reputation. Somehow, the image seemed immune to counter-evidence, so deeply was it entrenched in European common knowledge. As already pointed out (pp. 25–35 above), professional European historians picked up this "baggage," shared it with their non-European colleagues, and – almost without change – bequeathed it to students of Egyptian history, who still uphold it today.

To sum up, the demon-image of Abbas Paşa was the political and sociocultural product of both the Ottoman-Egyptian elite and the Europeans. The materials of which it was created were part and parcel of mid-nineteenth-century elite culture in Egypt and in Europe. Members of the viceregal family, high officeholders, and European consular and commercial agents were certainly the dominant political and cultural group in Egypt during the middle decades. However, faced with such a powerful and determined viceroy as Abbas Paşa, they had to adopt the indirect tactics of the weak. If, as we shall see later, the *fallāḥīn* and the urban lower strata resisted elite pressure by withholding their labor in various indirect ways, members of the Ottoman-Egyptian elite and their European collaborators denied Abbas their social approval. Whereas the former "voted" with their legs, the latter "voted" with their tongues.

Positive views about Abbas: the counter-evidence

The efficacy of indirect resistance must not be underestimated, though it is the tactics of the powerless. In fact, the Ottoman-Egyptian elite and the Europeans created an atmosphere in which positive information about Abbas Paşa could not survive long. My purpose in this section is to point out the range of such information and to note where and how it was readily available to any member of the elite and the European community. People who thought well of the viceroy were prominent Ottoman-Egyptians and Europeans, but their voices were drowned by the torrent of defamation. Hence, while Abbas and his men monopolized political power and dominated the economy, they were defeated in the social salons of Cairo, Alexandria, Istanbul, and the interested lobbies in Europe.

Positive information about Abbas was published in *The Times*, which officials and members of the public interested in Egyptian affairs could read. It appeared in consular reports, which decision makers routinely saw. And, it could be heard from a number of fairly senior government officials who served under Abbas. It is certainly true that men like Nubar, Hekekyan, ᶜAlī Mubārak, and other high-ranking officials who had served under Abbas could not freely voice their views about him after his death. They had nothing to gain by it and could lose Sait's favor. But during the reign of Abbas, they had everything to gain by telling whoever cared to listen about their experience in the service of the Paşa. Though evidence of the kinds mentioned thus far was not abundant, it was nevertheless substantive, indicative, and accessible. But it was ignored because Ottoman-Egyptians and Europeans, who together produced the demon-image, had a vested interest in portraying Abbas as unmitigated evil. They had no real opposition to contend with.

Thus, for example, those who were convinced that Abbas Paşa was an incorrigible Christian- and European-hater could still read in *The Times* that the viceroy was rather polite and courteous to his European guests. In November 1850, a formative period in the history of the demon-image, the paper reported that Abbas had given a lavish reception in celebration of the Kurban Bayramî, a Muslim high holiday. The Paşa rose from his seat every time a European consul entered or left, treated the consular corps and the Christian clergymen present with "great courtesy," and offered them pipes and coffee. In the same communiqué from Alexandria, it was also reported that when Abbas had heard that alabaster was required for some monuments in Rome, he gave orders to prepare six blocks of the finest and largest in the country and send them to the Pope as a present.[41]

In March and May 1851, as the crisis over the *Tanzimat* was intensifying, two letters to the editor were published in *The Times*. Both expressed enthusiastic support of Abbas's position. One of them favorably compared Abbas to Mehmet Ali, and listed six major achievements of his administration. Among other things, Abbas abolished monopolies, reduced taxes, improved the condition of the *fallāḥīn*, greatly developed transport facilities, and ensured perfect security in the country.[42] It is true that these letters were intended to mobilize the support of the British public and government in favor of Abbas, but the list of successes was not trumped up. Overall, such positive information was not out of context, for the overall reporting in *The Times* was generally favorable to the viceroy. Yet somehow it was not registered in people's minds, nor did it have any lasting impact. The fate of counter-evidence in diplomatic correspondence was much the same.

In the course of 1852, Colonel Hugh Rose was appointed as acting consul-general in Egypt. He replaced Charles Murray for a few months. Not new to the realities of daily life in the Ottoman Empire, Colonel Rose was well-equipped to pass an educated judgment on the situation in the Nile Valley. In one of his dispatches, he provided a warm and most laudatory endorsement of Abbas's rule. Rose's report to the Foreign Office combined an evaluation of the character and performance of the maligned Paşa, whom he judged to be "so little aggressive" on account of his mild treatment of his "treacherous relations." Rose discounted allegations that Abbas was contemplating revolt, which he deemed too ambitious for the viceroy's character. Praising the state of public security, Rose writes:

> As I came up the Nile, I saw the banks covered in many places with bales of cotton and other valuable produce of the country; An unarmed Peasantry had brought it there for shipment, and neither Store Houses nor guards were required for its protection. Can a clearer proof be required of order and security, remarkable anywhere, but peculiarly so in a Country like Egypt, to which Nature has certainly granted a noble River fertilizing and enriching all within its reach, but with a drawback of a Desert running along each bank, the abode of wild Bedouins, whose Revenue is plunder, and whose law is that of the strongest . . . That protection [of the route to India] is not due to Guards, for there are none, but to Abbas Pasha's authority which, hitherto, has been so efficient that the Transit passes through the heart of the Desert with more security than it would through the Centre of many European Capitals . . . the Authority of a Governor who protects so well such all important Interests, more especially as official documents prove that that Authority is maintained by a sparing use of punishment.[43]

But Murray returned, and so did his less enthusiastic dispatches. He remained for about a year and towards the end of 1853 was permanently replaced as consul-general by Sir Frederick Bruce.[44] After a short time, Bruce came to resent the fact that Abbas was not being as friendly to him as he had been to his predecessor. His ensuing bitterness is amply reflected in his reports. Before that, however, when all was new and promising, Bruce admitted that the country improved since he last visited it eight years before. He even complimented Abbas on that count, to which the viceroy replied: "We are not like you in England, we go very slow, but we advance a little. When we have finished the Rail-road, we will set about other improvements."[45]

Such favorable reporting about Abbas's government did not come as a surprise to the Foreign Office. It matched the generally positive coverage of the Paşa's rule by the British press.

However, this line was totally alien to French thinking, as reflected in the tenor of reports received at the Quay d'Orsay and articles published by the Paris newspapers. The French consul-general complained to his Foreign Minister in

1852 that Murray induced British papers to give Abbas a "good press," and that Palmerston helped by making positive statements about Abbas.[46] We may mention here the rumors that circulated among the French in Egypt, alleging that the correspondent of *The Times* in Alexandria was in the Paşa's pay. Indeed, the "softer" attitude towards Abbas is so remarkably absent in French sources, that such an allegation – quite unfounded, it appears – seems as almost the only explanation that could logically bridge the gap. The British, it was argued, had a vested interest in defending Abbas, their ally, so they covered up his horns and tail. In fact, however, there was no conspiracy to defend Abbas, and no concerted effort in English to prevent his character from being defamed in French. Only few statements, scattered here and there, dot an otherwise indifferent, often unsympathetic, presentation of Abbas Paşa and his reign by British writers.

On Friday, 1 February 1856, Nassau Senior was dining at Consul Walne's country house, not far from Cairo. Also present were Ayrton and Abdallah Bey. Walne had spent many years in Egypt, first as an eye doctor and then as a British consul; Ayrton had served as tutor to Ilhami Paşa, son of Abbas; Abdallah Bey had been Rickards, before he was converted to Islam and joined the administration of Abbas to manage the Transit Authority. They all had had personal contact with Abbas in their various capacities and remembered him quite favorably and fondly. Abbas had been dead more than a year and a half then, Sait was viceroy, times had changed: the English were out, the French were in. Abdallah had been dismissed, and Ayrton was then assisting Ilhami in his financial dispute with Sait over Abbas's estate. They talked about Abbas.[47]

Abdallah and Ayrton called Sait Paşa a tyrant, and accused him of cruelties of the kind and order previously attributed to Abbas. He was, they intimated, callous, capricious, murderous, and treacherous in the extreme.[48] This was their retort to the accusations which Senior brought up, provocatively, against Abbas. But the most revealing defense of Abbas came from Walne. The insights it affords, and its sensitivity, merit special attention. Said Walne:

> I knew Abbas well; we quarrelled from time to time, but I was one of the few foreigners with whom he was at ease. It is not true that he was cruel – that is to say that he had a pleasure in simply inflicting pain, or was even indifferent to it. But he was irritable, and affected to be so still more than he really was. I have known him send for people, fly into an apparent passion, and threaten to behead or beat them to death, and as soon as they were gone, confess that it was a farce.

Walne then talked about the low rate of capital punishments in Abbas's time by comparison with other periods in Egyptian and Muslim history, or even by the standard of most Christian countries. It was often rumored, he said, that Abbas had sent his enemies to the Sudan and had them poisoned or drowned on the way, but when Sait became viceroy, they all returned except one or two who had died of natural causes. Returning to Abbas's personality, Walne observed that,

> the most marked feature in his character was timidity. He had all the other faults to which that great fault is a predisposing cause. One of them is excessive severity, which looks like cruelty, but differs from it in not being wanton, in being prompted by an undue desire for safety – and of this he was guilty. Another is suspicion – and he was suspicious, as indeed are all his family.[49]

From this kind of personal defense of Abbas's character, we move now to another type of argument devised to vindicate the Paşa's rule. The gist of it was to attribute the negative aspects of Egyptian realities during his reign to the doings of Mehmet Ali and Ibrahim. Bayle St. John, for example, condemns some of the oppressive practices common in Egypt at the time and concludes that:

> in fairness, however, we must remind the reader that Abbas Paşa is only answerable for acquiescing in customs handed down. He has not established any new pernicious regulation that we have heard of; and even if he remain perfectly quiescent and leave things to go their own gait, King Log is better than King Stork.[50]

With regard to Europeans and Westernization, asserts St. John, Abbas did not carry out the reactionary views attributed to him before he became viceroy of Egypt. On many occasions, we are told, "he clearly showed a disposition to temporize between his prejudices and his interests." The author, who is very critical of European involvement in trying to modernize Egypt, credits Abbas with good sense and courage for his opposition to Mehmet Ali and Ibrahim, as for rallying a group of supporters around him to counter his predecessors' harmful policies. As for Abbas's alleged cruelty, St. John is convinced that "he has not by any means shown himself of a sanguinary disposition . . . I do not think that the present Viceroy has any disposition to be a tyrant. He wields the authority he has received with some moderation."[51]

We have already encountered Hekekyan's strong aversion to Abbas, but if we examine closely the views he expressed before his demotion, we may discover a different attitude towards the viceroy. Among the Hekekyan Papers, there is a short biography of Abbas, apparently contained in a letter addressed to two of Hekekyan's acquaintances in England.[52] The biography brings out the amicable relationship between Abbas and the Sukkias family. The father, who had been Tusun Paşa's banker, moved to Egypt when Abbas, Tusun's son, was six. Sukkias's sons, Artîn and Hüsrev, later became active in the administration, while their sister married Hekekyan. This document is devoid of the bitterness and hatred of Abbas that pervades the passages treated above (pp. 113–16). The atmosphere is serene, and the language intimate, though a case is mentioned in which Abbas, as a youth, went through a temper tantrum, which kept repeating itself in later life. Also described are Abbas's long-term relationships with three women, the second of whom gave birth to Ilhami Paşa. No insinuation whatever is made concerning homosexuality, bestiality, or any other deviancy.

As Hekekyan was discussing with Senior the characters of Abbas and Sait, he intimated that he had known both of them from infancy. He then observed that both were "charming boys and pleasing young men." In private life, he added, both would have been "amiable men," but power made Abbas into a tyrant, and with time Sait would possibly become "Abbas-like." This accords with a view expressed by Artîn Bey, Hekekyan's brother-in-law. Artîn had been Commerce and Foreign Minister to Abbas and his close adviser. But he fled to Istanbul when the Paşa accused him of embezzlement. Also speaking to Senior, Artîn said that Abbas "was good in private life," but that power spoiled him.[53] This was, then, another version of the familiar argument that power corrupts, and absolute power corrupts absolutely. In the same conversation, Artîn observed that Abbas was more literate than Sait and that his command of Turkish was quite good. Abbas also spoke Arabic and had a good traditional Islamic education.

The various references to Abbas in ᶜAlī Mubārak's *Khiṭaṭ* are all positive, and his own career during Abbas's reign is described in brilliant terms.[54] When writing about Alexandria in the time of Abbas, Mubārak devotes a few lines to a more general evaluation of the Paşa's reign. Abbas, says the author, followed the policies designed for Egypt by his predecessors, Mehmet Ali and Ibrahim. These policies proved highly favorable to commerce, and the country's wealth grew. Because he applied laws intended to protect and develop agriculture, the yields of the land increased. Abbas's liberal attitude made farming an attractive enterprise even to members of the elite, so large tracts of fallow land were brought under cultivation. Food was abundant, and prosperity included everybody, not just one group of the population. Abbas also reorganized and improved the army, and strengthened the coastal fortifications. Mubārak then lists specific exploration and development projects which Abbas introduced in the area of Alexandria, a city he allegedly shunned. In sum, the first three viceroys are lumped together, and the country's debt to them is jointly recognized.

In another place, Mubārak provides the biography of Shaykh al-Azhar at the time of Abbas Paşa, the eminent Ibrāhīm al-Bījūrī (sometimes al-Bājūrī). There he reports that after Abbas came to power, he used to go to the university-mosque of al-Azhar to attend classes taught by the famous shaykh. The shaykh, relates the *Khiṭaṭ*,

> would not rise [for the viceroy], but would have a chair, made of palm branches, brought for him to sit on for a little while, outside the class-[circle]. Afterwards, he [Abbas] would go outside the Azhar and distribute some Egyptian silver coins [as alms].[55]

Surely this does not seem like the terror-inspiring figure from whose shadow all cringed. Rather, this is a subdued, humbled ruler, interested in Islamic learning and able to follow it in Arabic, one who did not stand on ceremony out of deference to a highly regarded learned man and his teaching.

Yet, for the warmest and most striking defense of Abbas, we have to return to a politician, in fact, to one of the most prominent – and controversial – members of the Ottoman-Egyptian elite in the nineteenth century: Nubar Paşa. Nubar was very fond of Abbas Paşa, to whom he refers as "my master and benefactor." He admired his administrative skills and thought highly of his performance as Governor of Egypt. Nubar was also aware of Abbas's demon-image, which by the time he wrote his memoirs, at the turn of the twentieth century, had become an integral part of the annals of Egypt. The legend, complains Nubar, overshadowed Abbas's eminent qualities as administrator and his adherence to principles of order and economy. The French terminology employed by Nubar is almost the reverse of the language frequently used to criticize Abbas in French. Moreover, Nubar declares that he is happy to render legitimate though belated justice to the memory of Abbas.[56]

Nubar seems so sure of his positive view of Abbas, that any attempt to conceal unpleasant aspects of life under his rule becomes superfluous. Nubar's Abbas was first of all a competent ruler, intelligent, possessed of excellent common sense and of high Ottoman breeding, generous, thoughtful, kind, and forgiving to his close allies. This character description contains elements which are in full contrast to some of the basic features in the image of Abbas the demon. Nubar relates the story of how Abbas handled his cousin Mustafa Paşa, who at first was one of his most trusted supporters, but then betrayed him. The situation was politically complex and very delicate, and Abbas maneuvred with much skill to extricate himself from it. Nubar was so impressed, that he ends his account with an exclamation: "Quel travail continu dans ce cerveau d'Abbas, épiant tous, pesant tout, toujours en éveil!"[57]

For Nubar, Abbas personified "le grand seigneur, le véritable prince oriental": living in distant seclusion, yet ever commanding from the depths of his palaces with absolute authority, which is blindly obeyed by all. Yet we get much more than that: a highly personal image of the viceroy by a man who was emotionally attached to him. When Abbas died, Nubar was still in Vienna. He was recalled by Sait, who cancelled both his and his brother's posts in Europe. Nubar returned to a different Egypt, for the change from Abbas to Sait was remarkable in style and mood. The French loved Sait, as he was their man and was going to restore their lost position in Egypt. His winning personality and openness to Europe was in sharp contrast to Abbas's style. But in Nubar's eyes, the change was not necessarily for the better, and he never liked the new Paşa. For Nubar, a world had ended with the death of Abbas, whose style of government and *mentalité* he classifies with Mehmet Ali's and Ibrahim's. With Sait began what he called "a regime of laisser-aller, of complete lack of self-respect."[58]

Sait, of course, was spoiled by the love of the Ottoman-Egyptian elite and the Europeans. Some of Abbas's men were shunned for a while, but those who vowed loyalty to the new viceroy were reintegrated into the administration. Even Nubar was reappointed and promoted under Sait. A kind of harmony was

9 Nubar Paşa (1825–99)

restored at the top of Egyptian society and was maintained for the remainder of the middle decades. It is at this point, after Nubar's warm endorsement of Abbas, that the discrepancy between the man, his record, and his demon-image demand explanation most persistently. So we now turn to an explanation of the gap, in which the political will mesh with the socio-cultural to reconstruct the mood and rhythm of the dominant social group in mid-century Egypt.

6 The demon-image as a product of elite culture

As we now come to examine the origins of the demon-image of Abbas and the reasons for its development, we ought to draw a distinction between the personality, or character, of the viceroy and the record of his reign. These two elements are not completely separate, for treatment of one influenced the treatment of the other. There is also, to an extent, a causal relation between them: defamation of the character of Abbas was backed up by examples from his performance as ruler, and criticism of his government often mobilized as explanation aspects of his personality which conduced him to follow certain reprehensible policies. This is certainly true about *accounts* of the Paşa's character and performance. But when we study the evidence from that period, it is astonishing to discover how little actual relation there was between the two. That is, the record does not sustain the prevailing condemnation of Abbas's rule and should have produced a markedly different account of his performance. As for his character, things are more difficult to ascertain, and the picture that emerges from the evidence is both mixed and complex: while the demon-image is certainly unjust and completely distorted, it can be asserted with equal conviction that Abbas was not a saint either.

Thus, the gap which exists between the record and the demon-image suggests that what we have here is a case of character assassination. The questions that come to mind in this respect are: when and how did this happen? By whom and for what purpose was it done? And, not least important, why has the image so well endured the test of time?

Abbas had clearly acquired a distinct reputation well before he assumed power as viceroy of Egypt. That reputation was expressly negative in European eyes. It stemmed from the fact that Abbas stood out among members of the ruling family because he had so few associations with foreigners. His ignorance of Western languages classified him in European jargon as "reactionary"; his criticism of Mehmet Ali and Ibrahim's policies labelled him as anti-reformist. The group of like-minded persons who gathered around Abbas in those days was often called "the fanatic party." The negative image certainly had its roots in that period, but it did not yet amount to character assassination. For here we shall use this term to describe a very special situation, in which an irreconcilable gap exists between the image and the evidence. It is then that the image acquires a life of its own, takes over the historical record, and deliberately distorts it. In the case of Abbas Paşa, this did not happen until the first year or two of his reign. The reason was that both Ottoman-Egyptians and Europeans suspended judgement for a while, as they did not want to alienate the viceroy. Everybody waited to see how Abbas would manage the affairs of Egypt.

Eventually, Abbas changed much in style and less in content, but this was enough to end the grace period granted to him by these two influential groups. For one group, the senior officials and close associates of Mehmet Ali and Ibrahim, the damage was immediate and unmitigated: many of them lost their positions in the administration and all access to power and wealth. Members of the ruling family who were suspected of hostility to Abbas and considered as a political threat to his rule – often with good reason – were also alienated from government and moved to Istanbul. What they described as "seeking asylum" was, in most cases, no more than a desire to undermine the position of Abbas, and work in the Ottoman capital for his removal. The case of Mustafa Paşa, Ibrahim's son, indicates that Abbas was indeed willing to trust with his most guarded secrets even a potential rival who expressed loyalty. Mustafa later betrayed Abbas and joined the Istanbul group of malcontents.[1]

The strong motive for fighting the viceroy was born at that initial stage of his reign. It not only fed on political reasoning, but had a convincing economic aspect too. A major dispute developed between Abbas and members of the ruling family over the inheritance of Mehmet Ali. The Paşa was not necessarily bent on disinheriting his disgruntled relatives. Rather, the re-allocation of resources within the economy, and the solvency of the fisc, necessitated the expropriation of major assets held by these individuals as a result of land grants during the reigns of Mehmet Ali and Ibrahim. The dispute was later settled through the intervention of the sultan and the Porte. But before that, it fueled the anti-Abbas fire that burnt the midnight oil in many Istanbul salons. At this point, it is important to understand by what means the campaign to depose Abbas was actually waged; it is here that we also see the crucial role of image-building in this high-level game of Ottoman politics.

The reign of Abbas was destined to become a test case of Egypt's semi-autonomous position within the Ottoman Empire. Along with the – albeit different – Serbian precedent, the hereditary governorship conceded to Mehmet Ali, with great reluctance, by a sultanic *ferman*, was an unwelcome pattern in Ottoman eyes. Egypt was not Tunis, nor could Serbia equal its importance. The short reign of Ibrahim, and the fact that his illness was well-known in Istanbul, postponed the confrontation until the reign of Abbas. If the hereditary governorship could survive Abbas, it was felt, the institution would be likely to become a long-term reality. Because of the international sanction that guaranteed the settlement of the "Egyptian Question," the Porte realized that a direct challenge to the arrangement in Egypt would not be effective. However, the Ottoman government was ready to take advantage of any development that might call in question the wisdom that lay behind a solution which had been devised at the time under pressure to end a potentially disastrous internal conflict.

In Ottoman eyes, the best challenge to the principle of hereditary governorship could come through an Egyptian violation of the stipulations of the 1841 edict, for example, by maintaining a larger army than agreed, or by refusing to apply Ottoman laws in the *Vilayet* of Egypt.[2] Barring that, the incompetence of the hereditary *vali*, if it could be universally demonstrated, along with a concomitant, preferably incessant, strife within the viceregal family, was the next best thing. This could reopen for negotiation the whole question of the status of Egypt. Since Abbas showed no *overt* inclination to violate the edict, the only hope for the Porte remained in the second option. Through a series of miscalculated steps, which he took a short time after his accession, Abbas managed to alienate both the upper echelon of the administration and many of his relatives. Those steps consisted in the removal and appointment of high office-holders and in some financial decisions with strong personal implications for the same group of people. Thus, he presented the Porte with a golden opportunity to play its hand. The ensuing bickering among family members, their inability to settle matters within the family through compromise, and the flocking of the losing party to Istanbul, gave the Ottoman government a legitimate standing in the conflict that was evolving in Egypt.

At the same time, Abbas also dealt a major blow to French interests and prestige in Egypt, as he let go a number of French experts who had served his predecessors with much success. In addition, he suspended some of the projects associated with France's *mission civilisatrice* in Egypt. Then he was quite awkward in his attempt to sugar-coat the pill, and somewhat slow in courting British influence, which after some maneuvering, he managed to rally to his support. All these played into the hands of his Ottoman and Ottoman-Egyptian opponents, so that he was left exposed in a ruthless arena with few effective advocates to defend his cause. However, Abbas was by no means helpless, nor unskillful in handling the prolonged struggle. But he had to pay the price of his early mistakes and, perhaps, bled much more than was necessary. Those past mistakes, and a posture which he genuinely adopted on the issue of Western-style reform, also determined the "name of the game" and the main weapon of his enemies: character assassination.

How was this actually done? To answer the question we have to consider two separate, though certainly interrelated, arenas. The one, and from Abbas's point of view, the more important, was that of the political and social discourse of what I call the Grand Ottoman elite. The other was a European scene, divided between the foreign community in Egypt and the chanceries of Europe. The one operated by word of mouth and traveled the Nile and Mediterranean route from Cairo to Istanbul; the other fed on rumors manufactured in Egypt, then written down in consular dispatches to decision makers and articles in the European press. The mingling zones, where information flowed freely from one system to the other, were located in Cairo, Alexandria, and Istanbul. In the social and political salons of these cities, as in casual meetings over good Middle Eastern food and drink, or in smoke-filled government bureaus and embassy anterooms, information about political events and details of the social life of Empire grandees were exchanged. True, exaggerated, and fabricated stories served the double purpose of communication network and social lubricant.

It is here that the term "public opinion" becomes useful. What is meant by it is no more than the views that were current in the Ottoman-Egyptian elite, i.e. those positions that prevailed despite a measure of dissent. As we have already seen, the elite included officeholders of all levels, both army officers and bureaucrats. The lower strata of society, it is true, are excluded from this definition of "public opinion." This is done on purpose, not because such groups had no views about politics, or no interest in the intimate life of their rulers, but because their views are more difficult to glean, for those men and women rarely left a written record, and their "public opinion" very seldom decided the political and economic fortunes of the Empire. Their resistance to government oppression – treated in part II – was not effectively articulated within the political culture. During the middle decades, that culture was still dominated by the Ottoman-Egyptian elite and its modes of operation. In any event, soon after his accession to power, elite public opinion was overwhelmingly stacked against Abbas Paşa. And European public opinion – more easily definable because of the proliferation of newspapers[3] in Europe by mid-century and the existence of other types of sources – was in much the same mind about the third viceroy of Egypt.

The limited use of the printed press at the time further emphasized the role played by word of mouth in the Ottoman-Egyptian context. Only two papers, both official gazettes, were in circulation in Egypt and the Empire during the reign of Abbas Paşa: the Egyptian *Vekayi-i Mısır* (with its Arabic version, separately edited, *al-Waqā'iᶜ al-Miṣriyya*), and the Ottoman *Takvim-i Vekayi*. These gazettes were, of course, controlled by the government, which makes them quite difficult to use as indicators of public opinion. During the middle years of the nineteenth century, they are most useful for monitoring government appointments and official decrees. As for journals in European languages, only a few appeared at the time, mostly in Istanbul, none in Egypt.[4] Even so, in those years not many members in the circles we are concerned with here knew European languages. Hence, they mostly talked and corresponded with each other, as is amply clear from various contemporary sources – Hekekyan Bey, Yusuf

Kāmil Paşa, Arif Paşa, and Nubar Paşa record many examples of such communications.

The quality and reliability of the information traded in elite and foreign circles was often dubious.[5] Not that this made much difference: stories and rumors were as powerful and manipulable as the credibility attached to them by listeners and story-tellers. The actors in that socio-cultural environment were sufficiently well versed in its codes to be able to guage the limits of truth. But, since they often lacked any means to authenticate the stories they heard, they assigned truth-value to information according to what I shall call a "tacit principle of coherence." To make things a bit more specific: a story attesting the benevolence and immense kindness of Abbas Paşa had virtually no chance of being believed, if launched at any time after, say, late 1850. Conversely, from about the same time – when his demon-image had consolidated – any story alleging enormous cruelties, or sexual travesties, committed by Abbas had quite a good chance of being taken as true. Such stories would then be passed on as emanating from "good authority," or even as having been whispered by one of the Paşa'a close confidants.

The historicity of many of the horror stories that circulated about Abbas is much in doubt. Versions and circumstances varied considerably, and the sources were quite removed from the person and household of the Paşa. The reliability of such tales was broached in writing as early as 1873, by the French H. Couvidou.[6] In an original chapter entitled "Anecdotes," the author shows how most of the cruel deeds alleged to have been committed by members of Mehmet Ali's family were attributed to Abbas and the notorious Mehmet Paşa, better known as the *Defterdar*. Couvidou dismisses the stories altogether as a source for historical "truth," because of the great diversity of versions and the inability to trace the sources. The material suggests that, in the absence of acceptable criteria, it is virtually impossible to establish if there was any truth at all in such tales. However, my concern here is not to establish whether Abbas indeed ordered the stomach of a soldier to be split open so as to find if it contained stolen milk. The interesting question is not if Abbas actually had the feet of one of his runners hobnailed. Nor is it significant if it can be shown that a certain narrator admitted that he had invented stories, as Fouvidou and About claim.

Rather, what matters is that the stories were given credence by many and had wide circulation in Ottoman-Egyptian and European society. From the point of view of cultural history, the intriguing question is why these anecdotes were told and believed about Abbas. Or, in other words, why did they seem real to contemporaries who moved in those circles? Indeed, why did they make sense? This kind of concern is akin to that expressed by Robert Darnton when he tried to discover why a cat massacre seemed so funny to the apprentices and journeymen of a printing shop in Paris in the late 1730s.[7] The point is that the "objective" truth-value of the stories was irrelevant to their acceptability and durability. Their strength lay in coherence: they all cohered with each other and with what was "common knowledge" about Abbas. The name of the game was guilt by reputation. To get the flavor of the genre, let us consider for a moment three examples, named for convenience as follows: Abbas and Nazlı̇ Hanı̇m; Abbas and the show of marksmanship; Abbas and the sewed-up mouth.

Nazlı̇ Hanı̇m was the beloved daughter of Mehmet Ali and Abbas's aunt. She is the other contemporary figure whose character was slandered in similar ways. However, as a woman, the defamation of her character in a male-dominated society was not politically motivated, nor was it politically significant, as was the character assassination of Abbas. Therefore, it has to be understood in a different context, that of the place of women within the Ottoman-Egyptian elite. Here, we shall mention only the story of her relations with Abbas, relations of the two most vilified figures in the ruling family. According to both Nubar and Senior, one day, Nazlı̇ Hanı̇m had one of her lovers killed, as it was commonly believed she had done to several other men. When Mehmet Ali heard the story, he ordered Abbas to take her life. Appalled by the task confided to him, Abbas spent the entire night trying to persuade his grandfather to change his mind. By morning he succeeded, the order was rescinded, and, in the words of Nubar, Nazlı̇ owed her life to Abbas alone.[8]

However, when Abbas became viceroy and the princes who opposed him flocked to Istanbul, Nazlı̇ joined them. It was said that Abbas bitterly complained about her disloyalty and ingratitude. Some deep dispute between the two, probably related to Mehmet Ali's inheritance, must have caused her departure. The dispute became well-known at the time, for it figured in one of the more popular versions of Abbas's mysterious death. According to the story, Abbas was murdered by two mamluks, whom Nazlı̇ sent from Istanbul to infiltrate the viceroy's bodyguard and kill him. This story was so widespread that in 1866 Audouard appended it to an inverted version of the earlier stage in the relations of Nazlı̇ and Abbas. Accordingly, when Mehmet Ali heard of Nazlı̇'s alleged responsibility for the killing of her lover, he told Abbas "to settle the matter at once," which Abbas intended to do. However, when Nazlı̇ learnt of that, she threw herself at her father's feet and begged him to spare her life. Mehmet Ali immediately denied that he ever intended to have her killed.[9] Thus, Abbas was turned from the saviour of his aunt into the bloodthirsty nephew who was stopped by his grandfather from murdering his own aunt. The revised version might have been a mere figment of Audouard's imagination, but as it accorded so well with prevailing notions, she might actually have heard it from her informants.

An even stranger appendix to this story concerns Ibrahim Paşa, eldest son of Mehmet Ali and the second hereditary Paşa of Egypt. Nubar's account of the relations between Ibrahim and his sister Nazlî reveals a very close and affectionate bond. Nazlî nursed her ailing brother until his death, hardly ever moving from his bedside. However, in a book published in 1968, Ibrahim's great granddaughter, Emine Foat Tugay, tells a completely different story about Ibrahim and Nazlî. According to it, when Ibrahim heard of yet another travesty committed by his infamous sister, he went to see her and said: "If you do not die tonight I shall come and kill you in the morning." So Nazlî, who was no coward, took poison and died during that night. Tugay adds that everyone in her mother's family believed the legend to be true, although the fact was that Nazlî survived Ibrahim by some thirty years.[10] This vividly illustrates the gap that always exists between fact and fiction. It also declares the triumph of "coherent" fantasy over the historical record.

The name of Ibrahim is linked also to the story I entitled "Abbas and the show of marksmanship." This is another example of the difficulties presented by the kind of evidence we deal with. In his *Wanderings*, John Gadsby tells the following anecdote about Ibrahim, which he heard while traveling in Egypt during the reign of Abbas Paşa:

> This ferocious being [Ibrahim] often, in his day, amused himself by firing at the skins borne on the shoulders of the water carriers. If he hit the skin he would laugh heartily at the joke; and if he happened to wound the poor carrier, he would promise to support him for life; but, it is said, he always forgot his promise.[11]

With some variations, this anecdote is repeated in several sources about Abbas. One day, the story goes, Abbas was walking in his gardens with another man. As he boasted about his newly received French carbine, Abbas aimed it at a *fallāḥ*, who was toiling in the distance, and shot. The *fallāḥ* fell dead, but the Paşa appeared to be unaffected by what happened.[12] The story unmistakably belongs to the same genre as the one told about Ibrahim. A similar anecdote was also related about Sait. They were supposed to reflect crass cruelty and a complete lack of regard for human lives. Again, it is virtually impossible to establish the historicity of such tales, though their repeated pattern certainly casts grave doubt on their veracity. The use of familiar patterns, as in this case, conjures up the "categorized" image. So here European readers will intuitively associate the story with the heartlessness of oriental despotism.

We have already mentioned the story of the woman whose mouth was sewed up for having smoked in the harem contrary to Abbas's orders (pp. 118, 120 above). This was one of the more popular Abbas horror stories told and believed by foreigners and members of the Ottoman-Egyptian elite. Here, I do not wish to use the existing variety of versions in order to call in question the truth of the story, but rather to point out how well the anecdote typified the demon-image. Consul West's wife told Senior that she "knew" it to be true. She then employed it as corroborative evidence for another horror story, in which Abbas used to "build" men into the walls of his palaces, presumably as a form of punishment. What was done to the poor woman was not only cruel in the utmost degree, but literally bloody. In one version, Abbas himself did the sewing. "An Englishman," reported a French doctor, actually saw Abbas's hand covered with blood after he had performed the "operation." The woman could not eat and was left to starve, which made things look even worse. And, again, this abhorrent punishment was inflicted for a trivial matter – merely smoking in the harem.

In short, the story encapsulated the demon-image and perfected it to its fullest form. Even Nubar mentions it as fact, albeit in one sentence and without further comment. Sabry incorporated the anecdote into his narrative, thereby turning it into an historical fact. But we must also note that the idea of such an act was not new to Egyptian folklore. Egyptian Arabic has the saying that "he who enters the house of power gets his mouth sewed up with a thread."[13] In his analysis of colloquial Egyptian proverbs, Sha^clān classifies this saying with those denigrating the group of hangers-on, who live off the crumbs of the rich and powerful. They are censured as leading a dishonorable and parasitic life. If we assume that the saying predates Abbas, then the deed itself is a symbolic pattern, and the specific details about Abbas Paşa, the woman, and the smoking prohibition in the harem are the variant.

The variant which imputes the story to Abbas might have originated among the lower strata as an idiom about rulers and governments. It then could have been transmitted to members of the Ottoman-Egyptian elite and gained currency among them. Given the reputation of Abbas, the story must have been readily believed and incorporated into the demon-image. It was then whispered into eager European ears, and from that point on it stopped being a mere tale with well-understood cultural significance. Implanted in an alien cultural environment, the story was endowed with a positive truth-value that, perhaps, it was never meant to possess. It is at this point that a broader explanation of the whole question of image formation and consolidation might prove useful.

Cognitive studies discuss the way in which stereotypes about groups and individuals are formed in our mind. A stereotype of a group, or an image of an individual, are a cognitive representation of social information. These tend to be organized as a "category" according to the principle of feature similarity. What is called the associative network of semantic memory absorbs and assimilates into an image those qualities of an individual which have the greatest resemblance amongst them. By the same process, those qualities that do not yield to the principle of similarity are rejected and not incorporated into the image. Empirical findings show that stereotypical "categorization" is characterized by great reluctance to abandon a cluster of information, or an hypothesis, even for better or more reliable alternatives, once a basic set of notions has been internalized.[14]

When any person is assimilated into a group, his or her uniqueness is blurred.

But when one is assimilated into an outgroup, he or she tends to lose their individual characteristics even more than when assimilated into a stereotype of an ingroup. When we define the outgroup, or "the other," we tend to reduce and merge their qualities into simplified "outgroup schemata." The ingroup schemata, of which we have first-hand knowledge, are ever more complex and finely tuned than the outgroup schemata. An individual assimilated into an outgroup schemata is likely, therefore, to suffer the greatest distortion of character. Thus, for example, when an Egyptian ruler is described in the literature as a "typical Oriental despot," his individual traits are set aside, while the image with all its negative connotations is conjored up in the minds of European readers familiar with the term.[15]

These concepts are quite useful for understanding the development and survival of the demon-image of Abbas. At the crucial stage of image formation, the negative, indeed monstrous, features of the image were woven into the associative memory of the Ottoman-Egyptian and European contemporaries of Abbas, precisely because those features had a great deal in common: they were all evil and deviant. Positive information about the Paşa, such as his popularity with the lower classes and the traditional elements of society, was rejected as atypical, out of character, and banished from memory. For the Ottoman-Egyptian elite Abbas was not an outsider, but to Europeans he certainly was a member of the outgroup. Thus, his image suffered doubly: first, by being stigmatized through the elimination of positive information by the incorporation of correlating negative information; second, by being schematized at the hands of European writers as a member of the barbarous ilk of Oriental despots. One had to be special, promote European interests, and be open to Western culture, in order to be treated as a mild, enlightened, and "civilized" version of that rough category. Mehmet Ali, Ibrahim, Ismail, and even Sait were; Abbas was not.

Still, the crucial question is: how did it come to a breaking point, beyond which assigning truth-value to information became a fairly simple, intuitive matter? The answer lies in the years 1849 to 1851, when Abbas committed those initial errors which turned against him both members of his family and senior officials of previous administrations. The irreversible impact of that phase may be explained by the process of concept and impression formation. Initial messages enjoy enhanced recall within the linear order in which information is presented. They have what is called "primacy effect" and are crucial to stereotype formation.[16] Thus, the sheer quantity of slanderous information with which the group of injured individuals flooded elite circles must have been such, that, within the course of a year or two, the demon-image was inculcated in people's minds and the good name of Abbas was lost beyond retrieve. That was the point of no return at which the "nucleus of coherence" consolidated and the "category" was fixed and internalized.

The stories and allegations that emanated from the Ottoman-Egyptian elite were only reinforced by disgruntled European interlocutors, mostly of French origin. Then, as mentioned above, through official correspondence and the press, that oral information became reliable knowledge for decision makers and interested readers in Europe. All this was *not* a well-orchestrated campaign intended to have Abbas deposed by the sultan with European acquiescence. Rather, it began as an intense protest against grievances, both genuine and false, by a vociferous, influential group of Ottoman-Egyptians residing in Istanbul and Cairo. It then gathered momentum and, because conditions in Istanbul and Europe were ripe, assumed unexpected proportions. One may still doubt whether the propaganda success of Abbas's enemies would have been so great, had the Porte not connived in the campaign, and had Abbas been less inept at dealing with the French.

During the early stages of his reign, his relations with the Porte were excellent: Abbas was given a lavishly supportive welcome in Istanbul when he came to receive the edict of investiture. Consular reports were still minimizing the damage sustained by European interests, and the French consul-general was hoping to reverse much of that if *rapprochement* with the viceroy became possible. But all that was soon to change. Abbas refused to placate the Europeans, and continued to curtail useless projects. He also entered into a prolonged conflict with the Porte over the application of Ottoman penal legislation in Egypt. His close relations with Britain and the railroad concession were an added snub to the Porte and France. However, in the middle of 1852, the conflict with the Porte was resolved through mediation, and tensions were reduced considerably. As it became clear that Abbas lay safe on the throne of Egypt, the campaign to discredit him lost its political *raison d'être* and withered away. But the genie, once let out of the bottle, could not be put back again.

To be sure, Abbas fought his opponents with the same weapon that was being used against him. The viceroy was keenly interested in changing the rule of succession to primogeniture, which would have ensured that his son Ilhami Paşa succeed him, instead of Sait Paşa and Ibrahim's sons. If Ibrahim could be proven to have been a stepson of Mehmet Ali, it would have enhanced Abbas's scheme, since his own father, Tusun Paşa, would then be recognized as the eldest legitimate son of the Old Paşa. Arif Paşa, who was well-versed in the discourse of the Ottoman elite of the time, asserts that Abbas spent large sums of money in order to gain credence for various versions of Ibrahim's origin, and sponsored the publication of pamphlets that included all sorts of rumors on the subject. At mid-century, the people who had known the truth were already safely dead, so the move registered some success.[17] When Abbas died, it was believed that he was ready to launch his plan. Ilhami had just set out on a tour of European capitals, allegedly to add the final touch to his credentials. Some time earlier, the young prince had married the sultan's daughter Münire, which fully accorded with the master-plan attributed to his father. However, Abbas's death nipped the move in the bud, and Sait became viceroy.

In any event, we still need to gauge the atmosphere that enabled the demon-image to emerge as a "nucleus of coherence" in the lifetime of Abbas. In other words, how was it possible to convince people that the viceroy was a human monster capable of committing the worst abominations conceivable? What in the personality and behavior of that ruler conduced his contemporaries to take this image for fact? How did the Paşa gain notoriety as "le héros du mal," to use Olympe Audouard's words?

The fact is that few people knew much about Abbas during any stage of his life, and even fewer possessed reliable information about him after he became viceroy. Abbas was not a sociable person. He had few close friends or associates, and preferred to keep the public at a distance. He was accessible to his subordinates for the conduct of state affairs, but performed only those social obligations that were absolutely required of him by custom. With the exception of Murray, he received foreign consuls only when necessary for the exchange of diplomatic notes, or on official ceremonies. He rarely ventured on "fact-finding" expeditions in town and village, where people could see him transact the business of government in person, or execute justice in public. All this was in sharp contrast to the style of government exercised by Mehmet Ali and Ibrahim, and later by Sait and Ismail. In varying degrees, these rulers were accessible to Europeans and to their own officeholders. They were also sufficiently visible to the population at large. People did not need to see their ruler often, and many preferred to see him as little as possible.[18] But they needed to see the Paşa sometime, or know personally someone who saw him at least once and could describe basic features of his appearance. This was necessary in order to retain a human image of the ruler and prevents his dehumanization in the public mind.

Abbas's style of government was highly centralized, as were those of Mehmet Ali and Ibrahim. But he lacked public visibility, which made him highly vulnerable to the working of the imagination. Abbas operated through the services of a handful of loyal and efficient confidants. These men laid down an impressive network through bureaucratic and military channels, that fed information upward to the Paşa, and transmitted his orders downward. Mehmet Ali had a similar mode of operation, but he often bypassed levels of command to deal with matters directly when he deemed it necessary. As the material in the Egyptian archives amply proves, Abbas often occupied himself with minute details, normally not expected to attract the attention of a viceroy, but the actual contact was effected through his confidants, not directly. This was obviously the result of his personal disinclination to expand his relations with people in general. In the political circumstances that developed in Egypt at the beginning of his reign, Abbas's sharp departure from a visible style of government was incomprehensible to many. As things turned out, it could not be done without giving offence and paying a heavy price for it.

Abbas's propensity to isolate himself from the public produced two phenomena, both detrimental to his reputation. First, an acute scarcity of information about the ruler and his intentions was created. The following comment, attributed by Hekekyan to one of his sources, serves well to illustrate the point:

People are so interested in knowing everything that the Viceroy does and says, that even his most private and confidential menials are employed to divulge his most secret and trivial acts.[19]

Secondly, members of the elite and the foreign community felt rejected by the Paşa. In effect, it was the combination of the two that produced the demon-image of Abbas Paşa. The shortage of personal and polaitical information created the need to produce the scarce commodity by fabrication; the sense of alienation determined the negative nature of the material thus invented. An information vacuum was intolerable, if not downright inconceivable.

The departure point of fabricated information in mid-nineteenth-century Egypt was the scant substance that was actually "known" about Abbas. The tales that circulated revolved around the following themes: Abbas's hobbies of horse racing and breeding, bird watching, rearing of exotic animals; his preference for the open spaces of the desert, where he built several residences; and the fact that he recruited and trained his personal guard in a way that was reminiscent of the Mamluk system. This seemingly innocuous skeleton was fleshed out by the intensive work of the imagination. Every trait was augmented and blown out of proportion. The evil, the deviant, and the bizarre collapsed into a demon-image, while contradictory information was conveniently cast aside. The intensity of the selection process and its decidedly negative drift were conduced by a strong sense of being rejected. Both Ottoman-Egyptians and Europeans who lived and served in Egypt shared that feeling. Abbas's voluntary seclusion implied that society was not worth his time. His refusal to receive local grandees and foreign dignitaries alike, and his demeanor towards them when he condescended to see them, were a blatant affront. To both soften and avenge the insult, Abbas's distanced existence had to be interpreted in a derogatory way. It was thus contended that the Paşa isolated himself because he must have had a great deal to hide from the public, i.e. his deviant behavior.

Abbas was then rumored to prefer animals to humans, and the company of mamluks to women. To hide that, and his extreme cruelty, he chose to remove himself from society and dwell in the desert. Taken at face value, the viceroy's choice to live aloof and distanced was too offensive. So it was made to look as if solitary confinement was virtually imposed upon him by the need to conceal his vices from decent society. From the rejecting, Abbas became the rejected. However, such a dramatic inversion could not be achieved by anything short of perfect demonization. Abbas had to be completely dehumanized. This was done through hair-raising stories about his cruelty to humans and his simultaneous indulgence concerning animals. That extreme cruelty was almost invariably inflicted capriciously and for trivial offenses, or for no offense at all, as if there were cases in which such measure of cruelty could be justified. Many of these stories contained heavy innuendo about homosexuality and bestiality, though few were actually explicit. To be utterly repulsive, the demon-image had to be malicious and cruel beyond reason, sick and beastly beyond humanity.

But for the image to be fully effective, no extenuation could be allowed in the depiction of Abbas. He represented evil incarnate and, therefore, could have no redeeming features. Abbas had to be cruel to all, benevolent to none. As we shall see in part II, there is evidence to support the view that the situation of the *fallāḥīn* and the urban poor improved during the reign of Abbas. Be it solely for the peaceful conditions that prevailed and the reduction in public works, the burden was considerably eased for these very large groups in the population. However, not only do we find no trace of that in most stories about Abbas, but we actually read the reverse. We have already encountered the recurrent figment about the excessive heat that prevailed when he died, because the gates of Hell opened to receive his soul. Despite what we know about actual conditions, the sources that cite this story persistently attribute it to "the *fallāḥīn*." As the years passed by, Abbas's continued social disengagement provided no refutation of that unmitigated demonic image. Things only grew worse.

The period from the latter part of 1852 until Abbas's death in mid-1854 was detrimental to the atmosphere in the country. It perpetuated the demon-image even after the motive that created it – the desire to have Abbas deposed – was no longer practicable. With the settlement of the crisis over the *Tanzimat* and the railway, the need to conduct business with representatives of the European Powers in Egypt greatly diminished. As mentioned before, it was alleged that Abbas was planning to induce the Porte to change the order of succession in favor of his son. If so, he must have realized that European support was essential. But the matter could not be too pressing at the time, since Abbas himself was just nearing the prime of his life. The administration was running smoothly, and there was no imminent danger to his rule at home. Thus, Abbas could afford to further restrict his contacts with members of his own elite, and make himself even more inaccessible to Europeans. He gladly did both.[20]

But there was an additional factor that further soured the mood of the country. Abbas's style of government invoked the primordial fear of the unknown, the unpredictable, the uncontrollable. The fact that it was both centralized and authoritative, but that the top man was absent from public life during much of his last two years in power, had a devastating effect on the mood of the people. The lack of reliable, tangible, firsthand information about Abbas, and the concomitant abundance of false and exaggerated information about him, only increased the anxiety felt by many members of the Ottoman-Egyptian elite. It was partly because so few people knew where he was – physically – at any given time, that Abbas was said to be capricious and unpredictable. Even fewer people had a clue as to what his plans were, and only a handful of confidants had access to his person. Yet members of the elite had a sense that Abbas was virtually omniscient and ubiquitous. He could reach them anywhere, they believed, and nail them down for trying to deceive him, if they did. These feelings were clearly subjective, though not entirely divorced from reality. Indeed, Abbas Paşa controlled Egypt effectively until the day he died, and in a way, took advantage of the image he projected. But imagined or not, that fear was a living fact for the elite. In those days, their Egypt was compressed and silent.

As for members of the consular corps, many of them believed that if Abbas was invisible and inaccessible, he also abandoned the day-to-day government of his country. Consult were made to wait days for an interview with the Paşa, and not infrequently he simply refused to see them. Abbas learned to live with the bad press he received in Europe and occupied himself more with domestic issues. While the wounds of an excessively rapid modernization were gradually healing, the lower strata must have felt the mood pressure to a much lesser degree, as their condition improved and life was made easier for them in general. At the same time, their need for accessibility to the viceroy was minimal, and could be satisfied on public occasions, such as the reception of the pilgrimage caravan from Mecca, which Abbas always attended. However, the evidence available at present does not allow further generalization on this question.

Gradually, as the "silent" years crept by, some of Abbas's slanderers returned to Egypt, while others settled for good in Istanbul and other parts of the Empire. An attempted plot to overthrow the viceroy was effectively crushed in the Delta, but the man alleged to have been behind it, Sait Paşa, was allowed to remain in Egypt undisturbed. The country prospered economically, was well administered and safe. In 1853, Abbas sent a large military contingent to assist the sultan in his war against the Russians, thus becoming an ally in battle of both France and England. Abbas's authority was not questioned either in Egypt or in Istanbul. The hereditary governorship of Egypt became a fact of history for a full century to come. But the Paşa was liked by few – mostly those who were close to him – and his demon-image remained virtually unchallenged until it, too, became an historical fact.

PART II

The social divide and life of the lower strata

Introduction

When we consider Egyptian society as a whole, we must not forget that the viceroy and the Ottoman-Egyptian elite formed but a small, if politically and economically dominant, minority. The vast majority of the population was made up of various groups which had at least one thing in common – they did not belong to the governing elite and did not share its culture. Otherwise, that vast majority was anything but homogeneous. It consisted of a large rural population and a smaller, though significant, urban element. It was overwhelmingly Sunni Muslim, but Copts, other Christians, and Jews were well represented. That "silent majority" was Arabic-speaking, though Turkish, Greek, Slavic languages, Albanian, Kurdish, Circassian, Maltese, Italian, and other languages were also spoken by members of some of its groups. Large segments of non-elite Egypt lived on subsistence level, but others, mostly the rural nobility and the urban merchant class, led a comfortable life.

Although illiteracy predominated, religious and, gradually, modernized education could boast at mid-century an impressive network of schools. The Islamic network was headed by al-Azhar and controlled by the *ᶜulamā*; the modernized system consisted of military schools, government-administered, and private missionary schools. Intellectual leaders, such as Rifāᶜa Rāfiᶜ aṭ-Ṭahṭāwī and ᶜAlī Mubārak, were active in those years and already engaged in a major synthesis of traditional and Western knowledge. Thus, almost in every respect, in ecological, religious, ethnic, cultural, and economic terms, the non-elite majority was heterogenous. Nevertheless, its numerical core was quite distinct: born and bred in Egypt, it was Arabic-speaking, Muslim, uneducated, and poor. Within that cultural milieu, one group can be considered as a kind of "sub-elite." Socio-economically and culturally, it consisted of the rural notability, the urban rich, the educated, and the Muslim religious hierarchy. Yet, as pointed out in part I, these men were politically and economically subordinated to the Ottoman-Egyptian elite, and socio-culturally segmented from it.

While rural Egypt appeared to outside observers as fairly homogeneous, it was in the cities that the great variety of the human mosaic fully manifested itself. All social components mixed freely in the streets, the mentally conceived lines of place and station making themselves visible and audible in speech, dress, comportment. Flaubert was struck by the din of Cairo, the multi-lingual sounds, and the "harsh Semitic syllables" that "crack in the air like whiplashes." He added:

You brush against all the costumes of the Orient, elbow all its people . . . ; you see the Greek *papa* with his long beard riding his mule, the Albanian soldier in his embroidered jacket, the Copt in his black turban, the Persian in his fur pelisse, the desert Bedouin with his coffee-colored face walking gravely along enveloped in his white robes.[1]

Flaubert, St. John, and Gadsby – to mention some of the most keen European observers at mid-century – did not fail to notice the power relations which underpinned the colorful mosaic of Egyptian society. St. John saw the geographical division of Cairo and the "north–south relationship" it reflected:

In the southern quarters, inhabited by the wealthier classes, about the Birket el Fil, grave, respectable-looking men, are met, riding or walking slowly along; whilst towards the north is the region of dingy turbans, threadbare tarbooshes, blue shirts, ragged shawls, and naked feet. In the central portions the two classes, mixed with merchants, soldiers, Copts, Jews, asses, camels, and strangers, unite to form a huge, buzzing, brilliant, moving crowd.[2]

In this passage, however, St. John's recognition of economic and socio-cultural differences only touches the surface. Elsewhere, he corrects this benign picture, which Gadsby, in the following protest, puts in relief. It is cited in full for its concerned immediacy:

There is an Englishman beating his servant, merely for the amusement of his friends. Here is a Turkish officer unsparingly using his whip on the back of a poor half blind Arab, who, not having seen him coming, had not got out of his way. Yonder is a man with a koorbaj [whip] driving on boys and girls of only from three to six years of age, because they do not move fast enough with their little baskets of rubbish which they are carrying from that building belonging to the pasha. On this side is a poor fellow who has been nearly beaten to death because he had obeyed orders, as those orders had turned out to be wrong. On that side are a number of men at work in chains, merely because they are in debt to the government. Before you is a troop of men tied together by the neck, because the pasha wants them for soldiers in a far country; and these are followed by their heart-broken mothers and sisters, as I have just been describing. Hear thee not their lamentations? Do not the shrieks of the poor Arab under the bastinado lash vibrate in your hearts?

Gadsby's portrayal of power relations – across the social divide – between the Ottoman-Egyptian elite and the rest of the population is so harsh because it addresses only the element of exploitation and oppression. The other aspect, that which was manifested in patronage and the give-and-take of the elite household, has already been treated in part I of this book. However, the account was not balanced, and it is hardly worth denying that during the middle years of the nineteenth century a small Ottoman-Egyptian elite continued to monopolize political power in Egypt and freely disposed of all the country's economic resources. Skillfully manipulating the growing power of the state, the elite managed, appropriated, consumed, and redirected what the vast majority of Egyptians produced. They did this within time-honored Ottoman traditions, which also reflect distant remnants of past Near Eastern and Mongol concepts of state and society.[4]

According to these traditions, a strong causal relationship existed between the authority of the sovereign, his just application of the Sacred Law, the strength of the army, and the wealth of the fisc. The tax-paying, wealth-producing subjects owed complete allegiance to the sovereign. In return for the fruits of their labor and their loyalty, they deserved justice and protection, so that they could prosper, produce, and fill the state's coffers. With a solvent treasury, the army and governing elite could be supported, so that the subjects were justly and efficiently administered and properly protected from both internal and external enemies. Social harmony was maintained through an equilibrium of privileges and obligations, enshrined in a system of statuses and power symbols. Within this framework, "cultural meanings disguise and re-present economic and political relationships, define human power as divine order, subordination as duty and virtue."[5]

Yet social harmony did not always prevail in Egyptian society during the period considered in this work. Although open rebellion was relatively rare, resistance to official excesses was expressed in various other ways. The growing power of the state and its virtual monopoly over the use of violence made open resistance a costly and hopeless venture in mid-nineteenth-century Egypt. Nevertheless, a few uprisings did occur during the 1840s and 1850s in relatively remote provinces, but they were quickly suppressed by the government.[6] In the face of reality, resistance to government exploitation assumed less direct, more subtle forms. In a way, part II is a history of state encroachment and the resistance to it. In another, it is an account of access to and use of time, that is, the question to what extent, and for what purposes, the government "appropriated" time from the individual. And, concomitantly, how did people on the lower strata spend their "unappropriated" time? In yet another way, the story is about "the other side of the tracks," or the social divide, and, no less, about the nature of the divide itself.

Much of part II is an interpretation of popular behavior as reflected in Egyptian archival material. It is, of course, a most difficult task to accomplish, given the fact that the population under consideration was illiterate and left no written records. However, the unique quality of police reports affords some insights, which other, further removed, sources do not. A sentence uttered and transcribed by an officer, a situation described by witnesses, detectives, and *shaykhs*, are sometimes worth many tales culled from oral tradition in numerous versions. The fact that this mine of information is found in police files, or compiled in the course of criminal investigation, in no way detracts from its validity as a basis for general statements. The material is rich enough, covers broad grounds, and only marginally deals with offenders proper; it makes a whole society stand out in relief. The picture is further supported by an army of other sources, including archival material other than police records.

Taken as a whole, it appears that both the rural and the urban squeeze, or the demands put by the expanding state on its subjects, were great. They left most Egyptians with little control over their own lives. Nevertheless, the state knew its limits and rarely pressed the population beyond the threshold of endurance. In fact, during the reigns of Abbas and Sait, the lower strata were considerably relieved from Mehmet Ali's yoke. The peace that reigned in the middle years, scaled-down reform, and the reduction of urban – and possibly some rural – taxes,[7] made life less arduous. Hence, resistance was confined to draft evasion, desertion, abscondence from *corvée* sites when pay was inadequate, and application to the government for adjustment of pay to the cost of living. Petty crime, drunkenness, drug abuse, and the pursuit of "disreputable" professions, were also forms of resistance, but they remained on the margins of society. Thus, part II is devoted not only to state intervention, but equally to the impediments thrown in its way.

7 The great social divide in Egyptian society

If social strata are an abstract concept invented by social scientists, they are supposed, nonetheless, to reflect a tangible reality. In mid-nineteenth-century Egyptian society, the social divide between the Ottoman-Egyptian elite and the rest of the population was a vivid aspect of daily life. It was not only felt in economic terms, but also visibly expressed itself to the world. In speech, manners, dress, food, modes of transportation, and allocation of space, the social divide constantly represented itself to society. Roles and statuses were being acted out in subtle ways, too, but little was left to subtleties alone. Through a set of symbols understood by all, authority asserted itself everywhere. *Paşa*s, *bey*s, and *efendi*s were unmistakably *paşa*s, *bey*s, and *efendi*s, and everybody who was not was unmistakably not. Privilege and lack of privilege transcended the dry letter of the law; embodied in patterns of social interaction, they were deeply rooted in consciousness.

To foreign observers, often choosing to forget unpleasant realities back home, the social divide was a manifestation of oriental oppression. The more sensitive among them were less culturally judgmental, and some even used their descriptions of Egyptian society in order to direct harsh criticism at their own societies. In any event, before we set out to examine insiders' views, we ought perhaps to note some of the main features of the divide which were evident to foreigners who visited Egypt in the middle years of the nineteenth century. "Every man in the country," wrote John Gadsby, "is, in his way, a tyrant." He went on to explain that

> the Pasha issues his orders to his beys, or ministers. They again reissue them to their under officers, and so on until it comes to the poor sheikhs of the villages. However disreputable the order may be, *all* are compelled to obey . . . Thus all are bred and born in fear and distrust. The boys tyrannise over the girls, the men over the women and children, the sheikhs over the men, the nazirs over the sheikhs, the governors over the nazirs, and so on; and, to wind up, the pasha over all. To him the people are all slaves, and would soon be told so, if they dared to think otherwise.[1]

What Gadsby saw was a strict hierarchical order, a chain of command that bound all members of Egyptian society to both their superiors and their inferiors. But he did not only observe a bureaucratic hierarchy. It was more of a general hierarchy of power, for it included men's domination over women and children. Although Gadsby grasped a gradation of authority, his chain stopped with the village *shaykhs*. Under them came the vast subordinate population, the surplus-producing stratum. By incorporating the *shaykhs* and the *nazirs* – most of whom were of rural origins – this view blurs the social divide between the Ottoman-Egyptian elite and the rest of the population. However, it retains a certain distinction between governing and governed. It is at this point that Flaubert's observation on the subject is especially pertinent. "Officialdom is so far removed from the populace," he wrote, "that the latter enjoys unlimited freedom – of speech, that is. The 'most extreme excesses of our Press' would give but a feeble idea of the buffooneries that are allowed in the public squares. Hence the mountebank approaches the sublime in cynicism."[2]

For Flaubert, the divide was clearly between officialdom and non-officialdom. It is, however, not an oppressive divide but, in a way, a liberating one. The privilege of the powerless, it seems, was a freedom to caricature the powerful out in the open, thus giving vent to their frustrations. But Flaubert himself realized that this freedom of speech was bought at a heavy price: the acceptance of the existing order of things. "The general servility that prevails here (the baseness and cowardice)," he wrote elsewhere, "is nauseating – and on this score many of the Europeans are more oriental than the orientals."[3] Other visitors were also impressed by a seeming acceptance of the servile state. This was probably because of what they perceived as a completely different attitude towards authority in the post-revolutionary European societies from which they came. Having described the suffering of the poor and destitute, Gadsby remarked that:

> amidst it all, the poor people submit. If they cannot escape, they say it is the will of God, and have little thought of ascribing it to the wickedness of man. The main *qualification* that such people have for being ill used or beaten is that they have not courage to return the blow. Indeed, it would appear that the more roughly they are handled, the more readily they submit.[4]

A similar observation is made by Bayle St. John, one of the more sensitive and sympathetic visitors to mid-nineteenth-century Egypt. Unlike most Europeans, St. John was very critical of Mehmet Ali for what he believed to have been the inhumanity of his reforms. However, he was keenly aware that the Old Paşa was not unpopular in Egypt, and tried to reconcile the paradox as he wrote that:

> it would be a mistake to suppose, for example, that Mohammed Ali, in spite of the inexorable cruelty of his government, was personally hated by the fellahs. On the contrary, it must be confessed that they regarded him with a respectful awe which a just ruler would not, perhaps, have excited. 'T is pitiful, but 't is true. Men admire most what they understand best; and before we condemn these poor devils, let us be perfectly sure that

we are not ready, every one of us, to throw an heroic halo round the first successful adventurer who conquers a throne or endeavours to filch an empire.[5]

Leaving aside the self-criticism which rides on the author's statement, his point is clear. Put crudely, people understand the language of power, and they respect those whom they fear. Moreover, when control weakens, people often take advantage, and they lose respect for authority while they do. However, beyond the mere reality of power relations and domination, some Europeans noticed other differences across the social divide in Egypt.

Foreigners who came into closer contact with members of the elite observed the difference in etiquette and style. Writing about Abbas Paşa, the American consul-general, Edwin De Leon, noted that "his manners, like those of all high Turks, were bland and polished, for in all that constitutes perfect good breeding the Eastern surpasses the average Western man."[6] W. A. Bromfield, a British doctor and botanist who visited Egypt at mid-century, complimented the behavior of an Ottoman-Egyptian provincial governor who had assisted his party during a crisis situation in the Sudan. He wrote about him:

In countenance, address, and suavity of deportment, he would have passed as a perfect gentleman at any European court . . . There is something very prepossessing in the manners of the Turks of the higher class: we paid our respects severally to the governors of Ourdeh [New Dongola], Khartoum, and Berber, and found them all men of the world, polite, affable, and gentlemanly.[7]

We ought to remark that these provincial governors were not the most senior members of the Ottoman-Egyptian elite. Thus, even at the margins of its core, the cultural style of that elite was unmistakable. In this chapter, we shall explore some of the cultural differences which formed the social divide in mid-nineteenth-century Egypt.

Language as a social stratifier

As we move towards a cultural concept of class in mid-nineteenth-century Egyptian society, it is useful to begin with the important role of language. Perhaps the strongest characteristic of the Ottoman-Egyptian elite at the time was the use of Ottoman Turkish both for communicating and governing. The fact that the elite was Turkish-speaking, it should be stressed again, does not necessarily mean that it was Turkish. The former is a supraethnic distinction, while the latter is not. Rather, as argued above, the Ottoman-Egyptian elite comprised a number of groups whose culture was Ottoman and who spoke Ottoman Turkish. In fact, realities were even more complex than that. Not all Turkish speakers belonged to the elite, indeed quite a few of them inhabited the lower strata of Egyptian society. Whereas command of Turkish was a prerequisite of elite status, it did not automatically confer such status. In the running of government, Turkish was not really challenged until the late 1850s, that is, beyond the period under consideration in this work. Use of Turkish was imposed throughout the administration, though certain kinds of correspondence were conducted in Arabic. As growing numbers of Arabic-speaking officials were admitted to lower-level bureaucratic positions, a tendency to increase the use of Arabic was noticed. To remove all doubts, Mehmet Ali ordered, in October 1836, that all reports from Arabic-speaking officials be translated into Turkish.[8]

In the time of Abbas Paşa, the status of Turkish was actually strengthened, and its supremacy over Arabic is amply evident in the various contemporary collections at the Egyptian National Archives. It was only in 1858, during the reign of Sait Paşa, that the administration was ordered to switch to Arabic. However, the same archival collections demonstrate that the process was slow, and that Turkish did not give way to Arabic until well into the reign of Ismail. Not before the end of the nineteenth century, when the number of Turkish speakers in administrative positions declined substantially, was the language battle finally over.[9] But Turkish was not merely an administrative language. It was much more than that, as all live languages are. It was the language in which Ottoman-Egyptians thought, communicated, and socialized. If you could not laugh at a good inside joke told in Turkish, with puns and all, you simply could not belong. A brief example may illustrate the point.

On 2 March 1851, Hekekyan was invited by Abbas to participate in a consultation of senior ministers.[10] At the end of the meeting, Abbas wanted to have a few words with Hekekyan in private, and the two men moved to a side room. In the following passage, which Hekekyan noted in his diary after the interview, one can hardly fail to notice the importance of an intimate knowledge of Turkish.

> He [Abbas] took a turn up and down and asked me if . . . that doctor – what is his name – had gone. [Hekekyan:] "Beddan Bey," [Abbas:] "Aye Beddan Bey." I confess I did not at all like this manner. He knew Beddan Bey as well as his own father. Beddan signifying both in Persian and Arabic things which a Turk could not forget [testicles, "balls"]. He calls the German doctor Gressinger – "Gerisini iir" [literally, enter his rear end, or "bugger him"]. Mr. Gottier's name could never have been forgotten by a Turk [combination of *güt* (arse) and *eyir* (penis)].

In this passage, when Hekekyan wrote "Turk," he obviously meant Turkish speaker. This is, again, a supraethnic cultural distinction.

The formation of group solidarity in such a cultural milieu – mostly but not exclusively among men – made knowledge of Ottoman Turkish a *sine qua non*. So much so, that the linguistic category of Turkish speakers overshadowed ethnic categories. In fact, it assimilated into its ranks men and women from different ethnic backgrounds. Thus, those who spoke Turkish and whose culture was Ottoman were called Turks even if they were not. The relevant distinction in mid-nineteenth-century Egypt was the one between Turkish speakers (*turk*, or *ibn turk*) and Arabic-speaking native Egyptians (*ibn al-balad*, or sometimes in the plural *awlād ᶜarab*). The following event, a fairly typical scene in Cairo at the time, pitted the story of Mutawallī, an Egyptian servant of a certain Rüstem Bey, against that of some Turkish speakers.[11]

On 24 June 1851, Hasan Efendi, a middle-level bureaucrat, complained that the evening before, he had been assaulted and robbed by three drunkards near his home. He managed to recognize two of them, Mutawallī and a police guard named Salih, who was from Manastîr in Albania and spoke Turkish. Hasan Efendi's story was confirmed by his Turkish-speaking neighbors, who had saved him from the robbers the previous night. Salih and Mutawallī had different stories, but the one told by Mutawallī carried an added significance. He claimed that he was walking peacefully in the street leading to his master's house when he saw Hasan Efendi and Salih standing and talking. They were speaking Turkish, he said, so I did not understand what they were saying. Servants were addressed by their Turkish-speaking masters in Arabic when service was needed. Otherwise, they were excluded from the Turkish-speaking world around them by the sheer barrier of language. Whether true or invented, Mutawallī's story had to make sense if he had any chance of being believed. The picture of these two linguistically segregated worlds coexisting in the same space was very much a reality in Egyptian cities and towns at mid-century.

According to Mutawallī, Hasan Efendi and Salih parted ways at some point, but then Hasan said something to Salih, which Mutawallī again did not understand. At that point, Salih attacked Hasan and a brawl flared up. Mutawallī then ran to the two and attempted to separate them, a job that yet another person, unknown to Mutawallī, was also trying to accomplish. When asked to identify the man, he replied: "He was wearing the Ottoman dress, he was *turk*, not *ibn balad*, but I do not know him." Mutawallī could hardly be expected to distinguish an Albanian from a Bosnian or a Turk, but he could safely be trusted to tell a "cultural Turk" from a "cultural Arab." At times, that common distinction slipped also into official documents. In the "gun control" regulation mentioned below (page 164), the soldiers were referred to as "Turkish soldiers" (*türk asakirleri*), obviously not an ethnic term, but a socio-cultural one. There were many non-Turks in the army, and no ethnically homogeneous unit existed at the time. As the following case clearly indicates, ethnic categories were subordinate to the over-arching "Turkish" – but really Ottoman – socio-cultural category.

On 29 December 1853, the governor of Cairo received a petition presented by an Arabic-speaking Egyptian woman named Alfiyya.[12] The woman complained that her son Ḥasan, who had been employed at the government coach house, was beaten by one of the employees with a cart pole and died several days later. Alfiyya's story is not about safety measures and government compensations, nor about the tragic results of violence. It is really about the downward crossing of the social divide. Her husband, Hüseyin Ağa, had held a position in the provincial governorate of al-Gharbiyya. He died eleven years before in the town of Minya in Middle Egypt. When she petitioned the government, Alfiyya must have believed that if she could prove a "Turkish" status, she might fare better. So she made a point of mentioning that her dead son was actually *ibn turk*. His father Hüseyin Ağa, she added, was Kurdish (*jinsuhu kurd*). She thus made a distinction between ethnic identity (*jins*) and cultural identity (being *turk*).

To add further to the complication, Alfiyya went on to mention that she had another son, Muḥammad al-Mōralī. Muḥammad went with the army to the Hijaz four years before, and his mother had not heard from him since. Despite the sadness of the story, we must not fail to note the name of the second son. A Turkish speaker would have pronounced his name Moralı Mehmet, that is, someone, like many others in Egypt at the time, whose origins went back to the Morea. The text does not specify whether Muḥammad was not the son of the deceased Hüseyin Ağa, but it is likely that Alfiyya remarried someone whose agnomen was Moralı, whence the name of his son: Muḥammad, or Mehmet. We may safely speculate that, were Alfiyya to approach the government in connection with her son Muḥammad, she would have stated that he was *ibn turk*, whose father, she would have added, was a Greek from the Morea. But beyond the subordination of ethnic identities to a cultural category, this is indeed the story of an Egyptian woman who fell from elite status through the death of her husband, a middle-level provincial bureaucrat. By marrying someone who did not have elite status, however humble, she and her son descended beneath the social divide. Though both her husbands were Turkish-speaking, *ibn turk*, one was a member of the elite, the other was not.

Dress as a distinguishing mark

Dress was also one of the main markers of the Ottoman-Egyptian elite. If one had to speak to be identified as belonging to Ottoman culture, one's dress was a visual demonstration of status needing no further explication. However, not all people with means who dressed well were in fact elite members. There were certain distinguishing marks between members and non-members of the elite. These differences were known to all, indeed they were intended precisely for the purpose of drawing the status line. The initial distinction in mid-nineteenth-century Egyptian society is between well-dressed people and those who were not, mostly because they could not afford it. A well-dressed man was trusted to be honest and decent, or at least regarded as less likely to cheat other people.

Since well-dressed women mingled in public much less than poorer women, this was mostly a distinguishing mark for the male population.

In a number of cases recorded for Cairo at mid-century, thieves managed to sell their stolen goods to honest merchants despite a fairly regulated system of theft prevention. According to government policy, the blame for such sales devolved not only upon the thief, but also upon the merchant who bought from him the stolen articles. The valid assumption behind that policy was that some market dealers colluded with thieves, often taking advantage of their precarious predicament and buying stolen merchandise at cut prices. Shopkeepers and auctioneers in markets were required to use their "street knowledge" before making any transaction. That is, they were expected to look at their customers and assess if they were likely to be honest. Suspicious cases had to be reported to the police, which also had its own market connections and informers. In any event, people were encouraged, indeed in some circumstances obligated, to use a guarantor (*ḍāmin* in Arabic, *zamin* in Turkish) whenever possible.

In a large city such as Cairo, anonymity always provided opportunities for non-compliance. Still, life was made more difficult for thieves and their accomplices, and in smaller towns the system was considerably harder to defeat. When suspected merchants were questioned by the police, they were usually asked what led them to trust the man who sold them the stolen articles. In all cases which I have examined, the merchants invariably referred to the man's dress as the reason. The formulae they used varied slightly, but they all stated that the thief was well dressed and, therefore, trusted to be honest. The Arabic expressions employed by the merchants to describe the man who approached them were *lābis wa-mutahayya'*, *lābis ṭayyib*, *mutahayya' bi-l-libs*, and *mutahayya'*. There is no point in providing literal translations of these variants, as they all mean roughly the same thing: well-dressed (man). In one case, we also get an allusion to a specific – and significant – item of dress. The con-man referred to in that file was said to have worn a *ṭarbūsh*, better known in European sources as the *fez*, a red cap shaped like a truncated cone, which became the symbol of the modernized Ottoman elite (see pp. 8–9 above).[13]

In fact, the official uniform of the Ottoman-Egyptian elite became a major status symbol and a first-rate marker of that stratum. It distinguished the office-elite from those who also could afford to dress well but did not belong to the social center. Insiders and outsiders alike could easily tell elite members from those who were not. Thus, it is not unusual for an Egyptian of the lower strata to describe an elite member as "wearing the Ottoman dress" (*lābis al-ᶜOthmānlī*), or for Hekekyan to refer to two elderly gentlemen who were waiting with him for an audience with Abbas as "beys in appearance," without knowing them personally. Nor is it surprising to read in Maxime Du Camp the following anecdote. This publicist and photographer, who traveled in Egypt with Flaubert at mid-century, describes how, for a small remuneration, a policeman showed leniency when inflicting punishment on a culprit. "But as soon as a bey or pasha comes into view," wrote Du Camp, the officer returned to the original form of punishment "until the important personage is out of sight."[14] Elite dress, civilian and military, was recognizable to all, as indeed it was meant to be.

While *paşas* and *beys* dressed differently from other respectable or wealthy persons, no negative stigma attached to the dress of high-ranking *ᶜulamā* or rich merchants. However, what the vast majority of the population wore did carry such a stigma. For the elite, the real distinction, indeed a water-shed in social terms, lay between those who wore official dress and those who wore plain local clothes. These clothes were called "*fallāḥ* dress." They consisted of a felt skullcap (*libda*) and a woolen robe with a low neckline (*zaᶜabūṭ*), commonly referred to together – *libda wa-zaᶜabūṭ*. The worst form of punishment for members of the elite was to deprive them of their position in the administration or army, and order them to wear *fallāḥ* dress. This was an extreme measure which was rarely applied. The mere threat of such a penalty was usually enough to impose authority. However, both Abbas and Sait used it as an example and a deterrent.

According to one version of Abbas's mysterious death in mid 1854, his mamluks did it. As mentioned above (pp. 58–9), Abbas ordered that a number of them who had ridiculed their commander – a eunuch – be flogged. This was not the usual form of punishment for members of the elite. Infuriated by their insubordination and lack of respect, he also deprived them of their official status, ordered them to wear *libda wa-zaᶜabūṭ*, and sent them to work in the stables, a demeaning menial occupation.[15] These drastic measures were believed to be of a temporary nature, for a number of Abbas's closest allies persistently pressed him to reinstate the culprits. When he did, they came to his palace to pay their respects, but murdered him instead. The punishment inflicted upon these grandees was so patently humiliating because it infringed three crucial constituents of elite status at once – corporal punishment, loss of official dress, and forced menial work. It could be avenged only by shedding the viceroy's blood, or so those who believed the story and passed it on felt.

Sait preferred to make an example of a soldier, leaving the commanders to draw their own lesson from it. On 10 February 1856, he entertained a number of European guests, including Ferdinand de Lesseps, Nassau Senior, and Clot Bey. Senior reports that they were invited "to admire the *bonne tenue* of his recruits," who were drilling in the courtyard of the palace. As the guests were watching the soldiers, Sait related that:

> one of them amused himself the other day with abusing me and abusing the service to the others. I said that if he thought the life of a Fellah better than that of a soldier, he should enjoy it. So I put on him a Fellah dress, walked him up and down before the regiment for an hour, and then sent him to a village to work as a Fellah for a month. It had an excellent

effect. These young Sheykhs prefer perfect idleness to the service, but they prefer the service to work. This punishment alarmed them more than if I had given him, as most people would have done, a bastinado.[16]

In these two cases, Abbas combined the punishment usually reserved for non-elite groups – the bastinado – with that reserved for members of the elite – withdrawal of elite status. In his turn, Sait reversed the punitive measures. Instead of having the soldier flogged, as members of his stratum came to expect from superiors, Sait applied a concept borrowed from the symbolic world of the elite. Though we may accept his assessment that the punishment was effective, we should reject his explanation as to why it worked. A better reason is possibly related to the new career opportunities offered by Sait to sons of rural notables recruited to his choice regiments. Such young men and their families might have begun to see an advantage in that channel of mobility towards elite status which was opening up to them. To these recruits, unlike their predecessors, army uniforms represented the prospects of officer status beyond the lieutenant and captain level. Losing it may already have been for many of them most undesirable.

Army uniforms were made obligatory for the emerging civil bureaucracy in 1829. An order issued at the time stipulated which military rank was equivalent to what administrative status, and made the necessary adjustments in color of uniform and type of insignia.[17] Further information is not available at present about specific changes in official dress which may have occurred during the middle years of the nineteenth century. However, it is clear that there were many irregularities, and that members of the elite came to regard certain items as symbolizing their status more than others. In Egyptian society, the red felt hat, or *fez*, and the insignia (*nişan*) became largely identified with the Ottoman-Egyptian elite. These were worn with various items, such as jackets and trousers, often adopted from European fashions of the time. The existence of irregularities of official dress is attested not only by European travel accounts, but also by two orders issued in March 1849. In these orders, military and civilian officials were told to wear their ceremonial dress on all public occasions and on Islamic high holidays. Irregularly dressed officials were warned that they would not be admitted to ceremonies.[18]

The right to carry a gun – an elite privilege

Another important elite status marker, indeed almost as important as the official dress, was the right to carry arms. In cities and towns, these were mostly pistols of various makes; in the countryside, they were often muskets. The sharp distinction between those allowed and those forbidden to carry guns prompted Bayle St. John to remark that "fire-arms should seldom or never be regarded as weapons of offence in Egypt. If they are carried for other than sporting purposes, let it be as insignia of rank and respectability." Because of security problems and the increasing number of fatal accidents, Egyptian governments attempted to prevent the proliferation of fire-arms in the country.[19] This was extremely hard to impose in times of war, such as the period until the early 1840s. The introduction of a "gun control" policy in the middle of the nineteenth century at once turned the possession and display of arms in public into a privilege, indeed into a status symbol.

Originally, however, this policy had nothing to do with status. Rather, it seems that in addition to state control, concern for public safety figured high in government consideration of the issue. In 1849, an explosion in a store selling gunpowder caused a great deal of damage inside Cairo.[20] Consequently, the Council of Justice defined such stores as hazardous enterprises. The Council decided to forbid the sale of gunpowder in the city save at three specially designated points. Those places were to be secured so as to prevent a possible explosion from spreading around, and smoking was to be prohibited in them. The aim of these measures was specifically stated as the protection of the community. That increased awareness of the hazards of gunpowder and fire-arms was compounded by the government's desire to monopolize the use of such arms in order to make the emergence of effective opposition extremely difficult, if not totally impossible.

Repeated attempts and failures to enforce an effective "gun control" policy made guns an even more relevant status symbol. This meant that the legal carrying of fire-arms was at once a political and a social issue in the middle decades. Both those who were granted the privilege and those denied it were keenly aware of its existence. On 28 June 1849, the Council of Justice issued an order to all provincial governors, heads of police departments, the military authorities, and other government bureaus.[21] It addressed the increase in the number of rural murder cases in which fire-arms were used. The order further stated that inhabitants of Upper Egypt were known to buy their weapons in Cairo. Hence, the Council decreed that no fire-arms may be sold to a *fallāḥ*, or any other person besides bedouins and soldiers. These, too, were obliged to carry a permit either from their provincial governor, if bedouins, or from the commander of their unit, if soldiers.

Without an adequate permit, no one was allowed to buy a gun, nor to pass through the gates of Cairo or the various customs houses. Heads of guilds were told that fire-arms could not be repaired without a permit, and that guns presented to dealers without permits had to be reported to the authorities. Provincial governors were ordered to collect all weapons held by people not entitled to possess them. Thus, the Council drew a clear distinction between two groups: those in government service, including loyal bedouins who formed part of the concept of security, and the *fallāḥīn*, or simply put – everybody else.

Paşas, *beys*, and *efendis* who were not part of the military could obtain permits on the basis of need. This meant that if you had the right contacts you could easily obtain one. An interesting example of such a permit is found among the Hekekyan papers.[22] It is a very restricted permit, which allowed Hekekyan to carry a gun only for hunting purposes in the country. He was forbidden to use it inside Cairo, or near palaces, military barracks, and other government installations around Cairo. That permit was issued for a period of one year.

During the 1850s, serious attempts were made to enforce the policy, though they were not entirely successful. The provisions of a "gun control memorandum" were applied to offenders, and heavy penalties were imposed. In April 1853, for example, the director of the customs house at Giza, near Cairo, caught a boatman who was carrying a pistol and a rifle. The boatman claimed that the weapons belonged to a certain captain in the cavalry, that he himself was unaware of the prohibition, and that fire-arms were required for protection against robbers on the road. Nevertheless, the man was sentenced to six months' hard labor, the guns were confiscated, and a complaint was filed against the captain. In another case adjudicated about the same time, a man of *fallāḥ* status fired a gun accidentally and killed his wife. He pleaded guilty and reached an agreement with his wife's family regarding the payment of blood money. The arrangement was confirmed by the provincial court of Gharbiyya in the Delta and by the *Sharīʿa* court, but the Council of Justice threw out the settlement. In a harsh decision, the Council stated that the offender had carried a gun illegally and must be made to repent. In order to deter others, a heavy penalty had to be imposed, they added, and sent the man to prison for fifteen years.[23]

In the same year, it was reported that a platoon of eighteen soldiers under an officer was passing through a village near Ṭahṭa in the Delta. Suddenly, the officer spotted a *fallāḥ* carrying a gun. When he demanded that the gun be surrendered, the *fallāḥ* refused. In the ensuing skirmish between the soldiers and the villagers, one soldier and three of the *fallāḥīn* were injured. The Council of Justice found the officer at fault for taking the law into his own hands, instead of reporting the *fallāḥ* to the authorities. For his over-zealousness, he was given two years in prison and forced to pay heavy compensation to the villagers. All eighteen soldiers were jailed for one year, while the village head received seventy-five lashes for failing to prevent the incident.[24] The rash officer was clearly aware of the government policy and the zeal with which it was being pursued. However, he misjudged the commitment of the authorities to the maintenance of law and order and their willingness to defend the *fallāḥīn*.

Thus, in the countryside, "gun control" was certainly a live issue, which had a great deal to do with the state reasserting its right to monopolize the means of violence. But in the cities, the right to carry guns was less obviously related to questions of security and state power. A necessity-turned-privilege, it soon became yet another status marker which only members of the Ottoman-

Egyptian elite could acquire and which was forcefully denied to the rest of the population. *Paşa*s, *bey*s, and no few *efendi*s joined the pistol to the fez, as they strolled in the streets of mid-century Egyptian cities.

Transport, living spaces, and status marking

Along with language, etiquette, dress, and guns, what one used in order to move from one destination to another was a social statement. At mid-century, a keen observer of Egyptian society, Bayle St. John, captured both the visual aspect and the socio-cultural significance of transportation in Cairo, when he wrote that:

> there is no rumbling of carriage-wheels to deafen the ear. Now and then, it is true, a crazy vehicle, imported by some bey or effendi in obedience to the Pasha's command, "Let my people ride in carriages," comes jolting along over the mud pavement of the great streets, preceded by a running footman, who clacks a huge whip with a pistol-like report. Then the crowd *unwillingly* separates, tumbling into shops on either hand, or squeezing under archways, or making themselves thin against the walls. But this is a rare occurrence; and camels, which are the wagons, and donkeys, which are the cabs of the country, alone mingle with the mass of human beings.[25]

In a different, less crowded setting, by the Citadel, Flaubert recorded at the same time that "two or three carriages bearing pashas crossed the square, *attracting no attention*."[26] I italicized the two kinds of reaction in order to draw attention to both. Though seemingly conflicting in a sense, they are really not. Taken in conjunction, both reflect the common attitude towards the privileged core of the Ottoman-Egyptian elite. Load carts had been in use before, but it was during the middle years of the nineteenth century that horse-drawn passenger carriages began to appear in growing numbers to serve the more prominent members of the elite. Such carriages were an expensive and dangerous means of transportation. To warn the public and facilitate their passage through the narrow streets, they were preceded by yet another top elite status symbol – the running footman. These vehicles further removed those who could afford to ride in them from physical contact with the rest of the population. They formed yet another barrier.

The public's reaction to carriage transportation combined annoyance with indifference. The inconvenience to pedestrians described by St. John was the main source of annoyance, while the general resignation to the privileges and frivolities of the powerful and remote was captured by the sensitive eye of the young Flaubert. Alternative modes of transport did not afford a similar separation of space. Horses were ridden by the higher functionaries of government and were usually privately owned, not rented. In cities and towns, *paşa*s or *bey*s on horseback were elevated above street level, but they were still subjected to the impact of "street culture" with all its noise, dust, spattering mud, and smells.

Though for convenience and status, such dignitaries, too, were often preceded by footmen, they could easily stop for a moment to converse with passers-by. In the country, high-ranking officials rode in style, as Flaubert, again, recorded in his travel notes:

> *A rich man going home:* we see the Governor of Assiut leaving Esna on his way to sleep in the Government Palace. On horseback, with an escort, preceded by two men carrying torches. Only those two are visible, outlined against the wall by the blazing resin; all the rest move as darker shadows in the darkness of the night; particles of fire spiral upward and fall to the ground behind them.[27]

Nubar mentioned riding on horseback, Lane wrote that rich merchants and high-ranking *ᶜulamā* rode on mules, and Hekekyan talked about his donkey, and his donkey driver. Donkey riders were much closer to the street than horse riders. There was usually a donkey driver, whose services one rented with the "vehicle." Many of these were young boys who walked miles a day, making way for their animal and rider. "Most of the streets through which we passed were quite as crowded as those of Constantinople," wrote John Gadsby about Cairo at mid-century. But the people, he added

> skip from side to side like goats, when they hear, which they constantly do, the well-known warnings, "Schemalek," (Mind the left,) "Emenek," (Mind the right,) "O-a," (Take care,) "Errgah," (Look out,) "Reglek," (Mind your feet,) "Wishek, ya bint," (Mind your face, you girl,) &c. &c. . . . And, even when riding, we have to constantly "look out," or our legs would be grazed against a bullock cart, a carriage wheel, the panniers of a camel, or something equally inflexible; for neither camels nor *carriages ever stop for anybody*. Every animal seems to be in the way of every man and every man in the way of every animal.[28]

Some elite members owned donkeys and employed drivers on a permanent basis. Others rented them on occasions. Women rode either in carriages or on donkeys. The majority of the population, of course, walked on foot. Women of the elite rarely walked in the streets. But their fathers, brothers, and husbands boasted their elite status to the world and to themselves through the "prestige scale" of their means of transportation. Thus, human feet were lowest on that scale, then came donkeys, then horses, and finally, at the very top, carriages, especially closed ones. The higher one was on the scale, the more removed he or she was from street level and physical contact with whoever and whatever was there. Camels and carts were used for cargo, camels usually inside the city, camels and carts outside the walls. And, as Gadsby unwittingly observed, carriages never stopped for anybody.

The trouble really was that they drove too fast and caused accidents, at times fatal ones. Towards the end of August 1850, the Council of Justice was occupied with an accident which caused the death of a woman.[29] Three coachmen employed at the household of Mehmet Ali Bey, youngest son of the Old Paşa, drove a cart full of cut straw from Old Cairo into the city. As they drove near the palace at Azbakiyya, a funeral procession was passing by. The dress of a woman who was riding on a donkey was caught up in the carriage pole. Consequently, she fell off the donkey, was dragged on the ground until the cart stopped, and died. During a subsequent inquiry, four of the woman's blood relatives surrendered all claims against the coachmen. Since the offenders belonged to one of the ruling family households, the "out of court settlement" was probably reached under the irresistible influence of the patron house agents. The Mufti of Cairo was asked to give a legal opinion on the matter. He confirmed that from the point of view of Islamic law, there was no need for further intervention. The police, however, thought otherwise.

In a strongly worded decision, police authorities stated that the three coachmen were guilty of criminal negligence. Had they driven the cart more carefully in such a crowded area, the fatal accident could have been prevented. Therefore, and in order to deter other carriage drivers, the police recommended that the three be sent to prison for two years. Only two days later, the Council of Justice accepted that police recommendation. While the investigation of the case was being carried on, the police issued regulations aimed at preventing such accidents in the future. They stipulated that camels, horses, and carriages must not be driven at high speed through streets and markets. Speeding drivers were told that animals should be guided slowly through the city at all times. The public was warned that young children and old people were not to be left alone in streets where riding animals and carts usually passed.

It was further explained in the regulations that negligence of that sort was contrary to God's will and government view. Policemen and guards were ordered to enforce the law and keep an eye on young and old at dangerous places. This action was prompted by the aforementioned accident and by another tragic case, in which a little boy had been killed by a camel in the modern section of town – the Muskī. Almost three years later, in Alexandria, the horse driver of a certain *efendi*, accidentally hit an unknown man and killed him. Again, from the point of view of Islamic law, there was little to be done, since the man could not be identified and, hence, his blood relatives were unavailable for a settlement. However, the governor of Alexandria stressed that a severe punishment for the horseman was necessary in order to deter those who used to ride fast within city limits. Time and again, he wrote, orders were issued to this effect, but accidents still continued to occur. He recommended that the man be jailed for five years, which the Council of Justice fully accepted.[30]

As already mentioned, the growing use of passenger carriages by core members of the Ottoman-Egyptian elite further removed them from the rest of society. Moreover, it also distanced them from the less affluent members of the elite, thereby serving as an internal social stratifier. Driving faster than cargo carts, passenger carriages were more dangerous to the public. They also made more noise when preceded by running footmen, and, hence, in the Egyptian urban landscape, they constituted a loud and conspicuous reminder of social gaps. But they were in fact more than that. The increased use of carriages and the concomitant need to open up new roads and widen existing ones represented a quiet struggle for space in cities, especially but not only in Cairo and Alexandria. Wheeled vehicles pushed aside not only pedestrians or those using riding animals, but also artisans and shopkeepers, who used street space as an extension of their working area.

From mid-century on, these people were being regarded as intruding into the public domain. Through their recalcitrance, the refusal to make way for wheeled traffic, they were actually vying for essential space. From their point of view, the real intruders were the government and the modern transportation and infrastructure which the viceroys were introducing. From the reign of Ismail and into the present time, modern roads encroached on neighborhood streets and alleys that had been considered part of domestic space in poorer areas of Egyptian cities. At mid-century, however, the reform of urban pathways had a relatively marginal effect on domestic space, and the separation between the old and the modern city along the line which runs, through ᶜAbdīn palace, parallel to the Nile had not yet emerged. For Cairo, Raymond points out that, in the sixteenth to the eighteenth centuries, neighborhoods were segregated along socioeconomic lines. In the middle years, this segregation seems to have been somewhat less strict. In certain parts of the inner city, dilapidated dwellings existed next to mansions and palaces, as many addresses cited in court and police files indicate.[31]

There were, of course, richer and poorer areas, with concentrations of better and worse housing. Thus, for example, Azbakiyya was spacious and had more modern residences, while areas in Ḥusayniyya were poorer and more crowded. Perhaps the most significant difference between types of dwellings, was the space allocated to gardens. Palaces and elite mansions had gardens, which were smaller when within the city and larger when on the outskirts. Though not very many, there were some public gardens, which people from all walks of life could enjoy.

In general, the trend at mid-century seems to have been one which emphasized differences between the elite and the rest of the population. In the reassertion of Turkish, the regimentation of dress, the prohibition on fire-arms, the introduction of passenger carriages, and the predominance of houses built in the *Rūmī* style (see p. 55), in all these, the elite appeared to mark itself more sharply from those who did not have elite status. This, of course, went very well with the ceremonial government of Abbas and his successors. While being yet another aspect of the emerging dynastic order in Egypt, it might also be interpreted as the result of a different phenomenon. Perhaps the strongest distinguishing mark of the Ottoman-Egyptian elite during the reigns of Mehmet

Ali and Ibrahim was its external origin. That is, the fact that many of the leading members of the viceroy's governing elite came to Egypt from the outside. During the middle years of the nineteenth century, the Ottoman-Egyptian officeholders were effectively withdrawn from the Ottoman manpower pool. The viceroys became increasingly dependent on Ottoman-Egyptians, as the ranks of the elite were no longer being replenished from Istanbul or the Ottoman provincial service. Commitment to an Egyptian service made Ottoman-Egyptians less "outsiders," and "foreignness" lost much of its importance as a social stratifier. Consequently, there was need for other status markers, such as those mentioned above, in order to draw distinctions and ensure that social inequality was properly represented.

Inequality before the law

Social inequality in mid-nineteenth-century Egypt also had a legal dimension. As such, the law did not recognize social differences, and in principle all were equal before the court. In practice, however, discrimination existed nonetheless. Therefore, to discover social realities, one is ill-advised to comb the administrative or penal codes of the time. The administrative *kanuns* of vali and sultan were relatively free of economic, social, or cultural bias, though Islamic law, applied in Egypt by Ottoman *kadis*, still gave women, non-Muslims, and slaves only limited justice. Communal law among non-Muslims also discriminated against women and slaves. Important as it was, the law – administrative or Islamic – was only a declaration of intent, always subject to the work of social factors. Indeed, it would be quite unrealistic to expect that the power inequality which existed in Egyptian society would not create a corresponding inequality before the law. The relevant question is to what extent the powerless were denied justice, not if they actually were. And, in addition, to what degree was the due process of law impeded by social realities, by the pressure of the powerful to obstruct justice.

The first manifestation of inequality was the fact that, occasionally, members of the elite took the law into their hands, therein assuming the role of both police and court. For the purpose of our inquiry, we shall have to set aside the folk impressions of travellers, who invariably convey a picture of arbitrary rule on all levels of government in Eastern countries. Instead, we shall turn to police and court records in order to examine some explicit and implicit examples of this phenomenon. Such records, of course, reflect only those cases which came to police attention, leaving aside others which passed unnoticed or unreported. However, from the nature of the cases recorded, and on the basis of the discourse used in them, it is possible to provide a fairly reliable account of the situation that prevailed in the middle years of the century. True, circumstances varied from one area to another, from village to town, from governor to governor, but in the

1840s and 1850s, authority was centralized, control effective, and the country well policed.

In April 1852, the authorities in Cairo were informed that three ferrymen from a village north-west of the city were gravely injured as a result of brutal beating.[32] The detailed and arduous investigation which followed revealed a curious affair. It involved a prominent member of the elite, Mehmet Bey, the son of the late Hurşit Paşa. When we sum up fifteen dense pages of testimonies and reports on evidence, the following story unravels before us. Mehmet Bey, whose estate bordered on the banks of the Nile, decided to enter the business of operating ferryboats to transport passengers and goods from one bank of the river to the other. However, he apparently did not intend to enter into fair competition with the other ferry operators. Rather, he engaged in his service a number of ferrymen, who used threats and force to convince passengers to ride on their ferries and not on those of their competitors. Their fares for crossing the river were actually higher than those charged by the rest.

The head of the ferrymen's guild, whose son Ibrāhīm was the leader of Mehmet Bey's team of ferrymen, complained to the port authorities and warned the culprits that he would not defend them if passengers complained to the government of their illegal practices. At one point, someone indeed complained, and the matter was investigated by the port authorities in the presence of the guild head and his recalcitrant son, Ibrāhīm. At the end of the inquest, Ibrāhīm was found guilty and received ten lashes. He was released after Bilal Ağa had interceded on his behalf. Bilal was the chief eunuch of Mehmet Bey's mother, the senior female figure in the household. In the presence of Bilal, Ibrāhīm was made to sign a pledge of future good conduct. When the event was reported to Mehmet Bey, he reacted violently. On his orders, three of the "independent" ferrymen were taken by force to his estate, where the *bey* himself and some of his farmhands severely beat the men, leaving them wounded in one of the estate barns. The beaten men were later discovered by their friends, one had to be hospitalized for a fortnight, and the incident was reported to the authorities.

As the police doctor verified that the wounds of the three were caused by severe beating with wooden clubs, a story made up by Mehmet Bey to cover his deed collapsed. However, until the end of the investigation, he and his men continued to deny any involvement in the affair. At the beginning of the investigation, the *bey* requested that the matter be transferred to the Council of Justice, with which he claimed to have other dealings. This was not granted, and the investigation was completed by the police. Eventually, the case not only reached the Council, as all cases did, but was referred to the viceregal cabinet. Unfortunately, the final decision in this case could not be located in the archives. But curiosity aside, the existing documentation allows us to form some impressions. On the one hand, we have a case of what might be called legitimate intervention in the due process of law – that by Bilal Ağa. On the other, a clear obstruction of justice combined with flagrant violation of the law – that attributed to Mehmet Bey.

Bilal's appearance at the port in order to secure the release of Ibrāhīm was an acceptable intercession. It was not unusual to offer such assistance in a patron–client relationship, and the system treated such intercession as common practice. That action probably reduced the number of blows received by Ibrāhīm and hastened his release. The patron household in this case was a highly regarded one, and it was not uncommon for the mistress of the house to send her eunuch on such errands. On the other hand, Mehmet Bey's conduct caused a number of difficulties. He violated the law in public by sending his ferrymen to intimidate customers and force them, at higher rates, to use his ferry boats. According to one witness, that situation had been allowed to go on for about a year before the first complaint was filed. Although the livelihood of the other ferrymen was jeopardized by it, the *bey*'s peace was not disturbed by any of them. It went without saying that *bey*s had privileges and were allowed to break the law to a certain limit.

For it was precisely that limit which Mehmet Bey exceeded. The summary investigation by the port authorities of the first complaint filed against his men, and the punishment meted out to Ibrāhīm, signaled to the *bey* that he had in fact reached that limit. Failing to recognize the message – a socio-culturally coded one – Mehmet took the punitive action of a vigilante, crossing the point of confrontation with the government. He still believed that he could get away with it, if the case was passed on to the Council of Justice, where, presumably, he had powerful contacts. When his request was refused, he was given yet another hint as to the limits of his power and immunity. For throughout, as we must note, Mehmet Bey denied having committed the offenses attributed to him. He, too, realized full well that no *bey* could *legally* commit such acts. All he was doing from that point on was to negotiate a way out of the quandary. That is, to receive a symbolic statement that would pronounce his conduct acceptable by allowing him to go unpunished.

A less severe case took place in March 1852 at the sweet-sellers' market in Cairo.[33] One of the Finance Ministry officials, Abdülkerim Efendi, entered into an argument with one of the dried-fruit dealers. He said that the price he had been asked to pay for raisins was higher than the official price. As explained in the testimony of the head of the dried-fruit and sweet-sellers' guild, prices were then determined by the heads of guilds and recorded by the police. Passing by, the head of the guild, named Ḥamūda, joined the argument that flared up between the *efendi* and the shopkeeper. Shaykh Ḥamūda backed the dealer and suggested that the *efendi* should go to the police to check the price. when Abdülkerin asked Ḥamūda to accompany him to the police, Ḥamūda refused. If he wanted him to go to the police, said Ḥamūda, the *efendi* should produce an official summons from the police, otherwise he would not go. There are conflicting versions as to who hit whom first, but a policeman was soon dispatched from the station to bring Ḥamūda in for questioning.

The point to be noticed here is the nature of the confrontation between the Turkish-speaking, middle-level member of the elite and the Arabic-speaking Egyptian head of guild. The *efendi* was not trying to bargain in the market, which would have been quite acceptable. Rather, he was trying to point out that fraudulent trading was going on there. When he persisted in his accusations despite the fact that the guild head backed the dealer, he was in fact implying that the *shaykh* was guilty of complicity in that fraud. Later, at the police station, he further claimed that the inaccuracy of weights in that market had been well known for some time. Throughout, Shaykh Ḥamūda did not cringe before the *efendi*, though he might have been expected to. He was aware that Abdülkerim – elevated and privileged though he was – could not arbitrarily drag him to the police station. For that, an official summons was required. So he refused to comply with the *efendi*'s demand, at which, according to Ḥamūda, the latter hit him.

If indeed Abdülkerim Efendi struck Shaykh Ḥamūda first, which is much more likely, he must have assumed that this was acceptable behavior. He probably thought, as did Mehmet Bey in the case cited above, that he would get away with it when the matter reached the police. But here again, as with Mehmet Bey, he dared not admit that he had actually hit Ḥamūda first. Rather, he maintained that it was Ḥamūda who in fact assaulted him. Since nobody claimed that abusive language had been used as a prelude to the brawl, it is safe to assume that Ḥamūda's version was the more credible one. Abdülkerim was certainly testing the limits of privilege when he hit Ḥamūda, for Ḥamūda too had a semi-official status, being the *shaykh* of the dried-fruit-sellers' guild. It was probably acceptable for the *efendi* to strike the dealer, or hit him with a walking cane, to assert authority. But it was a violation of that unwritten social and cultural code to cause severe injuries by unlawful beating, as Mehmet Bey did to the ferrymen, or to hit men and women who were aware of their "rights" and willing to assert them, as did Abdülkerim to Ḥamūda.

That such were indeed the limits of elite privilege is attested also by the dispute which erupted in August 1853 between Salih Bey and Shaykh Salīm.[31] Salih Bey received a house in Cairo from Ömer Bey, the agent of the household of Zeynep Hanîm, daughter of Mehmet Ali Paşa and wife of Yusuf Kâmil Paşa. He had lived in the house for four years, and then moved to his country estate. When he returned to Cairo after some time, he discovered that the house was occupied by Shaykh Salīm. Inquiring around, he found Salīm at the shop of a certain tailor, and a heated argument flared up between them in the presence of a few witnesses. Salih reportedly cursed Salīm, calling him, among other things, "you pimp, you Jew, you foreigner." He then assaulted the *shaykh* with a wooden club, but when he tried to hit him with a chair, he was stopped by the witnesses. Shaykh Salīm complained to the police and an investigation of the incident, quite aside from the property dispute, took place.

During the investigation, Salih Bey, who was addressed with great deference by the officials, admitted that he had hit the *shaykh*. At that point, the investigator asked him why he did that, explaining very politely that if he had a legitimate complaint, he should have come to the authorities, for "it is the government that restores one's rights." Salih Bey apologized and said that he would have done so, had he known that this was the procedure in such cases. Later on, Shaykh Salīm told the police that at the end of the investigation, Salih Bey said to him that, had he known Salīm would complain to the police, he would have killed him with his gun. Salih denied that, but the police once again reminded him that he should not take the law into his own hands, since these matters were for the government to decide, not for individuals. Thus, again, we enter the twilight zone of elite privilege.

There are two levels of discourse in this case. One is the official, in which Salih Bey – unlike Mehmet Bey and Abdülkerim Efendi in the previous cases – admitted that he had hit Salīm, apologized to the police, and was verbally rebuked. Clearly, when avowed and overt violations occurred, no immunity could be granted. The other level is the unavowed one, that in which Salih expressed his regret for not having killed Salīm. Because he denied the allegation, he was not punished for it, as he might have been otherwise. He was only reminded, once again, of the limits of his privilege. Incidentally, even if Salih had actually said what was imputed to him, it was probably an empty threat. It seems more likely that had he known that Salīm would complain to the police, he would not have attacked him in the first place. In this case, as in the previous one, the *shaykh* made things difficult for both *bey* and police by asserting his declared legal right for protection against arbitrary use of force. This was, of course, less likely to come from people with no social standing in the community at all. The conduct of both *shaykh*s indicates that among the more assertive members of non-elite groups, there was sufficient confidence in the willingness of the authorities to impose the limits of privilege on members of the elite.

However, the police were not infrequently faced with attempts to obstruct such intentions. In cases involving the testing of privilege boundaries, elite members were not the most cooperative. If they could, *paşa*s, *bey*s, and *efendi*s preferred not to appear before the police in person, but rather to correspond with the official in charge of the investigation. At times they tried to prevent members of their household from giving testimony that might be damaging. At other times, efforts were made to reach "out of court" settlements, in which pressure was used to accept compensation and have the case closed to avoid embarrassment and possible punishment. The Council of Justice and police records are peppered with evidence of repeated requests to appear for investigation or to send witnesses needed for the completion of inquiries. But perhaps the saddest of all, are the cases of self-denial of basic rights among the powerless when confronted with the powerful.

Such cases fall into a number of categories. First in numbers come those for whom there can be no record. That is, all those instances in which people were abused and beaten by *paşas*, *beys*, *efendis*, or their men, but dared not report the offense to the police. These countless individuals either did not know better and believed that such was the law of the land, or feared worse consequences if they did complain. Such men and women had little confidence in the justice of the viceroys. Too weak to draw the line, they were the silent victims of social inequality. However, there is sufficient evidence to believe that such cases did not include murders. And there is also reason to argue that, for the most part, severe beating causing noticeable bodily injury did not go unreported nor passed without punishment. If medical attention was required, and certainly when the casualty had to be hospitalized, the authorities were usually notified and an investigation followed in due course.

The second category of self-imposed injustice can be gleaned from the grey area of accidents, especially those causing death or severe handicap. The difficulty was in establishing negligence, which was punishable by criminal law. The blood relatives of the victim had a certain role to play in the litigation, and if favorably disposed, could affect the outcome of both investigation and trial. In a number of cases examined, a pattern emerged whereby elite members tried to influence relatives of their lower strata victims to settle out of court. Such situations were often prone to illegal pressures and intimidation. The accident in which a woman was killed by a speeding carriage in Cairo has already been mentioned (see pp. 167–8 above). In that case, a settlement was reached between the household of Mehmet Ali Bey and four of the blood relatives, who renounced all claims for court-determined compensations. It was hoped – in that case in vain – that the settlement would free the negligent party from liability. In all likelihood it was purchased with money and intimidation.

On 23 April 1851, in Old Cairo, three porters were carrying a large wooden beam into the garden of the *kethüdâ paşa*, or deputy governor-general, one of the most powerful men in the Egyptian administration.[35] The beam was caught in the gate and fell off their backs. Falling down, the beam hit a twelve-year-old boy, Ibrāhīm, breaking his head and back. He died the following day. The boy's father, a marble carver in a Cairene workshop, was immediately fetched from work to examine the scene of the accident. In no time he was persuaded that the tragedy was unintentional, and that negligence was not involved. The boy's mother soon concurred in her husband's view. Thus, the way was cleared for the police physician to sign the necessary certificate confirming that the boy died as a result of an accident. It is difficult to imagine that the meeting between the clients and agents of such a powerful man as the *kethüdâ* and the poor parents of the victim was a meeting of equals. Even if the parents thought otherwise, they had little choice but to absolve the porters of any responsibility. They may have received some money or offered patronage in return for their cooperation. And, of course, the porters may well have been neither negligent nor careless. But the fact that blood relatives had any role to play in such cases exposed them to pressure, and often compromised their position.

The keynote to the actual nature of elite/non-elite relations during much of the nineteenth century was struck by the viceroys of Egypt themselves. Indeed, it was they who set the limits of privilege in Egyptian society as a whole. Personal example was important, but not less significant was the control the viceroy had over the elite. The less control the elite felt, the more likely it was to extend the privileges it enjoyed. As one of the instruments of power, the police were an effective tool in the hands of determined viceroys, whose views and policies they implemented. Under weak viceroys, the police merely applied the socio-cultural code, with all its biases unrestrained. In the reign of Abbas, the police were directly answerable to the Paşa and less susceptible to elite pressures. The limits of privilege in his time were trimmed, and the lower strata had easier recourse to justice. The years of Sait returned a broad smile to the faces of many *paşas* and *beys* and, concomitantly, witnessed the rise of privilege and elite immunity.

Not long after his accession, on 27 July 1849, Abbas issued an order to all provincial governors regarding criminal procedure. It enjoined the governors to follow the law with fairness and give justice to all. It made clear that the personal wish of the viceroy was to grant each person his or her rights and give each offender his or her punishment. Governors were told to be present when complaints were recorded in police registers and to recommend a penalty when forwarding reports to the Council of Justice. This was not an empty declaration of intent, but a serious attempt to regulate the system of justice in the country, especially outside the large cities, where opportunities to abuse power and privilege were greater. It was followed by recurrent, specific guidelines for the administration, the Council of Justice, and the police.[36] The results of that sustained policy can be felt in the proceedings of an interesting and complicated case which reached the high court in April 1854.

To simplify the story, we should note only that Selim Ağa and Ṣāliḥ Efendi had a long-drawn-out dispute over an unpaid debt, which resulted from a deal in livestock.[37] A third person was also involved, Ali Vehbi Efendi, a scribe at the viceregal Privy Purse. Ali Vehbi was the brother of Selim, who owed a large amount of money to Ṣāliḥ. One of the attempts to settle the debt ended in a fight, and there were, of course, conflicting versions as to who beat whom and even where. Afterwards, Ṣāliḥ went to the police and filed a complaint against Selim, but refrained from accusing Ali Vehbi of any offense, although he alleged that he had been beaten in Ali Vehbi's house. The reason for not including Ali Vehbi in the complaint against his brother was, Ṣāliḥ said, that his transgression was of a different kind. It was, he added, illicit intercession, and he intended to petition the viceroy himself in this matter. Furthermore, Ṣāliḥ objected to Ali Vehbi's presence at the police station, there being no complaint against him, but against his brother Selim alone. This was, he charged, yet another example of Ali Vehbi's interference in a matter of no direct concern to him.

Ṣāliḥ Efendi defined Ali Vehbi's interference in the case as "perfidy and protectionism" and stated that the viceroy explicitly prohibited such practices. He further said that the Paşa was personally opposed to protectionism since "we are all [equally] his subjects, and his [concept of] justice prescribes that *the high and the low are alike* [in the eyes of the law]."[38] Ṣāliḥ had the same concern for equality before the law when he demanded that the case be transferred to the *kadi* court. At first he claimed that the question of remission of debt (*ibrā'*) should be decided by the *kadi* according to Islamic law, not by the police or the Council of Justice, which was an administrative court. This was a classical example of the conflict between Islamic and administrative law, between *Sharīᶜa* and *Siyāsa*. However, the police official conducting the investigation stressed that the police protected the rights of all people just as well as the *kadi*. It was then that Ṣāliḥ stated his belief that at the court of the *kadi*, Ali Vehbi would not receive preferential treatment.

This insistence on equality before the court stemmed from a deep conviction that "protectionism" and patronage networks could and did obstruct justice. However, it also reflects the feeling that if one stood firmly on one's rights, he or she could receive justice. In this case, as in others, the disadvantaged party, Ṣāliḥ Efendi, invoked the name and known policy of Abbas Paşa. He did that hoping to countermand what he believed to be the propensity of the police to favor the well-connected Ali Vehbi Efendi. This is echoed in his angry exclamation at Ali Vehbi, which he later denied but witnesses confirmed: "You are also a protégé of the House of Abbas, and you, you think that you scare me with [the power of] that House. But I have chucked heads in this government [before], and God willing, I shall chuck your head too!"[39] Thus, it is clear that patronage was still very much a social fact in mid-century Egypt. Nonetheless, it was also clear that one could protest when legitimate patronage turned into protectionism. It was acceptable to be a protégé of the House of Abbas (*mansūb al-ᶜAbbāsiyya*), and benefit by it in many ways. But in the reign of Abbas, to use that in order to obstruct justice already scratched the limit of privilege.

The social divide at the periphery

Whereas the core of the elite was clearly marked from the rest of society, we could reasonably expect to find that distinctions at the periphery were not as sharp. However, although we can certainly say that there was a graded elite/non-elite social continuum in mid-century Egypt, real distinctions were also made at the margins, where fine social lines were drawn. A number of examples will serve to put things in focus. At the beginning of July 1849, the Council of Justice dealt with a case of insubordination referred by the Military Council.[40] A soldier misbehaved towards a captain, and a second-lieutenant was ordered to put him under arrest. As the lieutenant was accompanying the soldier to the place of detention, the latter tried to convince the former not to give testimony against him. The argument he used was that since both men were Arab and, therefore, different from Turks, they should not act against each other. When the lieutenant heard these words, he hit the soldier and further reported the incident to his superiors. The Military Council recommended that the soldier be sentenced to one year hard labor, and that the lieutenant be restricted to quarters for five days. The Council of Justice accepted the recommendation regarding the soldier, but decided that no penalty should be imposed on the officer. Though we have no further details regarding this case, it is still possible to draw some conclusions from what we do have.

The officers corps was made up mostly of elite members, though there were by mid-century growing numbers of non-elite members in junior ranks up to captain (*yüzbaşī*). The rank-and-file were by and large recruited from among non-elite groups, mostly from among the rural population. Our case is really the story of those junior officers, born and bred in the Egyptian countryside, who were at the lower end of the Ottoman-Egyptian elite. As the century wore on, these men were allowed to rise to the rank of colonel. The tensions that existed between them and the other and more senior officers constituted one of the main factors behind the events of the 1880s that led to the ᶜUrābī Revolt.[41] At mid-century, however, they were still making their first steps up the steep ladder towards becoming full-fledged members of the Ottoman-Egyptian elite. The soldier rightly detected the existing tension of roles and statuses in his lieutenant's heart. Harping on sentiments of local solidarity, he hoped to extricate himself from what he knew only too well was awaiting him at court. By misjudging the loyalties of his superior, by misreading the transformation which the lieutenant was undergoing, he in fact worsened his lot.

We must not underestimate the weight of our lieutenant's reaction in this case. He did not merely ignore the soldier's attempt to compromise him, which he easily could have done. He not only hit the man, but actually reported the instance to his superiors, thereby exposing the soldier to harsher punishment and inviting allegations that his own behavior facilitated that breach of military ethics. In fact, if the lieutenant was hoping to be rewarded for his "betrayal" of his countryman, he was very much in the wrong. For, the superior officers must have regarded his role unfavorably, as they convinced the military authorities to recommend some sort of punishment for him too. The use of force by officers against disobedient soldiers was common enough not to be the cause of punishment recommended for our lieutenant. Rather, it seems more likely that it was believed he may not have been sufficiently firm in the situation that developed between him and the recalcitrant soldier.

Whatever the fault that was attributed to the lieutenant, it is significant that the Council of Justice cleared him of all charges. In the centralized Egyptian state, the council was one of the main "interpreters" and enforcers of elite values. In its capacity as conciliar body, law-drafting agency, major channel of administrative power, and high court, the Council of Justice was the defender of elite culture, a sort of "Keeper of the Seal" in socio-cultural terms. The council was often concerned with the interpretation of the "spirit of the law," namely the guidelines provided by Egypt's viceroys. It was less bound by military considerations and saw the picture as a whole. Generally speaking, the council accepted the recommendations put to it by the various government bureaus. This was especially so in criminal cases, such as the one we have been discussing. Therefore, the council's decision to acquit our lieutenant was in fact a statement. By extension, it signaled to native officers that their military status should override their other group affiliations. This was a message of a self-confident center, of a power-elite not yet perturbed by the gradual rise of a local challenge. At mid-century, the Ottoman-Egyptian elite was still open to a controlled inclusion of rural Egyptians in the lower echelons of its officers corps. Although the period lies outside the scope of this work, we ought to note that all this was to change during the last third of the nineteenth century.

In another case, we read about a man named Salīm Sirrī, who retired from the army as a first lieutenant. In October 1853, he was mentioned as Shaykh al-Ḥāra in one of Cairo's neighborhoods. It was then that Salīm came to the police and filed a complaint against a man to whom, according to his testimony, he had lent a certain amount of money.[42] The two men used to frequent the same bar near Azbakiyya, but the last time they went there, things went very wrong. Salīm's friend had some *ᶜaraq* (Turkish *rakī*), and was certainly in no mood to be reminded of his debt to Salīm. When the latter, however, did mention the repayment of the debt, the debtor pulled out a knife, cursed Salīm, and assaulted him. He then escaped and was only brought in the following day. When we sort out the testimonies of eye witnesses, it appears that the offender cursed not only Salīm but the army, the police, and the government. There are two significant points in this case. The first is that although Salīm was no longer a junior officer in the army, in the eyes of his drinking-mate he was still a member of the military (*ᶜaskarī jihādī*). That is, he was very much identified with the government, and though a native Egyptian like his attacker, he did not belong to the Egyptian in-group; he was not "us," but "them."

It is reasonable to assume that Salīm was classed in that category because he had been an officer, rather than because he had been in the army as such. Obviously, the fact that he also held a junior administrative position as Shaykh al-Ḥāra helped to identify him with the governing rather than the governed.

Under the liberating influence of alcohol, a deep sense of alienation between the two came out. Though they inhabited the rock bottom of the Ottoman-Egyptian elite, men in Salīm's position were already once removed from the rest of their own people. According to one of the witnesses, the offender shouted at Salīm: "No one will ever boss me around! Shit on you and on the police!" (in colloquial Egyptian Arabic: *lam aḥad yaḥkum ʿalayya qaṭṭu, kharā fīk ū-fī 'ḍ-Ḍabṭiyya*). Not surprisingly, when interrogated, the man denied the accusation, but was nonetheless sentenced to a term of hard labor.

In both cases, that of the lieutenant and that of Salīm, we were not actually dealing with core Ottoman-Egyptians. Rather, we were touching the twilight zone which lay not only beyond that core, but at the very margin of the elite. That is, the ill-defined boundary which set those individuals apart from the bulk of their kith and kin. Even in those extended margins of the elite, people were fully aware of the divide. Though differences in material conditions were less apparent, and no language or culture barriers existed, important status distinctions were still made. Much more so at the core, where the divide covered all spheres of human activity. It consisted in differences of language and etiquette, of food, clothing, living conditions, inhabited spaces. The divide was not merely a representation of differences, but much more a manifestation of inequalities. It charted the limits of opportunity, the boundaries of hope, the very access to economic, political, and intellectual resources.

Although the elite and the lower strata of society were stratified within themselves and, in addition, borderlines at the margin were blurred, a socio-cultural divide was a fact of life in mid-nineteenth-century Egypt. Higher at the core, lower at the periphery, it was nonetheless very much there. In part, at least, the divide marked the "squeezing" line of the state. Whether in rural or urban Egypt, those who did not belong to the Ottoman-Egyptian elite were squeezed to a far greater extent than members of the elite. Although more limited in coping with central and local pressure, they nevertheless found effective ways to resist authority.

8 The rural squeeze – pressure and resistance in the countryside

Conscription

Mehmet Ali's decision to replace the mercenary army which he had inherited by a conscript army put an enormous burden on the lower strata of Egyptian society. It meant that the *fallāḥīn* and the urban poor had to furnish the bulk of the enlisted men and the lower ranks of the officer corps. With the sizable force that the viceroy required for his military operations, conscription affected the core of rural Egypt and had direct consequences for agriculture and the economy. It touched every village and hurt almost every family. Until then, military service was something other people did, not members of the ingroup. Men in uniform enjoyed certain rights which the rest of the population learned to accept, and the social barrier between them and those without uniforms appeared to the latter insurmountable. As the conscript army was being recruited – forcibly and with much pain – the realities of military life became known.

The service was long, hard, faraway. Not infrequently, it ended in death, and those who did return had little good to say about the army. In addition, economic and social hardships were to be endured by those who remained behind.[1] Consequently, people did whatever they possibly could to evade the draft. From self-maiming to absconding, from bribing to pleading, from violence in some cases to various tricks, the weak and poor stretched their resourcefulness to the limit in order to keep away from Mehmet Ali's new and glorious army. For its part, the government did all it could to impose its will on a recalcitrant population. Quotas were imposed on governors, who broke them down by villages, inflicting heavy penalties on village headmen who lagged behind. Recruiting officers and cavalry units were deployed in the countryside to catch evaders. As the outcome proved, the battle was not waged between equals and the new army marched on to victory and fame.

The end of the Syrian Wars, the limit put on the size of the Egyptian army, and the advent of peace in the 1840s eased the burden on the lower strata of society. Although still well in excess of the figures imposed by the Edict of 1841, the army was reduced to about a quarter of its maximal size, numbering around

100,000 men throughout the reign of Abbas and during most of Sait's reign. As the middle decades remained on the whole peaceful, general conscription drives became rare, and the conditions of service improved. For most of the period, Egyptian soldiers did not leave Egypt, and many were engaged in civilian projects rather than fighting an enemy or policing occupied territories. One major exception was the Crimean War, which in the mid 1850s brought back the horrors of conscription to the Nile Valley. Another was the unpopular service in the Sudan, where the viceroys maintained a large force to keep the peace.

Such improvements notwithstanding, the army remained unattractive for the lower strata of Egyptian society. However, for the sons of village *shaykhs*, or what is sometimes called rural notability, a limited, though significant, mobility into junior officer ranks became increasingly possible. For the rest, low pay and poor conditions meant marginalization in their own society. Until the late 1840s, soldiers were forbidden to marry, which increased the peculiarity of their position and further cut them off from the rest of society. Only in November 1848, deserving individuals were given permission to get married. Obedient, diligent, and clean soldiers could obtain such permission from their commanding officers. It was hoped that this would serve as an incentive to others, who would seek to improve their performance so that they could marry too.[2]

The original proscription of marriage was intended as a means of attaching the soldier to the service by overriding all competing commitments. Having a wife, and often children, it was thought, propelled the soldier towards desertion, which not infrequently arose from his family falling into economic difficulty. The change of policy must have resulted, at least partially, from the realization that the prohibition was not entirely effective. First, we have to assume that not a few soldiers had already been married when recruited. Second, even after the decision to allow marriage on a selective basis, soldiers were getting married without obtaining proper consent. In April 1853, for example, a second-lieutenant married without permission, through the mediation of another second-lieutenant.[3] As the man could not provide for his wife, he divorced her. In the process, he was also accused of falsification of documents. The Council of Justice dismissed him from the service, deprived him of his pay and savings, and distributed the money among his divorcee and creditors. His superior officers, a colonel and a major, were incarcerated for five days and fined; the other second-lieutenant, the match-maker, was also punished.

In principle, the method of recruitment introduced by Mehmet Ali remained the same during the reigns of Abbas and Sait. All able-bodied males between the ages of eighteen and twenty-two were subject to conscription. After quotas had been imposed on villages, men were chosen by a system of lot-casting (*qurʿa*). More men than actually required were assembled, and those not exempted for one of the stipulated reasons were mobilized. Bedouins, non-Muslims until 1858, students, and economic hardship cases from 1863 onward, were exempt from military service. It was also possible to avoid conscription either by paying a specified amount of money, or by providing a black slave as substitute. Thus, those who had the means could buy their way out of the service, but the vast majority, the lower strata, could not. At mid-century, the urban population in the major cities was more fortunate than the peasantry.

Early in December 1848, shortly after his accession to power, Abbas Paşa issued an order to release from the army all former residents of Cairo enlisted by Ibrahim. Recruitment of these people, numbering 400 in all, the viceroy argued, impeded commercial and industrial activity in the city and was detrimental to progress. This was a clear departure from Mehmet Ali's policy, which did not spare the urban population. In 1863, another order was issued to this effect, this time by Ismail Paşa. Exemption from conscription, and release of those already serving applied not only to the city of Cairo, but also to its suburbs of Būlāq and Old Cairo (Miṣr al-Qadīma). In obvious recognition of the rising importance of Alexandria at mid-century, its population was also included in Ismail's orders. Here, the exemption granted to the inhabitants of Istanbul served as the model for the major Egyptian cities.[4] It was an added incentive for migration from village to town.

In spite of the peace that prevailed in Egypt during much of the 1840s and 1850s, the records are peppered with incidents related to the draft. Because of the coercive nature of conscription and the obstinate resistance to it, the process was not infrequently attended by violence. In July 1849, it was reported that an accident occurred in the district of Ṭahṭa as the army was rounding up candidates for military service. When a large crowd of men was squeezed together, a gun fired accidentally, and one of the draftees was killed. In the same year, also in Upper Egypt, a quota of recruits was imposed on villages of the district of Sōhāg (Sūhāj). As often happened, the *fallāḥīn* fled to the mountains, and the village head, his son, and some of their men went after them. When the team approached the hiding place, one of the draft dodgers fired at them, killing one of the searchers and wounding the *shaykh*'s son.[5]

Indeed, the draft system placed a great deal of power in the hands of village heads, who could affect the selection process directly. But it also made them responsible in the eyes of the central government for any irregularities or disorder connected with such duties. A few examples may illustrate the point. In April 1854, during another conscription drive in Upper Egypt, new quotas were imposed on village heads.[6] As these were being filled, one of the lists remained short by one man. Lot-casting was then applied to provide the missing person, but as tensions rose and emotions ran high, a skirmish erupted. Shots were fired and public order was disrupted. The investigation concluded that the village *shaykh* was at fault for not complying with the law against possession of firearms. He was sent to prison for six months, and the governor of the province was ordered to collect all weapons held by the *fallāḥīn*.

In June 1849, a *fallāḥ* from a village in the district of Giza, not far from Cairo, complained to the authorities that he had been beaten and abused by his village *shaykh*. The *shaykh*, alleged the *fallāḥ*, had selected him for military service, but then asked for a hefty bribe, 250 *kuruş*, in order to have him released. The *fallāḥ* decided not to pay, but believing that the *shaykh* had caused the death of two persons in the past, decided to run away. After a reconciliation between the two, the *fallāḥ* returned to the village, only to find the agreement breached and to receive a severe beating from the *shaykh*. The Council of Justice sent both men to prison, the *fallāḥ* for six years, and the *shaykh* for three.[7] Both government and villagers assumed that dishonesty was common in the conscription process, though the authorities tried, as much as they could, to restrain the venality of village heads.

A few years later, the Council of Justice dealt with another case from the same district.[8] A village headman was accused of favoritism towards five members of his household. It was alleged that he had made it possible for his son, his servant, and three other relatives to evade the draft. The investigation revealed that the village quota for the draft in question was three men. The *shaykh*'s son drew the number four, thus falling out of the conscripted group. The servant drew the number three, but as he had no parents, he was excused. The three relatives of the *shaykh* were exempted from service by the government physician. One was too old and dejected, another was old and afflicted with scrofulosis, and the third had syphilis and required seven to eight months of treatment to be cured. Consequently, the council declared that the allegation against the village head was without foundation.

Talking in 1856 to friends of the late Abbas Paşa, Senior heard the following story about Sait's cruelty:

> What do you think of the execution of the two men in Tantah? The story that is told is bad enough, but the truth is worse. Their crime was this: One was the Sheykh of a village which I know well, near Tantah. Like the other Sheykhs, he was required to send a son to the army. He persuaded one of his neighbors to send a son in the place of his own. The young man was imprudent enough to let this out – Said hanged both fathers.

Indeed, it was in the early part of Sait's reign that an order was issued to draft sons of village *shaykh*s in order to upgrade the quality of the army. In addition, attempts were made to limit the service to one year, in principle, and conscription drives were carried out on an annual basis.[9]

The destitution of the peasantry and the urban poor played into the hands of the *shaykh*s, giving them a much needed leeway in the application of conscription policies. In the middle years of the nineteenth century, it was still reported that sheer necessity drove the poor to offer their sons to village headmen in return for money. The son of a poor family thus obtained would replace the son of a better-off family, eager to purchase the boy's freedom from military service.

The *shaykh* would then pocket the difference between what he received from the latter and what he gave to the former. Lane described the practice during the reign of Mehmet Ali Paşa as "selling" children, though the term more frequently used for it later was "hiring out" (the Arabic verb *akrā*). It seems to have been the result of extreme poverty and dire need, and – unlike the sale of children into slavery among the Circassians – not a socially acceptable phenomenon.[10]

Incidents of evasion and venality, such as those described above, were common in the middle years of the nineteenth century. Although the burden of conscription was significantly reduced, its harsh effects, and certainly the resistance to it, continued to be a source of friction between the government and the large population subject to the draft. The Crimean War and the decision to send an Egyptian expeditionary force to assist the sultan brought back bitter memories from the reign of Mehmet Ali and disrupted the viceroy's peace in the Nile Valley. Travel accounts written in that period are replete with descriptions of the forced draft, which to most Europeans represented one of the worst vices of life in Egypt.[11] During conscription, travellers relate, chained recruits were being marched or transported by boat from their villages to the training camps. They also tell of the mass flight to the mountains to escape the recruiters.

St. John, Bromfield, and Gadsby, among many others, report the effects of conscription during the 1850s. Whole towns were abandoned by the able-bodied male population, shops were closed, streets were deserted. "When I was on the top of the great peak . . . that overlooks the plain of Thebes," wrote St. John,

> a false alarm was raised at Gournou; and presently numerous long lines of men appeared hastening up the slopes, and plunging into the ravines – all bound for the tombs. When they reached their place of safety – from which they could always retreat farther into the desert, if necessary – they began rolling large stones down the slopes, to show that they were ready to defend themselves; and throughout the day occasionally we heard the crashing sound of these projectiles, as they jumped from crag to crag towards the plain. I believe in no instance did the recruiters venture a pursuit, being content to keep watch at the foot of the hills, and to catch any one whom starvation or weariness induced to descend.[12]

Some draft evaders sought refuge on river boats hoisting European flags and carrying European travelers. Bromfield and his party harbored four fugitives of this kind. "Once on board a boat under a consular flag," he wrote,

> the government cannot touch them; they are under the protection of that flag *pro tempore*, and are considered as servants in the pay and employ of the owner or traveller. These poor people work their passage to the capital by taking the oars with the rest of the men; they bring their own privisions (a little d'hourah merely), and all we give them is lodging on deck with our own people.[13]

Others, who were not so lucky, resorted to self-maiming. Although less pervasive, this was still practiced in the period under consideration.

To reduce the practice of blinding of one eye and cutting fingers, which were the most common forms of self-maiming in Egypt – intended to hamper the ability to fire a musket – Mehmet Ali and his successors imposed heavy penalties on offenders. They also enlisted such men and placed them in special non-combat units. Still, the practice was hard to defeat. It is not surprising to read in Maxime Du Camp's account of his travels with Flaubert, that "all our men [crew of the boat] except Rais Ibrahim, Bury and Aouadallah, had their right forefinger cut off to avoid being taken for military service." Sait authorized the conscription of men with slight leucoma in their left eye, or with a thumb, toe, or index finger missing, but demanded that men with fresh injuries of this kind be duly punished first. When Ismail Paşa came to power in 1863, he issued an order that all men who had been maimed to avoid the service would be drafted and sent to the railway works. It would appear that what perpetuated self-maiming was preference for non-combat duty, since it no longer ensured complete freedom from military service.[14]

Once in the army, no few soldiers tried to run away. Sarūjī asserts that men absconded from the service for a number of reasons: some committed an offense and feared retribution; some decided not to return to camp at the end of a home leave; and others simply could not hold out after long and arduous years of service. The number of deserters recorded in 1865 reached 1,048, while in 1871 it was as high as 2,071. The government tried to tackle these alarming proportions by strong deterring measures. Vigilant searches were launched to catch deserters, and heavy penalties were imposed on those who were caught. The most severe regulations were introduced in the reign of Sait. In adition to the penalty for desertion stipulated in the military code, offenders were to be sent to serve in the Sudan, their property was to be sold, and the returns credited to the Treasury. However, these harsh measures were suspended after a while, and the money collected on sold property was returned to the owners.[15]

A more common penalty was that imposed on two soldiers who were caught and tried in April 1849. Both belonged to the artillery unit stationed at Abū Qīr on the Mediterranean coast. One received 250 lashes, the other, who had a record of disobedience, was sent to prison for six months. Six months of hard labor became the standard penalty for deserters in the early 1860s. Convicts were also deprived of their pay, and the period spent in prison was added to the required term of military service. At the same time, the authorities felt that in order to discourage potential deserters, they had to deter would-be accomplices. Those harboring fugitives were made liable, as were local officials, if they failed to detect deserters in their area of jurisdiction. In an arbitrary measure during the early 1870s, deserters were to be replaced by their immediate relatives, regardless of culpability.[16]

In that way, the extended family was made responsible for the deserter's action. This notion was based on the likelihood, though not the certainty, that a runaway soldier would not survive long without a support system. In seeking to provide for himself, such a man was liable to raise enough suspicion in an alien environment, so that local authorities would become aware of his presence. Only a familiar environment could harbor such a person without it becoming known to the authorities. A different, albeit conceptually akin, approach was tried in the reign of Abbas. Then, it was the local tax-farmer (Turkish *müteahhit*, Arabic *mutaᶜahhid*) who was made responsible for deserters residing on his estate. The tax-farmer was informed of a desertion and given a number of months to search and find the culprit. If he failed to find him, the tax-farmer had to provide a substitute.

A clear precedent was set in the case of Sayyid ᶜAbd as-Salām, who had deserted from his infantry regiment early in 1849.[17] The tax-farmer of the area in which he had lived, a certain Cafer Bey, was given two months to find him. As he could not find the man by the end of the said term, he was ordered to supply another one in his place. Cafer Bey refused to do so and asked for six more months to search. He also notified the authorities that, unless ordered by the viceroy, he would not supply a substitute if his efforts still yielded no result by the end of the sought extension. The Council of Justice ordered Cafer Bey to supply a replacement for Sayyid ᶜAbd as-Salām immediately, thereby obligating all other tax-farmers to comply with such instructions in the future. By putting the onus on the stronger and more resourceful element on the scene, i.e. the tax-farmer, rather than on the deserter's family, Abbas's policy was more effective and eventually more humane than Ismail's.

At mid-century, the government began to conscript Copts regularly. The process was not without difficulties, since it was customary in the Ottoman Empire not to draft non-Muslims, and the Copts were reluctant to pay the price for what Europeans deemed as emancipation. St. John writes about the disaffection of the Coptic population in Upper Egypt when they were subjected to conscription in 1850–1. There is evidence that Copts were drafted nonetheless, and that they served in regular units side by side with Muslims. Because the issue was considered "Christian," European consuls saw in it an opportunity for intervention. In August 1853, a British consul reported that the Copts had been withdrawn from their units and placed as a contingent – numbering 2,400 in all – to work on the construction of the Alexandria–Cairo railway. However, this may have been a temporary measure. Responding to a query from the governor of Asyūṭ in 1858, Sait Paşa permitted the conscription of Christians, as a matter of routine, it seems.[18]

To sum up, conscription and war were a great burden on the lower strata during the reign of Mehmet Ali Paşa. In fact, this factor is estimated to have contributed significantly to the low rate of population growth in the first half of the nineteenth century. In addition to those who got killed in battle and died of war-time diseases, the loss in birth rate was also great, as the young men needed to maintain it were away from home for long periods of time. According to Justin McCarthy's figures, the population in Egypt grew during the middle decades at a rate 2.6 times that of the previous period. Considering that there were two major outbreaks of cholera in the 1850s, which claimed the lives of close to 150,000 people, the effect of the post 1841 peace on population growth is even more remarkable.[19] With all its vices, conscription was not the only affliction suffered by the *fallāḥīn*. The *corvée*, too, had a tremendous disruptive effect, and like the conscription, occurred in a mitigated form during the 1840s and 1850s.

The *corvée*

Corvée, or forced labor, was still common in Egypt during the middle years of the nineteenth century.[20] Contrary to a prevailing notion, forced labor was not unpaid labor. What made the *corvée* different from other kinds of labor was its involuntary nature. In addition, *corvée* was usually a large-scale operation, hence requiring elaborate organization and management. It often consisted in unskilled labor and, at least originally, was intended for public works. Classical examples of such projects are the Nile Barrages, the Maḥmūdiyya Canal and other irrigation works, the Alexandria–Suez railway, the paved roads' network, the fortification of the Mediterranean coast, and the Suez Canal. Most of these were either begun or completed during the period under consideration. The power to appropriate manpower lay with the state, and forced labor was usually allocated to projects considered necessary for the good of society. This power was delegated by the viceroy down the bureaucratic ladder, but was monitored by the central government. With time, however, forced labor came to be used also on private estates of, and construction projects for, members of the ruling family and prominent members of the Ottoman-Egyptian elite.

Unlike conscription, forced labor was imposed on the whole of the rural population. That is, not only men between the ages of eighteen and twenty-four, but men and women of all ages, including children and the old. Not infrequently, whole families were taken to forced labor, continuing to function as unbroken production units. In her book *Women in nineteenth-century Egypt*, Judith Tucker argues that "*corvée* labor could be extracted by the State precisely because the family remained more or less intact, carrying on the functions of production for subsistence, provision of shelter, care for the young, old, and sick, and social regulation."[21] Only in the early 1850s, an attempt was made to limit the population subject to forced labor. The more relaxed conditions that prevailed at mid-century made such moderate changes possible, although the *corvée* was still to survive for several decades.

As already mentioned, the *corvée* was not without cost to the beneficiary, whether the government or an individual. First, there was the cost of maintaining the workers, that is of providing food and shelter. Although the food was often of an inferior quality, it still cost something. There was also the cost of transportation from the village, at times quite remote, to the venue of work. As for wages on *corvée*, there is ample evidence that workers were paid, and though the pay was not high, it was competitive with going rates. For example, workers sent in 1849 to fortify the Mediterranean coastline were paid a monthly salary. At the same time, men and women who worked on the improvement of the Maḥmūdiyya Canal were paid 1 *kuruş* per day plus biscuit rations. A similar daily pay, from 1 to 1.25 *kuruş*, was also reported for the cotton factory at Būlāq, Cairo's main port. This was not all that bad if we consider that in the 1850s policemen and soldiers were paid from 15 *kuruş* per month for privates to 25 *kuruş* for corporals and 30 *kuruş* for sergeants.[32]

Although the wages cited above were the official ones, the workers frequently did not receive them in full. The government often tried to substitute food staples for cash payment, or simply accumulated arrears that were later paid at cut rates. Gadsby provides a vivid description of the practice at a sugar refinery, owned by Abbas Paşa, in the Middle Egyptian town of Minya:

> The officers profess to pay the men promptly, but when their time of servitude is up, there is always a considerable balance due to them. They, however, do not trouble about that being too glad to get away. Some time afterwards, the clerks, (Copts, – *Christians!*) receive the money, and then go to the poor fellows, and say, "Now, if you like, we will give you so much for your debt," being perhaps one-third. This is readily accepted; and thus are the people defrauded, while the Turkish governor and the enlightened "Christians" divide the spoil! This, I was told, is universally the case throughout Egypt. Sometimes, the people are paid in bread and sometimes in sugar, the payer always fixing the value, and keeping the balance.[23]

As we have already seen, the range of projects necessitating and permitting the use of forced labor was fairly limited, though it did expand with time. The traditional use of *corvée* in Egypt was related to the total dependency of its agriculture on the water of the Nile. Irrigation by canals required constant maintenance to prevent the blockage of water by deposits. There seems to have been little argument with the view that such seasonal labors were essential for the success of the crops. The work was hard and tedious, and the *fallāḥīn* were, understandably, unenthusiastic about it. But a strong, centralized state under Mehmet Ali Paşa ensured that they would still do the job. Contrary to most views, the viceroys of mid-century did not neglect the irrigation system. Rather, they fully recognized the damage that negligence might entail. The records mention orders to send workers to specific canals and dams as a matter of routine. They often refer in passing to persons being absent from their villages because of such projects.[24]

Negligence continued to be a grave offense and was punishable by imprisonment. In April 1853, for example, much damage to the fields was caused in two districts in the governorate of Giza. It was ascertained that a water passage in one of the canals was not properly dammed. Consequently, the river flooded the fields and destroyed the crops. In the event, action to repair the blockage was slow, and workers were not dispatched to the site immediately. The Council of Justice made the two districts liable for the cost of repairs and found the village *shaykh*s guilty of negligence. They were all sentenced to six months' hard labor. At the same time, it is true that the *scale* of canal dredging was reduced in the 1850s, thereby easing some of the burden regularly imposed on the *fallāḥīn*. Late in 1853, the government recorded a hefty loss, equivalent to more than 10,000 pounds sterling, because many canals were "cancelled out." This was the estimated value of the large quantity of biscuits which, left in government storehouses, were damaged and had to be discarded as a result of dredging projects being cancelled.[25]

Another use of forced labor was in defense projects. A good example of that is the order issued by Abbas Paşa on 31 July 1849 regarding the fortification of the Mediterranean coastline.[26] The viceroy's aim was to strengthen the coastal forts from Damietta through Abū Qīr to Alexandria. The work was to be carried out in the summer so as to be ready for winter. Adjacent governorates and artillery regiments were ordered to send 2,250 men at once, with the final target being a total workforce of 5,200. The project directors were instructed to provide food and medical care, to replace the workers every forty days, and to pay them on a monthly basis. To ensure sufficient and punctual provisioning, Abbas ordered that the workforce be supplied like an army unit. This was done out of recognition that Alexandria was crowded and expensive in summer, which might add to the usual difficulties facing the directors. Here, again, the responsibility of the government and the central organization are evident.

This is becoming less so as we move into the ill-defined use of *corvée* in agriculture. The problem here was the peculiar position of the tax-farmers, or holders of *ühde*s (Arabic *ᶜuhda*s). These members of the Ottoman-Egyptian elite were given large and medium-size estates, consisting of villages which had accumulated tax arrears. The purpose of the government was to make these men responsible for the regular flow of income to the treasury, the excess of which they could keep for themselves. They could also use the *fallāḥīn* in their estates in order to cultivate their private tracts of land, which they were assigned as part of the *ühde* benefits. That access to the labor of the *fallāḥīn* was hard to monitor and gave ample opportunity for abuse and exploitation. Gradually, holders of *ühde*s, instead of village *shaykh*s, were asked to supply men for *corvée* projects, to track down deserters from the army, and to assume responsibilities that they were not originally meant to have.

Because *ühde*s were not necessarily profitable and were often imposed on members of the elite against their will, not a few must have come to regard themselves as performing a public service when running their assigned estates. They had no qualms about using forced labor on their land. When in need of assistance, cultivators on the ruling family estates (*çiftliks*) were sent to work on *ühdes*, thereby reenforcing the notion that tax-farmers had about their job. ᶜAlī Barakāt observes that during the reign of Abbas, the government accepted responsibility for the supply of labor to large estates.[27] It was recognized that the state had a vested interest in the expansion of cultivable land, to which such labor was being supplied. In the middle years of the nineteenth century, land and agriculture became increasingly profitable, much as a result of government policy. By then, however, the *fallāḥīn* found themselves often forced to work for the tax-farmer's benefit, and his free access to their labor was hard to check.

And sometimes, none of the original public nature of the *corvée* remained, as was the case in the mid-1850s' story told by Barthélemy Saint-Hilaire.

> At one town, the name of which I forget, our boat stopped to take in coals; we were pressed for time; and our crew, being all very busy at the moment, could not land to get it on board. In a few minutes the order was given, and fifty or more men and children were set to work to carry the coal from the bank to our boat. This *corvée*, which they supposed would go unrecompensed, generally gave them little pleasure; and our chiaoux had to interfere and hasten the work. The loading of the coal however was speedily performed; and on returning from our walk half an hour afterwards, the steam was up, and we started.[28]

To round up the various types of forced labor in mid-century Egypt, we ought to mention that government factories and warehouses were also eligible to use such work. Gadsby mentions *corvée* laborers in the sugar refinery of Abbas Paşa at Minya, and in the cotton manufactories at Būlāq and Shubrā. Workers were annually sent also to the storehouses in Būlāq and other locations around Cairo. They came mostly from governorates in Upper Egypt and worked as porters. But workers in Cairo government factories were, for the most part, town people. As for the latter, it is not entirely clear whether their service was also of a temporary, though not necessarily seasonal, nature.[29] Be that as it may, resistance to the *corvée* in towns, especially in the larger cities of Cairo and Alexandria, generally differed from that in rural, distanced areas. The scope, method, and intensity of the workers' reaction to their exploitation varied according to the type of project and the laborers' perception of the government resolve to carry out the work.

Let us first dispense with the much smaller group of townsmen who worked at government manufactories. The few instances recovered indicate that the reaction of these workers was by more direct means than those employed by the vast majority of *corvée* laborers – the *fallāḥīn*. In May 1849, for example, workers at the textile factory of Kharanfish inside Cairo – not far from the palace of Abbas's youth – petitioned the viceroy because they had not been paid for some time. The Treasury claimed that there was no cash to pay them, but the Council of Justice urged the Deputy Minister to find the means, possibly through the government storehouses, i.e. by paying in kind.[30] Such direct tactics may have been better suited for dealing with the central government in Cairo, since a petition had a better chance of reaching the high authority it was addressed to. In the country, however, distance caused delays, and impediments could more easily be thrown in the way of petitions. Indirect tactics seemed perhaps more effective in that situation.

The two most common forms of *fallāḥīn* resistance to the *corvée* were evasion of orders to repair to work sites and, failing that, abscondence from the site itself. Most *corvée* work was carried out far away from one's village home, with all the hardships caused by temporary dislocation. Although attempts were made to use workers from villages near a project site, this was not always possible. Much of the workforce was required in Lower Egypt, for irrigation works, and around Cairo and Alexandria, where development and construction mostly occurred. Consequently, some shouldering of the burden was demanded from Upper Egyptian *fallāḥīn*. Such constant and draining demands on the rural population in general soon yielded quiet but obstinate resistance. It was more intense when the *corvée* was carried out away from home, but was essentially directed against inadequate pay and poor conditions. Even in its extreme form, however, protest against the *corvée* never reached the scale or intensity of the reaction against the draft.

The case of the Maḥmūdiyya Canal project may serve to illustrate this point.[31] On 8 March 1849, orders were issued for the widening and deepening of the Maḥmūdiyya to enable the passage of steamers. The total workforce was to consist of 30,384 workers. The quotas were allocated to seven Lower Egyptian governorates. Each had to supply from 2,072 workers (Giza) to 7,285 workers (Gharbiyya). Government engineers were put in charge of the men and women and were empowered to release them when the work was completed. However, six months later, the project was bogged down for manpower shortages. First, the governorates failed to send the full number of workers required of them. Second, because of inadequate supply of food and low pay, many of the workers who did arrive ran away. It became clear that strict orders were not enough, and that other measures had to be taken, if the target was to be reached.

The immediate need of the project was put at 860 workers, and the Council of Justice devised a plan to retain the men on the site and encourage them to work well. Accordingly, to maintain discipline and prevent the workers from absconding, their village *shaykh*s were to accompany them and remain on the premise. Initial pay was to be set at 1 *kuruş* plus half an *oka* (0.624 kg) of biscuits per person per day. On top of this, a productivity bonus was to be paid to workers according to the amount of mud taken out of the canal. These instructions represented a clear recognition that *corvée* had major limitations, which could not be overcome by mere coercion. It is hard to say how effective the new approach was. Whatever had been accomplished at the time needed constant maintenance, as the orders sent out about a year later prove. Negligence caused the Maḥmūdiyya to overflow, and a new dredging operation was announced.

Such resistance to the *corvée* manifested itself in many other instances during the 1840s and 1850s, as provincial authorities and estate holders were caught between the central government and the recalcitrant *fallāḥ*. It was often the case that quotas were not filled, a reality which the government must have come to accept as a common feature of forced labor. Orders were issued and reissued, and although strict measures were taken from time to time, the government seems to have been resigned to the fact that quotas had to be set at a much higher level than required in order to receive the needed number of workers. On 8 September 1848, for example, the governor of Daqahliyya was ordered to supply 2,181 men to pick up rice in the eastern "rice villages."[32] However, only about 300 appeared, some of whom were children and had to be sent back. A month later, on 11 October, the local authorities complained about the situation, but Daqahliyya did not respond. On 19 October, the viceroy's office interfered, demanded swift action, and threatened that any damage to the crops would be charged to the governorate of Daqahliyya.

In another province, that of Gharbiyya, orders were issued in the summer of 1849, imposing on tax-farmers, including members of the ruling family, quotas for forced works within the province. Again, a little over half the quotas were actually filled. About 20,000 workers were supplied, 19,618 more were needed. Despite recurring orders to provide the rest, the *ühde* holders in question did not respond. In August of the same year, a shortage of porters occurred at government storehouses in Būlāq and the Cairo area. Porters were usually provided under *corvée* from Upper Egypt, but although instructions had been sent, none arrived that year. In an attempt to alleviate the problem, orders were sent to the nearby governorates of Giza and Qalyūbiyya to provide 400 men immediately. Here, too, pay was tied to productivity and calculated per load. The authorities must have had grounds to believe that such an incentive would make it easier to attract the required number of workers in a relatively short time.[33]

But it was not enough to get the workers to the project site; they had to be kept there doing the job. In the middle decades of the nineteenth century, abscondence of *corvée* laborers was a common phenomenon, over which the authorities often agonized. As in the case of the Maḥmūdiyya Canal cited above, it was soon recognized, under Abbas Paşa, that workers had to be paid properly if projects were ever to be completed. At issue was the form of payment. To save cash, workers were paid partly in provisions or food staples, partly in government notes, and if lucky or on a high-priority project, partly also in cash. The real value of government notes was considerably lower than their nominal value, and money-changers would cash them for one-third of the amount stated on them, and often for much less. The government had a different pay policy for every project according to its importance and urgency. There were also accounting arrangements between the Treasury, the governorates, and the tax-farmers' estates from which the laborers came.

Workers on government construction projects were paid a third of their wages in agricultural produce and two-thirds in Treasury bills. In July 1849, the terms of payment were changed with the workers' consent and "in order not to act unjustly towards them." Thenceforward they were to be paid a third in cash and two-thirds in produce. The case of those working on the construction of the viceroy's palaces at ᶜAbbāsiyya and Qaysūn was recognized as special. On Abbas's personal instructions, efforts were made to shift gradually to full cash payment. The payment was to be charged to the tax accounts of the holders of the estates whence the workers came. In the same year, the Council of Justice dealt with pay arrears accumulated by the government in its construction operations, which at the time were being conducted on a large scale. It turned out that workers had not been paid for more than six months, except for those on "urgent projects," who had been given partial payment.[34]

The Council noted that the workers were very poor and could not be expected to cope without pay. Many had run away and it would be difficult, council members observed, to bring them back by force. The Superintendent of Construction reported that he had no cash left and suggested that the arrears be paid by Treasury bills. However, the Council of Justice decided to apply to those workers the same policy adopted with regard to *corvée* workers in government factories, i.e. a third of the pay in agricultural produce, two-thirds in Treasury bills. Significantly, a provision was made to obligate the tax-farmers from whose estates the laborers came to convert the bills to cash. A similar case occurred at the same time in the Būlāq dockyards. The work was brought to a halt because many of the unpaid *fallāḥīn* ran away, and those who remained were constantly complaining. The Council of Justice gave these workers the same deal as that of the factory and construction workers.[35]

It is quite clear from these and other mid-century cases that there was unrest on many of the government work sites. The records bear witness to growing protest on the part of *corvée* laborers against prevailing pay policies. That protest was not merely verbal, but manifested itself in mass desertion of projects. This slowed down progress considerably, sometimes bringing work to a complete stop. The situation forced the government to realize the limits of coercion. This much is stated in simple words. Consequently, pay policies were changed and the conditions of the workers were improved. Some form of negotiation with workers is implied in the documents of the time, as they occasionally mention that the consent, or approval, of the workers was obtained. Although there is no direct evidence that workers organized their action against the government, we may assume that some form of concerted, *ad hoc* action by workers did occur.

Thus, the involuntary nature of the *corvée* was being slowly eroded. However, not before the last quarter of the nineteenth century did it begin to lose its grip on the Egyptian countryside. It is true that work incentives and better pay gradually replaced the whip, but the need for a large workforce on projects of public works in Egypt ensured the continuation of the practice. Yet another factor helped the government, and the *fallāḥīn*, to overcome the labor shortage. The middle years of the nineteenth century were on the whole peaceful, and the army, still quite large, was frequently employed in civilian projects. As already mentioned in part I, this factor blurred the distinction between military and civilian officeholders, which increased the cohesion of the Ottoman-Egyptian elite. Here we note that military manpower was both more easily accessible and more transportable than the *fallāḥīn*. It was also better disciplined, more manageable on the job, and – being made up of the same population – quite familiar with the *corvée*. In a period which offered few combat challenges – save for the Crimean War effort – the government often used soldiers as a substitute workforce on public projects.

The 1850s also witnessed a more sparing attitude towards the weaker elements in rural society. It was Abbas Paşa who, in 1851, made a significant attempt to reduce the suffering attached to the *corvée*. He prohibited the use in forced labor of pregnant women, mothers of children under three years old, children under eight, men and women over seventy, and disabled or ill persons. Heavy penalties were to be imposed on those who sent such people to work on *corvée* projects. There are reports, however, that the order was not fully complied with.[36] Thus, the main trends in the appropriation of forced labor at mid-century are quite clear. As certain vulnerable groups in the population were being gradually excluded from the *corvée*, on humanitarian grounds, the uses to which forced labor was being put, as we have already seen, were expanding.

On the whole, the practice was as yet not about to disappear. Reflecting on the *corvée* at the end of the century, Nubar observed that the use of forced labor strictly for public works was justified and legitimate. However, he found its spread to serve private ends an "odious abuse."[37] His first sentiment was probably shared by most members of the Ottoman-Egyptian elite, while the second manifestly was not. That it was not accounts, at least in part, for the rural squeeze which made people leave their villages and migrate to other villages, to middle-size towns, and to cities. The life the migrants made and the difficulties with which they were faced in the big city are the subject of the following chapter.

9 Rural migrants and urban attitudes

From the countryside to Cairo

Internal migration from village to town and city has been identified as one of the on-going social and economic phenomena of nineteenth-century Egyptian history. Gabriel Baer showed that towns grew more rapidly during 1821–1846 than in the middle decades, which he linked to agricultural development combined with the decline of industry. He noted that mercantile centers of agricultural areas, such as Ṭanṭa, Manṣūra, Damanhūr, and Zaqāzīq, grew considerably in the middle years. Alexandria experienced a sharp rise in population in the reign of Mehmet Ali; and its population in 1846 was more than twelve times that in 1826, but then levelled off. On the other hand, Justin McCarthy's figures point out that Cairo's population increased in the middle years by a rate 1.5 times the rate during the preceding period. The period considered in this work saw the beginning of development in the area of Suez, the establishment of suburbs around Cairo, such as ᶜAbbāsiyya, the rise of Port Said towards the end of the 1850s, and the decline of certain towns, such as Rosetta (ar-Rashīd), which paid the price for the rise of Alexandria.[1]

The records examined for the present work leave little doubt that internal migration continued to occur during the middle decades. To avoid the perennial debate over the relation between village and town – was there a dichotomy or merely a continuum? – we shall examine only migration into Cairo and the effect it had on the migrants. In spite of obvious differences from town to town, we may assume that there were many similarities in what migrants experienced in Cairo, Alexandria, and medium-size towns. However, our sources limit the scope of questions that can be properly treated and my evidence is insufficient to deal fully with the cultural and psychological effects of migration. Hence, a comprehensive study of migration in mid-nineteenth-century Egypt will have to await future research. Still, we can look at our select group of migrants,[2] if not at migration as a whole, and attempt to discover some of the realities of their old and new lives. Who were these people? Where did they come from? What happened to them in the big city?

We should note at the outset that migration was a broad phenomenon, encompassing relocation to other large cities, as well as movement from village to village, from village to town, from town to town, from town to city, and from city to city. Not infrequently, it was a gradual process, in which one relocated to a village in another province, or to a provincial market town, on the way to the final destination. Thus, for example, we can trace the fortunes of a certain Muḥammad ʿAbd ar-Rahmān, who was born in a village near Fayyūm. When he was still a child, his parents moved to a village in the province of Giza. After a while, his father was conscripted and later died in the service. Afterwards, Muḥammad went to Cairo and began working in a workshop. When soldiers came to the manufactories to draft the workers, he escaped and found refuge with the bedouins in Giza. He then moved from town to town, taking on various jobs to make a living. In 1851, he ended up in Cairo again, and for a while worked in a bakery.[3]

Another typical case is that of Sayyid Yūsuf from a village near the town of Manṣūra. He worked at a government factory in that town. The labor was forced, so as one point he absconded and went to the town of Binha, where he stayed for a month. Sayyid Yūsuf then went to the village of Inbābā (Imbābā) not far from Cairo, stayed there for a fortnight, and then, in September 1851, moved on to Old Cairo, a suburb of the city. These were not unusual trajectories of migration at the time, with all their social and economic implications. They persisted despite attempts by the government to prevent the *fallāḥīn* from leaving their villages. In the mid 1840s, Mehmet Ali launched a cruel repatriation drive, aiming to track down migrant *fallāḥīn* in their newly adopted villages and return them to their original ones. One report estimated the number of people uprooted in the drive of 1844–5 at 12,000 men, women and children.[4]

In the 1840s and 1850s, Cairo attracted migrants from several parts of Egypt. Most of those seeking residence in the capital came from two areas – the governorates adjacent to it and the more remote Delta villages. Middle and Upper Egypt supplied a relatively small number of migrants in that period. Foremost among the newcomers were men and women from Gīza, Minūfiyya, Fayyūm, Manṣūra, Gharbiyya, Sharqiyya, and Qalyūbiyya. They came mostly from villages, much less from small towns. As could be expected, men clearly outnumbered women. Men and women migrated for different reasons. Most women who moved to Cairo did so because they followed their husbands, or because a resident of the city, or a migrant, married them and brought them over. In a society in which women were usually "attached," few could even contemplate migration on their own.

There were a number of reasons why men moved to Cairo, or were brought there and decided to stay. Those who came from the hinterland of the capital were the better informed migrants, for they had previous knowledge of the conditions and the opportunities in the city. They collected such information on their visits as they carried products and merchandise to trade, stayed a few days, and then returned to their villages. It was not uncommon for such men to form contacts in town, establish working relations, and then decide to move permanently. Their families, if they had any, followed immediately or after a while. Some of the migrants from Upper and Middle Egypt also had at least a limited impression of life in Cairo when they visited the Ṭanṭa fair and stopped in the big city on the way. Others, however, acquired a Cairene experience in less favorable circumstances, as when ordered by the government to come to the area.

In this category we find all those villagers who had been conscripted or taken to do forced labor. Military service brought quite a number of *fallāḥīn* to the barracks of ᶜAbbāsiyya and other locations around Cairo. Most of them had their basic training there, others were stationed in regiments deployed in the city or nearby. Thus they had occasion to get acquainted with city attractions. When discharged from the service, some of the men chose not to return to their villages but to seek their fortune in Cairo. Others returned home, but found that things had changed, or their tastes were no longer suitable to life on the land. They would then try their luck in the city, joining friends from their unit who had already settled there.[5] The social rupture that mobilization entailed must have made migration less traumatic. Once uprooted and resocialized, these men were better prepared to meet the challenge of city life.

At mid-century, many of the construction projects were carried out in and around the city of Cairo. During the reign of Abbas, the palace complex was being built in ᶜAbbāsiyya, with its surrounding military schools, hospital, and residences for members of the elite. Palaces were also under construction inside the city, and roads were being paved, including the one from Cairo to Suez. The Alexandria–Cairo railway began in the early 1850s, was completed at mid-decade, and extended to Suez towards the end of the decade. Parts of that project, lasting a few years, required work in the vicinity of the capital. Sait continued to build in and around Cairo, at Qasr an-Nīl and elsewhere. Thus, a large workforce, mostly recruited under the *corvée* and made up of *fallāḥīn*, became a permanent feature of the city's life well into the reign of Ismail. Although *corvée* laborers, like soldiers, had little spare time, they, too, wandered into town and watched its wonders. Some of them remained after their release, some returned when things at the village got too rough.

Women were not the only ones to follow a family member to the city, usually a husband. Not a few of the male migrants joined a brother, a married sister, a relative, or simply friends and acquaintances from their own village. Such a connection offered a base away from home in an alien environment and made absorption into urban life less painful. It offered the newcomer temporary shelter, basic city orientation, and often most importantly – a chance for employment. This was not merely through contact with a prospective employer, often the one employing the more veteran migrant and satisfied with his or her services, but much more than that. It was not easy to find a job without a guarantor (*ḍāmin*), someone willing to vouch for the worker and be responsible for any damage or misconduct. Men and women without a credible guarantor, i.e. employed and having no criminal record, had to settle for the least attractive, most temporary employment, or sometimes, to remain unemployed.

Shelter was also important because of security regulations in the city. Alleys and streets were locked after sunset and doormen slept at their gates. There were police patrols and those moving outside at night had to carry a light. Loitering was prohibited and could get one into trouble with the authorities. Towards dark, the homeless would drift to the mosques, mostly to al-Azhar, and camp for the night. Indeed, we find that many of the migrants populated such premises, or found temporary residence in cheap inns, or khans. The records mention that those who had relations or acquaintances would spend the night with them. It was not uncommon that even the most casual and newly made contacts would offer, or be asked to offer, a roof over the migrant's head for a few nights. Food seems to have been less of a problem, for the *fallāḥīn* usually came from the village with ample supplies to last during the initial period.

The migrants who appear in our records were usually employed. Only very few were defined as out of work (*baṭṭāl*). But the overwhelming majority were employed as unskilled workers performing menial services as boatmen, donkey drivers, grooms, servants, or watchmen. Few served as skilled laborers in workshops. Unskilled labor paid much less than skilled and could be obtained more easily. Thus, again as expected, migrants joined the bottom rungs of the social and economic ladder. Those who faced extreme hardship resorted to pilfering. At great risk, they then tried to sell the stolen items for cut prices in tightly controlled markets. To rid the city of vagrancy and assure the public safety, convicted felons were punished and then deported to their village. They were accompanied by a policeman to ensure that they reached their destination, but, at least in two recorded cases, the culprits returned to Cairo after a while and were again caught stealing.[6]

Migrants to Cairo continued to maintain contacts with their families back home and with other migrants from their village already living in the city. Family and friends used to visit their migrant relatives, spend time with them, and return to the village. Unmarried men often sought to marry a woman from their own village and bring her to Cairo. Such connections extended the population exposed to city life and created an ever-increasing pool of potential migrants. Failure to "make it" in the big city also resonated in the village, discouraging those who might have contemplated migration. On the whole, such setbacks did not reverse the trend of steadily growing flow from the country to the capital. After migration, the records reveal, migrants maintained close ties with individuals from their own village, either sharing a shelter, or a job, or both. This was a natural support system in an unfamiliar and demanding environment. It often proved an economic crutch and a comforting, familiar setup.

With time, however, gaps opened between veteran migrants and those who remained in the village. Still, the basic solidarity survived. In one case, a man came to Cairo from a village in Qalyūbiyya province and began studying at al-Azhar. Years later, another man approached him, claimed that he was also from the same village, and asked to spend the night at his place. The Azhar student did not recognize the newcomer – saying he was young when he left home and did not remember the man – but, nonetheless, let him stay under his roof. Yet the redeployment of village networks in the city was not without problems for all concerned. For one thing, not only the friendships of the old village were reproduced, the animosities were too. Old relationships were relived and blood-feuds resurrected. In one such case, a man from a village in the province of Gīza confessed to the murder of another man in Cairo. He said: "[He] had killed a relative of mine in my village, so likewise, I hit him and killed him, and now no one has any claim at all [i.e., the account is settled]."[7]

It is hardly surprising that migrants continued to rely on village connections while already living in Cairo. They clung so eagerly to old acquaintances because the environment to which they wished to be integrated was anything but welcoming to newcomers. Urban society was organized in a complex network of communal units, which the state created and absorbed into its own apparatus. While serving the needs of city dwellers, the system operated against those who were not already part of it, even if they truly wished to abide by its code of conduct. The following section attempts to describe how urban society excluded the "unknown faces," and why it was so difficult for migrants to lose their anonymity. The same anonymity that some regard as one of the liberating aspects of modern metropolitan life, was a great liability in mid-century Egyptian cities.

The known faces of society and the *Gharīb*

Neighborhoods, quarters, guilds, and to a lesser extent *ṣūfī* orders, were viewed by the government as instruments of control. Their *shaykh*s were regarded not only as the eyes and ears of the authorities on the streets and in the markets, but also as an extension of the government into the private domain of city dwellers. We shall deal with the urban control system in chapter 11, but need to point out here that the system must not be considered as merely imposed from above against the will of the people. Far from it, those forms of social organization were part and parcel of Egyptian culture in the middle years of the nineteenth century. They existed well before our period and survived into the British occupation. The system cannot be attributed to force of habit, nor to passivity or submissiveness of any kind. The lower strata of Egyptian society at the time appear to have willingly cooperated with a system that favored the *known*, the *familiar*, the *traceable* faces. That system enhanced their feeling of security by reducing the number of unknown faces in one's immediate environment, at home, on the job, and wherever possible. In that context, anonymity was not deemed a virtue; it was sheer vice.

Not only the neighborhood *shaykh* – and the village *shaykh* in rural Egypt – knew the personal history and whereabouts of each individual in their jurisdiction. Everybody else in what might be called a "unit of information" did. Villages, or demarcated parts thereof, neighborhoods, guilds, and *ṣūfī* orders constituted such units. Residential units of information were not only self-contained, but also physically separated by a gate, which at mid-century was still being closed after sundown. In his usual perception, St. John described how Cairo was changing with the setting of the sun:

> the streets rapidly empty; everyone goes home to supper; and in about an hour after total darkness scarcely any one remains abroad. All is then silent and desolate. The few passengers that from time to time move along, are preceded, if at all respectable, by a servant carrying a paper or glass lantern. Everyone is bound to have a light of some sort, under penalty of being arrested, lodged in the guard-house, and beaten or imprisoned next morning . . . At times the measured tread of a patrol, attended, perhaps, by a few police-officers, announces, in apparently deserted quarters, that the Government is watchful over the lives and fortunes of the citizens; and now and then a man of the party briskly waves a half-smothered torch, and a bright red flame bursts suddenly forth, and reveals the shining bayonets and white uniforms of the soldiers. Honest men hasten to announce their presence and display their lanterns; whilst thieves slink into bye-lanes, or endeavour to conceal themselves in the deep, gloomy doorway of some large house.[8]

Even during daylight, the labyrinth of streets and alleys which constituted Cairo and other Egyptian towns presented a real challenge to outsiders. Almost all travelers tell of being lost in it, having no sense of direction, not knowing how to get back, and impinging, in the process, on the privacy of residents. On 9 January 1850, Flaubert inscribed in his diary the following passage:

> I walk by myself in Cairo, in fine sunshine, in the section between the prison and the Bulak gate . . . I keep losing my way in the maze of alleys and running into dead-ends. From time to time I come on an open space with the debris of ruined houses, or rather with no houses; hens pecking, cats on walls. Quiet way of life here – intimate, secluded. Dazzling sun effects when one suddenly emerges from these alleys, so narrow that the roofs of the *moucharbiehs* (*sic*) [shuttered bay windows] on each side touch each other.[9]

Many neighborhoods consisted of no more than one street with a few diverging alleys. One gate usually sufficed to close them to passage, so that they were "locked up as a safe" (*inna l-ḥāra maḍbūṭa mithl aṣ-ṣandūq*). St. John believed that the tendency to shelter oneself from the outside concealed a "mania for complete privacy." In fact, what he noticed was the traditional distinction between the indoor (*juwwan*) and the outdoor (*barran*), which explains the allocation and usage of dwelling and public space in the Ottoman Middle East. Yet, alleys and blind alleys in a neighborhood were not considered as public domain. In them, women washed kitchen wares, children played, and men sat out and relaxed after a day's work. All met there and conversed with each other, thus using the *ḥāra*, or neighborhood, for social interaction. To keep strangers out, the neighborhood door-keeper (m. *bawwāb*, f. *bawwāba*), would close the gate at night, sleep by it in case someone was locked outside, and open it in the morning at prayer time, waking up those who wished to pray. Many neighborhoods also employed a regular guard (*ghafīr al-ḥāra*).[10]

Many people spent much of their life in the neighborhood in which they had been born. It was not uncommon for someone to say that he or she had lived in the neighborhood "from my childhood" (*min ṣughrī*), or to state that "I live in this neighborhood and was born [in it]" (*innī sākin wa-mawlūd fī hadhihi l-ḥāra*). There was some movement in and out of neighborhoods, but the new faces of those who managed to acquire residence were absorbed into the "known" reservoir of familiar faces. Because the *ḥāra* was a community, people knew who lived in each house, what were the relations in every family, what clothing and household effects their neighbors owned, and what was their daily routine. They often celebrated together the happy moments in their neighbors' life and shared the unhappy ones. They also knew all outsiders who had frequent recourse (*taraddud*) to the neighborhood, as well as the nature of relations formed between such outsiders and neighbors.

Relations with outsiders were either functional or "social." Functional contacts were formed mostly with people who provided various services, such as peddlers, repairmen, and servants not living in the household. "Social" relations were often defined in terms of mixing with someone, or keeping one's company, walking or sitting with someone, and going about the markets and *ḥāra*s with one (in Arabic, the terms *khulṭa*, *mashy*, *julūs* frequently occur).[11] Although this may seem a fairly limited range of social activities, it nevertheless covered all licit liaisons outside the family. The illicit ones, which were hard to conceal from neighbors, were often decribed in pejorative euphemisms. Thus, people were familiar with anything that was *regular* about life in the *ḥāra*. Hence they could easily detect any *irregularity*. By definition, irregularities were suspicious, unless satisfactorily explained. Reports about the latter soon circulated among neighbors, hardly ever failing to reach the *shaykh*.

The exact opposite of the familiar neighborhood mate was the "stranger," or the "outsider" (*gharīb*, pl. *aghrāb*). The *gharīb* was immediately noticeable, sticking out against the familiar background. Out of curiosity combined with suspicion, he or she was watched by neighborhood residents, talked to or about, and most significantly – remembered, at least for a while. Since some form of harmful conduct was often expected of strangers, they were marked for prevention and, failing that, tracing. The underlying assumption was that unknown faces had no legitimate business in the neighborhood. Presumably, *gharībs* came to the *ḥāra* to steal, attack a neighbor, or form some illicit liaison. When something of that nature occurred, the authorities invariably inquired if anyone had seen a *gharīb* in the neighborhood. Often, a detailed description by residents led to arrest and conviction.[12]

Some strangers belonged to a worse category, that of "suspicious persons" (*mashbūhs*). A man or a woman repeatedly spotted by neighbors and whose appearance in the *ḥāra*, or its vicinity, could not be accounted for was a *mashbūh*. From just *gharībs* they became *known gharībs*, their unfamiliar faces being recognized as such by residents of the neighborhood. Such *mashbūhs* were watched even more closely and treated with greater caution. They were often known to the police, although they had no record of having committed an offense. If part of a group of similar persons, they were sometimes referred to as "suspicious people" (*ahl ash-shubha*). There were, of course, "strangers" and even "suspicious persons" who were honest men and women, intending no harm to the peaceful residents of the *ḥāra*. They could be simply looking for employment, trying to peddle some merchandise, or merely looking for conversation to pass the time. If lucky, they might be offered a cup of coffee, a pipe smoke, or even a roof for the night.[13]

Wherever such people turned, they found it difficult to overcome the barrier of anonymity. One needed a guarantor (*ḍāmin*) or guarantee papers (*ḍamānāt*) in order to obtain a menial day job, to sell an item of some value, or to get a room in an inn. This was done to protect employers from unreliable workers, to prevent the sale of stolen goods, and to safeguard against squatting or establishing a base for illegal activity. Guild *shaykhs*, door-keepers, guards, as well as ordinary men and women, all helped to enforce these regulations, which they believed were intended for their own protection. They made it difficult for newcomers to be absorbed into society. The special predicament of strangers was even recognized by the government and duly recompensed. In July 1849, for example, a small group of skilled workers was sent to Suez to work on the construction of the new port. After some time there, they petitioned the government for a pay increase, claiming that as *gharībs*, their living expenses were higher. Their request was granted.[14]

Other strangers did not fare so well. ᶜĀ'isha and her husband al-Ḥāj Muṣṭafā came to live in Būlāq, the north-western port of Cairo. They built a shanty in an open space, so they did not belong to a neighborhood, and had no *shaykh*. They had no contacts with neighbors, since they were considered "strangers" (*aghrāb*). They used to sell sugar in various places, carrying with them their two-year-old baby. A certain camel driver owed them 10 *para*, a mere farthing, which he did not pay. An argument that erupted between them one day deteriorated into blows, and the camel driver hit the woman with a prop. ᶜĀ'isha fell to the ground with the baby in her arms, the baby was hurt and died a few hours later. The police arrested the camel driver, but the couple could not produce witnesses to the brawl, nor anyone who would testify to refute the camel driver's assertion that the baby had been sick and did not die from the fall. When she had to explain why no one would testify, ᶜĀ'isha said: "[Even] if someone saw [the brawl and the condition of the baby], he would not come to testify in our favor, because we are strangers in that place."[15]

Such a degree of alienation was perhaps an extreme case, but it occurred nonetheless. Even if ᶜĀ'isha was not telling the whole truth, her explanation was not rejected out of hand by the police as being impossible, or exaggerated. It seemed to have fit into what all concerned knew to be the lot of *gharībs* in society. That was so especially for people without any acquaintances in the environment to which they moved. Although we must not underestimate the suffering of such individuals, their difficulties were not insurmountable. Clearly, on the margins, the system was not as tight as it may seem. Honest strangers could still get employment, become "familiar faces," find a dwelling, raise a family, and be integrated into society. Dishonest *gharībs* could still find profiteering merchants who would buy pilfered property without guarantee, albeit at cut prices; and, surely, not all thieves were actually caught.

As the century wore on, the social tendency to favor the known and shun the unknown was gradually mitigated. This eventually happened with the marked improvement in transportation and the substantial increase in the migration from village to town. The last third of the nineteenth century saw not only the development of a modern railway network and the inauguration of the Suez Canal; it also witnessed the removal of gates inside cities, the opening up of enclosed neighborhoods, and the lighting up of large cities at night. If at mid-century, "the layout of the town repulsed the newcomer," in Jacques Berque's words, it too was thrown open during the reign of Ismail. All these changes legitimized the *gharīb* and reduced the individual's ability to control, or "know," his or her own social environment. Consequently, integration of newcomers into the host society was made easier and the stress of migration was reduced. A much greater degree of anonymity became the norm and an important measure of neighborhood and trade intimacy was lost.

Thus, the advent of modernity induced profound change in socio-cultural patterns. It came gradually, not abruptly, as a result of changing political and economic realities. As long as rural migration was fairly limited, the pattern of urban behavior towards migrants continued to hold firm. This was the situation during the middle decades, as reflected in this chapter. However, between 1882 and 1897, when circumstances brought to Cairo each year thousands of migrants, who needed food, housing, and employment, the cultural code began to be modified. If integration was difficult for rural migrants, life in general was not easy for the urban lower strata. Chapter 10 describes the urban "squeeze" and how the population coped with it.

10 The urban squeeze

The urban setting was not hospitable to outsiders, partly because city dwellers needed to maximize their own chances of coping with life. In previous chapters we dealt with the hardships of rural life and the difficulties of urban integration experienced by those who chose to leave their villages. In this chapter we turn to examine some aspects of urban life. Here I wish to deal with basics, with the simple issue of making a living. How did people find employment? What were the jobs they could find? How much, how often, and in what ways were the employed paid? How were pay demands raised by workers and how did the government deal with them? What happened to the unemployed, the poor, the homeless? These are some of the questions explored in the following pages.

Ways and means of finding employment

There were several ways in which day laborers could find a job. The government created most of the demand for labor in the economy, and what it could not get through the *corvée*, it was forced to obtain on the free market. Much of the skilled labor in industry and construction had to be recruited on a competitive basis. In addition, the various kinds of servants who were required by government offices and agencies came from the growing ranks of the urban poor and were not *corvée* laborers. But there was also constant demand for menial workers, both skilled and unskilled in the private sector. A significant share of that demand was generated by members of the Ottoman-Egyptian elite, who needed hands for the running of their households and had the means to hire them. Large households employed many cooks, porters, gardeners, guards, personal attendants, horse and donkey drivers, ostlers, water carriers, and other servants. Only part of that demand was supplied by slave labor.[1]

Certain services, however, had to be acquired outside the household. Thus, for example, if repairs or construction were needed, masons, carpenters, plasterers, and the like, would be hired on a daily basis, or per job. There were, of course, many smaller households, but even the modest ones employed servants and created a demand for free menial labor. Some of the workers employed in households, large or small, gained the confidence of their employers, with

10 The Gate of Matewaley (*sic*), Cairo, 1843, by David Roberts

which came also the security of long-term status. Many others, however, changed jobs frequently, having to find new employment when circumstances so decreed. An important share of the free labor market was dominated by the bazaar economy. That is, by the many kinds of small and professionally organized employers who owned stores and workshops in the traditional markets of Egyptian towns. For the most part, they manufactured and sold food products, clothing, and house wares.

According to time-honored practices, merchants, artisans, and craftsmen initiated apprentices into the secrets of their trade. They were organized in occupational associations which are commonly referred to in the literature as "guilds."[2] Guilds were still very much a feature of the Egyptian economy in the middle decades. As we shall see later, they played an important role in the job market. The process of becoming a master, or a skilled worker, within a guild, was long and demanding, the hierarchy was fairly strict, and the flow of labor tightly supervised. Yet movement was not impossible, and workers changed masters and trades, or simply moved to another town. And, there was certainly "unregulated" employment, especially for the unskilled, as one could offer his or her services and be hired to do a job. Employment agents operated in that market within set guidelines which the government supervised. But not everybody could find a job. Unemployment, both temporary and long-term, existed at the margins, though part of it was certainly voluntary.

The various ways of getting a job can be gleaned from the records. One would normally be looking for employment where work was being carried out, i.e. in the centers of business or around households. Thus, for example, at the beginning of 1851, a Greek lumber merchant was renovating his house in a northern neighborhood of Cairo.[3] He employed a master whitewasher and several workers for a period of twenty-five days. A certain ᶜAbdallah was passing by, when one of the merchant's servants approached him and asked if he would like to work with the whitewasher and his men. ᶜAbdallah agreed to begin work immediately. This seems to have been the most casual form of hiring. It was common on a short-term basis, and no references were required. That sort of employment was most suitable to workers who had no roots in the city, no persons who could vouch for them, and no verifiable record of employment. Employers in such a situation knew that they were taking a risk with an unknown quantity – as in this case, when ᶜAbdallah disappeared with some valuable belongings.

There were, of course, more active ways of looking for a job. The case of Muḥammad Muṣṭafā, a water carrier in Alexandria, was quite common. In November 1850, early in the pilgrimage season, he came to Cairo to work as a servant on the pilgrim caravan going to the Hijaz. In Cairo, he went to the depot of the chief packer, offered his services, and was hired. Though a longer-term employment, this was still a fairly loose association under the limiting and trying conditions of the pilgrimage, from which, incidentally, the chief packer himself did not return alive. For slightly closer associations, a guarantor (Turkish *zamin*, Arabic *ḍāmin*) was required by prospective employers. He or she was expected to vouch for the candidate's honesty and was accountable to the employer in case of irresponsible or dishonest conduct. Ibrāhīm al-Barbarī, who came to Cairo from Somali, was at a great disadvantage because no one knew him and he could not find a guarantor. There were many like him, who had to settle for the worst jobs.[4]

When labor was in short supply, or a job had to be done urgently, employers tended to take on workers without guarantors. Nevertheless, most of the time, inability to produce a satisfactory reference was a major impediment to employment. As already mentioned, those who suffered from it most were the newcomers, the rural migrants who came to town in search of a job. The system clearly favored town residents, veteran migrants, the "known" – and, therefore, trusted – faces around. Even employment agents, who almost by definition catered for job hunters, were obliged to demand a guarantor from all applicants before placing them. Both employers and the authorities held such agents responsible for the performance of workers placed by them. They, in turn, required guarantors in order to reduce their own risk element. But, in certain circumstances, agents and employers were willing to risk hiring "unknown" workers. The following examples may serve to throw light on some of the points raised here.

In May 1851, a high-ranking official approached the head of the employment agents' guild and asked for a groom. The groom was supplied as requested and began working for the official. After three days, however, he was sent on an errand, from which he never returned, taking with him the clothes that he was supposed to collect for his master. The first thing the official did was to complain to the agent, who immediately began to search for the groom. When he found him the following day, the agent brought the groom to the police station and left the matter to their care. In another case, about the same time, a woman named Zanūba came to a female employment agent to seek a servant's job. The agent demanded a guarantor, but Zanūba could not produce one. At the time, she was living with her mother and relatives in Būlāq, having recently left her husband of a month because he used to beat her.[5]

Sympathy aside, the agent refused to place Zanūba without a proper guarantor, so she sat outside the agency and wept. Another woman came to the agent to look for a dough kneader and saw Zanūba crying. When she heard the story, she offered to take Zanūba in temporarily. After the two had gone to the woman's home, they met a group of *ṣūfī*s, who offered to put up Zanūba at their lodge for a while. She indeed spent two nights there, but the woman who took her in became concerned that she might be exploited sexually.[6] So she went to the agent and urged her to get Zanūba out of the *ṣūfī* lodge. When the two were talking, a third woman came to look for a servant. The agent told her that she could give her Zanūba, but without a guarantor. At the other woman's suggestion, it was decided to hire Zanūba for a few days as a trial period. She was fetched from the lodge and was taken to her new employer's house.

After four days, however, Zanūba stole a few house wares and clothes, all worth 250 *kuruş*, and ran away. She went to the area of al-Azhar, where many poor people loitered. When she was asked how she had gotten the stuff, Zanūba put it all down and escaped. The stolen items were recovered in full, but the culprit was still at large. The interesting point here is that at that stage, the police notified the parties involved that it was the responsibility of the agent to find Zanūba and bring her to the police. As in the previous case, the agent set out to search for Zanūba, found her, and turned her in. The following case, which is even more complicated, reveals that whereas the police expected agents to produce the offenders for whom they were responsible, agents were also expected to keep the police informed and not to take the law into their own hands.

Aḥmad Ramaḍān came to Cairo from a village in Middle Egypt. In the summer of 1849, as he was looking for a job, he approached an employment agent and asked to be placed.[7] The agent knew about Aḥmad's indebtedness to his previous employer and told him he had to settle it first. Aḥmad offered to mortgage his wages until the debt was fully paid up. A few months later, an engineer from Minūfiyya asked the agent to send him a servant. When he was told of Aḥmad's predicament, he said he would like to try him, and if he liked his work, he would pay the debt himself. After only one day of work, Aḥmad stole 300 *kuruş* and ran away. He then went and purchased a few things in one of Cairo's markets, which was promptly reported to his agent. The agent contacted the Minūfiyya engineer, inquiring why the servant was given spending money before his debt had been settled. The engineer informed the agent of the theft and demanded the money from him.

At that point, accepting his responsibility for Aḥmad's conduct, the agent set out to search the culprit. When he caught him, he made Aḥmad resell the things he had purchased and returned the stolen money to the engineer. After that, Aḥmad disappeared, leaving no trace behind. About a year later, in November 1850, Aḥmad's sister-in-law came to the police to report him missing. The police summoned the agent and reprimanded him for not reporting the case to the authorities after Aḥmad's disappearance. They clearly did not regard the case as closed after the stolen amount had been recovered and returned to the owner. The agent asked for and received ten days to find Aḥmad. After some sleuthing, he discovered that Aḥmad had been drafted to the army and was still serving. The offender was brought to trial and jailed. Obviously, agents were responsible to their clients, but also to the government. Along with heads of guilds, *shaykh*s of quarters and neighborhoods, and *ṣūfī* orders, and other men and women in quasi-official capacity, such agents were part of an effective network of control, which enabled the authorities to maintain a high level of order and tranquility in Egypt at mid-century.

Perhaps the most important employment agents in the free labor market were the heads of the various guilds. In the middle years of the nineteenth century, they still controlled the flow of labor in manufacturing as in all services. In many trades, employers were obligated to hire and fire workers through the guild *shaykhs*. The *shaykhs* operated much like the employment agents mentioned above. They required a guarantor and were held responsible for the conduct and performance of guild members. An example of a common case might show the central role these men and women played in the job market. The owner of a coffeehouse in Cairo was in need of a coffee maker and server (Turkish *kahveci*, Arabic *qahwajī*).[8] Such a worker operated the coffee-making device (Arabic *ʿudda*) and served the guests, though often serving was done by waiters and not by the more skilled maker of the coffee. The owner applied to the head of the coffee-makers' guild and was assigned a worker. After a while, he fired the man and got another one, but this time without recourse to the guild head.

When the authorities later asked the owner to explain why he did that, the man said that he had acted out of charity. In fact, he asserted, his son was operating the coffee machine, so he hired a young boy as attendant and waiter. Thereafter he realized that the boy's father was in dire need, so out of pity, he hired him too. The latter he even hired without a guarantor. The police found that the owner contravened the accepted practice and fined him. He was told: "From now on you shall not hire a coffee maker without consulting the head of the guild nor without taking a guarantor for him according to the accepted rules of conduct." One had to demand a guarantor, it was stated further, for "if he [the worker] causes anything [i.e. damage or loss], his guarantor is responsible for whatever [damage] he causes."[9] In this case, much damage was caused indeed. The boy and his father disappeared with two silver-coated guns belonging to two discharged Ottoman soldiers who were passing through Cairo on their way from the Hijaz. The guns were recovered and the offenders were sent to prison.

Unemployment with all its social and economic effects was not unknown in Egyptian cities during the middle years of the nineteenth century. The industrial retrenchment of the 1840s and 1850s entailed the closure of most government factories and the gradual decline of local handicraft production. Consequently, many workers had to relocate and find a new job. With the considerable reduction in the size of the army, the ranks of job seekers swelled, and although most of the soldiers returned to their villages, not a few came to the large cities. Temporary and long-term unemployment resulted, as an even brief glance at the sources would indicate. Whereas temporary unemployment had always been the lot of unskilled laborers, it now afflicted also skilled workers. In the records of the 1850s, manufactory workers still appear, from time to time as unemployed (*baṭṭāl*), or as having obtained another occupation. Even carpenters, blacksmiths, and practitioners of similar trades are listed as unemployed. Long-term unemployment had all the negative social effects known to modern society. Poverty, begging, loitering, indebtedness, frustrating idleness, and crime come to mind first.[10]

Wages

For the lucky ones who found employment, there was the question of wages. Except for the army and the bureaucracy, there were no fixed pay lists. So, for wages of non-elite groups we have to rely on incidental data. To a certain extent, the records of the Egyptian National Archives, the Hekekyan papers, and some of the more observant travelers help to bridge this information gap. Thus, we can at least proffer some educated comments on how wages were determined and paid in mid-century Egypt. With more archival research, missing information might surface and a fuller picture could emerge. In any event, it is clear that wages were usually calculated on a daily or monthly basis. When disbursed by the government, they consisted of food rations, government notes, and – when the work was urgent or labor in short supply – straight cash, too. A mixture of the first two seems to have been the most common. Government notes, however, were especially unpopular with workers because they could be converted only at cut rates, as high as 33 percent, as low as 12 percent.

The private sector usually paid wage laborers a little better than the government. Nevertheless, the main advantage here was that pay was normally in cash, except for household servants, part of whose pay was given in "room and board." Foreign employers paid better and more regularly than local ones. Skilled workers were, of course, better paid and more secure in their jobs. Children received less than grown ups. Wages were calculated differently in different occupations. They were paid either per day or month of work, or per production unit. Thus, for example, in most of the services, as in construction, pay was per day of work, or per month on longer-term jobs. But porters were often paid per load carried, bakers by units baked, and irrigation canal diggers according to the length dug and/or loads of mud extracted. There were no strict rules, and though custom favored one method over another in a particular trade, it was often left to worker and employer to determine. Lastly, there was clear linkage between pay and living expenses, hence pay adjustments were made periodically to meet rising costs of food and clothing.

Average pay for unskilled laborers in construction and similar menial jobs was in the 1850s about 2 *kuruş* per day, the government paying about 1.5 *kuruş*.[11] During harvest, when demand for labor peaked, wages rose, sometimes by as much as 60 percent. Such wages were slightly above subsistence level, especially if we reckon that some food was usually provided by the employer. As prices had not changed much since the 1830s, we may use Lane's price lists to assess the buying power of these wages. Thus, for example, three eggs cost in Cairo 0.125 *kuruş*, fowls cost 1.25–1.5 *kuruş* each, mutton or lamb 1 *kuruş* a pound, beef 0.875 *kuruş* a pound, fresh and clarified butter 2–2.25 *kuruş* a pound, Egyptian sugar 2 *kuruş* a pound, coffee 6–7 *kuruş* a pound, and water 0.25–0.5 *kuruş* per goat's skin. Meat prices in the country were about half the prices in Cairo, and bread cost from a third to a half of what it cost in Cairo.

Skilled workers received from 3 to 4 *kuruş* per day. Workers with special skills could receive 9 *kuruş* per day, which some of them considered in the 1850s insufficient by Cairo standards. According to Lane's estimates, a "middle class" family of four required in Cairo in the 1830s about 7.5 *kuruş* a day for food, water, fire, and soap. Services rendered to Europeans carried higher remuneration, hence in the late 1850s, Western travelers paid 9 *kuruş per diem* to a "native under servant, speaking only Arabic, or a little of some European language," according to Wilkinson's travel guide. Servants with good knowledge of a European language, or cooks, received four to five times as much, a huge salary by Egyptian standards. As might be expected, however, European residents in Egypt, unlike travelers, paid considerably lower wages, perhaps no higher than members of the Ottoman-Egyptian elite paid their household servants.

Pay demands and cost-of-living adjustments

The first year of Abbas's reign saw a readjustment of the government pay policy. We have already mentioned the changes that took place with regard to wages of *corvée* laborers. The point to notice in relation to pay raises for voluntary work is the active role taken by the workers themselves to affect the change. The mechanism through which the workers could present their grievances was the time-honored Islamic institution of the petition (Turkish *arzuhal*, Arabic *ᶜardḥāl*). Petitions were direct supplications to rulers in order to achieve prompt rectification of wrongs. They were not ultimatums, but rather humble appeals to the sense of justice, either of the sovereign or of a high functionary. Numerous Islamic traditions throughout the ages extol the just and compassionate ruler, enjoining him to look after the poor and the weak among his flocks. He is expected to stand by his subjects and prevent his officials from oppressing them. It was quite common in the Ottoman Empire to present petitions, and "petitions and complaints registers" were kept as a matter of routine.

When Abbas came to power late in 1848, he inherited considerable pay arrears. The Treasury was indebted to military and civilian officeholders as to the many menial day workers hired for government employ. Since these people had been paid in Treasury bills which the government failed to convert to cash, Abbas decided to take a few measures to balance the books. Under his instructions the government offered to cash bills at the extremely low rate of 12 percent. However, at that rate, holders refused to turn in their bills. While officeholders had other means of recompensing themselves for their lost salaries, day workers were in dire straits, often barely subsisting. Officials reported to their superiors that such persons constantly came to complain of their situation and there was a feeling that something had to be done to ease the pressure. On 12 November 1848, the government decided that part of the pay of day workers would be converted to cash "on the basis of current prices," while the rest would still be convertible according to the previous, unacceptable offer.[12]

The complaints referred to above were in the form of verbal appeals rather than written petitions. However, in the course of the following year, petitions were presented by several groups of workers demanding pay increases or change of pay policies, especially with regard to the convertibility of Treasury bills. The Department of Education, for example, was short on cash and could not pay the daily wages of workers at the government press in Būlāq. Their monthly allowances were not paid either. So it was decided to give them at least something, and 20 percent of the monthly allowance was to be paid each month. However, since cash was unavailable, even that meager amount had to be paid in Treasury bills, so the modest gesture proved empty. The workers protested and presented a petition, which was considered by the Council of Justice in May 1849. Council members ruled that the promised 20 percent must be paid to the workers in cash.[13]

The Department of Education was not unique in experiencing cash flow problems. This was, in fact, the chronic state of much of the administration. It stemmed from stringent budgets imposed by the viceroys who ruled in the middle decades. Money was made available to priority projects only, as it was realized that otherwise the required workforce could not be obtained. But in that period, not only workers in dire need of money protested against their employers; those who simply wanted better and comparatively more equitable pay also petitioned the government. Thus, a group of eight skilled masons working for the Police Department demanded to have their pay raised to the level of skilled masons working for the Department of Construction. Acting on their petition, the Council of Justice ascertained that seven of them were receiving 2 *kuruş* per day, whereas one received 2.5 *kuruş*. The latter was recognized as the most skilled among the eight for his "expertise and aptitude." The Council found out that under the Department of Construction, masons with the seven men's qualifications were being paid 2.5 *kuruş* per day, while an expert was receiving 3 *kuruş*. Consequently, the workers' demand was accepted and their pay was raised accordingly.[14]

About the same time, ten carpenters and two master masons who were working at the construction site of the new Suez port presented a petition to the official in charge of the project. They demanded a pay increase of 0.5 *kuruş* per day. Their argument was that they had families to support and were regarded in the area as outsiders. This meant, presumably, that they did not enjoy the advantages that long-term custom conferred and had to pay more. They had, of course, additional expenses as their families were not with them. The interesting point is that the demand was based on a precedent of which these skilled laborers were keenly aware. They claimed that a similar pay increase had been given to skilled workers under the Ministry of War at the project of the Nile Barrages. Such information not only traveled fast, but was also accurate, for after reviewing their demand, the Council of Justice approved the increase. Their daily pay, it was argued, was fixed at Cairo rates, while Suez was – perhaps for difficulties of provisioning and rapid development – more expensive than other areas. In the same year, the Council of Justice granted pay increases to meet the higher cost of living in Suez also to fifty-one navy personnel who had petitioned the government.[15]

Another interesting petition, dating from the same year, was presented by the bedouins who conducted the government caravans from Cairo to Suez and across the Sinai desert. Their demand for a pay increase was based on a comparison between the rates paid by the government and those paid by non-government agents for the same services. The government indeed recognized that its rates had to be competitive, and it seems that the petition was a formal reminder that adjustments had to be made. On the whole, the rates appear to have been quite high, with some of the attendants and packers receiving 30 *kuruş* for the return journey from Cairo to Suez. Bedouins who worked as guards at the telegraph stations also petitioned the government around the same time and got redress. Their monthly wages were lower; they were paid only in biscuits, 15 okas (18.72 kg) per person per month.[16]

This form of pay "negotiations" continued well beyond the initial phase of economic readjustment following the accession of Abbas Paşa. In the mid 1850s, petitions were used not only by the workers themselves, but also by their managers, who sought to improve pay conditions on the shop floor and push up productivity. Thus, for example, in 1853, the master bakers at the large government bakeries of aẓ-Ẓāhir and Old Cairo demanded a pay raise for their workers.[17] Wages were set according to the level of production, but since Abbas had ordered the quality of bread supplied to the soldiers to be upgraded, more hands were required to produce the loaves and wages fell proportionately. The master bakers petitioned for a raise of the sum paid per unit in order to make up the loss of income for both skilled and unskilled workers. The additional cost to the government was put at 26,500 *kuruş* (about 250 pounds sterling), but the Council of Justice deemed the expense justifiable in order to maintain "the industrial calm," and the viceroy concurred.

Thus, in the middle years of the nineteenth century, petitions emerged as a useful and effective mechanism for adjusting wages in the public sector. Reflecting supply and demand, that sector was affected by, and in turn affected, the private sector. While *corvée* workers expressed their disaffection by walking out *en masse*, temporary workers in government employ petitioned the authorities, articulated specific demands, and argued their case cogently. Petitions could not be brushed aside. They were passed upwards in the bureaucratic hierarchy, usually ending up at the very top – the Council of Justice. When the matter had broad implications, the Council's recommendation was submitted to the viceroy, and a viceregal edict (*irade-i seniyye*) was issued. It is clear from the petitions that workers were well informed about pay policy and work conditions throughout the economy, not only in the public sector. For its part, the government was fully aware of the limit of exploitation; it recognized that wages had to be tied to prices and could not decline below subsistence level. Hence, we may say that in mid-century Egypt, a rudimentary form of linkage and indexation was in operation.[18]

Poverty

The "line of poverty" in mid-nineteenth-century Egypt is not so easy to define. Large sections of both the rural and the urban population existed on subsistence level, barely eking out a living. These men and women managed to have just enough to feed, clothe, and shelter their families. To European travellers, who were not always familiar with pauperism in their own countries, they seemed to be verging on starvation. A usually cautious observer of mid-nineteenth-century Egypt, the British Dr. Bromfield, took the chronic want of small coins, or change, as a measure of the poverty and destitution of the population in both village and town:

> Money is so scarce, that it is extremely difficult to get change for even a Mejeedie dollar of nineteen piastres, unless its value has been taken in goods; and it is only in the larger towns that change for so trifling a sum can be obtained at all . . . It is absolutely necessary on a journey to be furnished with a sufficient supply of five fuddah pieces [= 5 *para* = ⅛ of a *kuruş*], to pay for such trifling but necessary articles as milk, eggs, fowls, fruit, and bread, none of which can be had from the peasantry, or in the small provincial towns unless paid for in the lowest denomination of coin, or at most, in half piastre silver pieces of twenty fuddahs.[19]

One must realize, however, that very little was needed for subsistence in rural and, to a lesser extent, in urban Egypt at the time. In a village, one could live on less than a *kuruş*, or piaster, a day, and workers in towns often did not require more than a daily wage of about 2 *kuruş* to support their families. Hence, the measure of poverty has to be different. Here, we are not concerned with the vast majority of Egyptians, who, no matter how poor in European eyes, still managed to subsist, but rather with the smaller group which lived beneath the invisible, yet so tangible, line of subsistence. It is virtually impossible to assess how many people inhabited those economic and social margins of society at mid-century. For the moment, all we can do is to chart out the phenomenon, characterize those who were described in their own society as "poor," and throw some light on their living conditions. What can be said at the outset is that poverty was mainly urban, that it not infrequently accompanied migration, and that it seemed to be on the increase in the period considered here.

The Arabic word most frequently used to describe the poor was *faqīr* for a man, *faqīra* for a woman. It meant that persons thus described, either by themselves or by others, did not have sufficient income and, quite often, had no place to live. Some were said to have been "extremely poor," or *faqīr jiddan*. Others described themselves as "hungry" (*jawʿān*, in colloquial Egyptian *gaʿān*), and one man said that he used to sell his clothes to buy good (*wa-abīʿ hudūmī wa-ākul bihim*). The situation of some was referred to by the authorities as "possessed of absolutely nothing" (*lā yamtalik shay' muṭlaqan*). Two men said that they were beggars and had no money, "not even a farthing" (*lā yūjad ʿindanā walā nisf fiḍḍa*). Others simply described themselves as beggars, or said "we beg" (in colloquial Egyptian *b-nishḥat*). Of course, such statements were verified by the government before they were believed. Most of these people were vagrants, who had no recordable residence, and who were not attached to any particular neighborhood (*ḥāra*).[20]

In a society that favored the "known," the traceable, such individuals were "cut loose." The Turkish-speaking bureaucracy referred to them as "placeless," or "homeless" (*makansīz, kapīsīz*). In Cairo, as in other towns, one could find them camped out for the night in various parts of the city. The less fortunate would find a corner in a street, on the bank of the Nile in Būlāq or Old Cairo, or in the Mamluk cemetery. Those who managed to get a job for a few days could often receive permission to sleep on the premise until the work was completed. Others with small income, but not enough for permanent residence, rented a room in an inn, where some even stayed a number of years, rendering services to the owners as partial payment for accommodations. Peddlers who went from neighborhood to neighborhood, or from town to town, parked with their merchandise wherever they could.[21] But the most popular shelters for the homeless were the various mosques, which provided some protection against the cold in winter.

Foremost among the "open shelters" of Cairo was the mosque-university of al-Azhar. The poor and homeless would gather there before dark to spend the night in its courts and covered halls. In the morning they would disperse, going about their business, trying to find employment, food, perhaps a more suitable and longer-term lodging. Some tried to find an occasional job in the Azhar area, such as occurred at the frequent marriages, circumcisions, and other festivities around the celebrated mosque. The Azhar students themselves were not well-off, though many of them had a steady income and/or an occupation. There were several cases of theft perpetrated by the poor "guests" against students and faculty, and sometimes against other vagrants. The items stolen on such occasions only demonstrate how poor were all those involved. Such problems were often settled by the Azhar *shaykhs* without recourse to the police.[22] Generally speaking, God's poor were accepted as a permanent feature of His place of worship.

Some of the homeless rotated between several mosques and mausolea, spending a few nights in each. Those most frequently mentioned in the sources are the mosques of Ibn Ṭūlūn and al-Muᶜayyad, and the tomb of the Imām ash-Shāfiᶜī, but in almost all the larger sanctuaries, the poor and destitute found shelter. The government recognized this phenomenon as legitimate and did not try to prevent such usage of public space. In fact, it even moved to facilitate it. On 14 April 1849, for example, the authorities engaged a contractor to lay tiles in an area designated "for the poor" in the mosque of Ibn Ṭūlūn. In some measure, this reflects a realization that the government had a responsibility towards the homeless and could not simply turn them out at night. This attitude might have been guided by considerations of security and the desire to keep people off the streets after dark. To be sure, tile-laid grounds were not the most comfortable accommodation, and if adequate in summer, were quite cold in winter.[23]

There were a number of reasons why men and women fell below the line of poverty in mid-century Egypt. In other words, we should look for the conditions that impaired the capacity of these people to earn enough money to subsist. Almost all those considered poor were also unemployed. It was rare for someone to have a regular job, or to be frequently employed on a daily basis, and yet to be "poor" according to social convention. For an individual, trouble began when jobs became too few and far between, ultimately leading to long periods of unemployment. Soon after, resignation to one's inability to provide for him or herself followed. In many cases, debt was a precursor to poverty. That occurred, at times, in the interim period in which the unemployed still entertained hopes of rehabilitation and contracted debts in order not to slip further down. At other times, low pay or accumulated arrears forced a loan, which could not be repaid, or which required much of the wage to service.[24]

The story of al-Ḥāj ᶜAlī is an especially sad example of the consequences of indebtedness.[25] He had been a soldier in the regiment assigned to keep the peace in Cairo, but was released after a period of service. He then tried to make a living in the city by running a coffeehouse, which he rented for a monthly fee. It did not seem to work very well, and ᶜAlī fell into debt which he could not pay back. He also remained homeless. As a last resort, he hired out his young son to one of the village *shaykhs* to be enrolled in the army. Clearly, ᶜAlī's situation must have been desperate to resort to such an extreme measure. As we have already mentioned, village headmen did that when they needed to fill conscription quotas and wanted to replace sons of relatives and friends. In this case, ᶜAlī used the money to pay his debts but was left with nothing. Luckily for him, after the son's release from the army, an owner of a Cairene coffeehouse, who pitied the two, took them in and gave them employment and a place to stay. But not all the poor were as fortunate as ᶜAlī.

Those who had no one to turn to for help were prime candidates for perennial poverty. Sometimes, even the most modest income supplement from a relative could save a person in need. In one case, for example, a young man working at a factory in Būlāq occasionally asked his father for some money. The father managed to assist him from time to time, although he himself was only a servant and cleaner at the mosque of al-Ḥusayn in Cairo and must have been barely making ends meet. It was not people in similar situations who fell off the deep end, but rather those like Zanūba, mentioned above, who could not be hired as a servant because she had no guarantor. She was sitting and crying outside the door of an employment agent, knowing that she had nowhere to go from there. Like her, prime candidates for poverty were other divorced women with no relatives to turn to, villagers who emigrated to towns and cities without prior knowledge of urban realities and with no friends to assist them, the handicapped, slaves who had been manumitted or turned loose after the death of their owner, and deserters from the army or the *corvée*.[26]

What did the poor do to survive? Indeed, they begged, stole, or borrowed, and sometimes did all three. Borrowers rarely improved their condition beyond the short term, and often found themselves worse off than they had been before contracting the debt. As for begging, Edward Lane observed that it was the way in which many men and women of the urban lower strata in Egypt obtained their subsistence. He also believed that quite a few among them were impostors:

> their condition is not quite so bad as their appearance might lead a stranger to suppose. They are almost sure of obtaining either food or money sufficient for supplying the absolute wants of nature, in consequence of the charitable disposition of their countrymen, and the common habit which the tradespeople have of eating in their shops, and generally giving a morsel of their food to those who ask for it.[27]

Sometimes, poverty drove to crime, mostly to petty thievery, the booty of which was then sold illegally for a few piasters. Commenting on property offenses in rural Egypt, St. John took an unusual view among European travelers at the time. He wrote:

> In many cases the fellahs do not receive sufficient to support life; and are compelled to die or steal, if this word, as a term of depreciation, can be applied to the resumption of the product of their labour unjustly withheld.[28]

The same could be said of urban workers, whose wages were low and irregularly paid. If the *fallāḥīn* "stole" money from the government, land owners, or tax-farmers, wage laborers in towns pilfered from their employers, who often were well-to-do, but also from other poor people, who could ill afford it.

Generally speaking, the poor and homeless were regarded by the police as a suspect group. Since they did not belong to any specific neighborhood and were not accounted for by any *shaykh*, it was left to the police to keep track of them, at least in some measure. There were known places where such persons used to "hang out" during the day, usually in crowded city gates or markets. Detectives kept an eye on those who ganged together, especially children and young men, in order to prevent them from stealing or dealing in stolen goods. The police had its own sources within such groups and used them to detect offenders. Thus, thievery, too, was only a temporary relief to the poor who chose to pursue it. The experienced and adept could get away with occasional pilfering of small, inexpensive items. But, larger and frequent operations were difficult to conceal, as markets, neighborhoods, and potential offenders were fairly well monitored. In short, there was no easy way out of poverty, and it was even harder to escape for those born into it.

On the whole, life for members of the urban lower strata was not easy. Nevertheless, we ought to recognize that in this chapter, we have dealt mostly with the gloomy side of their lives. That is, with the factor of insecurity in their existence. The uncertainty of employment, the irregularity of day wages, and the unreliability of government as an employer were ever to be dreaded. To compensate for these, men and women eagerly attached themselves to those elements in their life that were stable. The family, the neighborhood, the quarter, the patron household, the guild, and the *ṣūfī* order, all served as social anchors. Those who had no attachments at all drifted to the very margins of urban society. In the following chapter we examine the urban network which provided such anchoring, but also served the government as an effective control system.

11 The network of urban control

We have already mentioned the important role of village headmen and the powers they acquired because the government delegated to them some major functions, such as the selection of *fallāḥīn* for military service and the *corvée*. A similar network of *shaykh*s was deployed by the government in Egyptian cities and towns. In the urban setting, however, these semi-official local figures had somewhat different tasks. In the middle decades, conscription was consigned to the rural population, and only small numbers of city dwellers were employed as *corvée* laborers, mostly in the few manufactories that still remained operative. Thus, the role of urban *shaykh*s differed in some ways from that of village *shaykh*s. To begin with, there were a few "kinds" of *shaykh*s in the city with different tasks and standing. There were mainly *shaykh*s of neighborhoods, of quarters, of guilds, and of *ṣūfī* orders.

Neighborhood and quarter *shaykh*s headed the residential units in town, or where one lived; guild *shaykh*s controlled occupational corporations, or various aspects of one's work; *ṣūfī shaykh*s presided over the orders which provided one with communal and spiritual activity. Thus, *shaykh*s accompanied city dwellers from womb to tomb. To the government, they were the eyes and ears, as well as the vehicles through which policies were implemented. In their various jurisdictions, they were an extension of the police and part of the control system that constituted the Ottoman-Egyptian concept of law, order, and prosperity (*asayiş ve rahat*). That concept recognized that public order and the welfare of the community were interdependent, and that social and economic disaffection could lead to crime and unrest. To the urban population, they represented authority, order, and stability, social anchors that aroused less antagonism than might be expected, considering their intrusion into the private domain.

In this chapter, we shall examine the role of neighborhood, quarter, and guild *shaykh*s, but not that of *shaykh*s of *ṣūfī* orders. The latter have been amply treated in F. De Jong's study of *Ṭuruq and Ṭuruq-Linked Institutions in Nineteenth Century Egypt*. De Jong shows that by the 1840s, the orders were brought into the realm of government control and a clear hierarchy under the Shaykh of the Bakriyya had been established.[1] This process continued throughout the middle decades and fully accords with the expansion of the state, as manifested also in the urban control network discussed in the following pages. It is clear, however, that the role of *ṣūfī shaykhs* in urban control was more limited than that of "residential" and guild *shaykhs*.

Quarter and neighborhood *shaykhs*

Before we proceed to discuss what quarter and neighborhood *shaykhs* actually did, we must clarify a few points of terminology.[2] There seems to be some confusion regarding the use of the terms *shaykh* and *ᶜumda*. Our archival sources leave little doubt that during the middle decades, the two were used interchangeably. According to context, both denoted "headman," whether of a village, an urban neighborhood, a quarter in town, a guild, or a guild-type group. Sometimes, the two terms appear together, as in "the *shaykhs* and *ᶜumdas*" of a certain quarter, or guild. In addition, there was a hierarchy within the structure of urban government.

In Cairo, for example, there were eight quarters, known as "eighths" (Arabic *thumn*, pl. *athmān*), following the system devised for the city during the French occupation. Elsewhere, such units were sometimes called *rubᶜ* (pl. *arbāᶜ*, literally "one-quarter," "one-fourth"). Below the *thumn* came the *ḥāra* (pl. *ḥārāt*), at times rendered as quarters, at times as neighborhoods.[3] Thus, the urban hierarchy of Cairo consisted of eight *shaykhs* of quarters, plus the *shaykhs* of the two suburbs of Būlāq and Old Cairo. Then came their deputies (*wakīls*), and the *shaykhs* of neighborhoods (*ḥāras*), who in some cases also had deputies. The latter usually appear in the records as substitutes when the *shaykh* was temporarily absent for some reason. However, it is possible that in larger *ḥāras* a permanent position of deputy *shaykh* existed. Other towns and cities had similar networks, mutatis mutandis.

Most *shaykhs* of quarters and neighborhoods were Arabic speaking, and socio-culturally did not belong to the Ottoman-Egyptian elite. To the local population they were the most immediate representatives of the government, though the contact was somewhat softened by the fact that they spoke the same language, in more than the lingual sense. It was to them that people in trouble turned for first "official help," often before they turned to the police. In the two suburbs of Cairo, Būlāq and Old Cairo, quarter *shaykhs* seem to have had greater authority *vis-à-vis* the local police than in the inner Cairo quarters. But everywhere, they had a small body of guards at their disposal, as well as a number of assistants. Variations aside, these often included a deputy, a guards' supervisor, and a midwife (*dāya*), for inspection of cases iunvolving women. Of course, all neighborhood *shaykhs* were at the disposal of the quarter *shaykh*, assisting him in his duties.

Although *shaykhs* of quarters were not as close to "street level" as *shaykhs* of neighborhoods, they were still fairly close to the scene of events.[4] They made frequent rounds in the streets and alleys under their jurisdiction, with or without police escort, dealing with occasional problems and minor disputes when such erupted, or were brought to their attention while making the rounds. Quarter *shaykh*s had the power to detain people, or take them to the police station for investigation. However, this was not often necessary, for the *shaykh*s carried enough authority to prevail, and to settle most disputes on the spot. Other cases, which they did not witness when combing their territory, were reported to them post facto, at any time of the day or night. They would then take action according to the circumstances. When necessary, the *shaykh* would proceed to the scene, listen to the parties, conduct an initial inquest, summon witnesses, and often impose a decision on all concerned without involving the police. Quarter *shaykh*s also had the power to prevent an "undesirable" person from residing in their quarter.

Serious offenses would be taken directly to the police, or reported to the quarter *shaykh*, and then by him to the police. Quarter *shaykh*s had access to scribes, for they often presented written reports to the authorities, as when passing a case to the police. Their observations were incorporated into case reports (*jurnāl*s), which at the end of an investigation, were put before the Council of Justice. But quarter and neighborhood *shaykh*s often had to respond to demands from police headquarters. In such cases, they were asked to supply missing information, conduct a search for escaping suspects, or carry out certain investigative chores on the scene. All such actions had to be reported to the authorities to prevent transgressions against the law and police practice. On 22 August 1850, for example, the police issued an order to all quarter *shaykh*s of Cairo and its suburbs to be on the lookout for a convicted thief.[5] The man had escaped from the Alexandria dockyard prison and was expected to seek refuge in the city or the adjacent Giza governorate. Such orders were quite common.

The police relied heavily on the quarter *shaykh*'s intimate knowledge of his territory. He, in turn, expected neighborhood *shaykh*s in his quarter to acquaint themselves with all individuals under their jurisdiction and keep him well-informed.[6] Neighborhood *shaykh*s had a more limited role in the actual investigation of misconduct, but could still play a significant part in settling minor disputes in their locales. There was great likelihood that they would be the first to reach the scene or a brawl, or a crime, because of their proximity. It was also likely that they would be told about events in the neighborhood early on and, thus, get a first chance to put things right. They were also expected to notice any illegal practices and report them to the authorities. Many of these, for example, were transactions which took place without a guarantor when one was required by local custom.

But the most important task of the *shaykh* was to collect accurate information on all individuals residing in his neighborhood. Furthermore, he was expected to maintain an unwritten neighborhood "archive," that is, a case history of each individual in his territory. This was in full conformity with a strong cultural trait which favored the *known* and strove to limit and exclude the *unknown* (see above, pp. 200–5). It also served some very practical purposes. First, unknown individuals were easily detectable. Since they were believed to commit most offenses, such persons were treated with suspicion and were the first to be detained when anything went wrong. Second, against a *known* background, wanted persons would immediately stick out and could be reported to the authorities. These could be deserters from the army or the *corvée*, draft evaders seeking refuge, escaped prisoners, or any other fugitives from the law. And third, such information was needed for testimony evaluation in criminal investigation.

For that purpose, neighborhood *shaykh*s were often called upon to testify to the character of various people. Such testimonies were expected to include details about the length of the person's residence in the neighborhood, his or her employment, circumstances of his or her movements in and out of the neighborhood, whether he or she had been involved in misdemeanors which were not recorded by the police, and, finally, the person's natural dispositions. To accumulate that kind of information, the element of continuity was essential. Hence, high turnover of neighborhood *shaykh*s was clearly undesirable. They were a fixture of the neighborhood, part and parcel of the local scene, available at all times of day and night, ever watching the life of "their" people. Indeed, neighborhoods became identified by the name of their *shaykh*s. It was not uncommon that an individual would give his or her residential address as such and such a place, "in the neighborhood [or jurisdiction] of *shaykh* so and so" (*shiyākhat fulān*).

The authorities demanded that neighborhood *shaykh*s remain vigilant and held them personally accountable. If they appeared remiss, they were reprimanded and forced to exert themselves until they obtained results, as the following case may illustrate. A woman was beaten by her husband in a Cairene neighborhood in November 1849.[7] There were conflicting versions as to the cause of death. The husband claimed he had hit her "lightly," and she could not have died from that, but probably as a result of her seven months' pregnancy. Although a doctor verified that the woman had died of beating, a few major gaps remained in the testimonies presented to the police. The neighborhood *shaykh* was severely castigated for failing to supply the missing evidence. He was told that he must fulfill his duties as *shaykh* and provide the necessary information. The *shaykh*, obviously under considerable pressure, promised to "investigate it from deep under (*abḥath min taḥt li-taḥt*)." He then undertook to question women and other involved persons, and was duly granted time to talk to the neighbors and produce results.

Much as we can learn from the record about what quarter and neighborhood *shaykh*s did, there is precious little information about who they were and how they were recruited. Their status was something of a hybrid. They certainly did not belong to the office holding Ottoman-Egyptian elite, but they did hold an official position. Thus, to the local population, they were law-enforcing agents who represented the viceregal government, without being part of the dominant, Turkish-based, Ottoman culture. Their position was akin to that of the Arabic-speaking junior officers in the army, in that they, too, were removed from their own people by dint of the function they filled. They were a non-elite, Arabic-speaking element, in the service of the elite. It is quite possible that honorably discharged junior officers were the "right material" for neighborhood *shaykhs*.[8] Others were probably local strongmen, or simply respectable and, in the eyes of the authorities, reliable individuals. In any event, they existed on the delicate borderline of group identity, walking the tight-rope between the Ottoman-Egyptian elite and the rest of the population.

As with so many official positions, a *shaykh*'s personality often determined his standing *vis-à-vis* the people in his territory, whose lives he followed from womb to tomb, and *vis-à-vis* members of the Ottoman-Egyptian elite, whom he served. There is evidence to suggest that those *shaykhs* who bowed before authority – whatever its caprice, excesses, or rapacity – were treated with contempt by members of the elite. On the other hand, those who stood up against flagrant violations of the law by elite members and demanded that due process be respected, received the support of the government (see pp. 172–7 above). This was the case at least during the reign of Abbas, who worked to check the power of the Ottoman-Egyptian elite and increase the capacity of government-controlled "intermediaries." To some extent, this was inadvertently reversed in the time of Sait, who relaxed controls over the elite. In both cases, the government called the tune, signalling to all concerned what its preferences were.

Guild *shaykhs*

The heads of local occupational corporations in mid-nineteenth-century Egypt formed an important part of the urban network through which the government implemented its economic policies and controlled both the bazaar economy and the labor market.[9] These corporations were common in all trades practiced in Egypt at the time. They were the basic occupational unit to which artisans, shop-keepers, and providers of most services belonged. Through them, the viceroy's men regulated – in varying degrees – commerce, handicraft production, and the services. However, the precise nature of these corporations, their origins, their history in various parts of the Islamic world, their structure, the extent of regulation they afforded, and other pertinent questions concerning their mode of operation have long been the subject of controversy among historians. The on-going debate about Ottoman and Egyptian guilds will not be treated in this section. However, some aspects of the role played by the corporations and their *shaykhs* in mid-century Egyptian society will be discussed in a limited fashion.

Before we can proceed, we ought to qualify our use of terms. This inevitably will reflect a certain viewpoint in the general debate, but after all, not all hard decisions can be avoided. One term that needs clarification is "guild," the other, "*shaykh*," requires some explanation. Even those who ardently defend the use of the term guild in an Ottoman or Egyptian context, would concede that there were clear differences between European guilds and Ottoman or Egyptian ones. The most striking feature of Egyptian local occupational corporations in the period discussed here is the fact that they were an articulation of government control. There was little of the voluntary about them, and they were not, for the most part, in a position to resist government policy. This distance from European guilds warrants some modification of current terminology.[10] To avoid cumbersome terms such as "local occupational corporation," we shall retain the term "guild," but keep in mind its inaccuracy.

In the Egyptian records from the middle of the nineteenth century, the terms most frequently used to denote guilds are the Turkish *taife* and the Arabic *ṭā'ifa* and *ḥirfa*. Members are usually referred to as *esnaf*, in Turkish, or simply by their profession, e.g. "the door-keepers" (*al-bawwābūn* or frequently *al-bawwābīn*). The head of such a guild is called *shaykh*, sometimes with *ṭā'ifa*, as in *shaykh ṭā'ifat al-bawwābīn*, or simply *shaykh al-bawwābīn*. *Ra'īs* and *mukhtār* are also used in similar constructs, though the latter is more common as *mukhtār al-bawwābīn*. The term *ᶜumda* also occurs in the documents, but it seems somewhat more ambiguous. For it often appears in the plural (*al-ᶜumad*) together with *shaykh* and could then mean "the *shaykh* and masters" of the guild (*ash-shaykh wa-l-ᶜumad*, or in Turkish *taifenin şeyhi ve umdeleri*). A term which was used on rare occasions is *muᶜallim*, as in *muᶜallim ṭā'ifat al-muballiṭīn* (head of the pavers/tile-layers' guild).[11] For the sake of simplicity, we shall use here only *shaykh* to denote the head of a guild, bearing in mind that other terms were also in use.

Before we delve into the realities of how guild *shaykh*s actually did what they did at mid-century, we should say a word about the state of Egyptian guilds during that period.[12] Mehmet Ali's reforms and failed industrial experiment of the 1820s and 1830s did not seriously weaken the guilds, perhaps with the exception of the weavers' guilds. Much of the rest lay outside the scope of his enterprise, since his factories operated in new fields of production, whose workforce had not been organized in guilds before. In addition, over half the number of guilds – with about two-thirds of total guild membership – were merchant and service guilds. These were not involved in production, hence only indirectly and mildly affected by the reforms. Even in those areas which were adversely affected by Mehmet Ali's industries, there is mid-century evidence of survival, if not revival.

Thus, after the gradual demise of his factories in the 1840s, some workers put their newly acquired know-how to private use, setting up their own manufactories. It is true that the unwitting result of Mehmet Ali's policies was to weaken local competition and lay the country open to European products. But there were local craftsmen who adjusted to the changing realities by introducing new products or finding new markets for their traditional manufactures. Having survived the reign of Mehmet Ali, the guilds would not be seriously challenged until later in the century. No new attempts at industrialization occurred in the reigns of Abbas and Sait, nor did the government wish to undermine the guilds, which perfectly served its needs. Sait indeed tried to limit guild monopolies, but he was unsuccessful, probably because he was not quite adamant about it.

It is not enough, however, to say that guilds continued to exist in mid-nineteenth-century Egypt. We ought to find out what these corporations were actually about and how they operated. Baer correctly observed that Egyptian guilds at the time possessed "no rigid system of apprenticeship, no clear cut distinction between apprentices and journeymen, and it was relatively easy for an apprentice or a journeyman to become master . . . and no sharp economic or social differentiation developed between the guilds' masters and the shaykhs . . . " In addition to the functions of guilds discussed in the following paragraphs, they also served as tax units, their *shaykh*s assessing and collecting from individual members their share of the total amount imposed on the guild. It is important to note that guilds were *local* corporations, neither integrated nor coordinated country-wide or even within one city. Baer seems to imply that guilds exercised a monopoly of their trades, but, at least for mid-century Egypt, this appears less strict and much more in line with the fairly relaxed nature of Egyptian guilds.[13]

We have already mentioned the important role of the guild *shaykh*s in the labor market (p. 211 above). Many of their other functions resembled those of neighborhood *shaykh*s.[14] Like them, they were expected by the authorities to prevent any violation of the law, and when such did occur to report the offenders to the police and assist in bringing them to justice. Guild *shaykh*s were summoned whenever information about one of their guild members was needed. They had to know every person, his or her history, character, and disposition, and supply such details to facilitate criminal investigations. Collection of such data was a matter of routine, for which the law obliged guild members to report any unusual or suspicious event to their *shaykh*. When a guild member was believed by the police to have committed a felony, the *shaykh* was ordered to track him or her down, or provide information that would lead the detectives to the fugitive. Conversely, guild *shaykh*s were also the channel through which information about offenses committed against members of the guild was passed on from the government to the victims.

The authorities relied on guild *shaykh*s to assist in the daily enforcement of laws and regulations relating to their various trades. Thus, for example, on 28 June 1849, the government sought to prohibit the proliferation of fire-arms.[15] Only soldiers and bedouin auxiliaries – specifically excluding the *fallāḥīn* – were allowed to carry such weapons. Without a valid permit, fire-arms were not to be sold to anyone, nor carried when passing through city gates. Weapons were to be collected from all those not allowed to carry them, and no repairs were to be made in illegally held arms. Quite obviously, the full cooperation of guild *shaykhs* was absolutely essential if the prohibition was to be effective at all. Accordingly, guild *shaykhs* of fire-arms sellers were ordered not to sell without permit, whils *shaykhs* of fire-arms repairmen were told to treat only licensed weapons and report all other cases to the authorities.

Guild *shaykhs* had a dual responsibility – to the government and to guild members. Their responsibility to the authorities meant that they had to ensure that all guild members abided by government regulations. Any violation had to be dealt with, first by reprimand, then by punishment, including expulsion from the guild, which was tantamount to loss of a job and diminished chances for future employment. Thus, for example, the police discovered, in December 1851, that a certain door-keeper (*bawwāb*) of an inn failed to require guests to produce a written statement from a guarantor. The *shaykh* of the door-keepers' guild – probably of that particular area in Cairo – was asked by the police to sack the culprit. The *shaykh* obliged and the man lost his job at the inn. In other cases, *shaykhs* were called upon to serve as guarantors for negligent guild members and vouch for their future good conduct.[16]

But *shaykhs* also had a recognized responsibility to protect the interests of guild members. They were expected to do that through legal means and by approaching the authorities whenever infringement of custom or right occurred. An interesting dispute which erupted in 1851–2 may illustrate the situation that prevailed in Egypt during the middle decades of the nineteenth century (see also pp. 171–2 above). A high-ranking member of the Ottoman-Egyptian elite, Mehmet Bey, tried to take over the business of transporting passengers and goods between Cairo and a certain village across the Nile.[17] This was to be done at the expense of the boatmen attached to that docking point, who belonged to a guild and had an officially recognized *shaykh*. Before the situation deteriorated to bloody violence, the *shaykh* made an attempt to persuade the *bey*'s boatmen not to disrupt the status quo. First, he notified the authorities of the situation. Then, he warned the rival boatmen that if passengers complained to the authorities of their higher fares and coercive conduct, he would not be able to protect them, as he had no power over them.

Here, the dual concept of *protection* and *jurisdiction* is vividly expressed. The guild *shaykh* could offer protection against complaints only to members of his guild, over which he had authority (here *ḥukm*). For, membership in a guild entailed submission to the *shaykh*, hence to the laws and regulations of the viceroy's government. If the public or the authorities complained of negligence or "malpractice" by any member of the guild, the *shaykh* had powers to investigate and present a case to vindicate or incriminate the person concerned. Without such power over his subordinates, the *shaykh* could not offer them protection. Guild members surrendered the freedom to act outside the system, without a limiting code of conduct, in return for corporate protection within the system. That was the essence of the trade-off. By turning against their fellow boatmen, Mehmet Bey's boatmen forced the *shaykh* to expel them from the guild, which in ordinary circumstances, would have been a serious deterrent. However, in this case, the men placed themselves under the protection of Mehmet Bey, whom they probably believed to be more powerful than the *shaykh*.

The "authority" to which the boatmen's *shaykh* referred was exercised by guild headmen through a "code of ethics" embodied in guild regulations, practices, and accepted customs. These, of course, varied from guild to guild and were modified from time to time to meet changes in economic policies and circumstances. For the most part, such codes of practice were not written, but orally transmitted from master to apprentice over the generations.[18] However, it stands to reason that, in addition to the records kept by the government and the courts, *shaykh*s kept for reference a record of government orders regarding their own guild. The term frequently used to denote such codes was *usûl*, which implies an unwritten convention. Thus, a *shaykh*, or a government agency, could accuse a shopkeeper, an artisan, or a servant of violating his or her "guild *usûl*" (as in the Turkish *taifenin usûlu*), and demand that he or she be punished according to the gravity of the transgression.

In addition to imposing the guild's code, *shaykh*s had other responsibilities, which might be termed "professional." In commercial and artisan guilds, these were quite specific, but in the services, such functions were less clearly articulated. In some trades, the *shaykh* and the masters of the guild actually set the market prices of goods. This, for example, was clearly the case in the dried-fruit business (Turkish *yemiş*). After the prices were determined by these men, they were reported to the authorities and registered with the police. Thenceforward, those prices were binding and any deviation from them became a punishable offense, not merely an ethical matter for guild discipline. The *shaykh*s of the butchers, for instance, were consulted when the contract to supply meat to the government was being negotiated. And, in disputes, as during criminal investigation, guild *shaykh*s were often called upon to provide a reliable estimate of the value of animals and goods handled by their respective guilds. A great deal depended on their expert opinion, which could determine not only the level of compensation to be paid by a convicted thief, for example, but also the penalty he or she would receive.[19]

Before we round up our account of the role of guild *shaykh*s as "social intermediaries," we ought to mention that in various towns there were also *shaykh*s of yet another kind. These were the bazaar *shaykh*s (*shaykh as-sūq*). It seems that such a position existed only in towns with one central market, which was small enough to be managed by one market supervisor. The central Egyptian archives for the period contain a number of references to the bazaar *shaykh* of the Nile Barrages (al-Qanāṭir al-Khayriyya).[20] The *shaykh* is mentioned along with the commander of the market police (*ḍābiṭ as-sūq*), whose subordinate he appears to have been. The police officer operated from a certain coffeehouse in the bazaar, where he could also detain suspected offenders, some of whom were discovered by the market *shaykh* and handed over to him. From the little that is known about the position, it appears that the *shaykh*'s functions resembled those of neighborhood *shaykh*s. It is not clear what were his relations with guild *shaykh*s in the bazaar, nor if he had "professional" responsibilities similar to theirs.

As mentioned above, a fundamental trade-off was embodied in the concept of mid-century Egyptian guilds. In return for surrendering a measure of their freedom, members received a measure of protection. This notion can now be extended to the other elements of the urban control network. Accordingly, neighborhoods, guilds and *ṣūfī* orders offered varying degrees of security in return for submission to government authority as enshrined in the laws of the viceroy. Guild codes were the most explicit of these undertakings, but the criminal codes of the period and unwritten conventions were as binding. The Paşa's peace which reigned in Egypt during the middle decades of the nineteenth century had its price. Its terms, however, seemed then more generous than before, the price not as high. If indeed "all culture is a defense of the social order against conflict,"[21] then mid-century Egyptian culture is a good example of it.

So far, we have dealt with the various manifestations of state and elite power, which squeezed the rural and urban lower strata. The relative absence of violent conflict, as we have seen,[22] was due to the possibility, acceptability, and efficacy of other, indirect, and non-violent modes of resistance. A degree of flexibility was manifest in that the state yielded to petitions, adjusted wages, and allowed a greater share of the surplus to remain with the producers, in that it recognized the limits of coercion in conscription and the *corvée*, and provided internal and external peace. All that accounts in large measure for a record of relatively undisturbed social relations in a society where inequality in all aspects of life was rife. But there is another factor that defused social tension in contemporary Egyptian society, namely the in-built cultural mechanism that enabled various forms of pastime to flourish with few impediments.

12 The use of unappropriated time

Members of the rural and urban lower strata had little time they could really call their own. Through its exploitative economic policies and aggressive intervention, the state, both directly and indirectly, controlled much of the time these men and women had. In rural Egypt at mid-century, one had limited options of spending his or her free time beyond games, conversation with neighbors and friends, occasional festivities, mostly related to the family, agricultural events, simulations of past regional rivalries, or a local saint, and activities of *ṣūfī* orders, where these were accessible.[1] On the other hand, the city offered a greater variety of diversions, including street entertainment, coffeehouses, public baths, and bars. In this chapter, we shall explore the urban opportunities for spending one's free time, with the intention of assessing the social significance of leisure.

Entertainment

In the middle of the nineteenth century, the streets of Cairo, as those of other towns in Egypt, were the place in which most Egyptians sought and found entertainment to pass their daily leisure. To outsiders, the proliferation of performances was overwhelming, as Gadsby vividly conveys:

> In almost every street, at different times of the day, you will see a variety of exhibitions. Men with learned dogs, or still more learned monkeys, or yet more learned boys; reciting tales, the same tales a thousand and one times over, and every time with the same marks of applause; wrestlers, conjurers, jugglers, buffoons, &c. One man had erected a tent in the Esbekiah Gardens, and had a figure at the entrance dressed up as a British Grenadier; and this attracted hundreds. It is surprising how light-hearted the people are, even under their heavy chains.[2]

Actually, this "theatrical escapism" might well have been one of the more effective means of dealing with a "chained reality." Thus, the more frequented passageways, often near mosques, markets, and other public places, served as an "open-air theater" for all sorts of performances. There were no designated spaces for that kind of social activity; the performers, their assistants, and their paraphernalia moved about, choosing when and where to exhibit their talents. The crowd would then assemble in a circle around them, and the show would begin. Such performances were mostly the result of private enterprise, but there is evidence to suggest that, from time to time, the government also sponsored public entertainment. Descriptions of the main types of street shows can be found in many travel accounts of the nineteenth century. Edward Lane provides the best and most detailed survey of such performances, which hardly needs repeating here.[3] Instead, we shall only mention the most popular performances and try to place them in a socio-cultural context.

For our purposes, this would mean an attempt to define the meaning that such activities had, or acquired over time, within the culture; that is, what significance they had beyond being "mere," or "just" entertainment. What were the mundane, or illegitimate activities that the attraction and socio-cultural legitimacy of entertainment either salvaged or covered up? In more specific terms, for example, farce shows masqueraded politics and often conveyed a political message that no other medium in a controlled society could. The powerful, fascinating, and dangerous world of the occult was represented by the various forms of fortune-telling. Dancing served as an artistic prelude to and play on female and male prostitution. And snake-charming, not merely a performance, elevated to an art an activity widely believed to result in the elimination of dangerous and frightening reptiles from the environment.

There were different reasons why entertainment had to camouflage such activities. To voice open, rather than humor-coded criticism of the government was often dangerous. As for prostitution, the indirect approach seems to have been culturally preferred. Furthermore, during long periods in mid-century Egypt, obstacles were thrown in the way of the practice, and it was even made illegal. The occult and snake-charming bordered on the fascinating and mysterious, harping on the hidden fears and hopes of many. Thus, performance was just the tip of an iceberg, betraying and legitimating a deeply rooted belief system. The major components of that system were shared by rich and poor, powerful and powerless, Westernized and traditional; they recognized no "high" of "low" cultural distinctions. Thus concentrated and sublimated, entertainment served as a "reality-away-from-reality," a fantasy acted out in public, but answering to inner, forbidden dreams. In the following pages, we shall mention some of the major types of performances, and then briefly venture into the realms they "conceal."

Among the most popular performers were the *ḥāwīs*, whom Lane calls "performers of sleight-of-hand tricks." They displayed various tricks with tamed snakes and other acts which we usually associate with modern-day magicians. There were also, observed Lane, "several indecent tricks which he performs with the boy [his assistant] I must abstain from describing: some of them are abominably disgusting." "Obscene" jokes, too, were acted out to amuse the spectators. The *qayyim*, another type of performer, had a great talent for guessing games, such as discovering a coin placed under one of twenty-nine stones, or telling the names of persons in the audience. As Lane found out, these men always used "undercover" assistants to ensure that they guessed correctly.[4] The Gipsy (*ghajar*) women were the leading fortune-tellers in Egypt. They employed a mixture of shells, pieces of colored glass, and money as their tools. "I perform divination! What is present I manifest! What is absent I manifest!", they used to announce in the streets, reports Lane.

The *bahlawāns*, or acrobats, were also mostly Gypsies. Their performance consisted of rope-dancing, tumbling, leaping through a loop, and other exercises. Another kind of performer was the *quraydātī*, or monkey-trainer, a category which encompassed animal-trainers of various sorts. Their monkeys, dogs, asses, or kids were dressed up in funny costumes and made to perform a few tricks. From them we move closer to theater performances in the realm of the *muḥabbazīn*, rendered by Lane as "players of low and ridiculous farces." Lane found their performances "scarcely worthy of description: it is chiefly by vulgar jests, and indecent actions, that they amuse, and obtain applause."[5] Another "extremely indecent" theater was the *karagöz*, or shadow puppet-show, an Ottoman art performed in Turkish at night. It was not intended for those who could not understand the language and had, therefore, a limited audience on "the high street."

All the performances mentioned so far were a matter of daily occurrence. However, they were concentrated and mounted on a much larger scale during Muslim holidays and other public festivities. The Prophet's Birthday, the month-long fast of Ramadan, the two holidays which follow it – ᶜĪd al-Fiṭr and ᶜĪd al-Aḍḥā – and the departure and return of the pilgrims' caravan were but the major ones. On such occasions, the streets were lit up, performers in large numbers would fill those spaces designated for public use and attract crowds of people from all walks of life. Processions were also common on festivals, as on happy viceregal events; they were a performance in itself, representing to society its own statuses and roles. Some of the ceremonies became known tourist attractions, such as the Dawsa (pronounced Dōseh), in which the *shaykh* of the Saᶜdiyya order rode on horseback over the backs of several dozen of his men, ecstatically prepared for the trying event. In those days of celebration, Cairo, and to a lesser extent other cities, would turn into a huge, exhilarating theater.[6]

We must remember, however, that what the lower strata could see only in the streets of Egyptian cities, members of the Ottoman-Egyptian elite could enjoy at home, or at the homes of their friends. Many of the performers were invited by such people to entertain their guests on special occasions, mostly holiday festivities, weddings, or circumcisions. The pay performers received in such cases must have been higher and the audience different. A trade practiced often at home, rather than on the street, was snake-charming. It belonged to those performing arts which, as mentioned above, were considered not only entertaining but also quite useful. Snake-charmers, called by European travellers "psylli," were popular and much in demand at mid-century. Their non-performing job was to lure serpents away from houses that were infested with them. That they did by an elaborate ceremony involving incantations, knocking on walls with a stick, and the like.

European visitors to Egypt were fascinated by snake-charmers and their accounts often include detailed descriptions of the practice. A sort of contest developed between performer and audience, as the latter were trying to discover any trickery which might explain the compelling sight of dangerous snakes being charmed out of their hiding holes in walls and floors, surrendering to the enchanters as if guided by an invisible force. Various restrictions were imposed on charmers to prevent deception. They were told to strip off their clothes and were thoroughly searched for hidden serpents, or were given different clothes by the owner of the house, or asked to enter the apartment without any clothes on. One who was convinced that it was pure talent was Dr. Bromfield. He wrote:

> Were the art of serpent-charming a mere juggling deception, how could it for so many ages have been exercised as a profitable employment by a particular tribe?; – it being, in fact, customary in Cairo to send to the serpent-charmer when a house is much infested with serpents, just as we should require the services of a rat-catcher, to rid our premises of those destructive animals . . . and were it *once* ascertained that conveying serpents to the premises to be cleared, was a usual, or even frequent practice, the poor, and generally covetous, and parsimonious Cairenes, would not give a *para* to have their houses stocked with noxious reptiles under the pretence of being rid of them.[7]

An additional "service" performed by snake-charmers was immunization from snake biting. This was a much more dubious practice, however. Unlike some Egyptians, Europeans might have found the ceremony amusing, if at times repulsive, but they certainly did not take it seriously. Those Egyptians who did could have been in real trouble, as we shall soon see. Flaubert's traveling companion, Maxime Du Camp, provides a representative account of the ceremony.

> The charmer then proposed to immunize me for the rest of my life against all kinds of bites, and to endow me with the power to handle with perfect safety all animals no matter how venomous. I accepted with pleasure, hoping for some kind of magical ceremony, and put myself in the boy's hands. I sat down cross-legged before him, he took my hand, pressed my thumb, wrapped a snake around my wrist, and addressed me in words that were rapid and staccato: he lifted the snake to my ear; it bit me hard; with a finger he took the blood from the bite and spread it on the ground; then he breathed twice into my mouth, made me breathe twice on the large black snake, which he had wrapped around my neck, twice rubbed my bloody ear with his hand that he had moistened with his saliva, once again asked me for "a big tip" – and the thing was done. Very simple, as you see: not a very perilous initiation.[8]

Perilous, though, it was, at least to those who took it seriously. One who did was Amīn, the servant who accompanied Bromfield on his trip to Upper Egypt and the Sudan in 1851. He was stung by a great yellow African scorpion, which one of the camel drivers had brought to show to Bromfield. The meticulous Bromfield relates:

Ameen, foolishly relying on a supposed immunity from the venomous effects of these and other noxious animals, which he believed had been communicated to him by a serpent charmer at Cairo for a consideration of eleven piastres, actually grasped the scorpion with his bare hand, and it instantly struck him at the root of the second finger of the left hand. He suffered intense pain for a few hours, with a feeling of great coldness all over, numbness on the left side of the body, indistinct vision, sickness, and other constitutional symptoms of rather an alarming nature.[9]

Amīn was lucky, however, to be serving a doctor who knew what to do and who ultimately saved his life. The same kind of trust was invested in another "useful" art – fortune-telling.

Fortune-telling, too, was not only a form of entertainment; it was practical and taken seriously in all walks of life in mid-nineteenth-century Egypt. In this category we also include astrologers, necromancers, and practitioners of other methods of predicting the future. For mere fun, people asked fortune-tellers about the distant future without letting the prediction affect their immediate daily conduct. However, specific questions about imminent occurrences were also put to fortune-tellers, and advice on such matters was taken into consideration by many people. No few individuals habitually consulted specific fortune-tellers, whom they brought into their confidence and, over time, came to trust with business and personal affairs. This attitude cut across economic, social, and cultural lines. It was common among members of the Ottoman-Egyptian elite as among the lower strata in Egyptian society.[10] It would seem, however, that within the elite and among high office-holders, astrologers enjoyed greater popularity, as they were considered more "scientific" and reliable.

Abbas Paşa was believed by Europeans and Westernized Ottoman-Egyptians to have been particularly "superstitious." But he was well within Ottoman tradition when he employed asıtrologers and consulted them before taking any important step. The Ottoman court had maintained for long the position of Chief Astrologer (*Müneccim Başī*) and astrology was well respected in the empire throughout the nineteenth century. The burden of decision-making and a cultural proclivity for the occult lay at the root of this phenomenon. Thus, for example, Yusuf Kâmil Paşa reports that astrologers were consulted even in order to determine the sailing time of Abbas's son Ilhami Paşa, when he departed from Alexandria to Europe in mid 1854. Nubar relates that he once surprised Abbas in his chambers as the Paşa was attentively listening to one of his Circassian generals, Hamza Bey, who was predicting the future according to the shape of the shoulder blade of a freshly slaughtered lamb. This, Nubar adds, was an ancient Circassian "art."[11]

Another type of "scientific" fortune-teller at mid mid-century specialized in predicting the location of buried treasures. The idea excited the imagination of contemporaries, though in this branch of the trade, deception was harder to conceal. Hekekyan alleged that Abbas himself tried his luck in the field, digging for gold in Heliopolis on the basis of some such prediction. Nevertheless, in spite of his reputation, it was Abbas himself who banished all fortune-tellers from Cairo and Alexandria. The thought must have been on his mind for some time, for he carried it out almost immediately upon his return from Istanbul, where he had just been invested with the governorship of Egypt. Furthermore, the record of some of his critics on belief in the occult was not impeccable, to say the least. Two examples – figuring Sait and Nubar – may serve to illustrate the point and show how deeply ingrained such sentiments were even among the most Westernized of Ottoman-Egyptians.[12]

In December 1855, Sait told Nassau Senior how Abbas, haunted by superstitions, surrounded himself with astrologers. They kept predicting that he would be assassinated, related Sait mockingly, ever prescribing strange and costly ceremonies to avert such an end. The viceroy then went on to say that he inherited from his predecessor one of those men, who was still at his court. The man had been sent to Abbas by the sultan of Bornu and prophesied the future for Sait too. "His last prophecy has about eight months to run," intimated the viceroy, "as soon as they are over, I shall give him a flogging and send him home." If Sait indeed had no faith in the man or the practice, the obvious question might be asked, why did he wish to wait for the time to pass? The answer is that, like many other Westernized Ottomans and Ottoman-Egyptians, Sait Paşa relinquished old beliefs only to a point. Beyond that, in his heart of hearts, he was not fully convinced that it was all nonsense. Like Abbas, Sait also believed – and said so – that the death of Ibrahim Paşa, even to the date, had been predicted by a fortune-teller.[13]

In his memoirs, Nubar professes unmitigated incredulity towards "*les sciences occultes*." However, he too, had a personal experience with fortune-telling, which betrays a rather different attitude.[14] It was customary, Nubar writes, that members of the viceroy's entourage who accompanied him to Istanbul for the investiture would receive a promotion. Accordingly, Nubar expected to be made a *bey*. When he was with Abbas in the Ottoman capital, his brother consulted an astrologer, who said: "No, he [Nubar] will not receive promotion in Istanbul. But, a short while after his return [to Egypt], he would become a bey, if when he falls from a horse, he does not die instantly." The prediction came fully true, continues Nubar. To begin with, he was the only member of Abbas's entourage not to have been promoted, the viceroy wishing to avoid offending more senior officials.

Not long after his return to Egypt, the sequence of events further unfolded, as the young interpreter's horse reared up in the Muskī and tripped over him. Nubar barely escaped the pommel, which hit his chest. He was on his back, unable to move, for three weeks. When he recovered, Abbas made him *bey* and First Viceregal Secretary. The story is told without any comment regarding the lesson which Nubar drew from it. It merely concludes the section on Abbas and the occult and the chapter devoted to the events of the year 1849. The reader is left with a clear impression of the ambivalence with which that prominent and highly Westernized man viewed the subject. This impression is supported by the observation which opens Nubar's discussion of the practice in Egypt. He explains that fortune-tellers of all kinds proliferate, "le merveilleux et l'inconnu ayant toujours eu le don de séduire *l'homme en général* et, en particulier, l'Oriental" (the italics are mine).[15] Thus, perhaps unwittingly, Nubar prepared to legitimate his own ambivalence towards the occult.

Story-telling and farce plays were often used to express criticism of the government. Both belonged to a distinct *genre* and were constructed along set patterns. However, story-tellers and players could bend the forms to make them specific, thereby beaming to the audience a recognizable reality. Listeners and spectators would relate to a discourse thus made relevant, reacting naturally to familiar situations, as well as to standard jokes. Lane reporduced the translated text of a farce show played before Mehmet Ali Paşa. The play was quite specific, pointing out the corruption of state officials and tax-collectors. But stories and plays were not intended for the viceroy and his officials; they were mostly intended for public consumption. They served as a kind of safety valve, letting off steam in a harmless way and enabling the weak "to get even" *openly* with the powerful, if only for a brief moment.[16]

The last type of performance to be treated here for more than its face value is public dancing. During the middle years of the nineteenth century, female and male dancers became increasingly identified with prostitution. In the reign of Mehmet Ali Paşa, public dancing, singing, and prostitution were, for the most part, distinct trades. Male singers, who often accompanied their singing with some musical instrument, were known as *ālātī*s. A female singer was called *ʿālima* (pl. *ʿawālim*). *ghāziya* (pl. *ghawāzī*) was a woman dancer, and a *khawal* or *jink* (probably from the Turkish *cenek*) a man dancer.[17] At mid-century, all trades became assimilated, by and large, to prostitution, it being understood that after dancing, and sometimes singing, in public, the performer would be available for a fee. Accordingly, with the exception of *ālātī*, all terms came to imply female and male prostitution. Increasingly, *raqqāsa*, a female dancer, and *raqqās*, a male dancer, were used as well-understood euphemisms. This gradual change was brought about by political, economic, and social developments.

In 1834, Mehmet Ali prohibited public dancing and female prostitution in Cairo and banished the women to Upper Egypt, where they continued to work.

Until then, prostitution was supervised, regulated, and taxed by the government, though its legality did little to improve its respectability in the eyes of the public. Some prostitutes moved outside Cairo, to small and less controlled towns, in order to evade such costly, and often corrupt, government interference. After the prohibition, Cairene prostitution went underground and continued to be practiced under various guises throughout the period considered here. St. John describes in much detail his early 1850s visit to what he called "the academy of Kafr Mustanat." In that small Delta village, young girls were being trained as dancers and prepared for prostitution. And Flaubert, who seems to have been obsessed with sexuality and prostitution, conveys a sense of the clandestine nature of prostitution during the reign of Abbas:

> La Triestine [both prostitutes mentioned here were "Turkish"] was violently afraid of the police, begged us to make no noise . . . in this brothel it is forbidden to dance or play music. Nevertheless she played the *darabukeh* [a kind of drum] on the table with her fingers, while the other rolled her girdle, knotted it low on her hips, and danced.[18]

There is evidence that in the early 1850s, prostitutes were still being occasionally banished from Cairo to Upper Egypt. However, supervision must not have been consistently strict. Not only the better off prostitutes continued to work, as Flaubert's notes would suggest, but that lower class prostitution was openly practiced outside city walls, along "Pharaoh's Aqueduct." Banuma Hekekyan complained to her husband of the impertinent behavior of a European guest towards the singers (Turkish, *alimes*) during a wedding in an elite household. This suggests that singing and probably also dancing performances continued in spite of the ban. In mid 1852, a case of high-priced prostitution in a private house was recorded by the Cairo police. However, the authorities appeared to have been concerned mostly with the cash and jewelry reported as missing, while paying little attention to the "moral offense" involved.[19]

But neither can it be said that mid-century governments winked at prostitution. In August 1850, Abbas ordered the police to act on information that employment agencies were "fronting" prostitution. Strict instructions were issued to *shaykhs* of the concerned guilds and neighborhoods to take precautions in order to prevent the practice. That type of "covert prostitution" could not be possible without the collusion of both customer and employment agents. Men would come to female agents and ask for "a servant, a dow-kneater, or a wet-nurse," and a prostitute would be supplied. After such agencies had been closed down by the police, male agents began to operate in the same way, producing forged guarantee papers to give the business a legitimate appearance. The new policy made stringent scrutiny of female employment seekers mandatory. That involved checking their past record and subjecting them to physical examination by upright women recommended by neighborhood *shaykhs*. Islamic condemnation of prostitution was specifically mentioned in the instructions.[20]

In her study of women in nineteenth-century Egypt, Judith Tucker treats prostitution in the context of growing state repression and the concomitant resistance to it. As other "crimes" committed by women, she argues, prostitution "can be interpreted as a form of resistance in some cases and a badge of deprivation and despair in others." Mehmet Ali's ban and the interventionist policy of the expanding state transformed the structure and nature of the trade. In the absence of systematic regulation during the early 1800s, Tucker asserts, women had considerable control over their earnings. She further observes that increasing state control under Mehmet Ali weakened prostitutes and made them vulnerable to arbitrary and corrupt officials. Consequently, a "shadowy network of pimps and procurers" developed as an "unpleasant and dangerous" protective measure against government intervention. The fact that prohibition and regulation forced prostitution into the underworld, Tucker concludes, made women ever more dependent on male guardians.[21]

Much the same may be said about male prostitution, although the number of men involved in it was considerably smaller. In both cases, men were the procurers and the customers. That phenomenon was part of the larger issue of male homosexuality, one that has received little serious scholarly consideration and too much fanciful treatment by travelers. For an example of the latter, we must turn again to Flaubert, if only for his superior literary talents and his ever-alert senses. Flaubert readily admits that he sought the experience in Egypt, though he gives no indication of having actually found it. In the following passage from a letter to a friend, written in Cairo on 15 February 1850, he is describing two male dancers who performed at the hotel where he resided:

> As dancers, imagine two rascals [Hasan el-Belbeissi and another dancer], quite ugly, but charming in their corruption, in their obscene leerings and the femininity of their movements, dressed as women, their eyes painted with antimony . . . From time to time, during the dance, the impresario, or pimp, who brought them plays around them, kissing them on the belly, the arse, and the small of the back, and making obscene remarks in an effort to put additional spice into a thing that is already quite clear in itself . . . I'll have this marvelous Hasan el-Belbeissi come again. He'll dance the Bee [an erotic dance in nude] for me, in particular. Done by such a bardash [male homosexual] as he, it can scarcely be a thing for babes.[22]

A socio-cultural consideration of male homosexuality in Egypt at the time certainly lies outside the scope of the present study. What can be briefly said here, however, is that on the few occasions it is mentioned in archival sources, homosexuality seems to have been deemed neither illegal nor socially reprehensible. In November 1853, Cairo police investigated a theft in which were implicated a number of boys and men professing to have been homosexual.[23] As in the prostitution case mentioned above, investigators were more concerned with the stolen money than with what the men in question did sexually. Two of the men said they were *puşt*, which a nineteenth-century Ottoman Turkish dictionary renders as "passive sodomite." One was said by his associates to have been a pimp (Turkish *pezevenk*). One of the *puşts* was presented once as a dancer and once as a singer.

In detailed statements, the men described how they spent the evening drinking arrack and then went to the Greek consulate, where one of them worked. They found a room and went to bed. "We did it together," one of them said, "the way the local boys (*ibn al-balad*) do it." These statements were not extracted under pressure, but rather volunteered as innocuous information. Frequently, when violation of the socio-cultural code was involved, even without infringement of the law, a police officer would lecture the culprits and recommend proper conduct in the future. However, nothing of the sort happened in this case, which might suggest that all was taken in his stride. It does appear that by comparison with European culture, male homosexuality in the Ottoman East bore a milder stigma and was accepted, within certain limits. These are, of course, only impressions formed on the basis of insufficient data. Deeper delving into the archives might yield a better understanding of the phenomenon and its social significance.

Most forms of entertainment discussed thus far entailed only limited participation by spectators. The performers occupied center stage, while everybody else watched, either in a passive way, or more actively by uttering a comment here and there. This did not make entertainment less important, for its public aspect served legitimate unspoken sentiments by drawing them out of the realm of the individual into the public domain. Public dancing and fortune-telling involved the public to a greater extent. The former held prospects of sexual contact with the performer, while the latter brought one person at a time into the center of attention, as his or her future was being predicted, the other spectators watching. This brings us to other kinds of activity which engaged members of the lower strata as participants rather than as onlookers and facilitated social contact during their free time. In mid-century Egypt, such activity took place in three important institutions – the public bath, the coffeehouse, and the tavern.

Public baths and coffeehouses

If street entertainment entailed only limited participation by the spectators, other ways of spending free time offered much greater involvement. Both public baths and coffeehouses provided the space and the facilities for important social interaction in mid-nineteenth-century Egypt. Only the wealthy had private baths in their homes, so the use of the public facility was widespread not only among the lower strata of society. But both baths and coffeehouses catered mostly, though not exclusively, for residents of the areas in which they were located. Hence, their clientele tended to reflect the social make-up of each particular neighborhood or quarter. While coffeehouses were a restricted male territory, baths offered women a congenial space for interaction, one of the few available to them at the time. In this section, we shall take a brief look at the socio-cultural aspect of these important institutions of Ottoman and Egyptian history.

There were several dozen "Turkish" baths (*hammams/ḥammāms*) in Cairo; Lane's estimate for the 1830s is between sixty and seventy, and quite a few in other Egyptian towns. They were of the vapor type and offered a variety of services. These included use of the steam hall and washing facilities, shampooing, and massaging. Coffee and pipe were served, or brought along, and patrons could receive a towel and a sheet. Public baths were staffed by a number of attendants, some of whom operated the heating and steam system, some served as masseurs, and some cleaned up the place and disposed of rubbish. Egyptian archival sources provide ample information about the operation of baths. They clearly point out their centrality in the social life of all strata. Within the bath, however, status differences found some expression in the quality of services provided. Going to the bath was a matter of routine, though schedules varied. Workers would take a bath early in the morning before going to work, or when they returned home in the evening. Men and women of greater leisure used the bath when in need of social contact and according to their means.[24]

Men and women bathed in different baths, or in different hours in a mixed bath, and were served by attendants of their own sex. Because women were excluded from male-dominated institutions, from the state downward, opportunities for social interaction such as those afforded by public baths were especially important to them. Like water fountains, local markets, and the home, they offered women a venue for meeting, where they could informally discuss matters that were of concern to them. Tucker observes that marriage arrangements, family disputes, business transactions, and many other social and economic issues which involved women were aired amidst the steaming setting of the bath. She further explains that "professional women bath attendants and female owners of some baths constituted a corps of female personnel who could function as a clearing house for information and contacts." Thus, argues Tucker, the bath is an example of a female informal institution which had a parallel and separate existence from formal male institutions.[25]

Some European travellers had occasion to use Egyptian public baths, which were a tourist attraction for the more adventurous and experience-seeking visitors. The 1856 edition of Wilkinson's guide book to Egypt, advises that the baths'

> heat, the system of shampooing, and the operation of rubbing with horse-hair gloves, contribute not a little to cleanliness and comfort, though it is by no means agreeable to have to undergo the operation of being shampooed by the bathing-men . . . You had always

better use your own towels, or promise an extra fee for clean ones, which you cannot be too particular in rejecting if at all of doubtful appearance.[26]

Writing in the early 1850s, Gadsby counseled caution, for he knew several Europeans who caught severe colds after using the bath. He did not seem to have cherished the experience, especially the massaging session.

You are thrown into a profuse perspiration, and then a powerful man rubs you unmercifully hard with very coarse gloves, and sometimes actually rubs off the skin. He then takes hold of you, limb by limb, and cracks every joint. It is exceedingly unpleasant during the operation, but afterwards the sensation is delightful, and, in that warm climate, greatly conducive to health.[27]

Flaubert, of course, did not fail to see the sexual opportunities offered by the public bath. It is not untrue that men seeking homosexual contacts could find them in those establishments. In a way, the tradition seems to have been carried on in Western countries well into the latter part of the twentieth century. Young Flaubert wrote to a friend in January 1850 that he strongly desired to add this to his sexual experiences in Egypt.

It's at the baths that such things take place. You reserve the bath for yourself . . . and you skewer your lad in one of the rooms. Be informed, furthermore, that all the bath-boys are bardashes [male homosexuals]. The final masseurs, the ones who come to rub you when all the rest is done, are usually quite nice young boys. We had our eye on one in an establishment very near our hotel. I reserved the bath exclusively for myself. I went, and the rascal was away that day![28]

Spicy anecdotes aside, baths did have great social importance for men too. Lane, whose account of public baths contains none of the comments of the European observers mentioned above, believed that men visited the *ḥammām* more frequently than women. However, he also noticed the distinctly social significance of bath-going for women. Men, of course, had an additional institution for transacting social and economic business – the coffeehouse. Lane estimated that in the 1830s there were "above a thousand" coffeehouses in Cairo.[29] These were small establishments which catered mostly for the local, neighborhood population, something of a "local pub." They were often owned and operated by the same person, but other arrangements were also common. Some coffeehouse owners preferred to hire another man to manage the shop for them. Others rented the premise out to operators, who were more dependent on steady custom. If income dropped, they fast found themselves out of business.

The "means of production" in the coffeehouse was the *ʿudda*, or coffee-making equipment, which after the shop itself, was the owner's most precious item.[30] Other paraphernalia included water pipes and some matting to cover the stone seats inside as well as outside on the street. Coffee, various kinds of tobacco, and *ḥashīsh* were the stuff that lubricated social contact in coffeehouses. Various kinds of games, including gambling, were popular among patrons, and at times musicians and story-tellers performed before them. Most of the customers were "regulars." Coffeehouses were open from early morning to late at night, so one could wander in at any hour and find someone, at least the owner or operator, to exchange words with. Some local figures, such as the neighborhood *shaykh*, the guard, or a policeman, spent much time in the coffeehouse, where they could always get the latest news. It is not uncommon to read in the sources that the *shaykh* was approached at the coffeehouse, for people knew that he could usually be found there. In one case, a room in a coffeehouse was used by a market police officer for temporary detention of offenders.

But coffeehouses were really an institution of the lower strata of Egyptian society. The Ottoman-Egyptian elite socialized mostly at home, as the male section (*selamlık*) of most elite houses could accommodate visitors quite comfortably. So it was for those with modest homes, or no home at all, that the coffeehouse was ever so important. "Everybody used to enter the coffeehouse all the time" – so one owner described daily routine in 1850 – "one would order coffee for a friend and in turn be invited by him." Thus, an informal and entirely voluntary setting provided opportunities to discuss politics, business, daily matters, and family affairs in a congenial atmosphere. This distinguished the coffeehouse from the guild and even from the *ṣūfī* ordr, both of which had involuntary and hierarchical elements. Where much time was either appropriated by the state, or subjected to one sort of formal organization or another, the coffeehouse alone provided respite and relaxation. Yet for some, this was not enough, and they sought to escape reality by more drastic means. If the use of opium was limited to the "down and out," alcohol was not.

Taverns and drinking

Drinking of alcoholic beverages seems to have been more common in mid-nineteenth-century Egypt than is usually believed. Travelers rarely report about people of any class drinking, and it is quite clear that the Muslim interdiction of wine drove drinking out of the public domain. Hence it became a private matter. Lane himself confessed that he had never seen drinks taken in his presence, but was aware that alcohol was being consumed and even described how it was served and when. But other Europeans were sometimes openly asked for drinks, or offered them to Egyptians as reward for services rendered. Gadsby reported that

> one of the officers on board the governor [of Esna]'s boat asked us to give him a bottle of *brandy*, so much have the Turks, I am sorry to say, like the *Christians*, learnt not only to add drunkenness to their thirst, (Deut. xxix. 19,) but, as a consequence, thirst to drunkenness.

And St. John, who knew Egypt well, had no qualms about sending his hosts from the Albanian garrison at Luxor "a couple of bottles of wine" in acknowledgment of their hospitality.[31]

If members of the Ottoman-Egyptian elite occasionally drank at home in private,[32] interested individuals among the lower strata seem to have had the option of the wine bars. These were scattered in various parts of town, but mostly in the more commercial areas, the Frank quarters of Cairo and Alexandria, and some of the less respectable zones. There were bars especially designated for Europeans, mostly in hotels used by them. But the majority were more of the "pub" type and frequented exclusively by men of non-elite groups and the lower rungs of the elite. There is mention in the sources of such men purchasing drinks at the grocer's (*baqqāl*) for home consumption, but drinking in bars appears to have been far more popular among members of these groups, i.e. the overwhelming majority of the population. Before we venture into that world, we should note that drinking of alcoholic beverages, socially and individually, was an almost exclusively male phenomenon set in an urban environment and cutting across ethnic lines.

Wine bars, or taverns, were called in Arabic *khammāra*s, in Turkish (from Persian) *meyhane*s. They served a variety of alcoholic beverages including wine (*nabīdh*), a beer-like drink (*būza*), and arrack (*ᶜaraq*, Turkish *rakı̄*). Bars catering for Europeans, and occasionally the better-supplied local pubs, served also brandy and other spirits imported from Europe. All these drinks were either sold in bottles, usually to a group of men, or poured into glasses and served individually. Taverns were open during the day too, but much of their business was after dark. Men went there to drink, smoke, play games, gamble, talk, and have a good time. Among the names of bar owners mentioned in the records, Christian emigrés appear in significant numbers, though there were also taverns owned by Muslims. Customers, on the other hand, came from all ethnic groups and all religions.[33]

Clearly, the government considered the production and sale of alcoholic beverages, and the existence of bars, as perfectly legitimate business. There is no evidence that the authorities tried to interfere with the consumption of alcohol in bars. In fact, at least one of these establishments was located not far from the Muskī police station in Cairo. The government even regulated the production and distribution of liquor through the *iltizam*, or tax-farming system. The production of spirits in any given area was granted to an individual by contract in return for a fixed sum. As was common under that system, the contractor kept whatever he earned above the amount he had undertaken to pay the government. Conversely, if his earnings fell short, he was still liable for the full amount. Thus, for example, in November 1850, a certain Hoca Tekfur was re-granted, for two more years, a concession to produce wine in Cairo, Alexandria, and some provincial towns in Lower Egypt. The amount he had to pay to the government over the whole period, in three installments a year, was approximately £2,000.[34]

At mid-century, rum, arrack, and other liquors were being produced by the household of Ismail Paşa, as well as by those of some other members of the ruling family. Wealthy households owned the necessary equipment and either leased it to contractors, or produced the spirits themselves. Taxes were regularly levied on income from such activities, including those pursued by the ruling family. It seems that the margin of profit in the industry was not very high, since when a number of production contracts came up for renewal not many people competed for them. In spite of notices being served to all potential takers, in no few cases the concession holder was renominated with some modification of the terms, at times in his favor. This might prove that revenues were lower than expected and the government realized that its income estimates were hard to meet.[35] This was also the case with contracts covering tavern operation.

The government regulated the operation of bars throughout the country. These taverns were not run directly by any government agency or department, but by contractors. Such contractors undertook to supply and operate local pubs for periods of two years. Much like production contractors, they could keep any earnings in excess of the amount due to the Treasury according to the contract. A distinction was maintained between wine bars (*meyhane*s) and beer cellars (*buzahane*s), but at times contractors bid for both, and terms were determined according to the financial considerations of the government and the contractors. Calculations were often quite complicated for they involved rent paid to the government for the use of the taverns and deals with guilds of transporters and suppliers. Thus, for example, on 8 April 1853, the Treasury granted a two-year concession for the operation of beer and wine bars in three towns, including Alexandria, and several provincial districts, for a sum of about £4,000.[36]

While in most cases concession holders made profits and bid for renewal of their contracts, some lost money and could not pay the government its due. In April 1853, the contractor of the Sudan bars defaulted on his payment. He was about £200 short, and the Council of Justice ordered that he be imprisoned until the end of the lease term. Then, the Council decreed, he could pay and apply for a renewal of the contract, or the management of the bars would revert back to the government.[37] In the latter case, the contract would usually be offered again to the highest bidder by auction. When the Treasury did not expect a contractor to recover and pay back after having defaulted, the guarantors (*ḍāmin*s and/or *kāfil*s) of the deal were approached. With such relatively high amounts of money involved, these were usually powerful and wealthy individuals whose sound financial situation was well known. One of the contracts mentioned above was guaranteed by Hayrüddin Paşa, another by the wealthy Jewish businessman Yaʿqūb Qattāwī.

At mid-century, drinking habits were certainly part of urban lower strata culture in Egypt. Pubs had their "regulars," men who would come there to drink several times a week, if not every night. People talked about frequenting a specific bar often, about circulating between bars, about meeting the same men and passing the evening with them. With these habits came drunkenness and its social effects. Some men got drunk occasionally, others much of the time. The terms used most frequently to describe the state of intoxication by alcohol are the Arabic *sakrān* and the Turkish (from Persian) *sarhoş* and *mest*. We can read in the archival sources of men losing control of their conduct as a result of drinking, and of the after-effects of drinking. "He used to drink and hang out with the riff-raff" seems to express almost a causal relationship. People associated irresponsible, unlawful, and violent conduct with excessive drinking. They often attributed such conduct to a man's drinking.[38]

When men were found drunk in the streets, night patrols would detain them at a nearby police station. This was a preventive measure, for getting drunk by itself did not constitute an offense. The drunkard would spend the night at the station courtyard, or in a side room, and wake up sober in the morning. If no reported crimes could be traced to him, the man would be free to go. Offenders, too, believed that being under the influence of alcohol was, in a way, a mitigating circumstance. Thus, a minor member of the elite, who had tricked a whole police shift one night, told investigators in the morning that he had some arrack the previous night, after which, "happened what happened, I know not how or why." Thus, also, the expression "they were drunk out of their senses" was used to explain why three men assaulted a middle-rank bureaucrat in front of his house at night and ran away after some neighbors intervened.

Although drunkenness was not a major social problem at mid-century, it nevertheless existed on the margins of society. Often begotten by destitution, it was a way for the poor and homeless to escape harsh realities. But not less frequently, it seems, drunkenness existed as a by-product of a form of entertainment and pastime which formed around the tavern. Soldiers and policemen also drank. They frequented the taverns with friends just as other men of the lower strata did. And some of them, too, did get drunk. There were several cases of drunkards in uniform, who had to be disciplined after committing offenses. Yet, by itself and when not entailing misconduct, drinking by policemen was not punishable. Their colleagues on the night patrol would pick them up on the street, take them to the station, and release them in the morning when sober. However, it seems that the army took a somewhat different view of drinking, especially when it concerned officers.

At least in one case, a junior officer and his friends were punished for drinking wine. In September 1852, the Council of Justice reviewed a file which had been referred by the Ministry of War. A first-lieutenant was accused of organizing a wine party with seven of his fellow officers on a holiday eve. The party took place in the house of one of the officers. Because the lieutenant had done so on several occasions previously, the military court recommended that he be demoted to a non-commissioned rank for three months. The other officers, the court suggested, should be imprisoned for a few days. The Council of Justice endorsed the military court's recommendation.[39] The ruling in this case seems an attempt to discourage such conduct and set an example to junior officers. Enlisted men, presumably, could still drink at pubs like policemen. Once again, it is possible to sense the peculiar position of junior army officers, being Arabic-speaking, native Egyptians, who did not belong to the Ottoman-Egyptian elite, yet were expected not to behave in certain respects as the lower strata from which they originally came.

For one group of men and women, drinking in public was acceptable almost as part of their trade. Those were the various types of entertainers. Dancers, musicians, singers were given to drinking alcohol in order "to get into the mood" required for their performance. Lane observed that male singers would "sometimes drink until they can no longer sing, nor strike a chord." Drinking by women in public was associated with prostitution, and the same observer believed that such women required "brandy and other intoxicating liquor" in order "to extinguish the last spark of modesty which they may yet sometimes affect to retain."[40] Put differently, one might argue that male and female prostitutes, but even more their clients, needed alcohol in order to reduce inhibitions and create a more relaxed atmosphere. Music and dance, which were common to all but the lowest form of street prostitution, played a similar role to alcohol.

Be that as it may, in mid-century Egypt public consumption of alcoholic beverages was not a "respectable" thing in the eyes of "polite society," which identified it with lower strata culture. Even among the latter, drinking was not a "main stream" phenomenon, but a marginal one. Much more so with regard to excessive drinking, or drunkenness, and its long-term consequence – alcoholism. To a large extent, these were culturally associated either with the poor and destitute members of society, or with the marvelous and forbidden, i.e. with entertainment and prostitution. However, as mentioned above, drinking in private, alone or in small male groups, did not carry the same social stigma.

Thus, the city offered its inhabitants a wide range of diversions, from street entertainment to coffeehouses, baths, and taverns. To enjoy in full the more participatory kinds, one had to pay for services rendered and beverages consumed. But the poor could still watch performances paid for by others, frequent a coffeehouse or a bar for the sake of company alone, and in the hope that the generosity of friends would quench his thirst. So means had something to do with the use of free time, as did one's gender. Women could enjoy street performances and bath socializing, but were barred from coffeehouses and taverns. Finally, processions and public ceremonies were open to all and, in a way, formed part of entertainment. At mid-century, the full variety was available only in Cairo and Alexandria, whereas small towns offered a much-reduced scale of opportunities.

The range of experiences examined in part II reflects the realities of those who belonged to what I called the non-elite groups, or the lower strata, of Egyptian society. At first glance, the story of the preceding pages is about domination and powerlessness. Indeed, both the rural and urban population of Egypt during the middle decades was squeezed and exploited by the Ottoman-Egypt elite. Conscription, *corvée*, taxation, and low wages were the four grand evils from which the overwhelming majority of the people suffered. However, on closer examination we note that violent resistance erupted in the mid 1840s in response to excessive oppression. As conditions began to improve from the last third of the decade on, resistance reverted mainly to those indirect modes to which the powerless were accustomed in a strong centralized state – desertion, abscondence, protest. Peace and waning fortunes, and later a different approach to reform, began to loosen the yoke.

In those years, conscription drives were becoming less frequent and limited in scope; less *corvée* was required for fewer projects were being launched; some taxes were abolished; and attempts were being made to increase wages and improve the pay system. As the burden was gradually becoming more tolerable, social tensions were reduced and passive resistance to conscription, *corvée*, and taxation was re-entrenched as an ongoing, long-term attitude to authority. Throughout the period, opportunities existed for sublimation of violent conflict. These were at hand and, in varying degrees, available to all. The same opportunities were also available to members of the elite, for many of whom the middle years were more stressful and trying than for members of the lower strata. Thus, the perennial contradiction remains: a society which is in many respects one, yet in others is divided, segmented, ridden with social inequality.

Epilogue

The demise of Mehmet Ali's mini-empire in 1841 inaugurated the period which I called "the middle decades." The accession of Ismail Paşa in 1863 and the resumption of Egypt's expansion marked the end of that period in Egyptian history. Between two modernizing thrusts lay a time of readjustment, recuperation, and repose. At the same time, the middle years witnessed the emergence of dynastic order in Egypt, the rise of the Ottoman-Egyptian elite, and the beginning of a meaningful penetration of the rural notability and the urban middle strata through the great social divide. These major socio-cultural processes had profound political consequences, which affected Egypt well into the twentieth century. All were closely linked to the consolidation of national identity, the ascent of a national leadership, and the formation of the *efendiyya* (sometimes *afandiyya*) – the urban bureaucratic and professional class, which from the 1920s onward, stood at the forefront of the national movement.

The entrenchment of dynastic order in Egypt meant growing *political* independence from the Ottoman government. However, in *social* and *cultural* terms, Egypt remained very much within the Ottoman orbit. Throughout the nineteenth century, the court and the elite continued to affirm their difference from non-elite groups by using distinctive language, dress, and etiquette. Nonetheless, their outlook and identity gradually became more Egyptian and less Ottoman. Concomitantly, more and more Egyptians not belonging to the elite managed to climb up the military and bureaucratic ladder to join elite ranks. The "localization," or "Egyptianization," of the Ottoman-Egyptian elite was accelerated under British rule. But the political culture remained Ottoman even under the British, and so did bureaucratic practices. Not only the titles and the *fez* survived, but also political perceptions and modes of interaction. Almost to the collapse of the empire, the Ottoman way continued to be the rallying point of opposition to European domination, political and cultural.

The dynamic processes described in this book may alter the prevailing view of the middle decades as a dull and uninteresting period of Egyptian history. Yet, we must not fail to note that a major feature of life in Egypt remained unchanged throughout the period – social inequality. The growing power and expansion of the state from the beginning of the nineteenth century ensured that, in Egyptian society, honor and privilege were largely confined to the Ottoman-Egyptian elite. A noted social scientist wrote that:

> the social functions of stratification are primarily to maintain the nexus of power, affluence, and privilege in complex societies, and equally to assure that there will be people so vulnerable, poor, and deprived as to have no choice but to occupy occupational roles that are dangerous, dirty, unpleasant, and demeaned.[1]

The evidence presented in this work amply supports the view that the state in the middle decades continued to organize and sustain inequality in Egyptian society.

If "Ottoman-Egyptian elite" and "lower strata" may seem merely analytic categories (etic), they were, nevertheless, quite significant for mid-century Egyptians too (emic). In an Ottoman context, elite members would refer to themselves and be referred to by members of the Ottoman elite as *Mĭsĭrlĭ* (Egyptians). Egyptians who did not belong to the elite often called Ottoman-Egyptians *ʿOthmānlī*s (Ottomans), or *Atrāk* (Turks, because of the language they spoke). All frequently designated non-elite Egyptians *abnāʾ al-balad* (native Egyptians), and if of rural origin, *fallāḥīn*. Whatever the term used, all could not but be keenly aware of the existence of a social divide. The rural squeeze (taxation, conscription, the *corvée*) and the urban squeeze (low wages, taxes, living conditions) were a constant reminder of the painful reality of stratification and inequality. Deprivation was resented by the *fallāḥīn* and the urban lower strata, and, as far as possible, was resisted. For much of the nineteenth century, resistance was mostly by indirect means, though at times direct confrontation also occurred.

Political and economic inequality in Egyptian society also had social and cultural dimensions, which were, however, not as harsh. Here, the elite household structure, patron–client relations, relatively long periods of economic prosperity, communal associations, and an ability to sublimate protest through various forms of entertainment, all mitigated the reality of everyday life in Egypt. They softened and lubricated contact between the privileged and the deprived. Society and the state tolerated the existence of two, possibly three, subcultures. These had distinct and autonomous cores, whose peripheries overlapped. While roles and statuses were quite well-defined, the lack of social segregation made cultural exchange possible. On the peripheries, in the absence of the artificial line separating elite from popular culture, a form of socio-cultural negotiation occurred.

It was there, at the socio-cultural "seam," that mobility was being facilitated. It began with the sons of rural notables entering the reformed educational system, going abroad on student missions, and acquiring the civilian or military skills with which they later joined the lower ranks of the Ottoman-Egyptian elite. As the century wore on, the Egyptian component in elite culture gradually grew, use of Arabic increased, and more Egyptians of non-elite background were seen holding high office in the army and bureaucracy. That dual process, which intensified towards the end of the century, was not merely a political development, but a social and cultural one as well. Through it were defined the new political classes of twentieth-century Egypt. As the Turkish-speaking, Ottoman component within the elite lost its hold over the major positions in government, more and more Arabic-speaking Egyptians could boast the titles of *paşa*, *bey*, and *efendi*, along with their version of an Ottoman-Egyptian lifestyle.

All this was taking place in an Egypt that, for her elite, was becoming increasingly cosmopolitan. An already large presence of various European communities only grew in importance under the British occupation. French, Italian, and English vied with Turkish for the status of lingua franca, and ultimately replaced it. Paris and London eclipsed Istanbul as the source of material and cultural fashion. Under cultural "Egyptianization," the political and the economic elites gradually merged. Out of the middle and lower ranks, *efendiyya* culture emerged. With a distinctly local and professional character, it also assimilated some European ways and not a few traits of a great Ottoman bureaucratic tradition. And, in the 1940s, an Islamic "counter-culture" – which had been marginalized since the fall of Abbas Paşa – was maturing as a viable political alternative to Westernism in Egypt.

Until well into the twentieth century, however, the majority of Egyptians, i.e. the *fallāḥīn* and not a few of the urban poor, remained – by and large – outside these processes. So much so, that a keen Egyptian observer of modern Egyptian society, who conducted a fascinating study in the 1960s, failed to note any significant change in their world view.[2] What is even more important is that attitudes of the middle and upper strata towards the lower strata remained much the same. The stereotypes of the *bāshā* (*paşa*), the *bey*, the *muwaẓẓaf* (government clerk, official, equivalent of the Ottoman *memur*), and the *fallāḥ* survived into contemporary language and culture. True, the *bāshāwāt* of pre- and post-revolutionary Egypt were not the same as the *paşa*s and *bey*s (the *zevat*) of the middle decades, the reign of Ismail, or even the turn of the century. Nor, for that matter, were members of the *efendiyya* akin to nineteenth century *efendi*s. But these "stratifiers" continued to have a socio-cultural meaning; they continued to reflect the distribution of power in Egyptian society.

In 1980, in Cairo, an Egyptian informant vividly remembered an incident that had taken place in 1953. She was then employed at a day nursery and considered herself and her colleagues as *muwaẓẓafīn*, i.e. holding a literate job in government employ. The nursery was run by a director (*mudīr*) named Muḥammad, and sponsored as a charity by one of the royal princesses, who remained in Egypt after the fall of the monarchy in 1952. One day, the princess paid a visit to the nursery. She was greeted at the door of her limousine by the director, while the employees, including our informant, were waiting in front of the building to pay their respects. The short exchange that followed left a profound impression on our informant, who saw herself then, as in 1980, as a devout revolutionary (*thawriyya*) and an admirer of the late President Gamāl ᶜAbd an-Nāṣir. She was bitterly reliving the memory as she alternately mimicked the princess and the director.

When the princess approached the gate, she addressed the director, by his first name, without any title, and in colloquial Egyptian: "How are you, Muḥammad?" The director answered: "Praise be to God, Your Highness" (using the Ottoman honorific *İsmetli* in its Arabic form *Ṣāḥibat al-ᶜIṣma*). Pointing to the group of nursery-staff members, the princess then inquired: "And how are your *fallāḥīn*, Muḥammad?" The director, trying to cover his embarrassment, said: "Those, Your Highness, are not *fallāḥīn*, those are *muwaẓẓafīn*." "No, Muḥammad," the princess retorted mockingly, "don't you know that all Egyptians are *fallāḥīn*?" ᶜAbd an-Nāṣir, our informant added, did not like royal titles nor upper-class etiquette, and, after a while, they gradually disappeared. Yet, when she was speaking ten years after his death, *yā bey*, *yā bāshā*, and even *yā saᶜādat al-bāshā* (the Ottoman honorific *saadetli*) were still quite common forms of address.

Surely the titles no longer signified what they had in mid-nineteenth-century Egypt, nor what they came to mean at the turn of the twentieth century or in the 1940s; but they still mark recognition of social status, of respect. Moreover, rhetoric aside,[3] the connotation of the term *fallāḥ* has not gained much prestige, though it lost some of the contempt previously attached to it. All this is not intended as an argument from a position of *plus ça change plus c'est la même chose*. Rather, one ought to look at what is changing underneath the patterns that remain, and, conversely, at what survives yet appears to be changing. Perhaps not least important, *change* should be value-free, not deemed positive or negative in itself, but first identified within the culture in which it occurs, then assessed in its own terms.

In my journey into mid-century Egyptian society, the works of Clifford Geertz and Robert Darnton served as a source of inspiration, with their sober, skeptical attitude to grand theory and their close relation to the historian's treatment of text. "Cultural analysis is (or should be)," Geertz writes, "guessing at meanings, assessing the guesses, and drawing explanatory conclusions from the better guesses, not discovering the Continent of Meaning and mapping out its bodiless landscape." Darnton employs the same metaphor, referring to *l'histoire des mentalités* as "unmapped territory." "History in the ethnographic grain," he writes, is an attempt to show how people "construed the world, invested it with meaning, and infused it with emotion." By working carefully through the archives, the historian tries "to discover the social dimension of thought and to tease meaning from documents by relating them to the surrounding world of significance."[4]

I also share Geertz's and Darnton's feeling that such endeavors are intrinsically incomplete and imperfect. At the same time, by treating specific individuals and their documented stories – what is sometimes called micro-history – we reduce the risks involved. But we do more than that. We humanize the *structure*, bring realities closer, make empathy more possible. Elites and lower strata, *paşa*s, *bey*s, the *fallāḥīn*, guilds, neighborhoods, or *ṣūfī* orders can come alive only when the men and women that hide beneath them are brought out of anonymity, given their real names, and are placed in their natural setting. Then, they may speak to us from the old records at the Egyptian archives in Cairo; all we need to do is listen.

Notes

Introduction

1 The translation quoted here is from Hurewitz 1975: I, 277. Arrival and promulgation of the *ferman* in Egypt are from FO 78/452, 134, Chasseaud to Palmerston, 16 June 1841.

2 FO 78/404, 1–5, Hodges to Palmerston, 4 January 1840.

3 Hodges, among others, described Mehmet Ali's bearing as "full of defiance and insolence." He added that "in his public conversations respecting both his own legitimate Sovereign, the Sultan, and the Allied Powers he expresses himself in terms most unseemly and reprehensible" (FO 78/404, 113–20, Hodges to Palmerston, 20 March 1840). The audience with Count Medem is in FO 78/406, 160–4, Hodges to Palmerston, 4 September 1840. The reference to "oppression" is in FO 78/404, 9–10, Hodges to Palmerston, 6 January 1840. The texts of the convention and the edicts are in Hurewitz, 1975: I, 271–8.

4 FO 78/451, 85–9, Barnett to Palmerston, 17 August 1841.

5 For the Mamluk sultanate, see Ayalon's works mentioned in the bibliography, and Petry 1981.

6 For the main works of Holt and Raymond, see Holt 1973: 151–251; Holt 1968: 79–90; Holt 1966: 71–101; Raymond 1973. For intellectual and cultural beginnings, see El-Shayyal 1962, Crecelius 1982, and Gran 1978.

7 For Raymond's (1973) views on this question, see Raymond 1973: I, 12–16. For a recent contribution on the structure of government and patterns of socialization in eighteenth-century Egypt, see Gabriel Piterberg 1987.

8 Halil Inalcık's article, "Centralization and Decentralization in the Ottoman Administration" (Inalcık 1977) is still the most perceptive explication of what is commonly referred to as the period of Ottoman decline.

9 For a summary of the writings on Mehmet Ali and my own assessment of his reign, see Toledano forthcoming.

10 Bromfield 1856: 93–4.

11 Gadsby 1860: 189.

12 The population estimates given here are from McCarthy 1976. Panzac's (1987) figures are somewhat higher: 5 million in 1840, 5.4 million in 1848. Panzac's estimates for the population of Cairo are somewhat lower than McCarthy's: 282,348 for 1865 (see

Panzac 1987: 15 and 30). For estimates of the size of the Ottoman-Egyptian elite and the armed forces, see below (pp. 69–70). The first estimate of literacy is in Baer 1969: 227 (quoting Artîn Paşa), the second in Heyworth-Dunne 1938: 10–11, 147–8. For education, see Heyworth-Dunne 1938: 1–95 (in the eighteenth century), 96ff. (reforms in education during the nineteenth century). For the press in Egypt, see ᶜAbduh 1951.

13 For the final stage of the "Egyptian Question" see Temperley 1964: 89–156. The table of contents of Temperley's book vividly reflects the declining status of the issue.

14 On the 1850–2 crisis between Abbas and the Porte, see Baer 1969: 109–32, and Rivlin 1961b. On the Suez Canal, see De Lesseps 1876; Farnie 1969; Landes 1958: 173–88; and index.

15 Officially, Ibrahim was *vali* for fifty days. On Mehmet Ali's industry and its decline, see Owen 1981: 69–73, Issawi 1982: 150ff., and Rivlin 1961a: 191–200.

16 For the monopolies see Mustafa 1968; Owen 1969: 58–88; and Rivlin 1961a: 105–18, 171–90. For budgets and loans, see Owen 1981: 122–7. Landes states that inflation occurred during the 1850s, and that in the early 1860s the *kuruş* was worth half as much as in the reign of Abbas (Landes 1958: 109, note 3).

17 See Hourani 1968, which is also discussed below (pp. 71–2). The last element of potential danger, the *ṣūfī* leadership, was effectively put under state control during the middle decades, though the original step in that direction had been taken by Mehmet Ali in 1812 (De Jong 1978: 54–69). On rural and urban unrest in nineteenth-century Egypt, see Baer 1969: 93–108; Baer 1982: 225–323; Schulze 1981: 79–94; and Lawson 1981. For comparison with the much higher frequency of urban revolts in seventeenth-century France, see William H. Beik 1987: 36–67. The author lists no less than fifty urban riots and uprisings between 1635 and 1660 in one region alone, under the title "Some Public Disturbances in Languedoc" (ibid., 37).

18 This is a difficult question which requires further research. The rise in world commodity prices during the 1850s and 1860s clearly benefited cotton and cereals producers (see Owen 1981: 67, table 4; 136, table 22, and references to Owen 1969 and other sources provided therein). How much of it actually reached the *fallāḥīn* is unclear, though probably more did than before, owing to the phasing out of the monopolies, which enabled producers to sell directly to local and European merchants and not through the government.

19 See, for example: Barakāt 1978; Baer 1969: 8–9, 23; Owen 1969: 58–64; Rivlin 1961a: 37–74; and Issawi 1982: 144. For the debate concerning the nature of land ownership in Egypt, see Cuno 1980. For the cooperation of the landed elite with the Europeans against Ismail, see Hunter 1984: 179–226. Estates were granted as *ühdes* (Arabic *ᶜuhdas*) from the early 1840s. Because they had usually accumulated large tax arrears, such "gifts" were not popular among high officeholders (e.g. FO 78/623, Barnett to Aberdeen, 16 April 1845). It was also in the middle decades that the amount of land held by members of the ruling family (*çiftlik*) increased substantially.

20 "Long term" and "structure" are defined and explained in Braudel 1958. Structure signifies, Braudel writes, "a reality which survives through long periods of time and is only slowly eroded" (411). Some twenty years later, in *The Structures of Everyday Life*, he wrote:

> Everyday life consists of little things one hardly notices in time and space. The more we reduce the focus of vision, the more likely we are to find ourselves in the environment of material life: the broad sweep usually corresponds to History with a capital letter, to distant trade routes, and the networks of national or urban economies. If we reduce the length of time observed, we either have the event or the everyday happening. The event is, or is taken to be, unique; the everyday happening is repeated, and the more often it is repeated the more likely it is to become a generality or rather a structure. It pervades society at all levels, and characterizes ways of being and behaving which are perpetuated through endless ages. (Braudel 1981: 29)

21 Barakāt 1978: 154.
22 On epidemics and diseases in the middle of the century, see Panzac 1987: 16–20. The author shows how the population growth rate increased dramatically in the 1840s. This he attributes to the disappearance of the plague and smallpox, which was part of a "profound alteration in the living conditions in Egypt."
23 On reforms in the area of public health until 1850, see Kuhnke 1971: 148–92, 227–74. We may note that during the 1850s there were two major outbreaks of cholera – which gradually replaced plague and smallpox as the epidemic dreaded by Egyptians – in which over 150,000 people were killed, most of them, naturally, from among the lower strata. For the demographic impact of cholera and the plague in nineteenth-century Egypt, see McCarthy 1976. See also Panzac 1987: 16ff.
24 In 1840/1 (1256 A.H.), for example, the "curriculum" for training bureaucrats in Mehmet Ali's administration was typically Ottoman. Thus it included the study of Turkish, Arabic, and Persian, drills in writing and calligraphy according to the *İnşa* of Rifat, and basic historical texts, such as *Naima Tarihi* (Deny 1930: 97).
25 Hourani 1981.
26 I borrow this term from Clifford Geertz in an attempt to apply it to historical material. Indeed, many of the documents consulted for the present book lend themselves to such an approach because of their detailed and multi-layered nature. It is quite possible to use these records in order "to break the cultural code," as suggested in Geertz 1973: 3–30.
27 St. John's reaction is in St. John 1852: I, 120. Flaubert's response is in Flaubert 1972: 79.
28 Fernand Braudel 1981: 29.
29 "Abbas-Pacha," I, 31. An entry on Abbas was published about the same time also in the great encyclopedic work of Larousse.
30 Brehier repeats the stories about the drowning of the innocent women and the exile of the flogged mistress to Esna. Abbas, asserts the author, resembled one of those Oriental despots who decapitated people with a mere nod, and knew no other rule of government but that of their own caprice (1900: 149–55). Though it may seem odd, we should note that Brehier's book purports to be an historical work based on archival sources, travel accounts, and historical studies. As for Cameron, he insists at the outset that "history must record that the first acts of Abbas were to undo all that his grandfather had done – good, bad, or indifferent," and that "in the eyes of Abbas whatever was, was wrong; he would have none of it." All these viceroys are then accused of

wreaking financial havoc on the country, while allowing her to fall prey to European ambitions. However, Cameron opines that there is much to be said in defense of Abbas. The viceroy recognized that the country needed peace and quiet, and that the removal of the commercial monopolies was essential to prosperity. Cameron adds that "Egypt was saved from foreign pillage under his reign – a contrast to the days of Sait and Ismail, who prided themselves on the adoption of an opposite policy." So, after all, some justice is done to the defamed Paşa, if at the expense of a certain inconsistency in the narrative (the above is based on Cameron 1898: 202–4, 226–9; on the responsibility for Egypt's financial problems, cf. *Histoire Financière* 1878: 1–10, which vindicates Abbas).

31 The quotation is from the *Encyclopaedia Britannica*, I, 9. Cameron's reference to Nubar reads as follows: "[Abbas's] character has been so generally painted in sombre colours that it is right to record the unique authority of Nubar Pasha, who still speaks of him as a true Turkish gentleman of the old school" (Cameron 1898: 227). The tenth edition of the *Encyclopaedia Britannica*, published in 1902, did not yet include a special entry on Abbas Paşa. However, he is mentioned in the entry devoted to his great grandson, the Khedive Abbas Hilmi II. Needless to say, the mention is unfavorable, and an air of a different era comes out of the old leaves, as we read that the khedive:

> was surrounded by intriguers who were playing a game of their own, and for some time he appeared almost disposed to be as reactionary as his great uncle [*sic*, but wrong for great grandfather] Abbas I. But in process of time he learnt to understand the importance of British counsels. (*Encyclopaedia Britannica* 1902: XXV, 3)

Incidentally, the fifteenth edition of the *Encyclopaedia Britannica*, published in 1974, improved the record of Abbas, and, noting some of his accomplishments, it concluded that "although Abbas's aversion to reforms won him the reputation of a reactionary, his curtailment of government spending benefited the poorer classes . . . A man of secretive nature, Abbas lived in isolation in his palace at Banha, where he was strangled by two of his servants" (I, 6).

32 *Encyclopaedia of Islam*, 1st edn, 1913 (*EI*[1]), I, 8–9. In 1950 this article was translated and reproduced in the *İslam Ansiklopedisi* (I, 10–11). The Turkish editorial committee added to the translation two references to Ottoman sources, namely Lutfi and Kâmil Paşa. In fact, these sources refer to marginal points and have nothing to say about Abbas's character. They certainly do not substantiate the assertions made in the original article.

33 According to Young, Abbas actually sinned by refusing to learn European languages. "As a man," continues the author, "he retired, a solitary sluggard, into the darkest depths of Muslem obscurantism . . . He flogged and drowned his women, lived with his horses and dogs, enriched his palaces, and impoverished his peasantry like any Mameluke" (Young 1927: 62–5). Young's Abbas cooperated with the landed elite in order to oppress the *fallāḥīn*, though so many of his critics claimed that he actually destroyed the basis of that same elite. But C. G. Elgood's Abbas could not do even that, for he was "an obscure and somber figure of history, out of humor with Egypt and out of sympathy with her people. He hated Europeans, he abhorred Christians."

Elgood, who wrote a number of books on Egyptian history, decribes Sait as "no idle debauchee like Abbas" (Elgood 1936: 71). In the *Enciclopedia Italians* (published in Milan in 1929), Ettore Rossi described the viceroy as "tiranico e violento" (I, 17). However, Rossi does grant that under his rule Egypt progressed, and mentions the example of the railway.

Having glorified Mehmet Ali's heroic attempt at modernizing Egypt, Dodwell deplores Abbas's counter-reformation. "Happily," he concludes, the Old Paşa did not live to witness how Abbas "betrayed him, abandoned his work, and in many ways frustrated his purposes" (Dodwell 1931: 261–2, 267–8). According to Joseph Cattaui Paşa, whose chronological survey of Egyptian history appeared in 1931 (listed under state papers, p. 303), Abbas regarded all bearers of new ideas, especially the Europeans, as enemies of the faith of Islam. Though Cattaui credits the viceroy with the abolition of monopolies and the construction of the railway, he believes that Abbas's "retrograde spirit" resisted all reform. Here, the story of Abbas does not end with the opening of the gates of Hell, but rather with the candid statement, which comes after the description of the Paşa's death: "L'Egypte ne le regretta pas." Quite naturally, the account of Sait's reign begins with a sigh of relief, things changed "heureusement" (Cattaui 1933: 369–70).

34 Owing to their profound patriotism, the author asserts, the French are prone to condemn any ruler who impedes the spread of French influence; they also unduly praise those who uphold French interests, Sait being a case in point. Although it did not conduce ar-Rāfi^cī to revise his assessment of Abbas, this observation is in itself noteworthy (references above are from ar-Rāfi^cī 1948: I, 10–22). In this, ar-Rāfi^cī follows Ismail Serheng, who wrote in 1894 that Abbas had been treated badly by French writers because he had driven many French experts out of his service (Serheng 1894: II, 262). As the work of the historians surveyed below amply demonstrates, such historiographical awareness is quite rare in the literature.

35 Sabry 1930: 14–16; the chapter on Abbas covers pp. 13–28. The author, a trained historian with a French *doctorat d'état*, also gained by King Faud I's interest in promoting the study of Egyptian history. Sabry's work is one of the few that actually rely on independent research into the period of Abbas, whereas so much of the rest is merely derivative. In this, Sabry stands out with the small group of scholars who wrote in the mid 1930s, and whose work influences Egyptian historiography to the present day.

36 Discussion of Abbas's reign is on pages 1–17. In Sammarco's (1937) account, the character of Abbas retains almost all the elements we shall identify later as comprising the demon-image of Abbas Paşa. His despotic and cruel instincts created a reign of silence and terror. The documents of the time, the author assures us, prove with "éloquence écraseante" the viceroy's financial abuses and waste of resources. "Abbas," he writes, "preferred to reside in arid and solitary places, and, as much as possible, avoided forming relations with other people, in order to live in the company of animals, mostly dogs and horses, of whom he raised many." Abbas's suspicion of Sait Paşa was without foundation, and Ismail's plotting against him was a defensive action to protect the interests of the "oppressed" princes (for these comments on Sait and Ismail, see Sammarco 1937: 19, and 108, respectively).

What is amazing about Sammarco's assessment of Abbas is not so much its negative tone, but the fact that it is so overtly emotional in its total condemnation of the viceroy. Although ostensibly the result of careful endeavors in many archives, the evaluation of Abbas's character and rule is cast in terms which, to a large extent, resemble the defamatory language encountered in travel accounts of the most simplistic nature. Professor Sammarco's sources are almost exclusively European consular reports, and his attitude towards them is entirely devoid of doubt, or question of motive. His account is, therefore, no more than a synthesis of these reports, whose bias towards Abbas he shared without compunction. Criticism of Sammarco's view of Abbas can be found in Heyworth-Dunne 1938: 290–1.

37 For the section on Abbas, see Charles-Roux 1936: 242–52. This multi-volume French enterprise, also sponsored by Kind Faud, was edited by Gabriel Hanotaux. Its sixth volume dealt with Egyptian history from 1801 to 1882, and was written by Charles-Roux, a former ambassador and expert on Egyptian affairs.

38 Sāmī 1936: III/1, 73 (listed under state papers, p. 303).

39 "ᶜAbbās Ḥilmī I," I, 13. Nevertheless, the article represents an improvement over Oestrup's piece in the 1913 edition of *EI*, though it, too, *laisse beaucoup à désirer*. Written more than twenty years later, Colombe's article was still based on the formative works of the mid 1930s by Sammarco, Charles-Roux, and Heyworth-Dunne. The author grants that the burden on the "poorest classes" was relieved in the reign of Abbas because of tax remissions, less *corvée* for less reform projects, and less conscription since times were peaceful. But he says that Sammarco "refutes" the claim made by Sabry and ar-Rafiᶜi that Abbas's anti-European stance was a barrier to Western involvement in Egypt, and therefore, a positive thing. In fact, Sammarco does not refute that assertion, but merely states his disagreement with it, with no sources to back his sıtrong conviction. His view was challenged by Heyworth-Dunne, which Colombe ignores, as he also evades Heyworth-Dunne's positive assessment of Abbas in general (see below, pp. 32, 34).

40 Vingtrinier 1886: 576; this quote was later used as a motto for Heyworth-Dunne's chapter on Abbas. Further references to Abbas and his relations with Süleyman Paşa are on pp. 556–8. Süleyman Paşa, who continued to command the army, was the most prominent European retained in Abbas's service. His relations with Abbas, as presented in this biography, show the viceroy in an interesting light. Far from the wild, unaccommodating despot, he is portrayed as a flexible and reasonable ruler, who could take an insult, even in public, from someone like Süleyman, whom he held in great esteem. In one instance, Abbas allowed his top general to contravene his orders and prevail upon him; in another case, Süleyman rejected a friendly gesture made by Abbas, but the viceroy ignored the insult; and on a third occasion, the general made an offensive comment to Abbas during an official reception, which Abbas let pass without comment. It is likely that Süleyman Paşa's situation was unique, but the fact that Abbas allowed such behavior is in itself indicative of a certain restraint and tolerance. In admitting this information, and in the different way it treats the reign of Abbas, Vingtrinier's work is without parallel in French writings of the nineteenth century, and even later.

41 Serheng, II, 260–4.

42 Young Abbas was not particularly keen on his studies, as we know from his grand-

father's letters of reproach. Several times, his uncle Ibrahim complained to Mehmet Ali about his performance under his command during the first Syrian War in 1831 (see Marsot 1984: 87–9). But in Zakhūra's laudatory biography of Abbas (Zakhūra 1897–1916: 29–30), we read that he was "an excellent student . . . and despite his young age, became famous, at the time, for his courage, intelligence and forbearance, high breeding, noble character, and delicate nature." We also learn that in the Syrian War of 1831 Abbas performed with great courage and intrepidity. We may note here that opinions differ concerning Abbas's performance during the Syrian War. Ibrahim had a great dislike for Abbas, favorite grandson of Mehmet Ali, and his letters to his father about Abbas should be treated with caution. For example, a French observer stated that when Abbas was put in charge of the siege of Acre – Ibrahim having advanced north towards Ḥamāh – he carried out his mission with "une vivacité étonnante; jamais la place n'a été autant bombardée et canonnée" (MAE/Turquie/263, 332–5, News from Syria, 16 March–20 April 1832, cited in Douin 1931: II, 174; see also ibid., 161, 197).

As viceroy, Abbas developed the country, says Zakhūra, and devoted his efforts to the welfare of the population: taxes were reduced, and complete security prevailed in Egypt. It is curious, and not really clear, why of all the rulers of the dynasty only Abbas and Mehmet Ali are referred to in this work by the epithet "residing in paradise" (Turkish *cennetmekân*, Arabic *sākin al-jinān*). The rest of the deceased rulers are introduced by the less majestic "the forgiven" (*al-maghfūr lahu*). Abbas is not accorded such preferential treatment by any other source.

Three years later, in 1900, the eleventh volume of Bustānī's *Dā'irat al-Maᶜārif* appeared in Cairo with a short biography of Abbas Paşa (Bustānī 1900: XI, 486–7). This is a matter-of-fact account of the reign of the viceroy, which, unlike Zakhūra's biography, does not abound in superlatives. The summation of the viceroy's reign is, nevertheless, quite complimentary. Bustānī asserts that Abbas "was bold and resolute, keen on strengthening the country's prestige and improving the condition of its people." A similarly disposed biography of Abbas appeared two years later in Jurjī Zaydān's popular biographical dictionary *Mashāhīr ash-Sharq* (Zaydān 1902: 201–2; the cumulative image of Abbas is reflected also in Ziriklī's *al-Aᶜlām: Qāmūs Tarājim*, q.v.). There, the Paşa is said to have been learned, articulate, and generous.

The same biography of Abbas was later reproduced by Zaydān, verbatim, in his three-volume *Modern History of Egypt* (*Tārīkh Miṣr al-Ḥadīth*), which was published in several editions from the early 1910s on. With very slight, cosmetic variations, this biography reappeared in 1926 in Zakī Fahmī's biographical dictionary *Ṣafwat al-ᶜAṣr*. It is interesting to note that of the two portraits of Abbas that have been published, all the Egyptian sources mentioned above provide the better-looking one. The other, an unattractive profile with a hooked nose, appears in Charles-Roux's unsympathetic account of Abbas's reign (compare pls. 3 and 8 above). If we consider the nature of this account *vis-à-vis* the Arabic biographies of Abbas, the choice of portraits is hardly surprising. Although, perhaps we should not make too much this point, it is still worth noting that instances in which the type of portrait and the drift of the account do not agree are rare.

We may note, in passing, that Ottoman biographical works have little to say about Abbas, and what they do say is either favorable or neutral. The standard Ottoman biographical dictionary *Sicil-i Osmani* devotes to Abbas three lines, with the conclusion that he was "honest and just" (III, 293–4). The multi-volume encyclopedia of Şemsüddin Sami, *Kamüsülâlam*, allocates a third of a column to the Paşa. After some biographical data, the author states that Abbas was corpulent, obviously mixing him with Sait, whom he commends for sound administration, some reforms, and the concession of the Canal (IV, 3061 [Abbas], and 2580 [Sait]). The few references to Abbas in Ahmet Rasim's *Osmanlı Tarihi* are cryptic, informative, and neutral (Rasim 1326–30: IV, 1957, 1962, 2003). It is obvious that the Istanbul encyclopedists at the turn of the century were not much interested in either Abbas or Sait.

We may also mention that, in 1915/16, the Ottoman Foreign Ministry published a lengthy memorandum on the Egyptian Question. Quite naturally, the authors were concerned with the international implications of the status of Egypt. In spite of the crises between the Porte and Abbas over the so-called *Tanzimat* and the railway concession, the period was regarded as one in which the relations between the central government and the province were stable and basically unchanged. The Ministry's book made no reference to Abbas's character (Bab-ı Âli, Hâriciye 1915–16: 30–2).

43 The author argues that many of Mehmet Ali's projects had been abandoned before Abbas assumed power, and that those which he himself terminated, he did with "sheer common sense." The reign of Abbas, continues Heyworth-Dunne, was peaceful and prosperous, and the Paşa had "a character of his own and a better knowledge of his country's needs" than many people around him. He then takes on Sammarco's views of Abbas (see p. 29 and note 36, above), upholds ar-Rāfiᶜī's claim that Abbas wisely discouraged European adventures in Egypt, and concludes that certainly in education, but also in general, Mehmet Ali's enterprise had failed. At this point, he asks rhetorically, "why should Abbas be made a scapegoat for this failure?" (Heyworth-Dunne 1938: 288–312).

44 Rifaat's Abbas was a "selfish, sullen and severe master, incapable of adapting himself to the new state of affairs created by his grandfather." It is, therefore, "extremely painful" for him to record how, during his reign of "gloom and rampant caprice," Abbas reversed Mehmet Ali's "inspiring work." However, Rifaat admits that Abbas's rule was not without "one or two redeeming features": the reduced burden on the population, and the abolition of monopolies. His reign, he adds, was not as bad as the Europeans generally portrayed it (Rifaat 1940: 93–5).

Another example is Raḍwān's impressive history of the Būlāq Press, published in 1953. It presents a picture of the press which is not all that negative. Nonetheless, the narrative is interlaced with commentary that is predicated on the pervasive view about Abbas. Although the press and other literary agencies continued to function in the reign of Abbas, the author intervenes to remind us that the period was generally one of retardation and retreat, "a lingering after the leap" which the country witnessed during the time of Mehmet Ali. By contrast, though the same level of activity was manifested at the time of Sait, a comment is inserted to the effect that "contrary to Abbas, Sait was enlightened." In the sentence immediately following this statement,

Sait is excused for having the same reactionary views about education and learning as Abbas, because he was more interested in the army. Still, Sait is called enlightened and Abbas reactionary (Raḍwān 1953: 156–8).

Rivlin's article about the construction of the first railway in Egypt at the time of Abbas Paşa appeared in the widely circulating *Middle East Journal*, while ᶜOmar's dissertation on the construction of the railway in its Anglo-Egyptian context between 1833 and 1858, written at the School of Oriental and African Studies, has not been published in full yet. Rivlin's concluding sentence declares that while "England got the railway, ᶜAbbās Pasha not only retained his throne but before the end of his reign made Egypt's autonomous position an incontrovertible political fact of life that no Ottoman administration would ever again challenge" (Rivlin 1961b: 380). As for ᶜOmar, at one point he even cites an unflattering observation by Consul-General Bruce – no great admirer of Abbas – which he prefaces with: "ᶜAbbās's career is to be judged from Bruce's words" (ᶜOmar 1966: 187; other references to Abbas and his reign appear on 119–21, 183–7).

45 Quotation and observation are from Holt 1968: 193–5. For P. J. Vatikiotis (1969 and subsequent editions to the present), Abbas was "generally reactionary and despotic," deliberately arrested the process of modern change, allowed schools, factories, and even the army to deteriorate, and "had left no appreciable mark on Egypt, except for a reputation as the dismantler of his grandfather's edifice" (Vatikiotis 1969: 76–7). Richmond (1977), whose account contains a number of inaccuracies, asserts that Abbas "had homosexual tendencies and his character was gloomy, suspicious and withdrawn. He preferred to live in remote palaces surrounded by Albanian guards," and, to boot, his suspicion of Sait was "near pathological" (Richmond 1977: 70–3). There are a few references to Abbas in *L'Egypte d'aujourd'hui*, published in 1977 by the French Near Eastern Studies Research Group. These are relatively balanced and attempt to throw in some of the viceroy's accomplishments (Groupe de Recherches et d'Etudes sur le Proche-Orient 1977, q.v.). Such an attempt certainly stands out against the backdrop of writings about Abbas in French. A. Marsot (1984), however, takes us back to the old image. In her book about the reign of Mehmet Ali, she opines that "Abbas seemed to be not only slothful, but a dunce," that he was certainly "cruel, inept, indolent and incompetent," and, of course, a homosexual. Her impressions of Abbas were formed on the basis of letters which Mehmet Ali wrote to him and his tutors when the young prince was in his teens. Marsot also drew on Ibrahim's letters to Mehmet Ali, complaining about Abbas's performance in the first Syrian War of 1831 (Marsot 1984: 87–90).

46 For Abdel-Malek's view, see Abdel-Malek 1969: 38–9, 151–2. Although Abbas cultivated and promoted another major figure in Egyptian intellectual history, ᶜAlī Mubārak, his treatment of aṭ-Ṭahṭāwī was not forgiven. In the eyes of forward-looking modern Egyptians, Mubārak somehow never came to possess quite the "chic" that Rifāᶜa Bey did. Consider, for example, Ḥusayn Fawzī's well-known collection of essays, *Sindbād Miṣrī*, published in 1961. In the chronological notes at the end of the book, Abbas's reign is described in the following four sentences, which point out the impression that the defamed Paşa had left in the mind of this leading Egyptian intellectual at the time:

1849–1854: Abbas I, son of Tusun son of Mehmet Ali, assumes the governorship of Egypt. Mehmet Ali died in the summer of that year, and his grandson set out to lay fallow what his grandfather had tilled, and to destroy the works and reforms that [still] remained. He banished to the Sudan the man who gave rise to the intellectual renaissance of Egypt, Rifāᶜa aṭ-Ṭahṭāwī, and his followers, among whom – the cream of the crop – Bayyūmī Efendi. Abbas I died at the hands of a group of his intimate friends and pleasure-pals; he was afflicted with a venereal disease. (Fawzī 1961: 382–3)

47 There is one notable exception to the modern writings about Abbas and the middle years in Arabic, namely the work of some historians of the Sudan and Africa. Of these, I shall mention here just three: Muḥammad Fu'ād Shukrī's work on Egyptian rule in the Sudan, Makkī Shubayka's book on the Sudan from 1819 to 1919, both published in the 1940s, and as-Sayyid Yūsuf Naṣr's work on the Egyptian presence in Africa (Shukrī 1948: 44–53; Shubayka 1947: 54–8; Naṣr 1979: 125–31). Naᶜūm Shuqayr's book on the Sudan mentions Abbas without evaluating his reign. However, he regards favorably the development of the country in his time, which he attributes to the governors-general of the Sudan, especially to Abdüllatif Paşa, who served from the beginning of 1850 to the end of 1851 (Shuqayr 1967: 524–33).

The work of the historians mentioned above is largely based on material from the Egyptian archives, as well as on European sources. They are aware of the negative views about Abbas's reign and openly reject them, both on the basis of his record in the Sudan and on broader grounds. Shukrī and Naṣr even engage in a strong defense of the viceroy's treatment of aṭ-Ṭahṭāwī, for whom they reserve words of criticism because of his behavior in Khartoum and his opposition to Abbas in Egypt. Obviously, these historians did not think that the Sudan was such a bad place, that prominent scholars and able administrators only came to it if banished from Egypt.

Interestingly enough, a history textbook for Sudanese students provides a convenient solution to the dilemma of how to present the reign of Abbas. It simply states that he was a reactionary who opposed progress *in Egypt*, but *in the Sudan* he introduced many important reforms, and was tough with any official who proved dishonest or rough on the local population (Bakht ar-Riḍā' 1969: 104–5, 129–30).

48 "Editorial introduction," *Encyclopaedia Britannica* 1910, I, xix.

Part I: The Ottoman-Egyptian elite in the middle of the nineteenth century

1 Dissent and opposition

1 See Findley 1980: 37–8. Findley's argument for the Ottoman Empire follows sociological literature, mostly the writings of S. N. Eisenstadt.
2 FO 78/404, 113–20, Hodges to Palmerston, 20 March 1840.
3 St. John 1851: 71.
4 Information in this paragraph is based on Nubar 1983: 49 (quoted), and Politis 1931: 175–81 (listed under state papers, p. 303). The situation in the 1840s is amply documented in the literature, though too often not given the appropriate interpret-

ation. For a good, concise account of the economic history of the period, see Owen 1981: 64–76.

5 In the following passages – except when specific references were necessary – use was made of the following sources: FO 78/840, no. 24, Gilbert to Palmerston, 7 August 1850; ibid., no. 29, same to same, 21 September 1850; ibid., no. 30, same to same, 23 September 1850; MAE/Egypte/21, 98–103, Benedetti to the Foreign Minister, 4 May 1849; ibid., 124–7, same to same, 9 June 1849; ibid., 151–4, same to same, 6 August 1849; ibid./22, no. 23, Le Moyne to the Foreign Minister, 12 April 1850; ibid./Caire/29, 1, no. 40, Delaporte to the Foreign Minister, 6 January 1850; Hekekyan 37452, fo. 8, notes dated 23 February 1851 (listed under private papers); ibid., fo. 10, of 26 February 1851; ibid., fos. 13–15, or 28 February and 1 March 1851; ibid., fos. 17–22, of 1 March 1851; ibid., fo. 33, of 14 March 1851; ibid., fo. 35, of 20 March 1851; *The Times*, 21 October 1850 (6f); ibid., 2 November 1850 (5c); ibid., 19 November 1850 (5a); Serheng 1894: II, 261; Nubar 1983: 59–107; Tugay 1963: 72–145.

6 Sāmī 1936: III/1, 11–12.

7 On that see Nubar 1983: 89–90, 111; Cevdet 1953–1967: I, 58–60; Bab-ı Ali, Hâriciye 1915–16: 31.

8 For French contracts, see MAE/Egypte/21, 98–103, Benedetti to the Foreign Minister, 4 May 1849. Hekekyan's list is in Hekekyan 37452, fo. 33, notes of 14 March 1851. There was a long-drawn-out dispute concerning the fate of Yusuf Kâmil Paşa, husband of Mehmet Ali's daughter Zeynep Hanım. For permission to leave Egypt for Istanbul, Abbas forced the couple to obtain a divorce. The story ended on a happy note, when Zeynep joined her husband in the Ottoman capital, where both had a brilliant career and social life (Tugay 1963: 118–27).

9 The following account is based on DWQ, S/7/35/7, 21 and 25 (no. 3), 13 M 1269/27 October 1852. The plot is also mentioned, with partial information, in FO 78/916, no. 19, Murray to Malmesbury, 5 May 1852, and ibid., nos. 14 and 17, Murray to Stratford Canning, 18 and 31 May 1852, respectively. A French account, written two years after the event, tied to the plot the hostilities which broke out between two large bedouin tribes (MAE/Egypte/25, 261–5, no. 82, Sabatier to the Foreign Minister, 22 June 1854). Nubar mentions the plot as a grave and potentially dangerous incident, but misdates it by more than a year (Nubar 1983: 105–6).

10 Sait's intimation is in Senior 1882: II, 193. Other information in this paragraph is derived from: MAE/Egypte/25, 58–61, no. 31, Sabatier to the Foreign Minister, 17 May 1853; and ibid., 23–8, no. 23, 17 April 1853, and 32–5, no. 29, 1 May 1853, from same to same.

11 The quote from Edwin De Leon is in De Leon 1877: 55. An example of relations in the ruling family during the reign of Sait is to be found in a conversation between the latter and Nassau Senior. In 1856, the heir apparent was Ahmet Rifat Paşa, Ibrahim's eldest son, who was killed in 1858. About him Said told Senior: "You know to whom I have to leave it [the government of Egypt]; you know whether I like him or not" (Senior 1882: II, 87). Information about appointments is based on the lists provided by Amīn Sāmī for the reigns of Abbas and Sait. For details, see Sāmī 1936: III/1, 11–12, 27, 36, 44–5, 60–1, 88–9, 130, 180–1, 234, 290.

12 He was certainly viewed as such by Sait, who said so to Senior. However, Sait was not impressed by his chances to cause him much trouble (Senior 1882: II, 193).
13 The makeup and rise of this "second generation" of officeholders was studied in detail by Hunter, though the author does not stress enough the unique impact of the reign of Abbas (see Hunter 1984: 80–122).
14 The following is based on Landes 1958: 97, 111–15, and Senior 1882: II, 190–3.
15 Upon the accession of Sait, his former tutor and later advisor, König Bey, told Nubar: "Nous n'avons que faire des idées d'Abbas, nous avons changé tous cela." Abbas was forgotten, lamented Nubar, no one spoke of him any more, one could say that he had never existed (Nubar 1983: 124).

2 *Creation of a dynastic order*

1 Geertz 1983: 124. For the purpose of comparison with developments in mid-nineteenth-century Egypt, we should look at the rise of the Ḥusaynids of Tunisia, as described by L. Carl Brown. Brown stresses some of the main processes that we have detected in Egypt, notably the creation of dynastic order and its ceremonial symbolism. His particular attention to the traditional political culture makes a comparative reading especially fruitful (Brown 1974: 27–40). Of course, dynastic order, with all its ramifications, had already been established in Tunisia during the first decade of the eighteenth century, more than a century before Egypt.
2 In this and my understanding of ritual and ceremony, I follow Peter Burke's approach as formulated in a paper delivered by him at Magdalene College, Oxford, on 12 March 1987.
3 Murray's comment is in FO 78/804, 244–6, Murray to Palmerston, 6 July 1849. For the frequency of festivities see also Berque 1972: 71.
4 Politis 1931: 184–5 (no. 175, report by the Greek consul, 2 July 1849; listed under state papers, p. 303). For some additional examples, see *The Times*, 2 November 1850 (5c) (lavish reception on an Islamic high holiday); Vingtrinier 1886: 556–8 (an exquisite lunch send to the field maneuvers of the young princes, but refused by Süleyman Paşa as unbecoming soldierly conduct); and MAE/Egypte/25, 23–8, no. 23, Sabatier to the Foreign Minister, 17 April 1853 (a caravan of 300 men and women organized to accompany Abbas's five-months-old son to the Hijaz, where he was to be raised among the bedouins).
5 A description of Ilhami's circumcision rites can be found in FO 78/804, 286–7, Murray to Palmerston, 30 September 1849. For circumcision celebrations in the Imperial Ottoman Family, see Alderson 1956: 104ff. Flaubert's impressions are in Flaubert 1972: 76–7, which also includes the following comment about a man Flaubert met at the ceremony: "Nubar Bey, a young Armenian with a Latin-Quarter air about him."
6 MAE/Caire/29, 32–3, no. 56, Delaporte to the Foreign Minister, 5 June 1850; *The Times*, 17 June 1850 (5c).
7 Nubar 1983: 96–7. For the whole conflict around that issue, see Baer 1969: 109–32.
8 The mosque inauguration is in Hekekyan 37452, fo. 42, notes dated 13 April 1851.

The betrothal of Münire and Ilhami is mentioned in FO 78/1035, no. 6, Bruce to Stratford Canning, 15 March 1854.

9 Gadsby, 195–6, 300–1. Bromfield provides a detailed botanist's account of the Shubrā gardens, in Bromfield 1956: 211–13.

10 Information on Abbas's palaces is based on Mubārak 1887–1889: I, 84; III, 108–9; IX, 88; Sāmī 1936: III/1, 71; Senior 1882: I, 140–1.

11 The above is based on Mubārak 1887–1889: I, 84; Sāmī 1936: III/1, 30–1 (construction orders dated Ş 1226/June–July 1850), 71; Abu-Lughod 1971: 100.

12 The above is based on Nubar 1983: 78; Mubārak 1887–1889: I, 84; Senior 1882: I, 112–14. Ismail Serheng called ^{c}Abbāsiyya palace "an example of beauty" (Serheng 1894: II, 260).

13 The following is based on Mubārak 1882–1889: I, 83–6; Lane 1973: 8; Gadsby 1860: 181; Clot Bey 1840: I, 179 (where he used "Constantinopolitan" instead of *Rūmī*); Abu-Lughod 1971: 94. The quote from Abbas is in Nubar 1983: 79. For comparison with Ottoman architecture of the same period, see Goodwin 1971: 421–50 (palaces, *konak*s, and *yalı̂*s), and Goodwin 1977: 183–7 (good photographs of nineteenth-century elite houses). Goodwin writes that "the mid-century produced no Ottoman work of value" (421), mostly because of European influence and attempts to imitate classical Western style (e.g. Dolmabahçe palace).

14 Findley 1980: 30–9; Hunter 1984: 14–32, 110–22.

15 Kâmil 1911–1912: 228–9.

16 See for example, Findley 1980: 48–51, 63–4.

17 These terms appear in many documents, most readily in lists of grants received by court personalities. For example, see DWQ, S/1/9/22, 1 (no. 1), 22 L 1265/10 September 1849. For comparison with the Imperial Harem, see Uluçay 1971: 39–147 (where the author deals extensively with *Valide Sultan*s, *Kadı̂n Efendi*s, *Sultan*s, *Usta*s, and *Kalfa*s).

18 On the structure of the imperial palace, see Gibb and Bowen 1950: I/1, 329–62. What Abbas might have aspired more realistically to achieve, at least in size and elaboration, was the household of the grand vezir, which is described in ibid., 363–4. Numbers of mamluks are cited in Hunter 1984: 100–2; his estimates are based on Douin. The last figure is somewhat curious, if we remember that Abbas was only twelve years old then.

19 Hekekyan 37452, fo. 10, notes of 26 February 1851.

20 Senior 1882: II, 117–19. For an example of the Ottoman phenomenon, see Inalcı̂k 1941: V, 614.

21 Nubar's statement is in Nubar 1983: 121. Serheng's story is in Serheng 1894: II, 264–5.

22 Nubar 1983: 22–3.

23 Kâmil 1911–1912: 228–9; Hekekyan 37452, fos. 75–6, notes of 11 June 1851. Hekekyan's source, an eye-witness, said that sometimes the mamluks wore women's clothes. This was probably the *şelvar*, known in the West as "harem pants," which appears specifically in Kâmil's description.

24 It is quite difficult to obtain figures on expenses incurred in this respect, especially since Abbas considered the whole enterprise as highly confidential. In one document,

an order from Abbas to his *Kethüdâ*, thirteen men are reported as having been posted to the private service of the viceroy. Their names are Circassian, Greek, and Slav. The salaries allotted to them were quite high, and Abbas ordered that they be paid from his private purse (Sāmī 1936: III/1, 16).

25 Information in this paragraph is drawn from Alderson 1956: 4–16. The author argues that, because of the leeway afforded by seniority, it in fact combined a hereditary with an elective principle, however limited (ibid., 8).

26 Owen 1981: 123.

27 Nubar 1983: 241. For Abbas's designs concerning the principle of succession, see also Kâmil 1911–12: 230–1; and Tugay 1963: 99.

28 The change in the Egyptian succession was confirmed by Sultan Abdülaziz (1861–1876). Both he and his predecessor Abdülmecit (1839–1861) tried to adopt primogeniture also in the House of Osman. Tradition was stronger and they failed. Alderson says that Abdülaziz granted Ismail his wish in the hope of creating a precedent that would assist his own case. He cites Giese, who claimed that both sultans were impressed by the Western model and wanted to emulate it (Alderson 1956: 12–13).

29 ʿAlī Barakāt's comprehensive study of land ownership in nineteenth-century Egypt (available only in Arabic) should be consulted in any discussion of the issue; specific references to this work are provided in this and other sections. Good surveys in English of changes in land tenure during the reign of Mehmet Ali are provided in: Hourani 1968: 45–7, 51–3; Owen 1981: 64–9, 74–5 (pertinent general points are also made in 1–56); Baer 1978. A valuable contribution is Kenneth Cuno's article (1980). Other works that treat the subject as a major concern are Richards 1982 and Gran 1978. A detailed and valuable survey of the system of land tenure and the state of agricultural commerce in mid-nineteenth-century Egypt is provided in the following dispatches from the British consul-general, Fredericl Bruce, to the Foreign Secretary, the Earl of Clarendon, in May–July 1854: FO 78/1035, nos. 22, 23, 24, 28, and 34, dated 30 May, 31 May, 1 June, 16 June, and 5 July, respectively.

30 Information in this and the following two paragraphs is based on Barakāt 1978: 75–7, 94–100, 103–4, 142–4, 158–62, 169–81 (grants by Abbas to specific officials), 310; Hunter 1984: 99–110. For the sake of simplicity, figures have been rounded to thousands of feddans.

31 Nubar 1983: 89. Examples of orders to resume *ühde*s are in DWQ, S/1/9/20, 126 (no. 656), 16 Z 1264/14 October 1848; and ibid., S/1/9/22, 6 (no. 28), 24 L 1265/13 September 1849.

32 The above is based on: Sāmī 1936: III/1, 21; Barakāt 1978: 97–9 (grants to women), and 136–40 (*vakıf*s).

33 The concentration of landed estates operated in conjunction with a strict system of state monopolies. Mehmet Ali effectively controlled the movement of produce from the fields to the markets, setting prices as he saw fit. European merchants had no direct access to the *fallāḥīn* and were obliged to trade with the government. From the mid 1840s onward, the monopolies system was gradually weakened. Abbas further relaxed it, thereby improving the state of the producers, but later resumed state control over the flow of agricultural goods in the economy. Economic historians believe that the system finally collapsed during the reign of Sait Paşa in the latter part of the

1850s. On the monopolies, see Owen 1969: 58ff., Owen 1981: 73–7, and the sources mentioned therein.

34 Information in this paragraph (in order of appearance) is based on: DWQ, S/1/9/22, 1 (nos. 1 and 2), 22 L 1265/10 September 1849; ibid., 34 (no. 203) 16 Za 1265/3 December 1849; ibid., S/1/9/24, 35 (no. 226), n.d.; and ibid., S/1/9/22, 24 (no. 141), 23 Za 1265/10 December 1849. For the sake of comparison, Abbas's own acknowledged and documented expenses during his investiture visit to Istanbul were 368,000 *kuruş*, though European estimates were far higher (ibid., S/1/9/21, 2 (no. 9), 27 R 1265/22 March 1849). The French consul-general estimated that Abbas's mother spent during her trip to Istanbul the enormous amount of 25,000 purses, or approximately £125,000 (MAE/Egypte/21, 135–7, Benedetti to the Foreign Minister, 10 July 1849). It would appear that such estimates are quite exaggerated.

35 DWQ, S/1/9/24, 34 (no. 216), 24 Z 1267/20 October 1851.

36 Information in this paragraph (in order of appearance) is derived from: DWQ, S/1/9/22, 1 (no. 1), 22 L 1265/10 September 1849; Hekekyan 37452, fo. 32, notes dated 11 March 1851. The settlement figure is from Nubar 1983: 111. Yusuf Kâmil put the total amount paid by Abbas to Mehmet Ali's heirs at 380,000 purses, or about £2,000,000 (Kâmil 1911–1912: 230).

3 *The mainstay of dynastic order – the elite*

1 Hunter translates *daire*s as "private Viceregal administrations" (Hunter 1984: 63), but this does not convey the full meaning of the term. It is clear that in an Ottoman context, and this is the relevant one here, *daire*s meant households (in Toledano 1984b: 387ff., I translated *daire*, when located within the palace, as "princely suite," but when it appears as a physically separate unit, "household" seems more appropriate). Example of "pecking order" is in DWQ, S/7/35/7, 47 (no. 12), 3 Ş 1269/12 May 1853. Example of viceroy's household topping the list is in ibid., S/1/9/24, 33 (no. 211), 1 M 1268/27October 1851. For lists of civil ranks and salaries, see Hunter 1984: 55, 81. Lists of military ranks and salaries are in Sarūjī 1967: 289ff. Sarūjī does not provide a list for the reign of Abbas, which may be examined in DWQ, S/7/35/1, 16 (no. 49), 17 Ca 1265/10 April 1849.

2 Hunter 1984: 80–2.

3 Data in this paragraph are drawn from: Sarūjī 1967: 357–64; Sāmī 1936: III/1, 10, 26, 35, 43, 52, 59, 86–7, 129, 179, 233, 289, 332, 350, 376, 408; Naṣr 1978: 31–2; Serheng 1894: 260–1. The figures provided in this section are rounded approximations derived from a comparative examination of these sources.

4 Hourani 1968: 40–1, 45–7, 51–6.

5 Ibid., 53.

6 For names of persons and details of the orders issued, see FO 78/404, 160–1, Hodges to Palmerston, 20 April 1840, and ibid., 197, Hodges to Palmerston, 26 May 1840.

7 Details of Abbas's attention to *ṣūfī* orders are provided by De Jong 1978: 77, 81, 93, 141, 150. In this, Abbas stands out from all mid-century viceroys. The three *ʿulamā* appointed to the Council were: Shaykh al-Azhar, the Ḥanafī Muftī of Egypt, and alternately either one of the heads of the two most important mystic orders, Shaykh as-

Sādāt and ash-Shaykh al-Bakrī (Sāmī 1936: III/1, 17). In what might have been also a gesture to *ṣūfī* sentiments, and to commerce and the lower strata, Abbas extended the annual celebrations of Mawlid al-Badawī by three days and nights (ibid., 32–3). *ᶜUlamā* who served the viceroys loyally were rewarded handsomely, as in the case of Shaykh al-Jirjāwī of al-Azhar, who received a large estate from Abbas (Barakāt 1978: 152). At the same time, during the reign of Abbas, the allowances paid to the Azhar *ᶜulamā* were suspended; they were restored only in the reign of Ismail (Mubārak 1887–9: XVII, 12).

8 On the bedouins, see Baer 1969: 3–16, Barakāt 1978: 263–87, and Sāmī 1936: III/1, 17 (order to prevent incursions on crops which had been sown). On the role of village *shaykhs* at mid-century, see Barakāt 1978: 234–6; Baer 1969: 30–61; and Hunter 1984: 85, 88.

9 For an account of the literature on and the controversy around this issue, see Findley 1980: 43–66.

10 Yapp 1975: 349–50. Further references to Yapp's observations in this paragraph are based on Yapp 1975: 335–42 (European armies), 346–53 (Ottoman armies), 362–5 (modernization and comment on Egyptian army).

11 For the artillery officer, see Hekekyan 37452, fo. 70, notes of 5 June 1851. The complaint of the *bey* is in Senior 1882: II, 27. An example of troops sent to work on an agricultural estate is in DWQ, S/1/9/27, 3 (no. 16), 17 Ra 1270/18 December 1853.

12 An example of social mixing of military and civilian officials is in DWQ, L/2/67/2, 84–6 (no. 40), 4 L 1267/2 August 1851. An example of a military *zevat* household and patronage is in ibid., L/2/63/1, 20–4 (no. 11), 15 R 1269/26 January 1853 (household of the Chief-of-Staff Süleyman Paşa).

13 DWQ, L/2/63/1, 6–10 (no. 5), 2 M 1269/16 October 1852.

14 For examples of high officials who had held military positions, see Hunter 1984: 25, 86–7. A prominent official who also merits mention is Abbas's *Kethüdâ*, Manastîrlî Hasan Paşa. He and Abbas each commanded a wing in the Syrian campaign under Ibrahim (Weygand 1936: II, 34). Instances of disaffection in the army towards Abbas are in Hekekyan 37452, fo. 48, notes of 27 April 1851, and Senior 1882: I, 27–9.

15 Abbas's letter to Sait is in Sāmī 1936: III/1, 25, 15 Za 1265/2 October 1849. On Abbas's attitude to the navy, see also MAE/Egypte/24, 48–51, Le Moyne to the Foreign Minister, 4 January 1852; Serheng 1894: II, 263.

16 Hekekyan 37452, fos. 17–22, notes of 2 March 1851. Hekekyan, who was educated in Britain, had grossly underestimated the size of the Roman armies. We could somewhat improve our rating of his historical knowledge only if we assume that he meant to say that the size of the elite guard of the Roman Empire was the number he quoted above. Abbas and his ministers believed, as Hekekyan reports from the same meeting, that if the Ottoman Empire had 400,000 men under arms, she could easily defeat the Russians.

17 In the following paragraphs, reference is made to theses expounded in Findley 1980: 201–18, and Hunter 1984: 80–110.

18 L. Carl Brown seems to take roughly the same view with regard to the political elite in Tunisia, which he calls "Ottoman-Tunisians" (Brown 1974: 41ff.).

19 Following Shils, Geertz, and Berreman, I take ethnicity to mean a shared cultural

heritage, manifest in "primordial sentiments." In Geertz's words, "these congruities of blood, speech, custom, and so on, are seen to have an ineffable, and at times overpowering, coerciveness in and of themselves" (Berreman 1981: 15–16). Thus, Hunter's ethnic "Turks," and even "Turco-Circassians," share some of the elements of what I term here "Ottoman-Egyptian" culture. However, the various sub-groups classified under "Turks" also had "primordial sentiments" which were not shared by the "Turkish group" as a whole. Furthermore, the group as a whole shared socio-cultural features which were neither "primordial" nor common to ethnic "Turks" who did not belong to the Ottoman-Egyptian elite.

20 Panzac estimates that in 1840 there were 22,000 Ottoman nationals in Egypt, not including native Egyptians. These were, according to his categories: 12,000 Turks, 3,000 Greeks, 5,000 Syrians, and 2,000 Armenians (Panzac 1987: 26). Obviously, most of these – perhaps to the exclusion of the majority of Syrians – were Turcophones, though only a minority belonged to the elite. The most accessible source for the variety of names with ethnic and geographic connotations is Amin Sāmī's lists of appointments, which for the mid nineteenth century are to be found in Sāmī 1936: III/1 under each year. One "external" example of the confusion which prevailed is Gadsby's comment that "the Albanian soldiers, to whom I have several times referred, are native Greeks" (Gadsby 1860: 376 n.).

21 For this episode, see Nubar 1983: 117–21.

22 For Nubar and Hekekyan's letters, see Hekekyan 37452, fo. 40, notes of 27 March 1851. For Nubar and Vichen, see ibid. fos. 34–5, notes of 19 and 20 March 1851.

23 Clot Bey 1949: 188–9.

24 Information in this paragraph is drawn from: Politis 1931, 185 (Cossiva to the Greek consulate, 2/14 July 1849); MAE/Egypte/22, 21–2, Le Moyne to the Foreign Minister, 30 April 1850; Hekekyan 37452, fos. 17–22, notes of 2 March 1851; Nubar 1983: 125ff.

25 Non-Muslims, like the Armenians and Greeks, were certainly part of elite political culture, although they did not necessarily share the explicitly Muslim components of Ottoman-Egyptian culture.

26 On attitudes to reform in the bureaucratic elite of Egypt, see Hunter 1984: 114. Additional references to Mehmet Şerif Paşa are in Hunter 1984: 154, 156.

27 Yet Nubar believed that the ideas of the *Tanzimat* reformers, and by extension presumably those of Mehmet Ali, could have been more palatable, hence more successful, had they been presented to the public in Islamic, not European-Christian terms (Nubar 1983: 98, note 1).

28 Hekekyan 37452, fos. 17–22, notes of 2 March 1851. After his audience with Abbas, Hekekyan joked with some of the viceroy's personal guards, whom he called the "pistol gentry." He told them stories about feats of strength and other great physical capacities, which he said they loved to hear. Clearly knowing who he was, a prominent Armenian and a Christian, they felt comfortable enough to say about one of the subjects of his anecdotes, a Muslim: "He was a brave and cunning Muslim who triumphed over the unbeliever," using the derogatory *gâvur*. Hekekyan did not seem to take umbrage.

29 For some of the versions, see Bab-ı Âli, Hâriciye 1915–16: 31; MAE/Egypte/21, the

French consul-general to the Foreign Minister, 5 March 1849 (also quoted by Sabry 1930: 21).

30 Sabry 1930: 22.

31 Nubar 1983: 72–3.

32 Information in this paragraph is partly based on Nubar 1983: 67, 92. For the story of Zeynep Hanım and Yusuf Kâmil Paşa, see also E. F. Tugay 1963: 118–27.

33 Nubar 1983: 110.

34 The correspondence is contained in DWQ, S/1/9/27. References to specific letters from this register will be made in the following paragraphs.

35 For a later version of the tradition of *jurnal*s and *jurnalcı*s, see Asaf Tugay, *İbret* n.d. I, Istanbul and 1962 II, Istanbul. The first volume deals with such reports and their writers, and provides the text of many reports that were presented to Sultan Abdülhamit II. These were often used for internal security and spying on officials.

36 DWQ, S/1/9/27, no. 72, 20 Ra 1270/21 December 1853. Examples of orders to supply detailed *jurnals* are in ibid., 3 (no. 13), 17 Ra 1270/18 December 1853, and ibid., 3 (no. 17), 20 Ra 1270/21 December 1853.

37 Replacement of casualties is in DWQ, S/1/9/27, no. 78, 11 L 1270/7 July 1854. Promotion of the two officers is in ibid. no. 65, 29 M 1270/1 November 1853. Replacement of the captain is in ibid., no. 70, 17 Ra 1270/18 December 1853 (in the margin, or postscript, *kenar* in Turkish).

38 Information in this paragraph is from DWQ, S/1/9/27, no. 67, 29 M 1270/1 November 1853. Examples of payments to officers and soldiers of the expeditionary force are also in ibid., 3 (no. 15), 17 Ra 1270/18 December 1853; ibid., no. 84, 19 Z 1270/12 September 1854; and ibid., no. 89, 5 Ca 1271/24 January 1855. Four-monthly payments to the whole force varied in 1854 and the beginning of 1855 from 3,000 purses (1,500,000 *kuruş*) to 3,500 purses (1,750,000 *kuruş*). One deficient payment in 1853 came to 968,083 *kuruş*).

39 Information in this paragraph (in order of appearance) is taken from DWQ, S/7/35/8, 135–6 (no. 13), 14 Ca 1270/12 February 1854 (example of the use of the expression *Usul-ı Mısriye*); DWQ, S/1/9/27, no. 73, 9 Ca 1270/7 February 1854; ibid. 2 (no. 11), 29 Ş 1269/7 June 1853. Another expression which appears in documents (e.g. DWQ, S/7/35/5, 44 (no. 93), 22 Z 1266/29 October 1850), is *Mısır perverde*, or someone “nourished, educated, and brought up” in Egypt. In other words, there was already, at mid-century, a group of Ottoman-Egyptians who had grown up in Egypt and, presumably, were more committed to life in the country. In the case mentioned above, the fact that the concerned middle-level official was *Mısır perverde* appears to have induced the government to grant him his request to open a pharmacy in Cairo.

40 See, for example, his requests for reports on casualties and runaways and on the system of payments: DWQ, S/1/9/27, no. 85, 9 M 1271/2 October 1854; and ibid. no. 89, 5 Ca 1271/24 January 1855.

41 For the latest account of the rise of Egyptian nationalism, see Gershoni and Jankowski 1986.

42 DWQ, S/1/9/27, no. 70, 17 Ra 1270/18 December 1853. Historical references are also in ibid. no. 72, 20 Ra 1270/21 December 1853, and ibid. no. 67, 29 M 1270/1 November 1853.

43 For a concise and revisionist account of the discovery of the Serapeum, see Malek 1983. A popular and recent history of Egyptology is Clayton 1982. For a succinct account of the history of photography and its connection with Egyptology, see Malek and Miles 1986. Du Camp's impressive photographic results are in Du Camp 1852. Gadsby, for example, wrote: "In 1852, I found that the pacha was causing the temple at Luxor to be excavated." The project was directed by the French archeologist M. Maunier, and the labor was forced (Gadsby 1860: 346 n.).

44 See Linant Bey's observation on the matter in Senior 1882: I, 56–7.

45 Information in this paragraph is from Malek 1983: 65–7.

46 DWQ, S/7/35/1, 37 (no. 125), 17 C 1265/10 May 1849.

47 Two examples of individual export permits are in Sāmī 1936: 15 (to the Austrian consul for seventeen pieces), and 23 (to a British subject, by personal request of Consul-General Murray, for two mummies). These two permits were issued before the instructions on antiquities referred to above.

48 As late as March 1840, the British complained that Mehmet Ali was carrying on negotiations with local figures in the Yemen and Muscat. They protested against his meddling and feared his unspecified designs (FO 78/404, 120–43, Hodges to Palmerston, 31 March 1840). For Egyptian–Yemeni relations during the reign of Mehmet Ali, see Batrik 1968.

49 Information in this paragraph is derived from: MAE/Egypte/21, 96–7, no. 4, Benedetti to the Foreign Minister, 30 April 1849; ibid. 144–5, no. 43, the Foreign Minister to Benedetti, 30 July 1849; MAE/Turquie/1846–1850, Benedetti to Aupick, 17 June 1849. See also Serheng 1894: II, 263. For Anglo-French rivalry in Tunisia during the nineteenth century, see Raymond 1955 and Raymond 1964.

50 For the standard biography of Abbas, see Sāmī 1936: III/1, 4–5. Hekekyan's version is in Hekekyan 37452, fos. 1–3, n.d., but probably written at the beginning of 1851.

51 Information in this paragraph is drawn from Sāmī 1936: III/1, 16. On 25 December 1849, Flaubert recorded in his travel notes that the son of the Sharīf of Mecca was visiting Egypt: "The son of the Sharif of Mecca with all his retinue, on horseback – cashmere turban, green *kaftan*, coffee complexion" (Flaubert 1972: 67). For the two ports, see Sāmī 1936: III/1, 14 (order of Abbas to the supervisor of customs at Sawakin, 14 M 1265/10 December 1848).

52 For passage of troops through Egypt to the Hijaz, see *The Times*, 18 August 1851 (5c). On the events of 1856–8 in the Hijaz, see Ochsenwald 1980.

53 General information in this and the following paragraph is based on Sāmī 1936: III/1, 24; Serheng 1894: II, 261; Shukrī 1948: 40ff.; Shubayka 1947: 54ff.; Naṣr 1979: 125ff.

54 These incursions into Ethiopia raised the suspicions of the British consul-general, who thought Abbas might be contemplating extending his rule in that region and bringing Islam farther south (FO 78/1035, no. 23, Bruce to Clarendon, 31 May 1854). At the same time, the French consul-general was worried that the raids into Ethiopia were coordinated with the British, because of frequent visits of British officials to the palace of Binha at the time (MAE/Egypte/25, 259–60, no. 13, Delaporte to the Foreign Minister, 22 June 1854). Such "second-guessing" seems to have been quite common in the reign of Abbas. The consuls knew then less than they did in any other reign in the nineteenth century.

4 The realities of office-holding

1 This is the standard form of *irades*; the specific example is taken from the register containing decisions submitted to Abbas by the Council of Justice, DWQ, S/7/35/7. Documents submitted in this way were often called "summary [decisions]" (*hulâsas*, as when submitted by the Council of Justice, or "draft [memoranda]" (*mazbatas*), in other cases.

2 DWQ, S/1/9/23, 4 (no. 25), 25 S 1266/10 January 1850. This and many other registers contain an ample number of similar examples to prove the point.

3 The following is an interesting example from the foreign correspondence of Abbas Paşa. Early in 1852, Abbas replied to a request from the East India Company, saying "*I* give you *my* word from now . . . " (*Şimdiden söz veririm*). Use of the informal address abounds in the registers. For quick reference see DWQ, S/1/9/21. A copy of Abbas's letter to Mr. Anderson of the East India Company in London is in BM, OR 12130, fo. 35, and is dated 3 R 1268/26 January 1852.

4 For development of the bureaucracy, see Hunter 1984: 41–70. For changes in the army, see Schölch n.d.: 32–7.

5 Hekekyan 37452, fo. 45, notes of 20 April 1850.

6 Nubar 1983: 21–2, 92, 119–20.

7 Ibid. 45–6.

8 Findley 1980: 37.

9 Hunter 1984: 76–7.

10 Senior 1882: II, 104–5.

11 Nubar 1983: 118.

12 Information in this paragraph is based on orders and regulations cited in Sāmī 1936: III/1, 20, 21, 24.

13 Information in this paragraph is based on Sāmī 1936: 18 (articles 6, 7, 8 of council regulations).

14 Information in this paragraph is based on Hekekyan 37452, fos. 23, 25–6, 33, letters to Abdi Paşa, Minister of Public Instruction and diary notes, 4 and 5 March 1851; Nubar 1983: 118–21; Mubārak 1887–9: IX, 46–9 (Mubārak's autobiography). See also Hunter 1984: 77 (for Ismail's reign).

15 Humiliation of Ibrahim's sons by Abbas is in Hekekyan 37452, fo. 16, notes of 1 March 1851. The complaint of the French consul-general is in MAE/Egypte/24, 54–63, Le Moyne to the Foreign Minister, 13 April 1852; a similar complaint by the British consul-general is in FO/78/1035, Bruce to Clarendon, 16 February 1854. Nubar's experience with Canning is in Nubar 1983: 100–1.

16 Hekekyan 37452, fo. 28, notes of 6 March 1851.

17 Cevdet 1967: IV, 61–2.

18 Senior 1882: II, 111. When an official was dismissed, the expression usually used was that he was deprived of his insignia and "driven out" (*nişanını alıp terd kılınması*, e.g. DWQ, S/1/9/24, 33 [no. 211], 30 M 1268/25 November 1851).

19 Findley (for the central government) and Hunter (for Egypt) have adequately dealt with *intisap* (Findley 1980: 33–5, and Hunter 1984: 110–12). The following paragraphs are meant as a modest addition to the concept. Findley translates *intisap* as

"connections," Hunter as "personal connections," but it seems to me that this is more what the term came to mean in a later context. Also, this rendering appears to me too technical, or mechanical, losing the affective aspect of *intisap* relations that "attachment" retains.

20 Information in this paragraph thus far is from Mubārak 1887–9: 54, and Nubar 1983: 123.

21 Nubar 1983: 34–5.

22 Hekekyan 37452, fos. 17–22, notes dated 2 March 1851.

23 For example, even operators of the sign telegraph system had to be selected from among those who could read and write (Turkish *okur yazar*), as instructions required (DWQ, S/7/35/5, 30 [no. 62], 3 Z 1266/10 October 1850).

24 For the Egyptian economy in the middle years of the century, see Owen 1981: 122–52. Owen stresses the increasing difficulties caused by foreign borrowing, but also points out the internal development which loans made possible in Egypt. In addition to steady growth in various sectors, two agricultural booms occurred as a result of the Crimean War in the mid 1850s and the American Civil War in the early 1860s. During the reign of Ismail, major construction and development projects were launched at great expense, but with long-term effects on the infrastructure of the country.

25 Information in this paragraph comes from Hekekyan 37452, fo. 60, to Harris (British Consulate), 26 May 1851; ibid., fo. 63, notes dated 2 June 1851; ibid., fo. 67, to Harris, 3 June 1851; ibid., fo. 83, notes dated 16 June 1851; MAE/Egypte/21, 134, no. 12, Benedetti to the Foreign Minister, 14 June 1849; Nubar 1983: 113; Hunter 1984: 55–6. It appears that pay arrears were an issue for both Abbas and Sait upon their respective accessions. Abbas offered to buy treasury bills at 12 percent (DWQ, S/1/9/20, no. 108, 15 Z 1264/12 November 1848), and Sait deprived officials of arrears by a decree (Senior 1882: II, 207).

26 For some pay scales, see Sarūjī 1967: 289–306; ᶜAbd al-Wahhāb 1977: 155–6; Hunter 1984: 55, 58. For irregularities in the appropriation of funds by officials, see Hunter 1984: 67. Ranks in the bureaucracy are listed in ibid., 81.

27 Archival sources are full of references to such contracts. For some examples, see DWQ, S/7/35/8, 70 and 102 (no. 10), 4 R 1270/4 January 1854 (supplying meat to the government in Cairo); S/1/9/27, no. 81, 5 Z 1270/29 August 1854, and no. 82, 12 Z 1270/5 September 1854 (replacing uniform of Egyptian army); S/7/35/8, 65 and 70 (no. 9), 20 S 1270/22 November 1853 (supplying gold and silver to the mint); S/7/35/1, 19–20 (no. 61), 23 Ca 1265/16 April 1849 (contract to pave floor for poor in a Cairene mosque); ibid., 47–8 (no. 158), 1 B 1265/23 May 1849 (contract to pave the road to Suez); S/7/35/2, 61–2 (no. 469), 19 N 1265/8 August 1849 (concession to pearl divers in Abū Qīr); S/7/35/7, 29 (no. 7), 17 C 1269/28 March 1853 (production of spirits); ibid., 84 (no. 15), 29 B 1269/8 May 1853 ("wine bars" in the Sudan); ibid. 84 (no. 16), 29 B 1269/8 May 1853 (same in Alexandria and provincial towns throughout Egypt); S/7/35/5, 54 (no. 122), 7 M 1267/12 November 1850 (same in northern towns). Factory operation contracts are from Giritlī 1952: 173–4. Case of a *paşa* holding a contract to supply the transit authority with meat is in Bromfield 1856: 29. For a recent contribution on *iltizam*, see Murat Çizakça 1986.

28 DWQ, L/2/67/1, 94–5 (no. 38), 9 B 1266/21 May 1850; ibid., 95–6 (no. 39), 18 B 1266/30 May 1850; ibid., 73–5 (no. 30), 10 Ca 1266/24 March 1850.

29 Abbas's orders and reasoning are in the following sources: Sāmī 1936: III/1, 21–2 (order dated 27 C 1265/20 May 1849); DWQ, S/7/35/2, 10–11 (no. 288), 2 Ş 1265/23 June 1849; ibid., 27 (no. 303), 13 Ş 1265/4 July 1849.

5 The demon-image of Abbas Paşa

1 Audouard 1865: 132. In her excellent work on Cairo, published in 1971, Janet Abu-Lughod included the following perceptive observation: "It is difficult to believe that any ruler could have been as completely unattractive as Abbas Pasha is pictured, for one searches in vain in Western literature for a sympathetic word or a redeeming virtue" (Abu-Lughod 1971: 99).

2 See for example, M. Tossizza (Greek consul) to the Ministry of Foreign Affairs, 876/61, Alexandria, 7/19 December 1848, in Politis 1931: 181.

3 For this affair, see Baer 1969: 113–19.

4 Cevdet 1967: IV, 58–61.

5 Hekekyan wrote at the time: "Abbas had declared, it is said, that he would spend twenty thousand purses to get him [Reşit] out of his place. Reşit said that he would not spend twenty paras to return the same act of kindness to Abbas" (Hekekyan 37452, fos. 13–14, notes of 28 February 1851).

6 Sait's comment is in Senior 1882: I, 113–14. *The Times*'s report is in the issue of 1 July 1850 (5c–d). Mubārak's observation is in Mubārak 1887–9: VII, 60.

7 Sait's observations are in Senior 1882: I, 112–14.

8 Information about Hekekyan is based on his own notes and letters in Hekekyan 37452. His secret request for British protection is in his letter to Briggs (his tutor in England and former consul-general in Egypt), 29 April 1851, in Hekekyan 37452, fo. 48. While remaining on the government payroll, Hekekyan knew that he was being watched by Abbas, that his Istanbul mail was being intercepted, and that he was expected to report to the Paşa any schemes which Artīn might be plotting against him in Istanbul. Understandably, this tight-rope walking caused Hekekyan a great deal of anxiety and led him to a deep hatred of Abbas. It even made him apply in secret for British protection. Ultimately, he was not harmed by the viceroy, who even allowed him to engage, unperturbed, in archeological excavations. The material used here covers both periods in Hekekyan's relations with Abbas: before and after he was "put on quarter pay." That was the practice with officials who lost the *valī*'s favor without incurring his unmitigated wrath. About a year and a half after the death of Abbas, Hekekyan told his friend Nassau Senior, a well-known British economist who was visiting Egypt in connection with the plans to dig the Suez Canal: "I am perhaps impartial [towards Abbas and Sait]; for if I have to complain of Abbas for having turned me out, I have to complain of Said Pasha for not having restored me." This somewhat naive statement was obviously intended to lend credence to his views. What it actually betrays is Hekekyan's awareness of how his unflattering comments about Abbas might be construed by his interlocutor. Quite naturally, Hekekyan's background and his position during the reign of Abbas conditioned his perception of reality.

9 The account of the meeting with Abbas is in Hekekyan 37452, fos. 17–22, notes dated

2 March 1851. He recorded the details of the meeting upon his return from the palace, and the notes reflect his fresh impressions of the viceroy. Generally speaking, Hekekyan knew Abbas more through the eyes of colleagues, friends, and family members than by personal daily contact. In fact, most people "knew" the viceroy precisely in that removed way, which did not prevent them from speaking and writing about him as if they had first-hand knowledge. Still, Hekekyan was better placed then others. His wife was Abbas's playmate when they were children, which, as viceroy, he must have remembered fondly when granting her a large estate. The young boy was a frequent visitor to the Sukkias home, as the mother of Artîn, Hüsrev, and Banuma Hekekyan always made sure he would be served pilav, his favorite dish. Abbas used to eat his pilav in a peculiar way, with three silver spoons, which Banuma saved as a souvenir.

In addition to his wife's childhood memories of Abbas, Hekekyan also benefited from the more mature political impressions of his brothers-in-law, Artîn Bey and Hüsrev Bey, who held high office under Abbas. And, of course, there were his own contacts with the viceroy when he served as President of the Board of Health. Such contacts must have been fairly limited, for, in the early years of his reign, Abbas was preoccupied with the reorganization of the administration, with the challenge to his authority by rival factions in the ruling family, and with the painful redefinition of his relations with the Porte and the European Powers. Although his administration was highly centralized, the Board of Health was not high on the agenda, and when problems arose, as in times of epidemic, most of the top-ranking officials would be involved in solving them. But even so, those were the times that Hekekyan was closest to the center of things. In those days, he served as a source of information and political gossip, rather than as a mere consumer, living off the crumbs with no real grasp on what was going on (for Abbas's childhood, see Hekekyan 37452, fos. 1–3; land grant to Banuma Hekekyan [300 feddans] is in Barakāt 1978: 200–1).

10 Turkish *meşlah*, Arabic *mashlaḥ*: a seamless, long, flowing cloak of wool or camel's hair, sometimes embroidered with gold. It was worn by local notables, rather than by members of the Ottoman-Egyptian elite.

11 Hekekyan 37452, fos. 75–6, notes from 11 June 1851.

12 Riding from Cairo to Heliopolis, Hekekyan heard the man's observation that

> Mehmet Ali was a "vely" [*vali*] indeed, and that the present Viceroy was idle. He said he was cruel towards the poor – putting them to hard labour in the deserts and paying them nominally nothing . . . He said that many of his countrymen died daily in the works of the Pasha's palaces. He had the good sense to think that His Highness should have laid out money in improving "massr" [Egypt and/or Cairo] than to build in deserts. He said that if the levies were abolished the Viceroy would "be pardoned his manifold sins".
>
> (Hekekyan 37452, fo. 26, notes from 6 March 1851)

It should be noted once again that the condition of the *fallāḥīn* and the urban poor actually improved during the middle decades, including of course the reign of Abbas Paşa.

13 Hekekyan 37452, fo. 24.

14 Both quotations are from ibid., fos. 54–5, notes dated 7 May 1851.

15 Dispatch of 3 July 1833, in Douin 1927: 146.

16 If only to get the flavor of some French rhetoric on the relation between France and Egypt, we should look at Gouin's introductory notes to his work on the history of Egypt. The author refers to Egypt as the Jeanne d'Arc of the Orient, as "notre fille adoptive" (Gouin 1847: 1–4), and adds:

> Descendue des faites lumineux à l'obscure barbarie, elle a su remonter et ressaisir sa place au soleil. Qui l'a découverte dans son lointain Vaucouleurs? Qui l'a été cherché dans son coin de ciel? Qui lui a tendu la main? La France.

17 MAE/Egypte/22, 5–11 (no. 23), to the Minister of Foreign Affairs.

18 Ibid., 33–6, Le Moyne to the Minister of Foreign Affairs (no. 37), 31 May 1850.

19 MAE/Egypte/25, 103–7, Sabatier to the Minister of Foreign Affairs, 7 July 1853.

20 Quotation from Clot Bey is in Clot Bey 1949: 316. That from Mougil Bey is in Senior 1882: I, 27–8.

21 Ibid., I, 210–11. Another version of the story, similar in principle but without the first-hand account by the Englishman, the blooded hand, or Abbas's self-incrimination, is related to Senior by Mrs. West, wife of the British consul in Suez (I, 151).

22 FO 78/757, Murray to Palmerston (no. 30), confidential, 6 July 1848. Seven years earlier, Sir Charles Napier also wrote about the fear that Abbas inspired. Following the emergence of a resolution to the Ottoman-Egyptian conflict early in 1841, Napier paid a cordial visit to Egypt. As a British naval officer, he had figured prominently in the showdown between the European Powers and Mehmet Ali in Syria during the last quarter of 1840. Napier came to Cairo towards the end of January 1841. He was received by Abbas Paşa, then governor of Cairo, with "tolerable politeness," as he put it. Still, in his two-volume work, *The War in Syria*, published in 1842, we read the following comments about his host:

> Abbas Pacha, the grandson of Mehemet Ali, has long been known for his hatred to anything having the resemblance of a Frank . . . His character is none of the best; he is devoid of talent, and much more feared than either loved or respected . . . His appearance is not much in his favor, being a dull heavy man, much more resembling a butcher than a Pacha.
>
> (Napier 1842: II, 84)

23 In one of his dispatches, Murray wrote:

> My previous dispatches will serve to convince Your Lordship that I have never been an admirer of the character or administration of our present Viceroy; still I must do him the justice to say that as far as England is concerned we cannot complain of him.
>
> (FO 142/16, Murray to Palmerston [no. 2], 17 February 1851)

Abbas, of course, never knew of these views, as time added a personal touch to his confidence in the British consul-general. He even made special humanitarian gestures when Murray's wife was taken ill towards the end of his stay in Egypt.

In this context, we should also note a few sentences in a book written by Edwin De Leon, American consul-general in Egypt. De Leon knew Abbas in his official capacity, and, as he himself admits, was never on close personal terms with him. He was much more intimate with Sait Paşa, Abbas's successor, as were almost all members of the European community in Egypt. In 1877, more than twenty years after Abbas had died, De Leon published an account of Egyptian history entitled *The Khedive's Egypt*. Although relatively balanced in his appraisal of Abbas's reign, the retired consul-general had few good words to bestow upon the viceroy's character. He did, however, contribute an especially unattractive physical description of Abbas, which complements the demon-image, by then already a legend:

> Abbas was a sullen, suspicious, timid tyrant . . . His complexion was much darker than that of the majority of his family . . . Abbas was swarthy, with a scanty beard, short and stout of figure, with a bloated, sensual face, and dull, cruel eyes. Yet there was both energy and intelligence manifested in this repulsive countenance, when warmed into interest or animation on any matter that touched him dearly . . . Of his morals, the less said the better . . . in his conduct towards his own people he was arbitrary, rapacious, and cruel to the last degree. (De Leon 1877: 50–1)

24 For reports in *The Times* referred to in this paragraph and note, see the following issues (page numbers and columns given in parentheses): 11 February 1850 (8e); 23 May 1850 (7b); 17 June 1850 (5c); 1 January 1851 (5a). It was rumored in French circles that the paper's correspondent was in the pay of the Paşa. Such a claim was made by Dr. Bourguières to Senior, who responded that "neither the *Times* nor any tolerably respectable English journal was purchaseable" (Senior 1882: I, 241). De Lesseps told Senior that a British correspondent used to receive £1,000 a year from Abbas, but Sait discontinued it. De Lesseps thought it was a mistake and payment should have continued (Senior 1882: I, 48). Given the French view of Abbas, their jealousy of the rising position of the British in Egypt, and the conspiratorial frame of mind not uncommon in such circles at the time, this contention is hardly surprising. It fitted their world view perfectly well. However, in the absence of any concrete evidence, one can only form an impression on the basis of the nature and quality of *The Times* reports over the period from 1847 to 1855. There is practically nothing that might lead the reader of these reports to accept such rumors.

The Jockey Club was contacted through Murray's good offices and invited to take up Abbas's challenge. After some deliberations, however, the club decided to decline, fearing the damage that might come to their expensive horses as a result of the long journey and the difference in food and weather conditions. *The Times* regretted their decision and appealed to the public to meet the Paşa's challenge. As for the dogs, Abbas must have found employment for some of them, because, about a year later, the paper reported that the Paşa was staying at his desert palace, hunting gazelles with English deerhounds sent to him some time earlier.

25 Senior 1882: I, 151.

26 Quotations are from Flaubert 1972: 82 (letter to Cloquet), and 95 (presentation of credentials).

27 Ibid., 65.

28 Ibid., 40.

29 Gadsby spent much time traveling in Egypt during 1846/7, 1850/1, and 1852/3, and his few remarks about Abbas's personality are innocently woven into the narrative,

reflecting what seemed to him common knowledge. He tells his readers about a problem he and a fellow-traveler had with their horses on the road from Suez to Cairo, and the good thrashing given to the driver by his travel companion. It then, quite naturally, springs to his mind that "the pasha was once going to his palace, when one of the horses began to kick. He immediately ordered the sais (ostler) to have 500 lashes" (Gadsby 1860: 225). Or, as Gadsby and his team were preparing to embark on a tour of the Sinai desert, they had to wait several days for the camels, "as they were kept in the desert, for fear the pasha might fall in love with them," and "seal them with his own signet," as he was "taking the *forced loan* of all he could hear of" (Gadsby 1860: 404).

30 Clayton 1982: 58. References to Gadsby in this and the previous paragraph are from Gadsby 1860: 407, 398–401 (in order of appearance). Another useful source, in many respects, is the letters written by British physician Bromfield to his sister. The few things he had to say about Abbas represent the inseparable combination of what he had heard from his European friends in Egypt and what he then saw for himself. As regards politics, Bromfield merely reflects what he heard when he asserts that the viceroy "has sunk to be the mere vassal and representative of his master the sultan, who it is rumoured, is far from being satisfied with his administration of affairs in Egypt." The sultan would have deposed Abbas, Bromfield added, had it not been for the European guarantees of hereditary rule in Egypt. As for the character of the Paşa, he thought it was "careless [and] unenterprising." At another point, the doctor diagnosed Abbas as "possessed of a perfect mania for palace building," some of which he then described (for the passages quoted above, see Bromfield 1856: 23, 63, 206).

The Russian Archimandrite Porphyre Ouspensky, who visited Egypt on a mission in 1850, also had something to say about Abbas's "mania" for building in the middle of nowhere. On his way to the monastery of St. Catherine in the Sinai, Ouspensky's party camped for the night near ʿAbbāsiyya, the new town established by Abbas and named after him. In those days, it was perched in the middle of the desert, north-east of Cairo, an area densely populated today. "What made Abbas construct that city in a place with neither water nor vegetation?" wondered Ouspensky. He then proffered an explanation that the viceroy might have done so as the desert air had a favorable impact on his health. "However, here too, death caught up with him; the new town differs from the old one [only] by the fact that it was a new coffin," observed Ouspensky, in a comment that his French editor qualified as "somewhat philosophical."

A few pages later, the Russian clergyman supplies us with two items which demonstrate the excesses commonly associated with Abbas's character. On the point of irrational extravagance, we learn that, while crossing the Gulf of Suez, Ouspensky saw the vessels which the viceroy had constructed especially for his mother, who wished to make the pilgrimage to Mecca. We then hear of Abbas's passion for pigeons and dogs, and of his cruelty to human beings. On that count, Ouspensky had learnt that the Paşa was unforgiving if anyone was negligent of his beloved animals. A short while before, we are told, he had ordered one of his generals to be given the stick thirty times, only because one of the dogs confided to his care had lost his collar (for Ouspensky's observations as edited and translated into French, see Volkoff 1972: 209, 212–13 [6, 26 respectively in the original Russian edition]). This account was published in Russian in 1856, but many of his readers were well-versed in the French writings of the time, and some of them were probably aware of what French travelers and journalists felt about the events of the 1850s in Egypt.

31 MAE/Egypte/21, 128–31, Artîn Bey to Odilon Barrot, 9 June 1849; ibid., 132–3, Abbas to same, [?] June 1849.

32 MAE/Egypte/24, 19–22, Le Moyne to the Foreign Minister, 16 February 1852; ibid., 32–3, the Foreign Minister to Le Moyne, 20 March 1852.

33 Ibid., Sabatier to the Foreign Minister, 2 November 1852.

34 What happened that night at Binha is still unknown, and may well remain so for ever. His close political allies concealed the fact of his death for a few days, in the hope of securing the throne for his son Ilhami Paşa. Thereby, they expected to prevent the accession of Sait, Abbas's arch-enemy. The body of Abbas was seated in a carriage and driven in usual procession to his palace in ᶜAbbāsiyya. However, the plot failed because the conspirators trusted the wrong man. They instructed the governor of Alexandria to send a veseel to recall Ilhami, who was then at sea on his way to England. The governor immediately notified Sait Paşa, who then proclaimed himself viceroy, receiving the active support of the European consular corps.

35 Barthélemy Saint-Hilaire 1857: 84–5.

36 Ibid., 88.

37 Merruau 1858: 7; other references to Abbas appear on 23–4, 100–2. This passage and more of Merruau's text are reproduced verbatim in A. P. De Sande e Castro 1901: 291–3, but are attributed to a certain Merman. The notion that Abbas was homosexual also survived him, as is attested by the amusing example in About. The author relates an imaginary exchange about a passer-by, whom the interlocutors pretended to recognize: "[Il a] bourrait la pipe d'Abbas Pacha," said one of them, in an unambiguous insinuation (About 1869: 67).

38 In 1873, H. Couvidou published a scathing review of her book in the preface to his *Etude sur l'Egypte Contemporaine*. He accused her of not knowing the country and of being overly suspicious. Audouard's imagination dominated her observations, added Couvidou (see Couvidou 1873: 13–14). However, for the stories which circulated in the milieu she moved in, Audouard is a good source.

39 Audouard 1865: 132. Material cited in this section comes from 131–5.

40 For some of the most popular examples of folk stories, see About 1869: 60–2, 294, 314, and Couvidou 1873: 20–3. For evaluation of stories about Abbas, see chapter 6 below. Quotation is from Wallace 1883: 304. Other references by Wallace to Abbas are in 301–4. The author provides an "oral history" of the reigns of Mehmet Ali, Ibrahim, Abbas, Sait, and Ismail, as told by ᶜAbduh, a storyteller from the village of Kafr Sulaymān in the Delta. According to ᶜAbduh, Abbas was the best ruler for the *fallāḥīn* (ibid., 266–7).

41 *The Times*, 2 November 1850 (5c).

42 Ibid., 31 May 1851 (5d); the other letter appeared on 26 March 1851 (6a).

43 FO 78/916, Rose to Malmesbury (separate and confidential), 14 April 1852.

44 We have already noted the fact that, in spite of Murray's good relations with Abbas, his reports to the Foreign Office were rather reserved on the point of Abbas's character, and only begrudgingly credited the Paşa for serving British interests in Egypt.

However, we should record two statements by Murray, which nevertheless reflect appreciation of Abbas's success in maintaining perfect security in Egypt. In July 1851, he wrote to Canning in Istanbul that the Porte should not interfere with the internal affairs of Egypt, until they

> can show any other Province under their own immediate Government in which once or twice a month a string of 200 camels can cross 84 miles of desert with no guard other than the ordinary Arab camel drivers, and bearing the richest, Indian merchandise, and sometimes four, five or six hundred thousand dollars in specie without the loss of a dollar.

And, in March 1852, writing to the Foreign Secretary, he praised the "unexampled Prosperity of this Country [Egypt], [that is] coupled with the unprecedented moderation which the Viceroy has hitherto shown in the exercise of this Power" (FO 142/16, no. 17, Murray to Canning, 23 July 1851; FO 78/916, no. 10, Murray to Malmesbury, 23 March 1852). The context here, as in the previous quotation, is the conflict between Abbas and the Porte concerning the power to execute convicted murderers.

James Outram visited Egypt in 1849/1850 and spent some time there. He wrote a long and detailed report on the state of the country, with special attention to the army. Outram was impressed with the strength and prosperity of Egypt at the time, which he appraised on the basis of his experience in the East (the report is contained in the records of the East India Company. Some of Outram's impressions are mentioned in his biography, published in 1882 by F. J. Goldsmid [1992: II, 31–41]. For these references I am indebted to Professor Malcolm Yapp).

45 FO 78/966, no. 1, Bruce to Clarendon, 27 December 1853.

46 The complaint of the French consul-general is in MAE/Egypte/24, 19–22, no. 189, Le Moyne to the Foreign Minister, 16 February 1852. An early example of a positive view of Abbas recorded by a British observer is A. A. Paton 1870: II, 241–2.

47 References to Abbas in their conversation appear in Senior 1882: II, 3–11. On the dispute between Ilhami and Sait, see Landes 1958: 112–16. It might be said that Abbas ultimately avenged himself on Sait through the financial incompetence of Ilhami, though he surely had not planned it that way.

48 There was at least one recorded case of murder attributed to Sait (FO 78/623, Barnett to Canning, 26 March 1845). It was reported then that the young prince had murdered a *fallāḥ* "with his own hands." The British consulate carefully investigated the story, which they thought his character rendered "but too credible." It was discovered that Sait killed the man with a wooden club (*nabbūt*).

49 Ibid., 4–6.

50 References to St. John and quotations in this and the following passages are drawn from St. John 1852: I, 77; II, 179–80, and St. John 1851: 71–2, 75.

51 St. John also treats differently Abbas's "notorious" hobbies, which in the accounts of the Paşa's defamers, form a sinister feature of the demon-image:

> His taste leads him to the most trifling amusements . . . he spends time and money in the undignified, though not inelegant, and certainly innocent occupation of a pigeon-fancier. Near the new palace which he is building . . . rises a magnificent square tower, entirely

devoted to the lovely winged favourites of His Highness the Viceroy, who is reported to be quite learned in this department of natural history. Another of his tastes, for which Englishmen will have more sympathy, is for horses; and the public will remember his bold challenge to the Jockey Club.

So it is really a matter of presentation, which results from the observer's general disposition towards Abbas, for precisely the same hobby is depicted in other accounts as a most bizarre and deviant aspect of his character.

52 Hekekyan 37452, fos. 1–3, a draft of a letter addressed on the back to Mrs. Melly of Melly Romilly and Company, Liverpool, and to George Melly, Esq., London. The letter is not dated, but contextually appears to have been written at the beginning of 1851. The biography covers the first sixteen years of the viceroy's life with some current information about his family life.

Another positive note in Hekekyan's diary refers to a conversation with Dr. Loria, a medical man who served in the health services of Mehmet Ali, Ibrahim, and Abbas. Hekekyan reports that he justified to Loria Abbas's opposition to the application of the *Tanzimat* penal code in Egypt, and argued that such a step would undermine the authority of the viceroy and the security of the country. Whereas Hekekyan expresses similar views in various other notes and letters, his reasoning in this instance is more forceful and direct:

I told Mr. Loria that the whole country was in perfect tranquility and the people as contented as people generally are in most countries. People always grumble at being overtaxed and detest conscription. The outcry raised against the Viceroy proceeded from individuals, principally persons in office, some for real wrongs, some for imaginary wrongs and mostly for apprehended evils. The government being respectable enough – judging from the general state of the country – it would be an evil to disturb it by introducing a Tanzimat . . .

(Hekekyan 37452, fos. 9, notes dated 24 February 1851)

Of course, when he himself became like those individuals, imagining wrongs and apprehending evils, Hekekyan was so immersed in his worries that he almost lost all awareness of the reality of things.

53 For Hekekyan's comment, see Senior 1882: II, 224; for Artîn's observations, see ibid., II, 178–9.

54 One of the realities of intellectual life in Egypt during the nineteenth century was the rivalry between two imposing figures and their disciples: Rifāᶜa Rāfiᶜ aṭ-Ṭahṭāwī and ᶜAlī Paşa Mubārak (on this, see for example Shayyal 1962; Abdel-Malek 1969: 145–63; and Delanoue 1982). It was Abbas who gave Mubārak his first real chance at prominence. It was also Abbas who sent Ṭahṭāwī to the Sudan on an educational mission regarded by many as exile. When Sait succeeded Abbas, he recalled Ṭahṭāwī and sent Mubārak to the Crimean War, a different kind of exile. Writing about Abbas, Mubārak ignores the negative image of his benefactor and avoids any direct comment on his character. Indirectly, however, one can still construct a portrait of Abbas according to the *Khiṭaṭ*. The result is an impersonal list of actions, reported in a dispassionate manner. This is partly so because of the many years that intervened between the reign of Abbas and the writing of the *Khiṭaṭ*; by the 1880s, the issue was

dead for Egyptians and Europeans alike. References to Mubārak's view of Abbas in this paragraph are based on Mubārak 1887–9: VII, 60.

55 Ibid., IV, 40.

56 Nubar's assessment of the reign of Abbas is clearly expressed in the following passage:

> Son regne, en effet, non seulement marque une des principales étapes dans l'histoire de la transformation de l'Egypte, mais encore il est peu ou mal connue, et le caractère d'Abbas est faussement apprecié par les générations actuelles . . . La légende s'est emparée d'Abbas et, laissant dans l'ombre ses éminentes qualités d'administateur, ses principes d'ordre et d'économie, ne semble s'être attachée qu'a mettre en lumière les côtés de son caractère qui donnent prise à la critique. On ne voit généralement dans Abbas que le sombre chatelain de l'Abbassieh ou de Benha [two of his isolated palaces], enfermé dans son palais, sous la garde de ses mameloucks . . . ; mais on oublie que jamais la securité en Egypte n'a été aussi grande que sous son règne, et que jamais également vice-roi ne fut plus économe des derniers de l'Etat, plus soucieux des intérêts du pays. (Nubar 1983: 124)

Nubar, however, is not trying to "cover up" the negative aspects of Abbas's character. We are told how Mehmet Ali Paşa himself confided to Nubar his grave worries about the future of Egypt after his own death. These emanated from his sense that Abbas was indolent (*happa*) and incapable of governing the country. Nubar does not seem to take this observation too seriously, but rather relies on his own first-hand impressions of Abbas. He concedes that the Paşa could be cruel at times, and that he endowed with much emotion his relations with all people, both those he felt close to and those he believed – with or without good reason – to be his enemies.

In several passages that betray the realities of life in the Ottoman-Egyptian elite, Nubar admits that the viceroy's demand of complete loyalty, almost above all, assembled around him a group of obedient but unenterprising individuals with few original ideas. True, Abbas preferred a solitary life in his isolated palaces, but it did not prevent him from keeping a close watch on all that was going on in every corner of Egypt. Indeed he was somber, and the country was shrouded in fear: everyone spoke in a low voice, including Nubar himself (for more details, see Nubar 1983: 35–6, 67, 85, 91–2, and 113).

The story about Abbas being described by Mehmet Ali as *happa* has a curious postscript. The Old Paşa supposedly said that when reflecting about the future of Egypt after his return from a trip to Istanbul. He then told Nubar that Ottoman suzerainty was the only guarantee against European domination, since he was old, Ibrahim ill, and the progeny unworthy. A book published in 1915–16 by the Ottoman Foreign Ministry about the Egyptian Question repeats the story, but leaves out Abbas, who according to Nubar, was then called *happa*. Instead, Mehmet Ali is quoted as saying that he and Ibrahim can ensure the independence of Egypt, but they are both old, and who would after that ("*ondan sonra kim var ki*")? (Bab-ı Âli Hâriciye 1915–1916: 30–2).

It is appropriate to mention here that Yusuf Kâmil Paşa, later Ottoman grand vezir, who began his training as an interpreter in the service of Abbas, also made a positive, though qualified, statement about the character of the viceroy. In his political history,

Tarih-i Siyasi, he wrote that Abbas was highly intelligent and ardent (committed, dedicated), but also suspicious, though not without good reason (*pek fatin ve mutaassıp olmağla beraber müvesvis dahi olup ancak bunda haksız değilidi* [Kâmil 1911–1912: 230]).

57 Nubar 1983: 107. Another story takes us to the Palace of Shubrā, Mehmet Ali's residence, on 28 November 1848. The Old Paşa was by then mentally incapacitated, still obsessed with the idea that Ibrahim Paşa, his son and successor, had ordered him to be locked up. Ibrahim had just died, and Abbas came to bid his grandfather farewell before departing for Istanbul to receive the investiture edict from the sultan. "I have cursed Ibrahim because he had me locked up, so God took his soul" said Mehmet Ali to Abbas. "Do not treat me the same way, if you do not wish me to curse you too." "You are and shall always remain our master," Abbas assured him, as he bowed to kiss the old man's hand once again (ibid., 52). The gesture of the visit, and the sensitivity he showed towards his grandfather – for whom he must have harbored ill feelings – are hardly what one would expect from a barbarous savage.

Nubar's Abbas was also kind and generous, though his kindness and generosity were calculated. Twice he had paid Nubar's debts from his own pocket, and each month he would ask him if he owed any money. Because of that, Nubar was too embarrassed to contract new debts. Abbas did the same to other members of his entourage, not wishing them to fall into personal debt, for fear of being thus compromised (Nubar 1983: 79). When he heard that Nubar's father-in-law had not allowed his daughter to join Nubar in Egypt, he wrote to him in Istanbul expressing his anger. Nubar – then in London on a mission – was understandably moved at the gesture, and wrote about it to his wife: "I am happy and proud; my Paşa loves me, and to please me, he did for me what he would not do for many others." At this, even the unintruding editor of Nubar's memoirs, Mirrit Boutros Ghali, was compelled to comment that this story sheds unexpected light on the character of Abbas, who was more humane and kind than he is reputed to have been (ibid., 110–11).

When Nubar's brother, Arakel, was removed from his position at the Ministry of Commerce and relegated to a lesser post, both he and Nubar resigned from Abbas's service. As they were making their way to Alexandria, with the intention of leaving Egypt for France, they passed the Paşa's steamer and were recognized by him. Nubar was subsequently summoned to the viceregal boat, and in the ensuing interview, Abbas offered to restore him to his previous position. Nubar told the *vali* that he felt he should leave Egypt for a few months, but would be happy to resume his responsibilities afterwards. Abbas then offered to appoint Nubar and his brother as agents and representatives in Vienna and Berlin, which Nubar most gratefully accepted. Deeply moved, Nubar regarded that gesture as a sign of Abbas's great generosity, for he not only magnanimously ignored the offence caused by Nubar's resignation – tantamount to betrayal – but also rescinded his earlier decision to demote Nubar's brother (Nubar 1983: 117–22).

58 Ibid., 124.

6 The demon-image as a product of elite culture

1 See, for example, Nubar 1983: 104–7.

2 The basis for future claims of this nature was laid down in the edict itself ("if a single

one of them [the conditions set in the edict] is not executed, that privilege of hereditary succession shall forthwith be abolished and annulled"). For an English translation of the text, see Hurewitz 1975: I, 277–8.

3 Nassau Senior commented that Egyptians attributed far greater significance than was warranted to what was being published about Egypt in European papers. Although these letters and communiqués, he argued, "are harmless with us, they do great mischief here . . . The real fact is that the English public know nothing of Said Pasha and very little of Egypt" (Senior 1882: I, 115).

4 For the press at the time, see ᶜAbduh 1951 and 1943. ᶜAbduh's view of Abbas is derived from Merruau, but his description of the press is adequate.

5 In February 1856, the British consul-general, Bruce, told Senior, as they were discussing the mysterious death of Abbas Paşa: "In this country direct evidence can seldom be procured on any subject whatever, and the little that you get is always contradictory" (Senior 1882: II, 22). This is certainly a sweeping statement, but it nevertheless reflects the prevailing view among Europeans – as well as among no few Ottoman-Egyptians – about the quality and availability of information at the time.

6 Couvidou 1873: 19–23.

7 Darnton 1985: 79–104.

8 See Nubar 1983: 21, and Senior 1882: I, 236.

9 Audouard 1865: 136.

10 For Nazlī and Ibrahim, see Nubar 1983: 49; for the story of Khedive Ismail's granddaughter, Ibrahim's great granddaughter, see Tugay 1963: 117–18.

11 Gadsby 1860: 398 (note).

12 See for example Couvidou 1873: 21, and Audouard 1865: 134–5.

13 Transliterated from the colloquial it would read: *Illī yikhush beyt l-imāra yikhayyaṭ buqquh bi-dūbāra* (Shaᶜlān 1982: 65).

14 For illumination and discussion of the ideas offered in these passages and expounded in the sources cited in this and the following notes, I am indebted to Rachel Giora and Mira Ariel. Some examples of empirical findings can be found in W. Lilli and J. Rehm 1986; and L. Z. McArthur and S. A. Friedman 1980: 615–24.

15 For some works dealing with ingroup and outgroup categorization, see Secord, Bevan and Katz 1956; P. W. Linville and E. E. Jones 1980; Henri Tajfel 1982; A. W. Kruglanski and T. Freund 1982; and R. S. Wyer and S. E. Gordon 1984.

16 See for example S. E. Asch 1946.

17 Arif's information is quoted by Tugay 1963: 99.

18 The alienation and distance between governed and governing in Egyptian tradition are amply reflected in oral culture, as studied, for example, by Shaᶜlān 1982: 57–66. See also part II below.

19 Hekekyan 37452, fo. 34, notes from 15 March 1851. For an interesting discussion of the importance of information, albeit in a different setting, see Clifford Geertz 1979: 123–235.

20 As consular reports from 1853–4 indicate, Abbas continued to travel in the country and participate in some of the main public ceremonies. However, his distance from the elite and the Europeans was felt much more acutely than before, regardless of fact. On growing consular intervention from the mid 1850s onward, see for example Owen 1969: 83–8.

Part II: The social divide and life of the lower strata

Introduction

1 Flaubert 1972: 80.
2 St. John 1852: I, 121. On the economic division of quarters, see Berque 1972: 94.
3 Gadsby 1860: 398.
4 For Ottoman and Mongol traditions, see Lewis 1968: 1–17, 99–100; and Ayalon 1971–3.
5 On Ottoman political and economic thought, see Inalcîk 1977: 65–9; Thomas 1972: 78; and Itzkowitz 1972: 87–9. The quotation is from a review of Geertz's *Local Knowledge* by Roger M. Keesing 1985.
6 See, for example, DWQ, S/7/35/9, 2 (no. 25), 6 Ş 1270/4 May 1854. This is a report about a rebellion at Qina and Esna in 1854, in which men armed themselves, built fortresses, and spread "disobedience and corruption" in the countryside. The Council of Justice imposed long prison terms in the Sudan on twenty-two of the main figures in the case. Some unrest was caused by the bedouins during the same year (see two versions of the events in Senior 1882: I, 179–81, 257–61). This developed into a major clash between the bedouins and Sait's government after the Paşa ascended the throne (ibid. and Serheng 1894: II, 267). See also resistance to conscription in 1848 in Upper Egypt (Tucker 1985: 140). On the question of rural and urban revolts in nineteenth-century Egypt, see Baer 1969: 93–108; Baer 1982: 225–323; Lawson 1981; and Burke 1983.
7 The level of taxation in the middle decades remains to be explored by further research. In this book, I deliberately chose to avoid a detailed discussion of the system of rural and urban taxation. This complex issue, often incomprehensible in its detail but fairly well understood in principle, has been treated by a number of scholars. Through the 1840s and 1850s, taxes continued to be collected both in cash and in kind. Some sources claim that the tax burden was decreasing in the 1850s, but this is hard to establish for the rural population, although the position of the *fallāḥīn* must have improved, as the monopoly system was gradually breaking down and European merchants were gaining direct access to producers. Nevertheless, most of the *fallāḥīn* remained on subsistence level. In the city, other kinds of taxes were levied, the major one being the poll-tax (*firda*). The tax units were various guilds, whose *shaykhs* were charged with individual assessment and collection. Other "intermediaries" also collected urban taxes, as in the case of the *shaykh* of the Rifāᶜiyya order, who was charged by Mehmet Ali Paşa with the collection of the *firda* from acrobats, jugglers, and snake-charmers (De Jong 1978: 37). In town, too, it is clear that taxes and various duties were a heavy burden on members of the non-elite groups. Urban taxes were gradually being reduced by Abbas and Sait. For information on taxation, see Owen 1969; Baer 1969: 20–6, 46–9, 150ff.; Nubar 1983: 82–3, 86, 133–5; Senior 1882: II, 181; Wallace 1883: 266–7, 303; MAE/Caire/29, 326, no. 157, Delaporte to the Foreign Minister, 31 July 1854; DWQ, S/1/9/21, 9 (no. 56), 1 Ca 1265/25 March 1849; ibid., L/2/67/4, 1–5 (no. 1), 8 M 1270/11 October 1853.

7 *The great social divide in Egyptian society*

1 Gadsby 1860: 205.
2 Flaubert 1972: 80.
3 Ibid., 82.
4 Gadsby 1860: 387.
5 St. John 1852: II, 121–2.
6 De Leon 1877: 50.
7 Bromfield 1856: 139, 141.
8 Sāmī 1936: II/3, 6.
9 Barakāt 1978: 188.
10 Hekekyan 37452, fos. 17–22, notes from 2 March 1851.
11 DWQ, L/2/67/2, 77–9 (no. 35), 23 Ş 1267/23 June 1851.
12 DWQ, L/2/67/4, 11–13 (no. 6), 27 Ra 1270/28 December 1853.
13 See for example DWQ, L/2/67/2, 38–41 (no. 12), 18 S 1267/23 December 1850; ibid., 79–80 (no. 36), 23 Ş 1267/23 June 1851; L/2/67/3, 14–15 (no. 9), 12 M 1268/7 November 1851; ibid., 74–6 (no. 37), 27 Ş 1268/16 June 1852.
14 Example of description as *lābis al-ᶜOthmānlī* is from DWQ, L/2/67/2, 77–9 (no. 35), 23 Ş 1267/23 June 1851. Hekekyan's comment is in Hekekyan 37452, fos. 17–22, notes of 2 March 1851. Du Camp's description is from *Le Nil, Egypte et Nubie*, as translated in Flaubert 1972: 167–8.
15 Serheng 1894: II, 264–6.
16 Senior 1882: II, 84–5.
17 Sāmī 1936: II/2, 352.
18 Ibid., III/1, 20.
19 The quotation is from St. John 1852: II, 92. Examples of accidents involving illegally held fire-arms are in DWQ, S/7/35/2, 4 (no. 265), 30 B 1265/21 June 1849; ibid., 14 (no. 303), 4 Ş 1265/25 June 1849; ibid., S/7/35/7, 42 (no. 2), 29 C 1269/9 April 1853; ibid., 56 (no. 6), 8 Ş 1269/17 May 1853.
20 DWQ, S/7/35/2, 7 (no. 278), 30 B 1265/21 June 1849.
21 DWQ, S/7/35/2, 19 (no. 325), 7 Ş 1265/28 June 1849.
22 Hekekyan 37465, fo. 31, 3 S 1267/8 December 1850.
23 One of Hekekyan's sources, a certain Mr. Gomez, told him that only less than one-third of the fire-arms were turned in as ordered by the government. Those were mostly useless and worn-out pieces, the rest being buried in case of need (Hekekyan 37452, fo. 8, notes of 23 February 1851). Even if true, this still must mean that enforcement was effective, for people had to conceal their guns and were not free to carry or use them as before. The customs house case referred to in this paragraph is in DWQ, S/7/35/7, 35 (no. 2), 29 C 1269/9 April 1853. The case of the *fallāḥ* who killed his wife is in ibid., 32 (no. 3), 29 B 1269/8 May 1853.
24 Ibid., 93 (no. 21), 25 Za 1269/30 August 1853. Other examples of attempts to enforce the prohibition are in: ibid., S/7/35/9, 1 (no. 23), 5 Ş 1270/3 May 1854; ibid., (no. 24), same date; ibid., 4 (no. 14), same date.
25 St. John 1852: I, 127–8.
26 Flaubert 1972: 38. On the use of carriages in mid-nineteenth-century Cairo, see Abu-

Lughod 1971: 94–5. See also Raymond's articles in the two collections published by the Groupe des Recherches et d'Etudes sur le Proche-Orient.

27 Flaubert 1972: 161.

28 Lane's reference to mules is in Lane 1973: 139, and his description of donkeys and donkey riding is in Lane 1973: 139–41. The quotation is from Gadsby 1860: 177. The italics are mine, for emphasis. *Shmālak*, *ū*ʿ*ā* and *iw*ʿ*ā*, *irga*ʿ (meaning "move back"), *riglak*, and *wishshek*, are better approximations of colloquial Egyptian Arabic. Compare these expressions with a fuller list in Lane 1973: 140–1, note 2.

29 DWQ, L/2/65/1, 18 (no. 156), 16 L 1266/25 August 1850; ibid., 23 and 29 (no. 196), 17 L 1266/26 August 1850; ibid., 28 and 35 (no. 313), 24 L 1266/3 September 1850; ibid., 36 (no. 202), 27 L 1266/6 September 1850.

30 Ibid., S/7/35/7, 54 (no. 17), 24 Ş 1269/2 June 1853. Examples of some other fatal accidents are in: ibid., S/7/35/2, 80 (no. 523), 14 L 1265/2 September 1849; ibid., L/2/67/3, 108–10 (no. 46), 9 Za 1268/25 August 1852; ibid., S/7/35/5, 6 (no. 12), 6 Za 1266/13 September 1850; and ibid., S/7/35/7, 45 (no. 25), 9 April 1853.

31 On spaces and transport intrusion, see the interesting works of Hani Fakhouri 1985, Nawal Nadim 1979, and Sawsan el-Messiri 1978, cited in the bibliography. On the emergence of the "two distinct physical communities," i.e. old and modern Cairo, see Abu-Lughod 1971: 98ff. For Raymond's views on space allocation in Cairo, see Raymond 1984, especially his comments on residential areas, pp. 55–90.

32 DWQ, L/2/67/3, 83–97 (no. 39), 25 N 1268/13 July 1852.

33 Ibid., 43–5 (no. 27), 16 Ca 1268/8 March 1852 (first version), and ibid., 61–73 (no. 35), 21 Ş 1268/8 August 1852 (second, enlarged version).

34 DWQ, L/2/63/1, 36–8 (no. 14), 6 Za 1269/11 August 1853.

35 DWQ, L/2/67/2, 73 (no. 30), 9 B 1267/10 May 1851.

36 Abbas's order is in DWQ, S/7/35/2, 53 (no. 449), 7 N 1265/27 July 1849. A code devised in March 1849 for one of the newly created councils included the following article (no. 9): "Members of the council are obliged to defend not only the rights of the government, but also to protect the rights of the people. They must make justice and compassion their torch in judgement" (Sāmī 1936: III/1, 18).

37 DWQ, L/2/67/4, 28–40 (no. 11), 24 C 1270/24 March 1854.

38 Stated in Arabic: *wa-innanā min jumlat ra*ʿ*āyāhu wa-min* ʿ*adālatihi innahu al-jalīl wa-l-haqīr* ʿ*alā hadd siwā* (p. 32 in the register).

39 In a mix of colloquial Egyptian and standard Arabic: *inta kamān mansūb al-*ʿ*Abbāsiyya wu-khāṭir bi-fikrak innak tkhawifnī bi-l-*ʿ*Abbāsiyya yā ammā anā akalt ru'ūs fī hadhihi al-ḥukūma inshallah ākol ra'sak ayḍan.*

40 DWQ, S/7/35/2, 21 (no. 332), 11 Ş 1265/2 July 1849.

41 On that, see Schölch n.d.: 127ff.

42 DWQ, L/2/67/4, 5–7 (no. 2), 26 M 1270/29 October 1853.

8 Rural squeeze – pressure and resistance in the countryside

1 For example, a donkey-driver told Hekekyan in 1851 that, if the levies were abolished, Abbas would "be pardoned his manifold sins – it was unjust and cruel to deprive parents of the services of an only son for whom they would willingly pay 1,000 piastres

rather than lose their aid in agricultural labours" (Hekekyan 37452, fo. 26, notes from 6 March 1851).

2 Various decisions concerning the permission to marry are in DWQ, S/1/9/20, 112 (nos. 573, 574), 16 and 17 Z 1264/13 and 14 November 1848 respectively; and Sāmī, III/1, 9 (decision of 14 Z 1264/11 November 1848).

3 DWQ, S/7/35/7, 50 and 52 (no. 11), 2 B 1269/11 April 1853.

4 Abbas's order is in Sāmī 1936: III/1, 14, *İrade* to the Minister of War, 6 M 1265/2 December 1848. Ismail's is in Sarūjī 1967: 69–70 (Ismail to the Minister of War, 1 Ş 1279/22 January 1863).

5 The accidental killing is in DWQ, S/7/35/2, 28 (no. 355), 14 Ş 1265/5 July 1849; the incident occurred in 1848. The confrontation at Sōhāg is in ibid., 3–4 (no. 264), 30 B 1265/21 June 1849.

6 DWQ, S/7/35/9, 7–8 (no. 44), 20 B 1270/18 April 1854.

7 DWQ, S/7/35/2, 6 (no. 275), 30 B 1265/21 June 1849. Both the *shaykh* and the *fallāḥ* had committed offenses in the past, which accounts for the heavy penalties imposed by the council.

8 Ibid., S/7/35/7, 59 (no. 6), 29 B 1269/8 May 1853.

9 Information in this paragraph is based on Serheng 1894: II, 274, and Sarūjī 1967: 63–5. The quotation is from Senior 1882: II, 10 (the story was told by Abdallah Bey, a British convert to Islam who had served as Director of Transport under Abbas).

10 Information in this paragraph is based on Lane 1973: 194–5; DWQ, L/2/67/3, 103–8 (no. 45), 26 L 1268/13 August 1852. For the slave trade among the Circassians during the same period, see Toledano 1982: 148–91.

11 The historical difference which existed between the British and the French approach to conscription is reflected in a report about the draft in Egypt. In his letters from Egypt, published in English translation in 1857, Barthélemy Saint-Hilaire commented on *l'impôt du sang* [the draft]:

> The blood-tax is still more legitimate and useful than the money-tax. Unless all defence of society, or rather of the community, against the enemy without, and the no less formidable internal enemy, is abandoned, an army is necessary; and the most equitable, as well as most national means of raising it is by conscription. It has taken many centuries for this terrible, but noble state necessity to assume its proper light, and for the world at large to submit to a *corvée*, so frequently fatal. But in most civilized nations the resolution necessary has been bravely taken, and the military service is accepted without much trouble, even when it does not appear to the poor conscript in the light either of honour or duty.

The English translator could not resist inserting the following note:

> These arguments in favour of a conscription will, it is presumed, find little favour with English readers. They are reproduced here, but under the strongest protest against their validity. The conscription is equally odious and pernicious on moral, economical, and political grounds. (Barthélemy Saint-Hilaire 1857: 171–2)

12 St. John 1852: II, 85–6. For more descriptions, see ibid., 81–93, 109, 141; St. John 1851: 74; Gadsby 1860: 385–8; Bromfield 1856: 150–1.

13 Ibid., 151.

14 The quotation is from Flaubert 1972: 228 (Maxime du Camp, "The Crew of the Cange"). Sait's order is in Sāmī 1936: III/1, 273 (to the governor of Asyūṭ, 16 B 1274/2 March 1858). Ismail's order is in Sarūjī 1967: 80–1.

15 Information in this paragraph is derived from Sarūjī 1967: 83–7. Examples of search for deserters can be found in DWQ, L/2/65/1, 3 (no. 42), 5 (no. 174), 6 (nos. 187 and 188), 7 (no. 100), 8 (no. 119).

16 The case of the two soldiers is in DWQ, S/7/35/1, 25–6 (no. 83), 3 C 1265/26 April 1849. Otherwise, information is based on Sarūjī 1967: 83–7.

17 DWQ, S/7/35/1, 60 (no. 197), 15 B 1265/6 June 1849.

18 Reaction of the Copts in Upper Egypt is in St. John 1852: II, 281. Mention of Copts sent to work on the railway is in FO 78/966, Green to Addington, 18 August 1853. Reference to Copts serving in mixed units is in DWQ, L/2/67/1, 33–4 (no. 17), 23 S 1266/8 January 1850. Sait's reply to the governor of Asyūṭ on 16 B 1274/2 March 1858 is in Sāmī 1936: III/1, 273.

19 Population figures and the effect of war on growth rates during Mehmet Ali's reign are from McCarthy 1976: 15–24.

20 For the *corvée* in the reign of Mehmet Ali, see Rivlin 1961a: 243–5, and Owen 1969: 21, 47–8.

21 Tucker 1985: 42.

22 On the low quality of the food supplied to *corvée* workers – and, incidentally, to soldiers – see Hekekyan 37452, fos. 27–8, notes of 6 March 1851. Hekekyan relates a conversation he had with the Italian supervisor of the viceroy's ovens. The man intimated that the size of loaves was cut down, not an unknown modern practice, and that unsaleable wheat was being mixed with barley, beans, and the chaff and bran from the officers' flour. In addition, the ovens were too small and too hot, so that the final product was barely edible. In 1853, however, Abbas instructed government bakeries to upgrade the quality of bread supplied to the soldiers (DWQ, S/7/35/8, 24 [no. 1], 8 Za 1269/13 August 1853). The rest of this paragraph is based on the following: wages on the fortification project, see DWQ, S/7/35/2, 59 (no. 462), 11 N 1265/31 July 1849; wages on the Maḥmūdiyya project, see ibid., 81 (no. 527), 15 L 1265/3 September 1849; wages of a worker in the cotton factory at Būlāq are mentioned in Gadsby, 249; police and army pay scales, to be found in ᶜAbd al-Wahhāb 1977: 155; workers who were told to load and unload boats at the government warehouse in Būlāq were paid 7 *kuruş* per *ardabb* (originally *irdabb*, a dry measure equalling 198 liters), 10 *kuruş* if the work took place in other areas near the capital (DWQ, S/7/35/2, 72 [no. 496], 27 N 1265/16 August 1849).

23 Gadsby 1860: 383 n.

24 A few examples can be found in DWQ, S/7/35/1, 32 (no. 109), 12 C 1265/5 May 1849; ibid., 55 (no. 181), 11 B 1265/2 June 1849; ibid., L/2/67/3, 83–97 (no. 39), 25 N 1268/13 July 1852; ibid., S/7/35/7, 35 (no. 4), 29 C 1269/9 April 1853.

25 The case of the two Giza districts is in DWQ, S/7/35/7, 35 (no. 4), 29 C 1269/9 April 1853. The loss of biscuits is in ibid., S/7/35/8, 9 (no. 4), 3 C 1269/14 March 1853, and 6 S 1270/8 November 1853 (*İrade*).

26 DWQ, S/7/35/2, 59 (no. 462), 11 N 1265/31 July 1849.

27 Barakāt 1978: 346.

28 Barthélemy Saint-Hilaire 1857: 171. The author concludes this passage with the following comment: "I mention only those circumstances which I witnessed; but the reader may easily imagine what must be the *corvée* for the more arduous labours connected with the village itself, or the demands of the government."

29 More research into the phenomenon is needed. It may well lead to the conclusion that urban forced labor was essentially different from rural *corvée*, and that it might require the use of a different terminology.

30 *Corvée* in factories is mentioned in Gadsby 1860: 249, 301–2, 383. *Corvée* in government storehouses is mentioned in DWQ, S/7/35/2, 72 (no. 496), 27 N 1265/16 August 1849. Information about the Cairene origin of factory workers in Būlāq is based on ibid., S/7/35/1, 45–6 (no. 154), 1 B 1265/23 May 1849. The petition of the Kharanfish workers is in ibid., 31 (no. 103), 10 C 1265/3 May 1849.

31 Information in this and the following paragraph is based on DWQ, S/7/35/1, 1–2 (no. 1), 13 R 1265/8 March 1849; ibid., S/7/35/2, 81 (no. 527), 15 L 1265/3 September 1849; ibid., S/7/35/5, 66 (no. 159), 27 M 1267/2 December 1850.

32 DWQ, S/1/9/20, 68 (no. 327), 21 Za 1264/19 October 1848.

33 *Corvée* in the province of Gharbiyya is in DWQ, S/7/35/1, 55 (no. 181), 11 B 1265/2 June 1849. *Corvée* at the government storehouses is in ibid., S/7/35/2, 72 (no. 496), 27 N 1265/16 August 1849.

34 Information in this paragraph is derived from DWQ, S/7/35/2, 20 (no. 328), 11 Ş 1265/2 July 1849; ibid., S/7/35/1, 72 (no. 234), 22 B 1265/13 June 1849.

35 Ibid., S/7/35/1, 45–6 (no. 154), 1 B 1265/23 May 1849. It is difficult to say how effective were the accounting arrangements between the government and the tax-farmers. About the same time, the government decided to pay two-thirds of the factory workers' wages in cash. The Treasury accounts of the tax-farmers of these workers' villages were to be adjusted accordingly. But on 8 July 1849, a query from the governorate of Daqahliyya asserted that the accounts had not been adjusted as expected. Nevertheless, the Council of Justice reaffirmed the details of its previous decision (DWQ, S/7/35/2, 30 [no. 367], 17 Ş 1265/8 July 1849).

36 For Abbas's order and its application, see Tucker 1985: 41.

37 Nubar 1983: 83–4.

9 *Rural migrants and urban attitudes*

1 Baer's relevant studies are in Baer 1969: 133–48, and Baer 1982: 63–78. See also Panzac 1987: 28–32. McCarthy's estimates for Cairo are in McCarthy 1976: 29–31.

2 Conclusions about migrants in the following pages are drawn from information culled out of thirty-six case files. The files contain data concerning over fifty individuals who migrated to Cairo in the 1840s and 1850s. The exact number is hard to determine because there are ambiguities with regard to a number of persons. Some of these people appear in the police and court records as offenders, some as victims of crime, some as witnesses, and some are simply mentioned in the background, as part of the life stories told by the above. This information is unique and of superior quality to that contained in any other source I have seen for this period. Since data are scattered and had to be assembled piece by piece, I chose to list the relevant files, instead of

encumbering the text with endless notes. Only in a few points, when deemed necessary, references to specific documents are provided. All files are from DWQ and are listed in chronological order. The date is that of the final report, and events mentioned in any report may have taken place days, months, and years before: S/7/35/1, 26 (no. 84), 3 C 1265/26 April 1849; ibid., 71 (no. 227), 21 B 1265/12 June 1849; L/2/67/1, 10 (no. 4), 4 Z 1265/21 October 1849; ibid., 31–2 (no. 16), 18 S 1266/3 January 1850; ibid., 38 (no. 20), 6 Ra 1266/20 January 1850; ibid., 67–71 (no. 28), 7 Ca 1266/21 March 1850; ibid., 73–5 (no. 30), 10 Ca 1266/24 March 1850; ibid., 86–92 (no. 45), 14 C 1266/27 April 1850; L/2/65/1, 13 (no. 146), 21 N 1266/31 July 1850; ibid., 19 (no. 121), 4 L 1266/13 August 1850; ibid., 16 and 21 (no. 294), and 25 (no. 240), 6 L 1266/15 August 1850; L/2/67/2, 1–13 (no. 1), 12 Za 1266/19 September 1850; ibid., 19–24 (no. 4), 14 Z 1266/21 October 1850; ibid., 34–6 (no. 10), 16 M 1267/21 November 1850; ibid., 36–8 (no. 11), 3 S 1267/8 December 1850; ibid., 49–50 (no. 15), 6 Ra 1267/9 January 1851; ibid., 50–1 (no. 16), 19 Ra 1267/22 January 1851; ibid., 60–2 (no. 21), 26 Ca 1267/29 March 1851; ibid., 62–4 (no. 22), 28 Ca 1267/31 March 1851; ibid., 64–6 (no. 24), 7 C 1267/9 April 1851; ibid., 66–7 (no. 25), 10 C 1267/12 April 1851; ibid., 76 (no. 33), 24 B 1267/25 May 1851; ibid., 80–2 (no. 38), 29 Ş 1267/29 June 1851; ibid., 82–4 (no. 39), 6 N 1267/5 July 1851; ibid., 96–101 (no. 46), 7 Za 1267/3 September 1851; L/2/67/3, 12 (no. 5), 4 Z 1267/30 September 1851; ibid., 28–9 (no. 17), 11 Ra 1268/4 January 1852; ibid., 29–30 (no. 18), 11 Ra 1268/4 January 1852; ibid., 45–8 (no. 28), 17 Ca 1268/10 March 1852; ibid., 97–9 (no. 40), 27 N 1268/15 July 1852; L/2/63, 19–20 (no. 10), 7 R 1268/18 January 1853; ibid., 25–34 (no. 12), 28 B 1269/7 May 1853; ibid., 35–6 (no. 13), 10 Ş 1269/19 May 1853; ibid., 38–41 (no. 15), 19 Za 1269/24 August 1853; L/2/67/4, 28–40 (no. 11), 24 C 1270/24 March 1854; ibid., 57–8 (no. 15), 23 N 1270/19 June 1854.

3 DWQ, L/2/67/2, 96–101 (no. 46), 7 Za 1267/3 September 1851.

4 The story of Sayyid Yūsuf is in DWQ, L/2/67/3, 12 (no. 5), 4 Z 1267/30 September 1851. Mehmet Ali's repatriation drive is in FO 78/623, Barnett to Canning, 16 March 1845.

5 An interesting account of relations between ex-soldiers who moved to Cairo can be found in DWQ, L/2/67/3, 103–8 (no. 45), 26 L 1268/13 August 1852.

6 Examples of deportation are in DWQ, L/2/65/1, 16 and 21 (no. 294), 6 L 1266/15 August 1850 (duplicated on 25 [no. 240]); ibid., 19 (no. 121), 4 L 1266/13 August 1850; ibid., S/7/35/7, 36 (no. 7), 29 C 1269/9 April 1853. In the first and last cases, the persons returned to Cairo from their villages in the Delta after the deportation.

7 The case of the unrecognized visitor, who indeed was from the same village but ended up stealing from his benefactor, is in DWQ, L/2/67/2, 82–4 (no. 39), 6 N 1267/5 July 1851. The blood-feud is in ibid., L/2/63, 35–6 (no. 13), 10 Ş 1269/19 May 1853.

8 St. John 1852: I, 128–30. With regard to the attitude reflected in this passage, Gadsby accurately observed that "the people have an idea that a man who is afraid to show a light can be after no good, and they therefore secure him" (Gadsby 1860: 191). On lighting regulations and the closure of neighborhoods during the reign of Mehmet Ali Paşa, see Lane 1973: 4, 119–20, 151–2, and Legh 1816: 25ff. For a curious incident related to lighting regulations in the time of Abbas Paşa, see above, p. 75.

9 Flaubert 1972: 77. The bracketed explanation appears in the English translation used throughout this work, and the correct term should be *mashrabiyyas*.

10 Observations in this and the following paragraph are based on extensive reading of the Egyptian archives register series mentioned in the bibliography. Some specific examples for reference can be found in: DWQ, L/2/67/1, 3–10 (no. 3), 27 Za 1265/14 October 1849; ibid., 86–92 (no. 45), 14 C 1266/27 April 1850; ibid., L/2/67/2, 1–13 (no. 1), 12 Za 1266/19 September 1850; ibid., L/2/67/3, 26–8 (no. 15), 18 S 1268/13 December 1851; ibid., 28 (no. 16), same date; ibid., 33–8 (no. 22), 17 R 1268/9 February 1852; ibid., 58 (no. 32), 26 B 1268/16 May 1852; ibid., L/2/67/4, 7–8 (no. 3), 6 S 1270/8 November 1853; ibid., 41–4 (no. 12), 17 Ş 1270/15 May 1854. The quote is from St. John 1852: II, 118. A number of recent studies, based on social anthropology, have dealt with neighborhood structure and culture in present-day Cairo. Many of the observations made in these studies are borne out by the historical record of mid-century Cairo. They all stress the private nature of *ḥāra* space, which served as an extension of the dwelling units (see, for example, works by Nawal Nadim, Sawsan el-Messiri, Hani Fakhouri, and Janet Abu-Lughod, cited in the bibliography). Fakhouri describes the struggle for space between residents and encroaching outsiders (pedestrians, cars, etc.) brought in by modernity (Fakhouri 1985: 121–3).

11 One can read, for example, the following statement, uttered by a man who wished to stress that he had no association whatsoever with another man: "I neither mix, nor walk or sit with him, and I do not go about the markets and neighborhoods with him" (*lā lī khulṭa maʿahu wa-lā mashy wa-lā julūs wa-lā amshī maʿahu fī l-aswāq wa-lā fī l-ḥārāt*). This example is taken from DWQ, L/2/67/2, 77–9 (no. 35), 23 Ş 1267/23 June 1851.

12 Observations in this and the following paragraph are based on extensive reading of the Egyptian archives register series mentioned in the bibliography. Some specific examples for reference can be found in DWQ, L/2/67/2, 60–2 (no. 21), 26 Ca 1267/29 March 1851; ibid., 82–4 (no. 39), 6 N 1267/5 July 1852; ibid., L/2/67/3, 73–4 (no. 36), 25 Ş 1268/14 June 1852; ibid., 100 (no. 42), 17 L 1268/4 August 1852.

13 Observations in this and the following paragraph are based on extensive reading of the Egyptian archives register series mentioned in the bibliography. Some specific examples for reference can be found in DWQ, L/2/67/1, 94–5 (no. 38), 9 B 1266/21 May 1850; ibid., L/2/67/3, 7–10 (no. 3), 29 Za 1267/25 September 1851; ibid., 31–3 (no. 21), 13 R 1268/5 February 1852; ibid., L/2/67/4, 7–8 (no. 3), 6 S 1270/8 November 1853.

14 Some examples of the requirement of a *ḍāmin* can be found in DWQ, L/2/65/1, 30 (no. 159), 20 L 1266/29 August 1850; ibid., L/2/67/2, 69–72 (no. 28), 27 C 1267/29 April 1851; ibid., L/2/67/3, 100 (no. 42), 17 L 1268/4 August 1852. The petition of the workers sent to Suez is in DWQ, S/7/35/1, 78–9 (no. 247), 27 B 1265/18 June 1849. Accepting their demand, the Council of Justice stated that the cost of living in Suez was higher, though the workers' petition was based on the above-mentioned argument *and* a comparison with workers at the Nile Barrages project, who were in a similar situation.

15 DWQ, L/2/67/3, 99–100 (no. 41), 5 L 1268/23 July 1852. The text in Arabic reads:

idhā kāna aḥad naẓar lam yaḥḍur wa-yashhad maᶜanā bi-sabab innanā aghrāb fī tilka al-maḥall. The irregularities are in the original.

10 The urban squeeze

1 On slavery in nineteenth-century Egypt, see Baer 1969: 161–89. Baer estimated the number of slaves in Egypt during the 1850s at between 20,000 and 30,000, a little less than half of them in Cairo itself (ibid., 168). On the Ottoman slave trade in the nineteenth century, see Toledano 1982: 14–90.

2 For reasons that are explained elsewhere in this part (see pp. 225–6 below), the use of the term "guilds" to describe Ottoman occupational associations is problematic. Still, to avoid confusion and awkward substitutes, I retain it hereafter, nonetheless, bearing in mind that Ottoman "guilds" differed in a meaningful way from European guilds.

3 DWQ, L/2/67/2, 42–5 (no. 13), 28 S 1267/2 January 1851.

4 The story of Muḥammad Muṣṭafā is in DWQ, L/2/67/2, 38–41 (no. 12), 18 S 1267/23 December 1850. That of Ibrāhīm al-Barbarī is in ibid., L/2/67/3, 100 (no. 42), 17 L 1268/4 August 1852.

5 The groom's case is in DWQ, L/2/67/2, 75 (no. 32), 17 B 1267/18 May 1851. The female servant's case is in ibid., 73–5 (no. 31), 10 B 1267/11 May 1851.

6 There had been accusations that some of the women agents were running their offices as a cover for prostitution. The government was aware of this and issued strict instructions to prevent such practices. On that, see DWQ, L/2/65/1, 30 (no. 159), 20 L 1266/29 August 1850. See also below, p. 238.

7 DWQ, L/2/67/2, 30–2 (no. 8), 29 Z 1266/5 November 1850.

8 DWQ, L/2/67/3, 103–8 (no. 45), 26 L 1268/13 August 1852.

9 The Arabic of the two quotations is, as usual in these texts, a mixture of colloquial Egyptian and literary Arabic. It reads as follows (in order of appearance):
(1) *wa-kadhalika min al-'ān wa-ṣāᶜid lam tuḥḍir nafar qahwajī min ghayr iṭṭilāᶜ ash-shaykh wa-'akhdh aḍ-ḍamān ᶜalayhi ḥukma 'l-uṣūl*
(2) *idhā kāna yaḥṣul minhu shay' fa-yakūn ḍāminuhu huwa 'l-ladhī malzūm bi-mā yaḥṣul minhu*

10 Unemployed persons were also occasionally described by terms other than *baṭṭāl*, e.g. *dā'ir bi-lā khidma*, which means "roaming without work." On economic conditions in the 1840s and 1850s and their effects on industry and the handicrafts, see Owen 1969: 58–88, Owen 1981: 74–6, and al-Giritlī 1952: 169–87. For some examples of unemployment and its social effects, see DWQ, L/2/67/2, 32–4 (no. 9), 29 Z 1266/5 November 1850; ibid., 51–3 (no. 17), 27 Ra 1267/30 January 1851; ibid., 95–6 (no. 45), 3 Za 1267/30 August 1851; ibid., 96–101 (no. 46), 7 Za 1267/3 September 1851; ibid., L/2/67/3, 7–10 (no. 3), 29 Z 1267/25 September 1851; ibid., L/2/67/4, 18–28 (no. 10), 14 S 1270/16 November 1853.

11 Information in this and the following paragraph is based on the following sources: DWQ, S/1/9/20, no. 108, 15 Z 1264/12 November 1848; ibid., S/7/35/1, 73–4 (no. 238), 23 B 1265/14 June 1849; ibid., 38–9 (no. 132), 21 C 1265/14 May 1849; ibid., 78–9 (nos. 247 and 248), 27 B 1265/18 June 1849; ibid., S/7/35/2, 17 (no. 314),

5 Ş 1265/26 June 1849; ibid., 72 (no. 496), 27 N 1265/16 August 1849; ibid., 81 (no. 527), 15 L 1265/3 September 1849; ibid., S/7/35/8, 24 (no. 1), 8 Za 1269/13 August 1853; ibid., L/2/67/1, 83–5 (no. 33), 1 C 1266/14 April 1850; ibid., L/2/67/3, 103–8 (no. 45), 26 L 1268/13 August 1852; ibid., L/2/67/4, 1–5 (no. 1), 8 M 1270/11 October 1853; Hekekyan 37452, fos. 26 and 27 (notes dated 6 March 1851), 31 (notes dated 10 March 1851), 32 (notes dated 11 March 1851), 83 (notes dated 16 June 1851); *The Times*, 4 May 1850 (5d); Lane 1973: 312, 574; Wilkinson 1858: 115; and Bromfield 1856: 62.

12 Information in this paragraph is based on DWQ, S/1/9/20, no. 108, 15 Z 1264/12 November 1848.

13 Information in this paragraph is based on DWQ, S/7/35/1, 38–9 (no. 132), 21 C 1265/14 May 1849.

14 DWQ, S/7/35/1, 79 (no. 248), 27 B 1265/18 June 1849.

15 Information in this paragraph is derived from DWQ, S/7/35/1, 40 (no. 138), 22 C 1265/15 May 1849, and ibid., 78–9 (no. 247), 27 B 1265/18 June 1849. Incidentally, the wages cited for these skilled workers were quite high: 4 *kuruş* plus clothing, which was raised after the petition to 4.5 *kuruş* per day. The petition of the fifty-one navy men in Suez indicates that petitions could be presented also by soldiers. See also the case of 172 men and foremen employed at the navy's date-stone-crushing mill, in ibid., 68 (no. 220), 20 B 1265/11 June 1849.

16 Petition of the caravan bedouins is in DWQ, S/7/35/1, 73–4 (no. 238), 23 B 1265/14 June 1849. Petition of the bedouin telegraph guards is in ibid., S/7/35/2, 17 (no. 314), 5 Ş 1265/26 June 1849.

17 DWQ, S/7/35/8, 24 (no. 1), 8 Za 1269/13 August 1853.

18 "Going prices" (Turkish *cari esâr*) was the term most frequently used by the government in wage adjustment cases, e.g. DWQ, S/1/9/20, 16 and 184, 1 M 1265/27 November 1848.

19 Bromfield 1856: 199–200. The want of change seems to have been a perennial problem in modern Egypt. It might have resulted from an inadequate minting policy, from hoarding, or possibly from noth. One still tackles the problem in Egypt even today.

20 Information in this paragraph is based on DWQ, L/2/67/1, 12–13 (no. 6), 14 Z 1265/31 October 1849; ibid., L/2/67/2, 13–15 (no. 2), 14 Z 1266/21 October 1850; ibid., 32–4 (no. 9), 29 Z 1266/5 November 1850; ibid., 45–8 (no. 14), 29 S 1267/3 January 1851; ibid., 59 (no. 19), 12 R 1267/14 February 1851; ibid., L/2/67/3, 12 (no. 5), 4 Z 1267/30 September 1851; ibid., 58–9 (no. 33), 10 Ş 1268/30 May 1852; ibid., L/2/67/4, 11–13 (no. 6), 27 Ra 1270/28 December 1853; ibid., S/7/35/7, 36 (no. 7), 29 C 1269/9 April 1853.

21 Gadsby observed that Egyptians divide their property into three parts: money, which they bury; jewels, which they carry; and merchandise, which they trade. When in need, he wrote, "they will sell anything and everything sooner than their jewels, as they can carry them about their persons" (Gadsby 1860: 180). Information in this paragraph is based on DWQ, L/2/67/1, 18–19 (no. 11), 11 M 1266/27 November 1849; ibid., L/2/67/2, 38–41 (no. 12), 18 S 1267/23 December 1850; ibid., 64 (no. 23), 3 C 1267/5 April 1851; ibid., 76–7 (no. 34), 17 Ş 1267/17 June 1851; ibid., 80 (no. 37), 28 Ş 1267/28 June 1851; ibid., L/2/67/3, 26–8 (no. 15), 18 S 1268/13 December 1851;

ibid., L/2/67/4, 8–9 (no. 4), 13 S 1270/15 November 1853. The term *kapısız*, homeless, could also mean unemployed.

22 Information in this paragraph is drawn from DWQ, S/7/35/1, 71–2 (no. 230), 21 B 1265/12 June 1849; ibid., L/2/67/1, 22 (no. 13), 14 M 1266/30 November 1849; ibid., 92–3 (no. 36), 16 C 1266/29 April 1850; ibid., L/2/67/2, 68–9 (no. 26), 14 C 1267/16 April 1851; ibid., L/2/63, 18–19 (no. 9), 4 Ra 1269/16 December 1852.

23 The paving contract is in DWQ, S/7/35/1, 19–20 (no. 61), 23 Ca 1265/16 April 1849. In 1850, the government decided to furnish soldiers with mattresses to help them overcome the tiled floors at the barracks, which were too cold in winter (Sāmī 1936: III/1, 29, order dated 29 S 1266/14 January 1850).

24 Information in this paragraph is based on DWQ, L/2/67/1, 79–83 (no. 32), 28 Ca 1266/11 April 1850; ibid., L/2/67/2, 49–50 (no. 15), 6 Ra 1267/9 January 1851; ibid., 89–93 (no. 43), 11 L 1267/9 August 1851; ibid., 95–6 (no. 45), 3 Za 1267/30 August 1851; ibid., L/2/63, 38–41 (no. 15), 19 Za 1269/24 August 1853.

25 DWQ, L/2/67/3, 103–8 (no. 45), 26 L 1268/13 August 1852.

26 The mosque servant who helped his son is mentioned in DWQ, L/2/67/3, 59–61 (no. 34), 12 Ş 1268/1 June 1852. The woman who could not be hired is mentioned in ibid., L/2/67/2, 73–5 (no. 31), 10 B 1267/11 May 1851. Other information in this paragraph is derived from ibid., S/7/35/1, 51 (no. 172), 6 B 1265/28 May 1849; ibid., L/2/67/1, 34–7 (no. 18), 29 S 1266/14 January 1850; ibid., 85–6 (no. 34), 4 C 1266/17 April 1850; ibid., L/2/67/2, 15–19 (no. 3), 14 Z 1266/21 October 1850.

27 St. John 1852: I, xvii.

11 The network of urban control

1 De Jong 1978: 40–95.

2 For various definitions of the terms discussed in this and the following paragraph, see Abu-Lughod 1971: 84; Messiri 1978: 26–7; Berque 1972: 94; Baer 1969: 217–18; Nadim 1979; and Fakhouri 1985. For an example of the interchangeability of *shaykh* and *ᶜumda*, see DWQ, L/2/65/1, 30 (no. 159), 20 L 1266/29 August 1850.

3 To avoid the ambiguity that pervades the literature, I shall hereafter render *thumn* as quarter, *ḥāra* as neighborhood. This obviously reflects my feeling that, at mid-century, *ḥāra*s were smaller units, though they should not be confused with the other meaning of *ḥāra* – an alley. There were, of course, small and large *ḥāra*s, but a "neighborhood" was still, at the time, a manageable unit. Lane writes that "quarters (*ḥāras*) mostly consist of several narrow lanes (*ᶜatfas*), having but one general entrance, with a gate, which is also closed at night; but several have a by-street (*darb*) pasing through them" (1973: 4; I have inserted the Arabic terms in parenthesis according to Lane's own note 3 on the same page). Baer translates *shiyākha* as "subquarter," which would suggest that these were somewhat large neighborhoods in my usage. To form a general idea of the size of such units, we may note that in 1897, there were 195 *shiyākha*s in Cairo, 108 in Alexandria (Baer 1969: 218).

4 For examples of functions of quarter *shaykh*s described in this and the next paragraph, see DWQ, L/2/67/1, 86–92 (no. 45), 14 C 1266/27 April 1850; ibid., L/2/67/2, 1–13

(no. 1), 12 Za 1266/19 September 1850; ibid., 53–9 (no. 18), 7 R 1267/9 February 1851; ibid., 66–7 (no. 25), 10 C 1267/12 April 1851; ibid., L/2/67/3, 25–6 (no. 13), 11 S 1268/6 December 1851; ibid., 48–54 (no. 29), 17 C 1268/8 April 1852; ibid., L/2/63, 20–4 (no. 11), 15 R 1269/26 January 1853; ibid., 25–34 (no. 12), 28 B 1269/7 May 1853.

5 DWQ, L/2/65/1, 14 (no. 104), 13 L 1266/22 August 1850.

6 Examples of the evidence which forms the basis for the evaluation of the role of neighborhood *shaykhs*, offered in this and the following paragraphs, can be found in DWQ, L/2/67/2, 34–6 (no. 10), 16 M 1267/21 November 1850; ibid., 87–9 (no. 42), 7 L 1267/5 August 1851; ibid., L/2/67/3, 14–16 (no. 9), 12 M 1268/7 November 1851; ibid., 59–61 (no. 34), 12 Ş 1268/1 June 1852; ibid., 110 (no. 47), 14 Za 1268/30 August 1852; ibid., L/2/63, 1 (no. 1), 26 Z 1268/11 October 1852; ibid., 1–4 (no. 2), 7 Z 1268/22 September 1852; ibid., 18–19 (no. 9), 4 Ra 1269/16 December 1852.

7 DWQ, L/2/67/1, 19–22 (no. 12), 11 M 1266/27 November 1849. The neighborhood is Qā'itbāy.

8 This was specifically so in one recorded case (DWQ, L/2/67/4, 5–7 [no. 2], 26 M 1270/29 October 1853). One case is obviously not enough to support any general statement, but may still serve as "food for thought." Incidentally, it is also in this case that we clearly see how the lieutenant-turned-*shaykh* was fully identified with the government (see pp. 179–80 above).

9 André Raymond's work on eighteenth-century Cairene guilds is invaluable as background to the nineteenth century (Raymond 1973: II, q.v.). The most comprehensive studies of Egyptian guilds in the nineteenth century are Baer 1964 and Baer 1969: 149–60. (The study of 1969 includes substantial additions.) For a brief review of the controversial points debated among scholars over time, see: Baer 1982: 213–22 ("Ottoman Guilds – A Reassessment"), and the works mentioned therein; and Akarlı 1987.

10 Engin Akarlı takes issue with Baer's usage of the term "guild" for the Istanbul *esnaf*. He disagrees with their portrayal by Baer as highly structured and monopolistic organizations and argues that artisan groups became gradually better structured only from the eighteenth century. This development peaked in the reign of Mahmut II (1808–39) [Akarlı 1987: n. 16].

11 Examples of terms mentioned in this paragraph can be found in DWQ, L/2/67/1, 67–71 (no. 27), 7 Ca 1266/21 March 1850; ibid., L/2/65/1, 30 (no. 159), 20 L 1266/29 August 1850; ibid., L/2/67/2, 42–5 (no. 13), 28 S 1267/2 January 1851; ibid., L/2/67/3, 29–30 (no. 18), 11 Ra 1268/4 January 1852; ibid., 83–97 (no. 39), 25 N 1268/13 July 1852; ibid., L/2/63, 36–8 (no. 14), 6 Za 1269/11 August 1853; ibid., L/2/67/4, 28–40 (no. 11), 24 C 1270/24 March 1854; ibid., 44–54 (no. 13), 4 L 1270/30 June 1854.

12 Information about guilds in this and the following paragraph is based on Baer 1964: 16–48, 127–53, and Baer 1969: 149–56. Evaluation of Mehmet Ali's industrial experiment with its impact on handicraft production is based on Owen 1981: 75–6. Raymond (1973: II, 506–7) divides Cairene guilds into four categories: artisanal (over 38 percent), commercial (over 33 percent), service (over 20 percent), and entertainment (over 5 percent).

13 Quotation is from Baer 1969: 153, while other information in this paragraph is from ibid., 150–1. For Akarlı's view on guild monopoly, see Akarlı 1987: n. 16.
14 Information in this paragraph is based on DWQ, L/2/67/1, 72 (no. 29), 9 Ca 1266/ 23 March 1850; ibid., L/2/67/2, 68–9 (no. 26), 14 C 1267/16 April 1851; ibid., 75 (no. 32), 17 B 1267/18 May 1851; ibid., 95–6 (no. 45), 3 Za 1267/30 August 1851; ibid., L/2/67/3, 74–6 (no. 37), 27 Ş 1268/16 June 1852; ibid., 100 (no. 42), 17 L 1268/ 4 August 1852; ibid., L/2/63, 19–20 (no. 10), 18 January 1853.
15 DWQ, S/7/35/2, 19 (no. 325), 7 Ş 1265/28 June 1849.
16 The door-keeper's case is in DWQ, L/2/67/3, 26–8 (no. 15), 10 S 1268/13 December 185. Incidentally, the man claimed that he had received from the guests verbal statements of guarantee. An example of a *shaykh*'s guarantee (Turkish *kefalet*, Arabic *kafāla*) is in ibid., S/7/35/1, 68 (no. 219), 20 B 1265/11 June 1849.
17 DWQ, L/2/67/3, 83–97 (no. 39), 25 N 1268/13 July 1852.
18 This was quite different from the situation of the Istanbul *esnaf*, as is pointed out by Engin Akarlı, the sultan granted *nizam*s which lay down the ground rules of conduct. Akarlı takes a view similar to that expounded in the previous paragraph regarding the relation between the protection that a guild offered and the limitation it imposed on its members. For the code of the dealers in white slaves, see Toledano 1981: 60–2.
19 Price setting in the dried fruit business is in DWQ, L/2/67/3, 61–73 (no. 35), 21 Ş 1268/8 August 1852. Negotiation of the meat supply contract to the government and the city is in ibid., S/7/35/8, 70 and 102 (no. 10), 4 R 1270/4 January 1854. Examples of expert opinion rendered by guild *shaykh*s are in ibid., L/2/67/1, 15–16 (no. 9), 7 M 1266/23 November 1849; ibid., L/2/65/1, 23 (no. 194), 12 L 1266/ 21 August 1850.
20 See for example DWQ, L/2/67/1, 96–8 (no. 40), 25 B 1266/6 June 1850; ibid., L/2/67/2, 53–9 (no. 18), 7 R 1267/9 February 1851.
21 Eric Gans 1985: 301.
22 Note again the low incidence of rural and urban revolt during the middle years in Baer 1969: 95–103, and Schulze 1981: 79–94.

12 The use of unappropriated time

1 For games played in rural and urban Egypt, see Lane 1973: 344–52. For simulations of regional rivalries, see Berque 1972: 127–30.
2 Gadsby 1860: 235.
3 In early 1849, the government supplied a European acrobat named Romanini with a band, a tent, wood, and soldiers to facilitate his performance. The man then went to Syria, leaving behind unpaid debts (DWQ, S/7/35/1, 38 [no. 130], 19 C 1265/12 May 1849). Lane's account of the various types of performances is in Lane 1973: 383–90.
4 Cf. Gadsby 1860: 141–4. Gadsby studied with much attention the performance of a well-known magician in mid-century Cairo. He followed Lane's observations, checked them, and pronounced his own judgment on the matter.
5 See also Flaubert 1972: 37–9.
6 Lane's detailed descriptions of the festivals during the reign of Mehmet Ali are in Lane

1973: 425–99. Most of what he relates seems to have continued into the middle years of the century, as many accounts confirm, e.g. St. John 1852: I, 139ff., and Wilkinson 1858: 138–41. For *ṣūfī* celebrations and processions, see De Jong 1978: 54–69, and Berque 1972: 69–71.

7 Bromfield 1856: 220.

8 Flaubert 1972: 89. Flaubert himself wrote about the ceremony: "It was great fun – the men who engage in such sinful enterprises practice their vile arts, as M. de Voltaire puts it, with singular competency" (ibid., 86). Bromfield relates of a similar ceremony which he himself had experienced (Bromfield 1856: 221). Nubar mentions a somewhat different ceremony which one of his friends, a certain Latif Efendi, underwent in Baghdad when nine years old. However, unlike the Egyptian initiations, that one was not supposed to apply to spiders and scorpions (Nubar 1983: 75).

9 Bromfield 1856: 117–18.

10 On the occult among elite members, see Nubar 1983: 74–6. On the adaptation of Islam to the rural belief-system, see Berque 1972: 65–9.

11 Yusuf Kâmil's comment is in Kâmil 1911–12: 231. Nubar's story is in Nubar 1983: 75. On Ottoman astrologers and the Court Astrologer, see Pakalîn 1946–56: II, 616–20 ("Müneccim" and "Müneccim Başî").

12 Information in this paragraph is drawn mainly from Nubar 1983: 74–7. It remains to be investigated whether or not the California "gold rush," which occurred during the reign of Abbas, was known in Egypt and had any relevance to the Egyptian phenomenon of the same time.

13 For the above, see Senior 1882: I, 113–14.

14 Nubar 1983: 76–7.

15 Ibid., 74.

16 Lane's text is in Lane 1973: 388–90. For storytelling, see St. John 1852: II, 198ff. Textual analysis of stories and farce plays is well beyond the scope of the present work. For an idea of what can be done with such material in cultural history, see Taylor and Rebel 1981.

17 For terminology and description of these trades in the reign of Mehmet Ali, see Lane 1973: 355–6, 377–82.

18 For the dancing-girls' "academy," see St. John 1852: I, 22–31. Flaubert's preoccupation with the sensualities of Egypt is amply documented in his Travel Notes, e.g. Flaubert 1972: 67–9, 83–7, 110–22. The quotation is from ibid., 40; another example can be found in ibid., 68.

19 Mention of deportation of five women to Esna is in DWQ, L/2/67/2, 62–4 (no. 22), 28 Ca 1267/31 March 1851. Cheap prostitution along the Aqueduct, catering for soldiers and men of the lower strata, is mentioned in Flaubert 1972: 76. Banuma Hekekyan's criticism is in Hekekyan 37452, fo. 14, notes of 28 February 1851. Case of expensive prostitution is in DWQ, L/2/67/3, 76–83 (no. 38), 23 N 1268/11 July 1852.

20 DWQ, L/2/65/1, 30 (no. 159), 20 L 1266/29 August 1850.

21 Tucker 1985: 134, 150–5.

22 Flaubert 1972: 83–4. A detailed description of the dancers' clothes and the songs which accompanied them is in ibid., 69–70. For the debate about Flaubert's own

erotic preference, see his editor/translator's note (ibid., 204) and the reference made therein to views expressed by Sartre and others on the matter.

23 DWQ, L/2/67/4, 18–28 (no. 10), 14 S 1270/16 November 1853.

24 A bath in a simple *ḥammām* could cost as little as five *para*, or one-eighth of a *kuruş* (DWQ, L/2/67/4, 17–18 [no. 9], 11 Ca 1270/9 February 1854). An employed person could afford that amount – about 15 to 20 percent of daily city subsistence – without much difficulty. There were, of course, more expensive baths, and extra services that one might purchase for a fee. Lane's estimate of the number of baths in Cairo is in Lane 1973: 336. His meticulous and detailed description of the *ḥammām* is still the best available (ibid., 336–43). References to public baths are scattered in a variety of archival documents. Ready examples for information mentioned in this and the following paragraph can be found in DWQ, L/2/67/1, 75–9 (no. 31), 19 Ca 1266/2 April 1850; ibid., L/2/67/2, 1–13 (no. 1), 12 Za 1266/19 September 1850; ibid., 15–18 (no. 3), 14 Z 1266/21 October 1850; ibid., 38–41 (no. 12), 18 S 1267/23 December 1850; ibid., 50–1 (no. 16), 19 Ra 1267/22 January 1851; ibid., 64 (no. 23), 3 C 1267/5 April 1851; ibid., 69–72 (no. 28), 27 C 1267/29 April 1851; ibid., 87–9 (no. 42), 7 L 1267/5 August 1851; ibid., L/2/67/3, 1–7 (no. 1), 22 Za 1267/18 September 1851; ibid., 13 (no. 8), 8 M 1268/3 November 1851; ibid., 40–2 (no. 24), 9 Ca 1268/2 March 1852; ibid., L/2/67/4, 7–8 (no. 3), 6 S 1270/8 November 1853; ibid., 17–18 (no. 9), 11 Ca 1270/9 February 1854.

25 Tucker 1985: 108–9. See also Hattox 1985: 124, 160 n. 20.

26 Wilkinson 1858: 134.

27 Gadsby 1860: 192.

28 Flaubert 1972: 84–5.

29 Lane 1973: 333. His account of "the use of tobacco, coffee, hemp, opium, etc." is in ibid., 331–5. On the introduction of coffee in the sixteenth century and the social importance of coffeehouses, see Hattox 1985.

30 Observations in this and the following paragraph are based on extensive reading of material contained in the Egyptian archives series mentioned in the bibliography. Some examples for reference can be found in: DWQ, L/2/67/1, 67–71 (no. 28), 7 Ca 1266/21 March 1850; ibid., 75–9 (no. 31), 19 Ca 1266/2 April 1850; ibid., L/2/67/2, 15–19 (no. 3), 14 Z 1266/21 October 1850; ibid., 30–2 (no. 8), 29 Z 1266/5 November 1850; ibid., 53–9 (no. 18), 7 R 1267/9 February 1851; ibid., L/2/67/3, 15–23 (no. 10), 18 M 1268/13 November 1851; ibid., 102–3 (no. 44), 26 L 1268/13 August 1852; ibid., L/2/63, 25–34 (no. 12), 28 B 1269/7 May 1853; ibid., L/2/67/4, 58–60 (no. 16), 3 Z 1270/27 August 1854. See also Lane 1973: 344–52 (on games and gambling); Flaubert 1972: 95; Fakhouri 1985: 122; and Toledano 1984a: 157ff.

31 For Lane's observations, see Lane 1973: 149–50. The quotation is from Gadsby 1860: 356. St. John's gesture is in St. John 1852: II, 72.

32 See, for example, Lane 1973: 149–50.

33 A few examples of terms and usages mentioned in this and the following paragraph can be found in DWQ, L/2/67/1, 23–31 (no. 15), 12 S 1266/28 December 1849; ibid., 83–5 (no. 33), 1 C 1266/14 April 1850; ibid., L/2/67/2, 27–30 (no. 7), 23 Z 1266/30 October 1850; ibid., L/2/67/3, 59–61 (no. 34), 12 Ş 1268/1 June 1852.

34 Location of the bar in Muskī is in DWQ, L/2/67/1, 18–19 (no. 11), 11 M 1266/

27 November 1849. The wine production contract is in ibid., S/7/35/5, 54 (no. 122), 7 M 1267/12 November 1850.

35 The farming out of wine and spirit production was common also in the reign of Mehmet Ali (FO 78/433, 52, translation of a report from Cairo, dated 19 March 1841). Involvement of Ismail Paşa and the royal households in the production of spirits is described in DWQ, S/7/35/7, 29 (no. 7), 17 C 1269/28 March 1853.

36 DWQ, S/7/35/7, 84 (no. 16), 29 B 1269/8 April 1853.

37 DWQ, S/7/35/7, 84 (no. 15), 29 B 1269/8 April 1853.

38 A few examples of terms and usages mentioned in this and the following paragraph can be found in DWQ, L/2/67/1, 19–22 (no. 12), 11 M 1266/27 November 1849; ibid., L/2/67/2, 77–9 (no. 35), 23 Ş 1267/23 June 1851; ibid., L/2/67/3, 48–54 (no. 29), 17 C 1268/8 April 1852; ibid., 54–5 (no. 30), 1 B 1268/21 April 1852; ibid., 55–8 (no. 31), 18 B 1268/8 May 1852; ibid., L/2/63, 6–10 (no. 5), 2 M 1269/16 October 1852; ibid., L/2/67/4, 5–7 (no. 2), 26 M 1270/29 October 1853; ibid., 18–28 (no. 10), 14 S 1270/16 November 1853.

39 A few examples of drunk policemen can be found in DWQ, L/2/67/4, 14–16 (no. 7), 19 R 1270/19 January 1854; ibid., 58–60 (no. 16), 3 Za 1270/27 August 1854. The case of the merry officers is in ibid., S/7/35/7, 8 (no. 9), 8 Z 1268/23 September 1852.

40 For drinking among entertainers and prostitutes, see Lane 1973: 354, 379 (quoted in this paragraph); Flaubert 1972: 116; and DWQ, L/2/67/3, 110–12 (no. 48), 23 Za 1268/8 September 1852.

Epilogue

1 Berreman 1981: 13, following Herbert Gans and Michael Lewis.

2 Sayyid ᶜUways 1978: 377. This study examined the notes of request and complaint sent to the tomb of the Imām ash-Shāfiᶜī.

3 President Sādāt used to boast about his rural origins by often saying in public "I am a *fallāḥ*." At least half the members of the Egyptian parliament (*Majlis ash-Shaᶜb*) are required to be *fallāḥīn* and *ᶜummāl* (workers).

4 Quotations are from Geertz 1973: 20, 29, and Darnton 1985: 11–15.

Bibliography

Archival sources

*Egyptian National Archives, Cairo (*Dār al-Wathā'iq al-Qawmiyya, *abbreviated as DWQ), Cairo*

Police records (*Ḍabṭiyyat Miṣr*): these registers are marked L (Arabic *lām*)/2, which designates the second division of the Local Administration series (*Wathā'iq al-Idāra al-Maḥalliyya*)

Council of Justice records (*Majlis al-Aḥkām*): these registers are marked S (Arabic *sīn*)/7, which designates the seventh division of the Political series (*al-Wathā'iq as-Siyāsiyya*)

Cabinet records (*Maʿiyya Saniyya*): these registers are marked S/1, which designates the ninth division of the Political series

Cabinet records (*ad-Dīwān al-Khidīwī*): these registers are marked S/2, which designates the second division of the Political series

Cairo Province records (*Muḥāfazat Miṣr*): these registers are marked L/1, which designates the first division of the Local Administration series

Most of these registers are in Ottoman Turkish, the rest are in Arabic, or in a mixture of Ottoman Turkish, Arabic, and colloquial Egyptian. The full list of records can be found in the mimeographed catalogue at the Archives under Wizārat ath-Thaqāfa/Dār al-Wathā'iq al-Qawmiyya, *Qawā'im bi-Niẓām Tartīb Sijillāt ad-Dār*, Nuskha Tajrībiyya, February 1970.

Public Record Office, London

FO/78: consular reports from Egypt to London and Foreign Office instructions to British representatives in Egypt

FO/195: consular reports from Egypt to the British Embassy in Istanbul and instructions from the Embassy to British representatives in Egypt

Ministère des Affairs Etrangères, Paris (often referred to as the Quai d'Orsay, abbreviated as MAE)

Correspondance Politique/Egypte: consular reports from Egypt and instructions from Paris to French representatives in Egypt marked in references as MAE/Egypte

Correspondance Commerciale, Le Caire: reports and instructions exchanged between Paris and French representatives in Egypt, marked in references as MAE/Caire

Archives des Postes/Affaires Etrangères/Ambassade Turquie/Correspondance avec les échelles/Alexandrie et Le Caire: reports and instructions exchanged between the French Embassy in Istanbul and French representatives in Egypt, marked in references as MAE/Turquie

Private papers

British Library, London (BL, Add. MSS 37448–37471) Hekekyan Papers: marked in references as Hekekyan, followed by number of volume

British Library, London, Oriental Manuscripts, OR 12130: register containing drafts of outgoing correspondence of the Egyptian government during the middle years of the nineteenth century

Griffith Institute, Ashmolean Museum, Oxford: manuscript, painting, and photograph collections of the Egyptological archives

Edited collections of state papers

Cattaui, René. 1933. *Le Règne de Mohamed Aly d'après les archives russes en Egypte*, Rome

Politis, Athtnase G. 1931. *Le Conflict Turco-Egyptien de 1838–1848 et les dernières années du Mohamed Aly d'après les documents diplomatiques grecs*, Cairo

Sāmī, Amīn. 1936. *Taqwīn an-Nīl*, vols. I–III, Cairo

Newspapers and magazines

The Times, London

al-Waqā'iᶜ al-Miṣriyya/Vekayi-i Mısır, Cairo

Revue des Deux Mondes, Paris

Books and articles

ᶜAbbās, Ḥamid Muḥammad Ra'ūf. 1973. *an-Niẓām al-Ijtimāᶜi fī Miṣr fī Ẓill al-Milkiyya az-Zirāᶜiyya al-Kabīra*, Cairo

ᶜAbd ar-Raḥīm, ᶜAbd ar-Raḥmān. 1974. *ar-Rīf al-Miṣrī fī al-Qarn ath-Thāmin ᶜAshar*, Cairo

ᶜAbd al-Wahhāb, Bakr Muḥammad. 1977. *al-Būlīs al-Miṣrī 1805–1922*, unpublished M.A. thesis, ᶜAyn Shams University

Abdel-Malek, Anouar. 1969. *Idéologie et renaissance nationale*, Paris

ᶜAbduh, Ibrāhīm. 1943. *Tārīkh al-Waqā'iᶜ al-Miṣriyya*, Cairo

1951. *Taṭawwur aṣ-Ṣiḥāfa al-Miṣriyya 1798–1951*, Cairo

About, Edmond. 1869. *Le Fellah, souvenirs d'Egypte*, Paris
Abu-Lughod, Janet. 1971. *Cairo: 1001 Years of the City Victorious*, Princeton
1987. "The Islamic City – History, Myth, Islamic Essence, and Contemporary Relevance," *International Journal of Middle East Studies*, 19/2, 155–76
Akarlı, Engin. 1987. "Gedik," *Jahrbuch*, Wissenschafts Kolleg zu Berlin, 223–32
Alderson, A. D. 1956. *The Structure of the Ottoman Dynasty*, Oxford
Asch, S. E. 1946. "Forming Impressions of Personality," *Journal of Abnormal and Social Psychology*, 41, 258–90
Audouard, Olympe. 1865. *Les Mystères de l'Egypte dévoilés*, Paris
Ayalon, David. 1977. *Studies on the Mamluks of Egypt (1250–1517)*, London
1979. *The Mamluk Military Society: Collected Studies*, London
1971–3. "The Great Yāsa of Chingis Khān: A Reexamination," *Studia Islamica*, 33 (1971), 97–140, 34 (1971), 151–80, 36 (1972), 113–58, 38 (1973), 107–56
Bab-ı Âli, Hâriciye Nezareti. 1915–16. *Mısır meselesi*, Istanbul, 1334 A.H.
Baer, Gabriel. 1962. *A History of Landownership in Modern Egypt 1800–1950*. London
1964. *Egyptian Guilds in Modern Times*, Jerusalem
1969. *Studies in the Social History of Modern Egypt*, Chicago
1982. *Fellah and Townsman in the Middle East*, London
Bakht ar-Riḍā, Shuᶜbat at-Tārīkh. 1969. *Tārīkh as-Sūdān*, Khartoum
Barakāt, ᶜAlī. 1978. *Taṭawwur al-Milkiyya az-Zirāᶜiyya wa-Atharuhu ᶜalā al-Ḥaraka as-Siyāsiyya (1813–1914)*, Cairo
al-Barāwī, Rashīd and ᶜAlīsh, Muḥammad Ḥamza. 1954. *at-Taṭawwur al-Iqtiṣādī fī Miṣr fī al-ᶜAhd al-Ḥadīth*, Cairo
Barthélemy Saint-Hilaire, J. 1857. *Egypt and the Great Suez Canal, A Narrative of Travels*, London
el-Batrik, Abdel Hamid. 1968. "Egyptian–Yemeni Relations (1819–1840) and Their Implications for British Policy in the Red Sea," in P. M. Holt (ed.), *Political and Social Change in Modern Egypt*, London, 281–90
Beik, William H. 1987. "Urban Factions and Social Order during the Minority of Louis XIV," *French Historical Studies*, 15/1, 36–67
Bercher, Jean-Claude. 1985. *Le Voyage en Orient*, Paris
Berque, J. 1977. *Egypt: Imperialism and Revolution*, English translation, London
Berreman, Gerald D. 1981. "Social Inequality: A Cross-Cultural Analysis," in G. D. Berreman (ed.), *Social Inequality: Comparative and Developmental Approaches*, New York, 3–40
Braudel, Fernand. 1958. "History and the Social Sciences: The Long Term," in Fritz Stern (ed.), *The Varieties of History*, New York, 404–29
1981. *The Structures of Everyday Life*, London
Brehier, Louis. 1900. *L'Egypte de 1798 à 1900*, Paris
Bromfield, William Arnold. 1856. *Letters from Egypt and Syria*, London
Brown, Leon Carl. 1974. *The Tunisia of Ahmad Bey, 1837–1855*, Princeton
Burke, Edmund III. 1987. "Understanding Arab Protest Movements," *Arab Studies Quarterly*, 8/4, 333–45
Burke, Peter. 1983. "From Pioneers to Settlers: Recent Studies of the History of Popular Culture," *Comparative Studies in Society and History*, 25, 181–7

Bustānī, B. 1900. *Dā'irat al-Maʿārif*, Cairo
Cameron, D. A. 1898. *Egypt in the Nineteenth Century*, London
Cevdet Paşa. 1953–67. *Tezakir*, ed. Cavid Baysun, 4 vols., Ankara
Charles-Roux, F. 1936. *L'Egypte de 1801 à 1882*, Paris (vol. IV of Gabriel Hanotaux [ed.], *Histoire de la nation égyptienne*)
Çizakça, Murat. 1986. "Resource Allocation in the Islamic Societies of the Past," *Boğaziçi Üniversitesi Araştırma Raporu*, ISS/E, no. 4
Clayton, J. W. 1854. *Letters from the Nile*, London
Clayton, Peter A. 1982. *The Rediscovery of Ancient Egypt: Artists and Travellers in the Nineteenth Century*, London
Clerget M. 1934. *Le Caire*, 2 vols., Cairo
Clot Bey, A. B. 1840. *Aperçu général sur l'Egypte*, 2 vols., Paris
1862. *Relations des phases parcourues par l'institution médical en Egypte sous les gouvernements d'Abbas et de Said Pachas*, Marseille
1949. *Mémoires de A.-B. Clot Bey*, ed. Jacques Tagher, Cairo
Couvidou, H. 1873. *Etude sur l'Egypte contemporaine*, Cairo
Crecelius, Daniel. 1982. *The Roots of Modern Egypt: A Study of the Regimes of Ali Bey al-Kabir and Muhammad Bey Abu al-Dhahab, 1760–1775*, Chicago
Cuno, Kenneth M. 1980. "The Origins of Private Ownership of Land in Egypt: A Reappraisal," *International Journal of Middle East Studies*, 12/3, 245–75
Darnton, Robert. 1985. *The Cat Massacre and Other Episodes in French Cultural History*, Middlesex
Deherain, Henri. 1936. *Le Soudan égyptien de Mohamed Aly à Ismail Pacha*, Paris (vol. IV of Gabriel Hanotaux [ed.], *Histoire de la nation égyptienne*)
De Jong, F. 1978. *Ṭuruq and Ṭuruq-Linked Institutions in Nineteenth Century Egypt*, Leiden
Delanoue, Gilbert. 1982. *Moralistes et politiques Musulmans dans l'Egypte du XIXe siècle (1798–1882)*, 2 vols., Cairo
De Leon, Edwin. 1877. *The Khedive's Egypt*, New York
De Lesseps, Ferdinand. 1876. *The Suez Canal: Letters and Documents Descriptive of Its Rise and Progress in 1854–1856*, London (reprinted edition, Wilmington, Delaware, 1976)
Deny, J. 1930. *Sommaire des archives turques du Caire*, Cairo
De Sande e Castro, A.P. 1901. *Egypte*, Paris–Lille
Desgenettes, M. 1802. *Décade égyptienne*, Paris
Didier, Charles. 1856. *Cinq cents lieues sur le Nil*, Paris
Dodwell, Henry. 1931. *The Founder of Modern Egypt, A Study of Muḥammad ʿAlī*, Cambridge
Douin, Georges (ed.). 1927. *Le Mission de Baron de Boislecomte: l'Egypte et la Syrie en 1833*, Cairo
1931. *La Première Guerre de Syrie*, Cairo
Du Camp, Maxime. 1852. *Egypte, Nubie, Palestine et Syrie: dessins photographiques recueillis pendant les années 1849, 1850 et 1851*, Paris
Eccel, Chris A. 1984. *Egypt, Islam, and Social Change: al-Azhar in Conflict and Accommodation*, Berlin

L'Egypte d'aujourd'hui, *see* Groupe de Recherches et d'Etudes sur le Proche-Orient
Elgood, P. G. 1935. *Egypt*, London
Encyclopaedia of Islam. 1954– . 2nd edn, Leiden (1st edn, Leiden and London, 1913–38)
Fahmī, Zakī. 1926. *Ṣafwat al-ᶜAṣr*, Cairo
Fahmy, Moustafa. 1954. *La Révolution de l'industrie en Egypte et ses conséquences sociales au 19ᵉ siècle (1800–1850)*, Leiden
Fakhouri, Hani. 1985. "An Ethnographic Survey of a Cairene Neighborhood: The Darb el-Ahmar District," *Journal of the American Research Center in Egypt*, 22, 119–27
Farnie, D. A. 1969. *East and West of Suez: The Suez Canal in History, 1854–1956*, Oxford
Fawzī, Ḥusayn. 1961. *Sindbād Miṣrī*, Cairo
Findley, Carter V. 1980. *Bureaucratic Reform in the Ottoman Empire*, Princeton
Flaubert, Gustave. 1972. Translation by Francis Steegmuller, *Flaubert in Egypt, A Sensibility on Tour*, London
Gadsby, John. 1860. *My Wanderings, being Travels in the East in 1846–47, 1850–51, 1852–53*, London
Gans, Eric. 1985. *The End of Culture*, Berkeley
Geertz, Clifford. 1973. *The Interpretation of Cultures*, New York
1979. "Suq: The Bazaar Economy in Sefrou," pp. 123–235 in Clifford Geertz, Lawrence Rosen, and Hildred Geertz (eds.), *Meaning and Order in Moroccan Society*, Cambridge and New York
1980. *Negara: The Theatre State in Nineteenth-Century Bali*, Princeton
1983. *Local Knowledge*, New York
Gershoni, Israel and Jankowski, James P. 1986. *Egypt, Islam, and the Arabs: The Search for Egyptian Nationhood, 1900–1930*, New York
Gibb, H. A. R. and Bowen, Harold. 1950–7. *Islamic Society and the West*, vol. I, pt. 1 (1950), vol. I, pt. 2 (1957), London
Al-Giritlī, ᶜAlī. 1952. *Tārīkh aṣ-Ṣināᶜa fī Miṣr fī an-Niṣf al-Awwal min al-Qarn at-Tāsiᶜ ᶜAshar*, Cairo
Goldsmid, F. J. 1882. *James Outram*,. 2 vols., London
Goodwin, Godfrey. 1971. *A History of Ottoman Architecture*, London
1977. *Islamic Architecture: Ottoman Turkey*, London
Gouin, Edouard. 1847. *L'Egypte au XIXᵉ siècle*, Paris
Gran, Peter. 1978. *Islamic Roots of Capitalism*, Austin
Group de Recherches et d'Etudes sur le Proche-Orient. 1977. *L'Egypte d'aujourd'hui, permanence et changements 1805–1976*, Paris
1982. *L'Egypte au XIXᵉ siècle*, Paris
Hattox, Ralph S. 1985. *Coffee and Coffeehouses: The Origins of a Social Beverage in the Medieval Near East*, Seattle
Heyworth-Dunne, J. 1938. *An Introduction to the History of Education in Modern Egypt*, London
Histoire financière, *see* J. C. (J. Claudy)
al-Ḥitta, Aḥmad Aḥmad. 1958. *Tārīkh Miṣr al-Iqtiṣādī fī al-Qarn at-Tāsiᶜ ᶜAshar*, Cairo
Holt, P. M. 1966. *Egypt and the Fertile Crescent 1516–1922, A Political History*, London
1968. "The Pattern of Egyptian Political History from 1517 to 1798," in P. M. Holt (ed.), *Political and Social Change in Modern Egypt*, London, 79–90

1973. *Studies in the History of the Near East*, London

Hourani, Albert. 1968. "Ottoman Reform and the Politics of Notables," in W. Polk and R. Chambers (ed.), *The Beginnings of Modernization in the Middle East*, Chicago, 41–68

1981. "The Ottoman Background of the Modern Middle East," in A. Hourani (ed.), *The Emergence of the Modern Middle East*, London, 1–18

Hunter, F. Robert. 1984. *Egypt under the Khedives 1805–1879*, Pittsburg

Hurewitz, J. C. 1975. *The Middle East and North Africa in World Politics*, vol. I, New Haven

Inalcîk, Halil. 1941. "Hüsrev Paşa," *İslam Ansiklopedisi*, vol. V, Istanbul

1970. "The Ottoman Economic Mind and Aspects of the Ottoman Economy," in M. A. Cook (ed.), *Studies in the Economic History of the Middle East*, London, 207–18

1977. "Centralization and Decentralization in the Ottoman Administration," in T. Naff and R. Owen (eds.), *Studies in Eighteenth Century Islamic History*, Carbondale and Edwardsville, Illinois

İslam Ansiklopedisi. 1941– . Istanbul

Issawi, Charles. 1982. *An Economic History of the Middle East and North Africa*, New York

Itzkowitz, Norman. 1972. *Ottoman Empire and Islamic Tradition*, New York

J. C. [J. Claudy]. 1878. *Histoire financière de l'Egypte depuis Said Pasha, 1854–1876*. Paris

Jallād, Fīlīb. 1890–2. *Qāmūs al-Idāra wa-l-Qaḍā'*, 4 vols., Alexandria

Kâmil Paşa, Yusuf. 1911–12. *Tarih-i Siyasi-yi Devlet-i Aliye-yi Osmaniye*, Istanbul, 1327 A.H.

Kessing, Roger M. 1985. Review of Clifford Geertz, *Local Knowledge*, in *American Ethnologist*, 12/3, 554

Kruglanski, A. W. and Freund, T. 1982. "The Freezing and Unfreezing of Lay-Sentences: Effects on Impressional Primacy, Ethnic Stereotyping, and Numerical Anchoring," *Journal of Experimental Social Psychology*, 19, 448–68

Kuhnke, Laverne. 1971. *Resistance and Response to Modernization: Preventive Medicine and Social Control in Egypt, 1825–1856*, unpublished Ph.D. dissertation, University of Chicago

Landes, David S. 1958. *Bankers and Pashas*, London

Lane, Edward William. 1973. *Manners and Customs of the Modern Egyptians*, 5th edn, Dover Reprint, New York

Lawson, Fred. 1981. "Rural Revolt and Provincial Society in Egypt, 1820–1824," *International Journal of Middle East Studies*, 13/2

Legh, Thomas. 1816. *Narrative of a Journey in Egypt and the Country beyond the Cataracts*, London

Lewis, Bernard. 1968. *The Emergence of Modern Turkey*, Oxford

Lilli, W. and Rehm, J. 1986. "Judgmental Processes as Basis of Intergroup Conflict," in W. Stroebe, A. Kruglanski, D. Bar-Tal, and M. Hewstone (eds.), *The Social Psychology of Intergroup and International Conflict: Theory, Research, and Applications*, Berlin

Linant de Bellefonds, M. A. 1872–3. *Mémoire sur les principaux travaux d'utilité publique exécutés en Egypte*, Paris

Linville, P. W. and Jones, E. E. 1980. "Polarized Appraisals of Out-Group Members," *Journal of Personality and Social Psychology*, 38, 689–803
Mahfuz, N. 1935. *The History of Medical Education in Egypt*, Cairo
McArthur, L. Z. and Friedman, S. A. 1980. "Illusory Correlation in Impression Formation: Variations in the Shared Distinctiveness Effect as a Function of the Distinctive Person's Age, Race and Sex," *Journal of Personality and Social Psychology*, 39, 615–24
McCarthy, Justin. 1976. "Nineteenth-Century Egyptian Population," *Middle Eastern Studies*, 12/3, 1–39
Malek, Jàromir. 1983. "Who Was the First to Identify the Saqqara Serapeum?" *Chronique d'Egypte*, 58/115–116, 65–72
Malek, Jàromir and Miles, Elizabeth. 1986. "Nineteenth-century 'studio photographs' of Egypt in the collection of the Griffith Institute of Oxford," *VA*, 3, 121–6
al-Sayyid Marsot, Afaf Lutfi. 1984. *Egypt in the Reign of Muhammad Ali*, Cambridge
Mueruau, Paul M. 1858. *L'Egypte contemporaine, 1840–1857*, Paris
el-Messiri, Sawsan. 1978. *Ibn al-Balad: A Concept of Egyptian Identity*, Leiden
Mubārak, ᶜAlī. 1886–9. *al-Khiṭaṭ at-Tawfīqiyya al-Jadīda*, 20 vols., Cairo
Mustafa, Ahmad Abdel-Rahim. 1968a. "The Breakdown of the Monopoly System in Egypt after 1840," in P. M. Holt (ed.), *Political and Social Change in Modern Egypt*, London, 291–307
1968b. "The Hekekyan Papers," in P. M. Holt (ed.), *Political and Social Change in Modern Egypt*, London, 68–75
Naaman, Antoine Youssef (ed.). 1965. *Les Lettres d'Egypte de Gustave Flaubert, d'après les manuscrits autographes*, Paris
Nadim, Nawal al-Messiri. 1979. *The Concept of the Ḥāra: A Historical and Sociological Study of Al-Sukkāriyya*, Cairo
1985. "Family Relationships in a 'Harah' in Cairo," in N. S. Hopkins and S. E. Ibrahim (eds.), *Arab Society*, Beirut, 212–22
Napier, Charles. 1842. *The War in Syria*, 2 vols., London
Naṣr, as-Sayyid Yūsuf. 1979. *Juhūd Miṣr al-Kashfiyya fī Ifrīqiya fī al-Qarn at-Tāsiᶜ ᶜAshar*, Cairo
Nubar Pacha. 1983. *Mémoires de Nubar Pacha*, ed. Mirrit Boutros Ghali, Beirut
Ochsenwald, William. 1980. *The Hijaz Railroad*, Charlottesville
ᶜOmar, ᶜOmar ᶜabd al-ᶜAziz. 1966. *Anglo-Egyptian Relations and the Construction of the Alexandria–Cairo–Suez Railway (1833–1858)*, unpublished Ph.D. thesis, University of London, School of Oriental and African Studies
Owen, Roger. 1969. *Cotton and the Egyptian Economy 1820–1914*, Oxford
1981. *The Middle East in the World Economy 1800–1914*, London
Pakalîn, M. Z. 1946–56. *Osmanlî tarih deyimleri ve terimleri sözlüğü*, Istanbul, 5 vols.
Panzac, Daniel. 1987. "The Population of Egypt in the Nineteenth Century," *Asian and African Studies*, 21/1, 11–32
Paton, A. A. 1870. *A History of the Egyptian Revolution from the Period of the Mamelukes to the Death of Mohammed Ali*, 2 vols., London (first edn, 1863)
Petry, Carl F. 1981. *The Civilian Elite of Cairo in the Late Middle Ages*, Princeton

Piterberg, Gabriel. 1987. "Egypt in the Eighteenth Century: An Ottoman Province or a 'Mamluk State'?," unpublished M.A. thesis, Tel-Aviv University (in Hebrew)

Raḍwān, ᶜAbd al-Futūḥ. 1953. *Tārīkh Maṭbaᶜat Būlāq*, Cairo

ar-Rāfiᶜī, ᶜAbd ar-Raḥmān. 1948. *ᶜAṣr Ismāᶜīl*, 2 vols., Cairo

Rasim, Ahmet. 1326–30 A.H. *Osmanlı Tarihi*, 4 vols., Istanbul

Raymond, André. 1955. "Les Tentatives anglaises de pénétration économique en Tunisie (1856–1877)," *Revue historique*, 204, 48–67

1964. "La France, la Grande-Bretagne et la problème de la réforme à Tunis (1855–1857)," *Etudes Maghrebines: Mélanges Charles-André Julien*, Paris

1973. *Artisans et commerçants au Caire au XVIIIᵉ siècle*, 2 vols., Damascus

1984. *The Great Arab Cities in the 16th–18th Centuries, An Introduction*, New York and London

Richards, Alan. 1982. *Egypt's Agricultural Development, 1800–1980: Technical and Social Change*, Boulder

Richmond, J. C. B. 1977. *Egypt 1798–1952, Her Advance Towards a Modern Identity*. London

Rifaat Muhammad. 1940. *The Awakening of Modern Egypt*, London

Rivlin, Helen. 1961a. *The Agricultural Policy of Muhammad Ali*, Cambridge, Mass.

1961b. "The Railway Question in the Ottoman-Egyptian Crisis of 1850–1852," *Middle East Journal*, 15/4, 365–88

Sabry, M. 1930. *L'Empire égyptienne sous Mohamed-Ali et la question de l'Orient 1811–1849*, Paris

1933. *L'Empire égyptienne sous Ismail et l'ingérence anglo-française 1863–1879*, Paris

St. John, Bayle. 1851. "Egypt under Abbas Pasha," *Sharpe's London Magazine*, and *Eclectic Magazine*, New York

1852. *Village Life in Egypt*, 2 vols., London (reprinted New York, 1973)

Sami, Şemsüddin. 1894. *Kamüsülâlam*. Istanbul

Sammarco, Angelo. 1937. *Histoire de l'Egypte moderne depuis Mohammad Ali jusqu'à l'occupation britannique 1801–1882*, vol. IV, Cairo

Sarhank/Sirhank *see* Serheng

as-Sarūjī, Muḥammad Maḥmūd. 1967. *al-Jaysh al-Miṣrī fī al-Qarn at-Tāsiᶜ ᶜAshar*, Cairo

Schölch, Alexander. (n.d.). *Agypten den Agyptern! Die Politische und gesellschaftliche Krise der 1878–1882 in Ägypten*, Zurich and Freiburg

Schulze, Reinhard. 1981. *Die Rebellion der Ägyptischen Fallahin 1919*, Berlin

Secord, P. F., Bevan, W., and Katz, B. 1956. "The Negro Stereotype and Perceptual Accentuation," *Journal of Abnormal and Social Psychology*, 53, 78–83

Senior, N. W. 1882. *Conversations and Journals in Egypt and Malta*, 2 vols., London

Serheng, Ismāᶜīl. 1894. *Haqā'iq al-Akhbār fī Duwal al-Biḥār*, 2 vols., Cairo, 1312–1314 A.H.

Shaᶜlān, Ibrāhīm Aḥmad. 1982. *ash-Shaᶜb al-Miṣrī fī Amthālihi al-ᶜĀmmiyya*, Cairo

Shaw, Stanford J. 1962. *The Financial and Administrative Organization and Development of Ottoman Egypt*, Princeton

1968. "Landholding and Land-Tax Revenues in Ottoman Egypt," in P. M. Holt (ed.), *Political and Social Change in Modern Egypt*, London

El-Shayyal, Gamal El-Din. 1962. *A History of Egyptian Historiography in the Nineteenth Century*, Alexandria
Shubayka, Makkī. 1947. *as-Sūdān fī Qarn 1819–1919*, Cairo
Shukrī, Muḥammad Fu'ād. 1948. *al-Ḥukm al-Miṣrī fī as-Sūdān, 1820–1880*, Cairo
Shuqayr, Naᶜūm. 1967. *Jughrāfya wa-Tārīkh as-Sūdān*, Beirut (reprint of 1903 edn)
Taifel, Henri. 1982. *Social Identities and Intergroup Relations*, Cambridge
Taylor, Peter and Rebel, Hermann. 1981. "Hessian Peasant Women, Their Families, and the Draft: A Social-Historical Interpretation of Four Tales from the Grimm Collection," *Journal of Family History*, 6, 347–78
Taymūr, Aḥmad. 1945. *Tarājim Aᶜyān al-Qarn ath-Thālith ᶜAshar wa-Awā'il ar-Rābiᶜ ᶜAshar*, Cairo
Temperley, Harold. 1964. *England and the Near East – The Crimea*, London
Thomas, Lewis V. 1972. *A Study of Naima*, ed. Norman Itzkowitz, New York
Toledano, Ehud R. 1981. "Slave Dealers, Women, Pregnancy, and Abortion: The Story of a Circassian Slave-girl in Mid-nineteenth-century Cairo," *Slavery and Abolition*, 2/1, 53–68
1982. *The Ottoman Slave Trade and Its Suppression, 1840–1890*, Princeton
1984a. "Law, Practice, and Social Reality: A Theft Case in Cairo, 1854," in G. R. Warburg and G. G. Gilbar (eds.), *Studies in Islamic Society: Contributions in Memory of Gabriel Baer*, Haifa, 153–74
1984b. "The Imperial Eunuchs of Istanbul: From Africa to the Heart of Islam," *Middle Eastern Studies*, 20/3, 379–90
forthcoming. "Muḥammad ᶜAlī," *EI*²
Trollope, Anthony. 1950. *An Autobiography*, Oxford
Tucker, Judith. 1985. *Women in Nineteenth-Century Egypt*, Cambridge
Tugay, Asaf. 1962. *İbret*, 2 vols., Istanbul (n.d. and 1962)
Tugay, Emine Foat. 1963. *Three Centuries: Family Chronicles of Turkey and Egypt*, Oxford
Uluçay, Çağatay. 1971. *Harem*, vol. II, Ankara
ᶜUways, Sayyid. 1978. *Rasā'il ilā 'l-Imām ash-Shāfiᶜī*, Cairo (first edition 1965)
Vatikiotis, P. J. 1969. *The Modern History of Egypt*, London
Vingtrinier, A. 1886. *Soliman Pasha (Joseph Sève)*, Paris
Volkoff, Oleg V. 1972. *Voyageurs russes en Egypte*, Cairo
Wallace, D. Mackenzie. 1883. *Egypt and the Egyptian Question*, London
Weygand, Le General. 1936. *Histoire militaire de Mohammad Aly et de ses fils*, 2 vols., Paris
Wilkinson, John G. 1858. *A Handbook for Travellers in Egypt*, London (ten editions were published between 1843 and 1900)
Wyer, R. S. and Gordon, S. E. 1984. "The Cognitive Representation of Social Information," in R. S. Wyer and Thomas K. Srull (eds.), *Handbook of Social Cognition*, vol. II, ch. 2, Hillsdale, N.J.
Yapp, Malcolm E. 1975. "The Modernization of Middle Eastern Armies in the Nineteenth Century: A Comparative View," in V. J. Parry and M. E. Yapp (eds.), *War Technology and Society in the Middle East*, Oxford
Young, George. 1927. *Egypt*, London
Zakhūra, Ilyās. 1897–1916. *Mir'āt al-ᶜAṣr*, 3 vols., Cairo

Zaydān, Jurjī. 1902. *Mashāhīr ash-Sharq*
1925. *Tārīkh Miṣr al-Ḥadīth*, 3rd edn, 3 vols., Cairo (1st edn., 1911)
Ziriklī, Khayr ad-Dīn. 1980. *al-Aʿlām: Qāmūs Tarājim*, 5th edn, 8 vols., Beirut

Index

9 NORMAN N. LEWIS
Nomads and settlers in Syria and Jordan, 1800–1980

8 OLIVIER ROY
Islam and resistance in Afghanistan

7 JUDITH E. TUCKER
Women in nineteenth-century Egypt

6 RAYMOND A. HINNEBUSCH JR
Egyptian politics under Sadat
The post-populist development of an authoritarian-modernizing state

5 HELENA COBBAN
The Palestinian Liberation Organisation
People, power and politics

4 AFAF LUTFI AL-SAYID MARSOT
Egypt in the reign of Muhammad Ali

3 PHILIP S. KHOURY
Urban notables and Arab nationalism
The politics of Damascus 1860–1920

2 NANCY ELIZABETH GALLAGHER
Medicine and power in Tunisia, 1780–1900

1 YORAM PERI
Between battles and ballots
Israeli military in politics